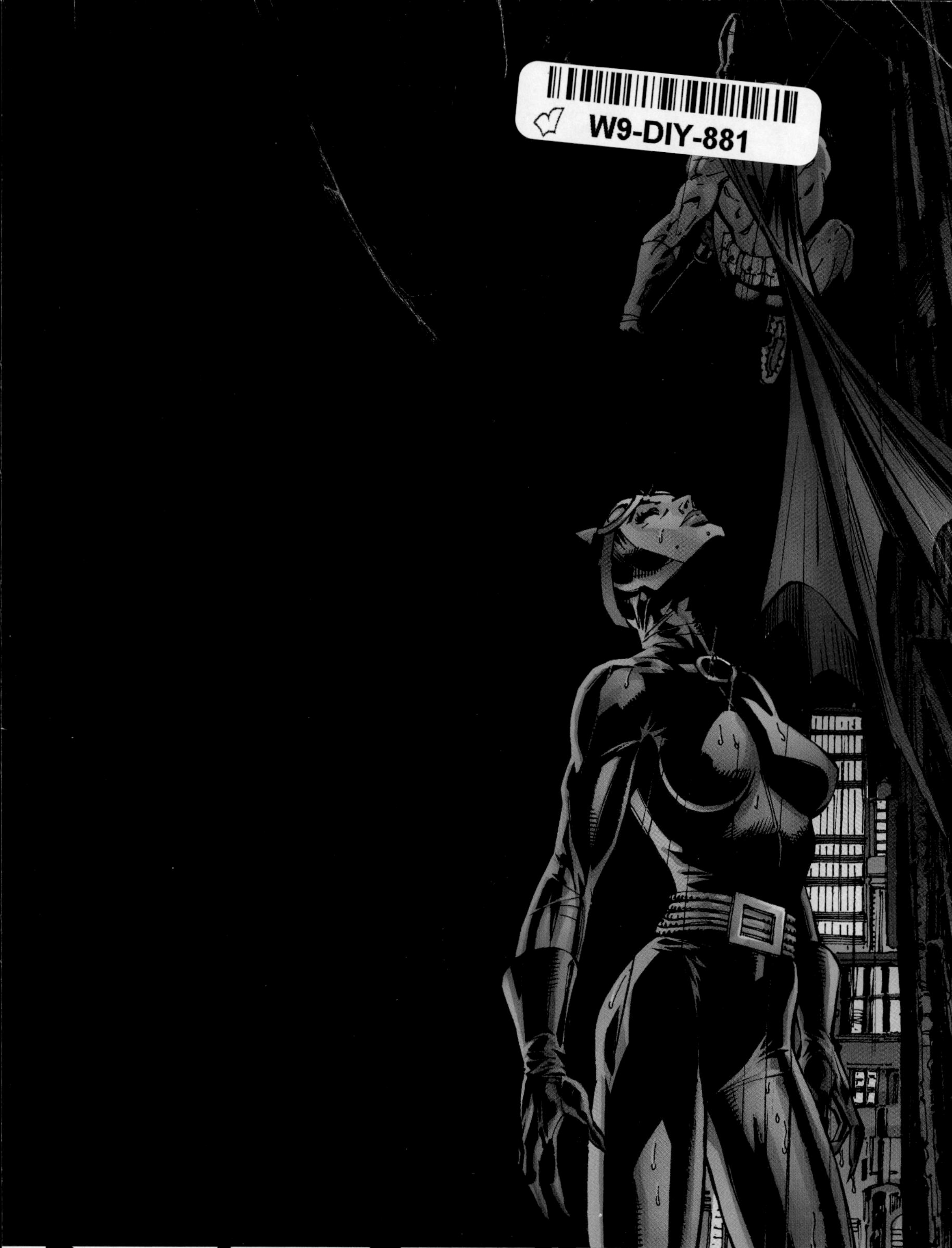

B A T M A N
HUSH
VOLUME TWO

Dan DiDio
VP-Executive Editor

Bob Schreck
Editor-Original Series

Robert Greenberger
Senior Editor-Collected Edition

Robbin Brosterman
Senior Art Director

Paul Levitz
President & Publisher

Georg Brewer
VP-Design & Retail Product Development

Richard Bruning
Senior VP-Creative Director

Patrick Caldon
Senior VP-Finance & Operations

Chris Caramalis
VP-Finance

Terri Cunningham
VP-Managing Editor

Alison Gill
VP-Manufacturing

Rich Johnson
VP-Book Trade Sales

Hank Kanalz
VP-General Manager, WildStorm

Lillian Laserson
Senior VP & General Counsel

Jim Lee
Editorial Director, WildStorm

David McKillips
VP-Advertising & Custom Publishing

John Nee
VP-Business Development

Gregory Noveck
Senior VP-Creative Affairs

Cheryl Rubin
Senior VP-Brand Management

Bob Wayne
VP-Sales & Marketing

BATMAN: HUSH VOLUME TWO

Published by DC Comics.
Cover, introduction, and compilation copyright
© 2003 DC Comics.

Originally published in single magazine
form as BATMAN 613-619, Wizard 0.
Copyright © 2003 DC Comics. All Rights Reserved.

DC Comics
1700 Broadway
New York, NY 10019

A Warner Bros. Entertainment Company
Printed in Canada.
Third Printing.

ISBN: 1 4012 0092 3
ISBN 13: 978 1 4012 0092 3

Cover illustration by Jim Lee
and Scott Williams.
Cover color by Alex Sinclair.

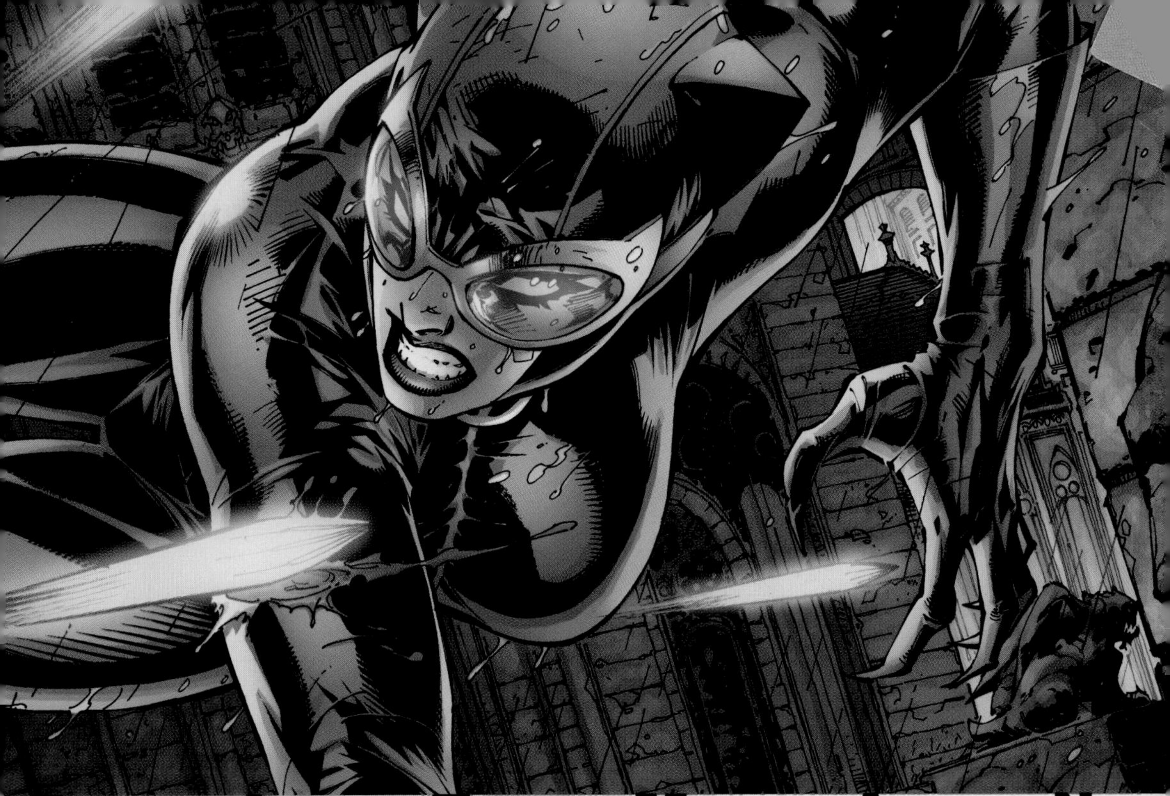

BATMAN

VOLUME TWO

HUSH

Jeph Loeb
Writer

Jim Lee
Penciller

Scott Williams
Inker

Richard Starkings
Letterer

Alex Sinclair
Colorist

Jim Lee & Scott Williams
Original Series Covers

Batman created by Bob Kane

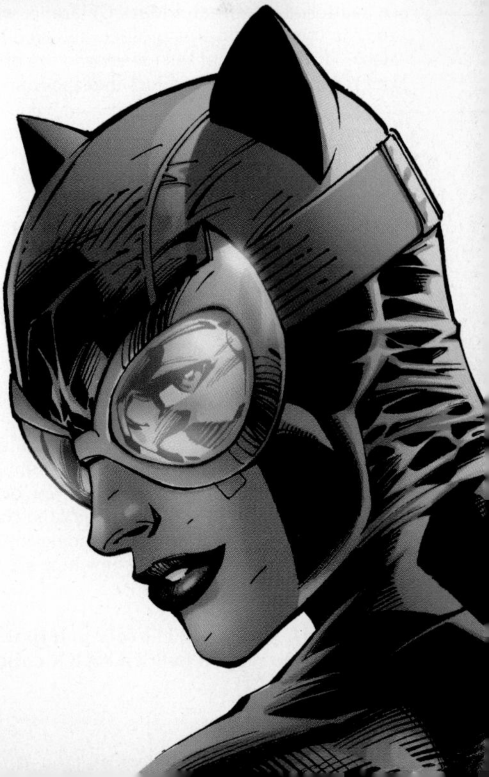

"HUSH"

"...the name of the villain is Hush."

I grinned ear to ear. Keeping projects secret in the world of comics is no mean feat — especially in a world of cell phones, IMs, message boards and online gossip hounds.

Yet writer Jeph Loeb and I had managed — for over a year — to keep our Batman project ultra top secret. Over a year!

But we hadn't come up with a name we were crazy about for the villain. And now, months into the project, Jeph had come through with the perfect one. A name not only for the villain, but also a name which completely captured the secrecy and spirit of the entire project.

Hush.

"How about a nice miniseries with extra glossy covers..."

"Or how about doing a one-shot graphic novel; sure would look nice on a coffee table."

INTRODUCTION BY JIM LEE

VOICES

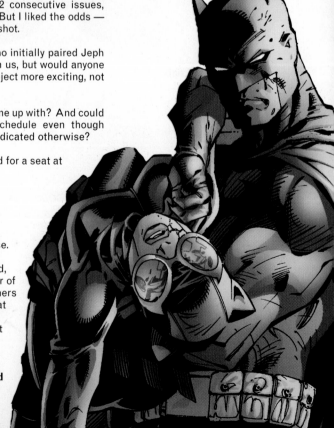

Everyone had wanted me to do this run, not as a monthly but as a special project, and although I knew dead certain that I could draw every book and make my deadlines for 12 consecutive issues, virtually no one else seemed to believe it. But I liked the odds — the payoff — if we managed to hit the long shot.

DC editorial art director Mark Chiarello, who initially paired Jeph and me together on this project, believed in us, but would anyone else? The audacity of the idea made the project more exciting, not just to me but to the retailers and the fans.

What kind of story would these creators come up with? And could they meet the demands of a monthly schedule even though common sense and conventional wisdom indicated otherwise?

Stubbornly, we stood our ground and waited for a seat at the Big Boys' table.

We wanted a shot at *Batman*.

The regular *monthly* title.

One of *the* flagship titles of the DC Universe.

There would be no wiggle room. If we failed, we would have self-combusted at the center of a three-ring circus in plain view like few others had before us. But if we *succeeded* (and that would be the only real way of silencing the critics and naysayers)...who knew how *big* it would eventually get.

"HAHAHA you loser! ! ! I told you that there was no way in hell XXXXX could really be Hush!"

Hush.

The name instantly created the air of mystery we wanted for the project, inciting readers all over the world to argue, fight, kick and claw one another on the message boards over the true identity of the bandaged man. It instantly created anticipation for the run, silencing the crowd before the performance began in earnest. It spoke of seriousness, of romance, of broken promises, and of old childhood secrets – themes that resonated throughout the storyline. But as secrets were exposed, new ones were created, further fueling fandom's fire.

It brought Jeph and me together on our very first collaboration. I had long admired his incredible work with artist extraordinaire Tim Sale on THE LONG HALLOWEEN, DARK VICTORY and SUPERMAN FOR ALL SEASONS. I will admit, I was initially worried about how we would work together. My sensibilities are nowhere near Tim's.

While he could create drama, mood and tension in a damn kitchen for God's sake with a confident, terse line, I would struggle. While he could make the rafters of Wayne Manor soar into the darkness, I would struggle. While he could make the black shadows of Batman's world seemingly come alive — I would struggle.

But my fears would be silenced — I was working with a professional; Jeph wrote to *my* strengths. I would joke on panels at conventions that that resulted in a book which needed no sense of storytelling — all sizzle with no steak. Only the humorless naysayers held onto this point of view.

Meanwhile, Jeph was pushing the fans' buttons, one at a time; slowly at first, but then at a manic pace, driving them back in droves to the world of Batman as they saw Batman's world literally turned upside down as he fell from the skies above Gotham, nearly to his death.

Jeph got into Batman's head like few other writers, exposing with deceptive simplicity the depths of the Dark Knight's sorrows, the frustrations of his mission, the love for his friends — unlocking the passions of one of the most stoic characters within comics.

And he could not have done it without the talents of letterer Richard Starkings. Superstarkingsman was only one of many nicknames Jeph coined for Richard, in tribute not only to his lettering skills but for his ability to make Jeph's writing look that much better on the page. Again, not only in appearance, but in tone. Unflinching in his feedback, Richard worked in tandem with Jeph and editor Bob Schreck to make the scripts sing.

"Don't change it. I always thought it was cool when I was a fan when the art changed and evolved over the course of an artist's run on a book."

"Hmm...but it looks odd to me, Scott..."

Hush.

Scott Williams was pulling Batman artwork from my hand, urging me to reconsider redrawing panels that I thought looked odd. Given the lead time on Batman, we, for the first time in our careers, had the luxury of going back and reconsidering the work we had done months ago. The pages weren't bad per se, but with the passage of time, I could see that the way I was drawing Batman had changed. The look we ended up with was very different from how we started. Batman had become leaner, his nose sharper, the shadows larger, the world darker. I was tempted to redraw some shots.

But Scott was right. Drawing comics is not about hitting the note every time the same way. It's not about making things look mechanical and as if they were processed by a cookie cutter.

Especially on Batman.

He would also decide to ink mostly with a brush and use technical pens for the details rather than his traditional, trusty crowquill nib — a first for him over my pencils. Again, those doubts. But Jeph and I were blown away by the results.

Blown away.

I always knew Scott was the best. Who knew he would be so versatile as well?

"Dude."

"Let's get it done right. I can stay up longer."

Hush.

It's true most comics are collaborations. All the creators have simple, clean titles under their names — writer, penciller, inker, letterer, colorist. But the truth is that we all are stepping on one another's toes, pitching in our two cents, sometimes — well, most times unsolicited. Sometimes we have to stop cc-ing those people. Sometimes they're right. So we have to fix and change things on the fly. Most times, the changes take all night.

It's also true the last man in the workflow gets stuck holding the bag. And Alex Sinclair, the colorist of the book, was the man most of those times on our run on Batman. And it was 4 a.m. and he was calling me out. In a nice way, of course, but essentially telling me not to call it a day (or night as the case may have been) and to stay up as long as it took to get the color proofs looking the way we wanted them to.

All artists have their own peculiar tastes vis-à-vis coloring, and I know I pressed Alex to make his own palette align more with mine. That took a lot of time and work and, most of all, patience on his part. And supreme dedication. But it went faster and easier as the issues passed by, not just because Alex was learning my tastes, but because I was learning his, and I know this run would look nowhere near as good without his tremendous coloring. Computer coloring has redefined the look of comics, and Alex was instrumental in redefining the look Scott and I were creating on Batman.

"Very nice. If we make shipping, everyone gets a big, wet sloppy kiss from me..."

Hush.

Editors have many hats to wear, many responsibilities to fulfill. Chief among them is to motivate the talent and to help focus and shape the creative process which BATMAN editor Bob Schreck did with aplomb. His honesty, wisdom and good humor were much appreciated as he and his assistant, Michael Wright, kept the motor running and the ship on course, making sure we focused on the important stuff and setting us straight when we frittered away time on the nonsensical. They plied us with reference and advised us on continuity so we looked like the experts we wish we were. You couldn't have asked for more.

"Adam...I don't think I have any new ways of saying thanks to all the fans and retailers for their support. [laughter]"

Hush.

When it first came out, it hit with a big splash, but then something strange happened: it just kept getting bigger and bigger, taking on a life of its own. Adam Philips of DC's marketing department was calling me every week (or so it seemed) for a new quote for press releases as BATMAN was tearing up the sales charts every issue. And it literally got to the point where I had run out of ways to rephrase my genuine excitement and astonishment at the phenomenon it had grown to be.

All I knew was that this was a special moment so I started to save and record bits and pieces of my memories from working on this book, some of which I have included here in this introduction. Because I didn't do that before when I worked on the *X-Men*. Or WILDCATS. Or DIVINE RIGHT. Or any other series I had ever worked on. So that when I flip through these pages again in the future, I will see more than just the words and pictures, I will see and hear the people who made this book come alive.

"Hush...the show is just starting."

— Jim Lee
San Diego, California
September 2003

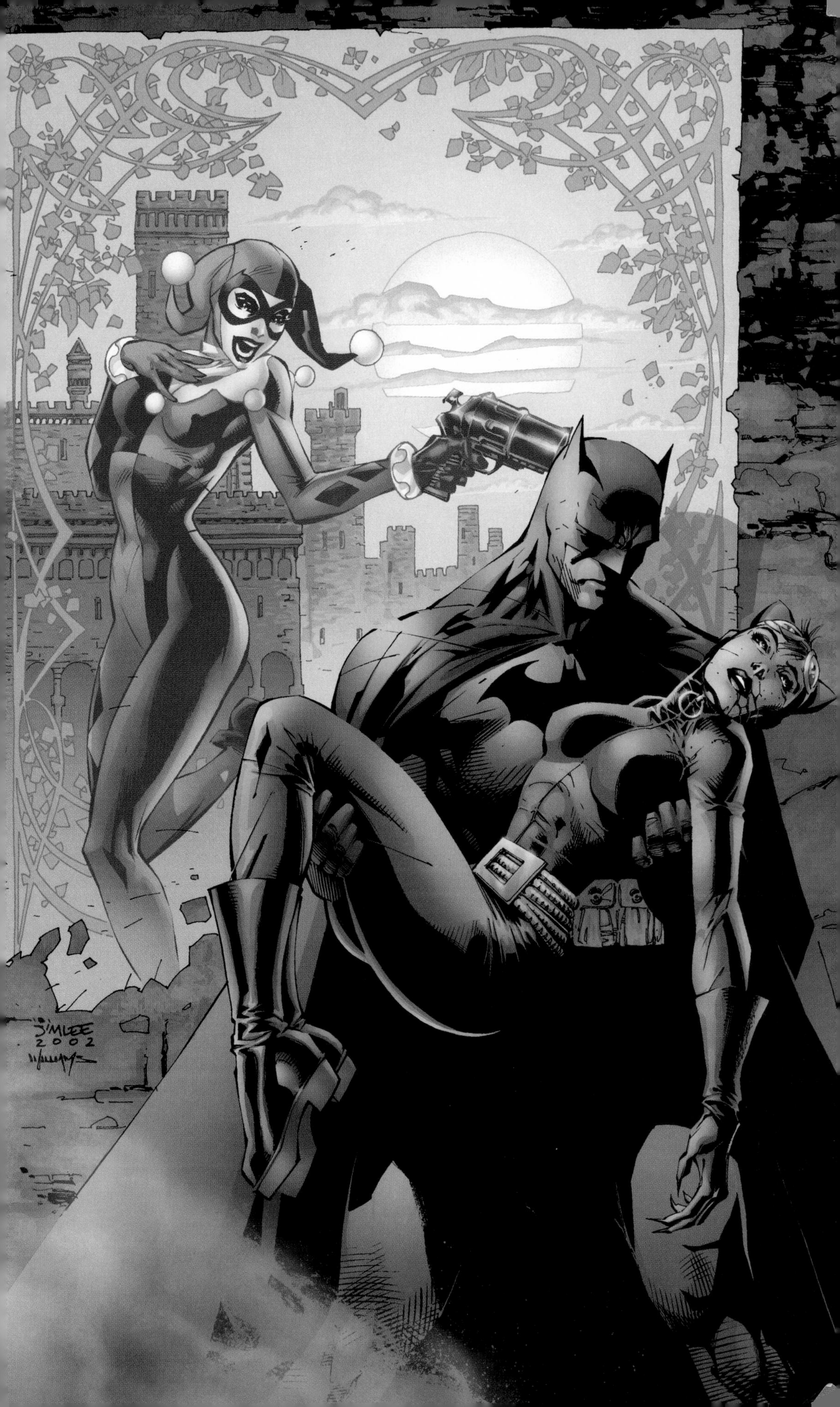
JIMLEE
2002

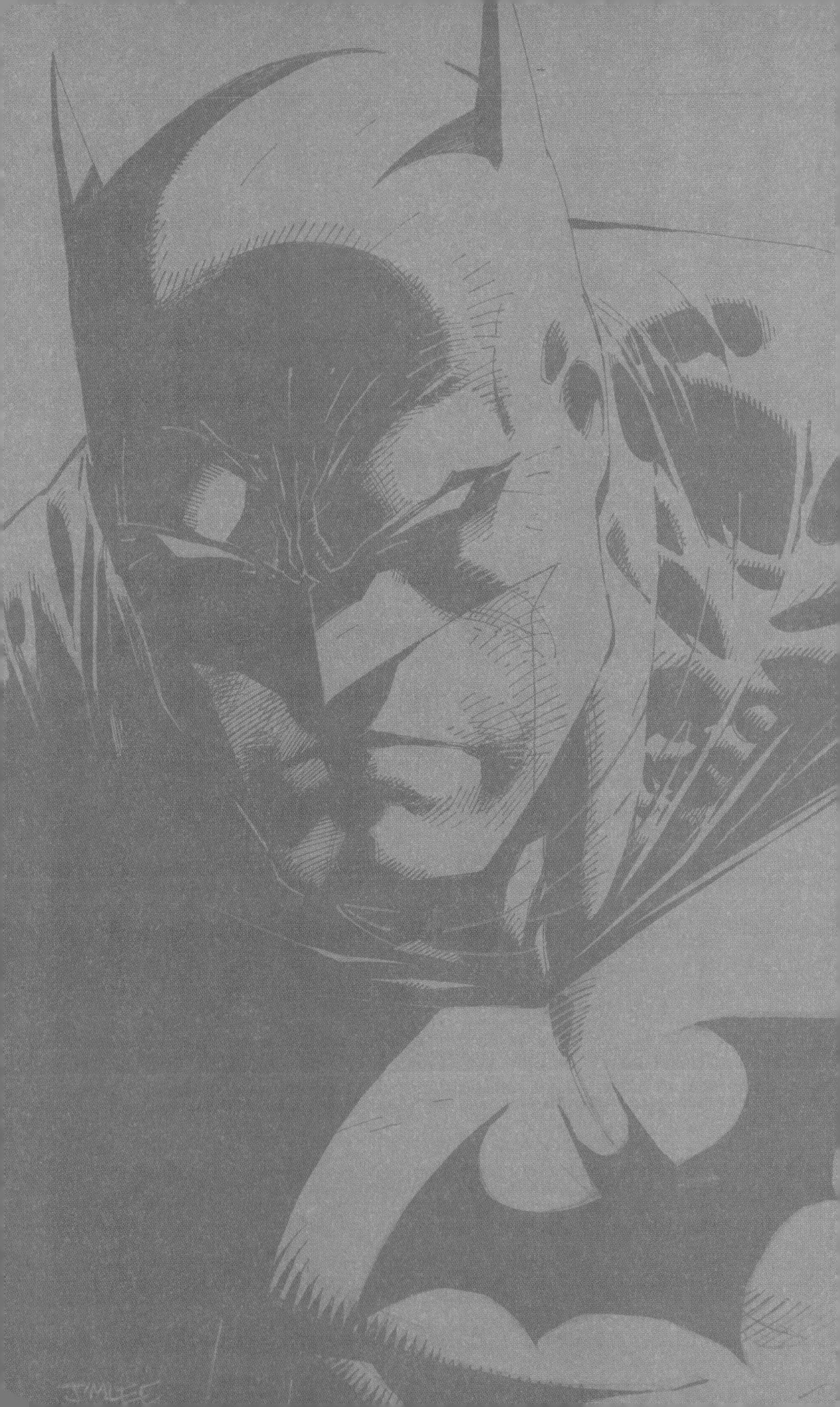

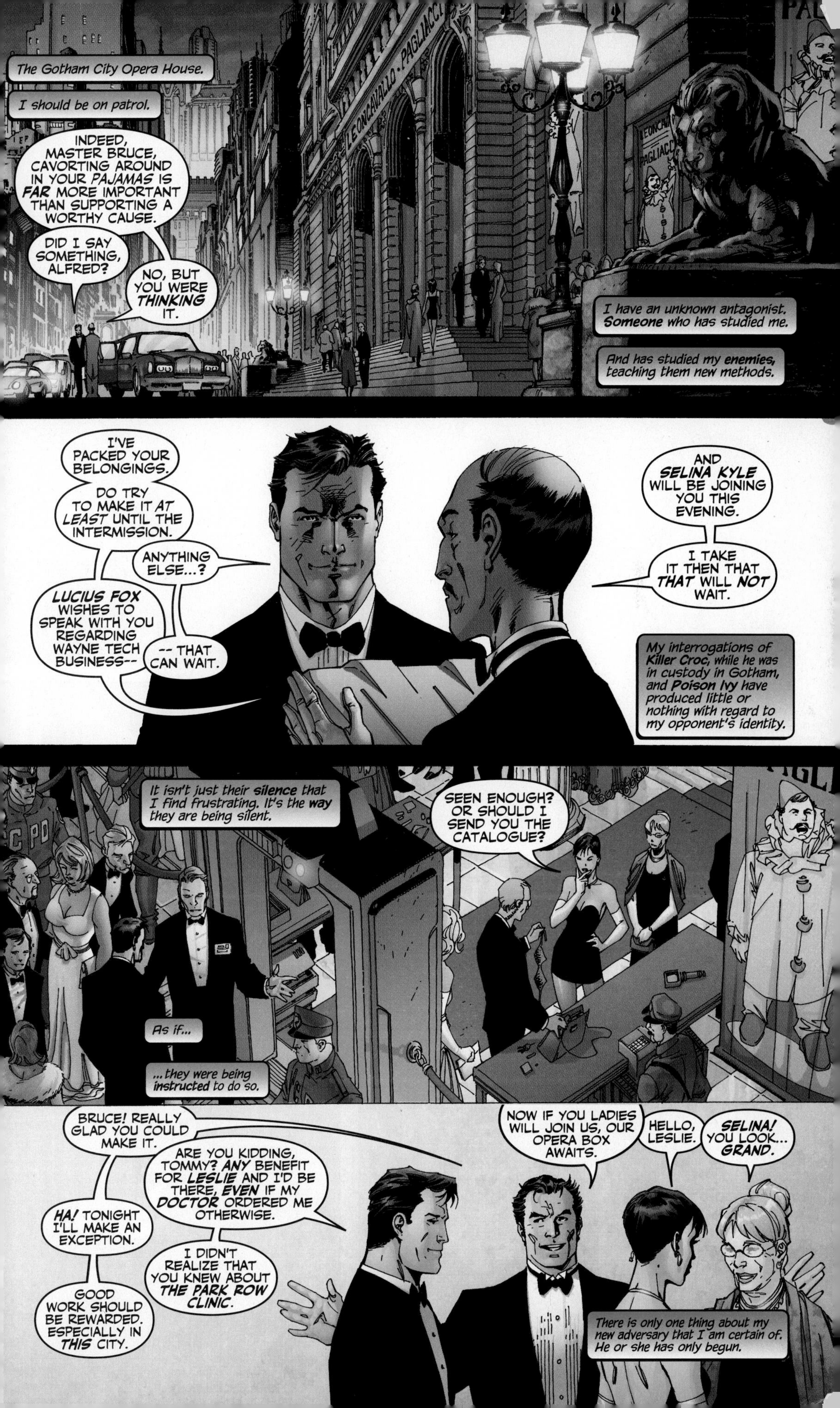
The Gotham City Opera House.
I should be on patrol.
INDEED, MASTER BRUCE, CAVORTING AROUND IN YOUR PAJAMAS IS FAR MORE IMPORTANT THAN SUPPORTING A WORTHY CAUSE.
DID I SAY SOMETHING, ALFRED?
NO, BUT YOU WERE THINKING IT.
I have an unknown antagonist. Someone who has studied me.
And has studied my enemies, teaching them new methods.
I'VE PACKED YOUR BELONGINGS.
DO TRY TO MAKE IT AT LEAST UNTIL THE INTERMISSION.
ANYTHING ELSE...?
LUCIUS FOX WISHES TO SPEAK WITH YOU REGARDING WAYNE TECH BUSINESS--
-- THAT CAN WAIT.
AND SELINA KYLE WILL BE JOINING YOU THIS EVENING.
I TAKE IT THEN THAT THAT WILL NOT WAIT.
My interrogations of Killer Croc, while he was in custody in Gotham, and Poison Ivy have produced little or nothing with regard to my opponent's identity.
It isn't just their silence that I find frustrating. It's the way they are being silent.
SEEN ENOUGH? OR SHOULD I SEND YOU THE CATALOGUE?
As if...
...they were being instructed to do so.
BRUCE! REALLY GLAD YOU COULD MAKE IT.
ARE YOU KIDDING, TOMMY? ANY BENEFIT FOR LESLIE AND I'D BE THERE, EVEN IF MY DOCTOR ORDERED ME OTHERWISE.
HA! TONIGHT I'LL MAKE AN EXCEPTION.
I DIDN'T REALIZE THAT YOU KNEW ABOUT THE PARK ROW CLINIC.
GOOD WORK SHOULD BE REWARDED. ESPECIALLY IN THIS CITY.
NOW IF YOU LADIES WILL JOIN US, OUR OPERA BOX AWAITS.
HELLO, LESLIE.
SELINA! YOU LOOK... GRAND.
There is only one thing about my new adversary that I am certain of. He or she has only begun.

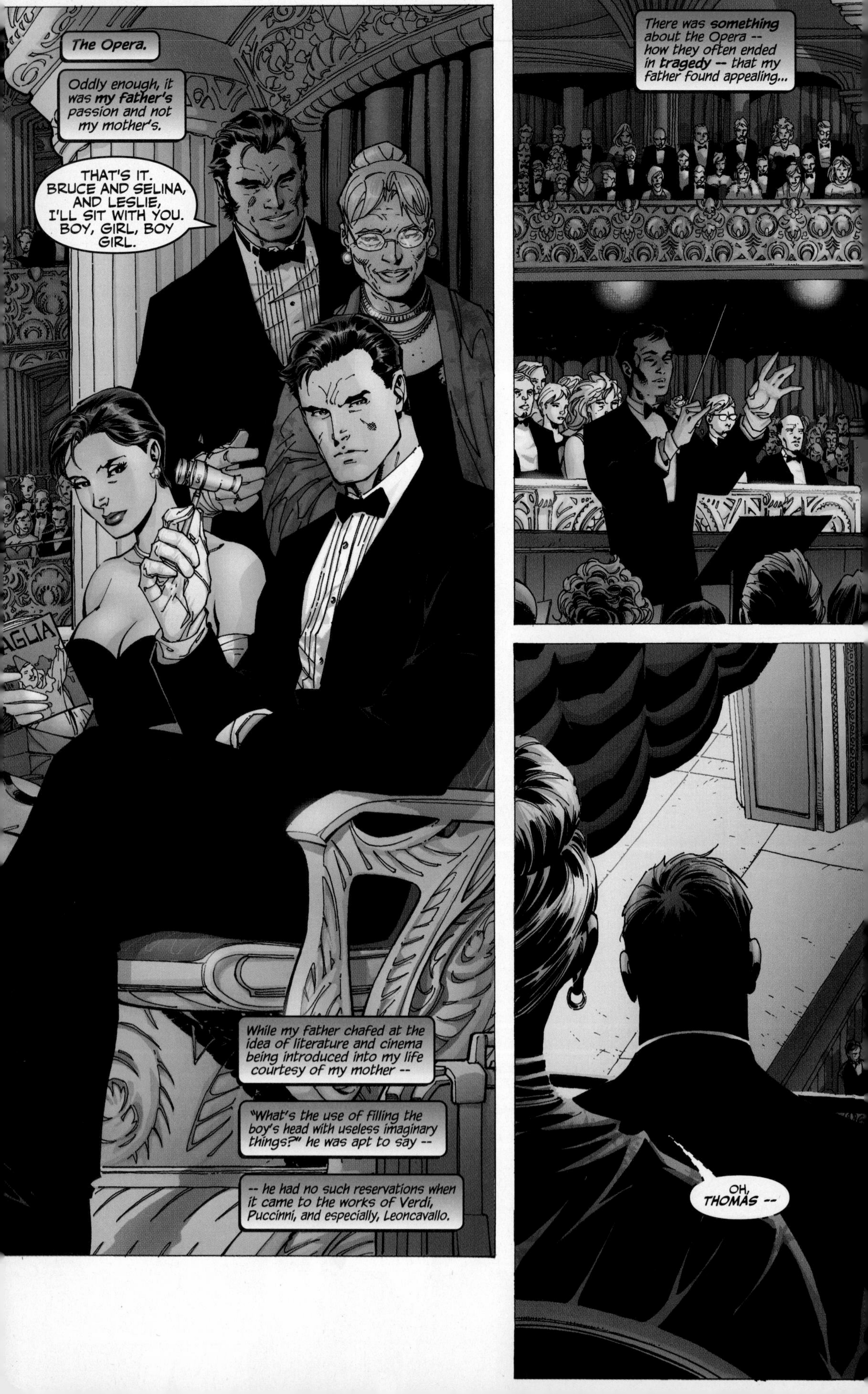
The Opera.
Oddly enough, it was my father's passion and not my mother's.
THAT'S IT. BRUCE AND SELINA, AND LESLIE, I'LL SIT WITH YOU. BOY, GIRL, BOY GIRL.
While my father chafed at the idea of literature and cinema being introduced into my life courtesy of my mother --
"What's the use of filling the boy's head with useless imaginary things?" he was apt to say --
-- he had no such reservations when it came to the works of Verdi, Puccinni, and especially, Leoncavallo.
There was something about the Opera -- how they often ended in tragedy -- that my father found appealing...
OH, THOMAS --

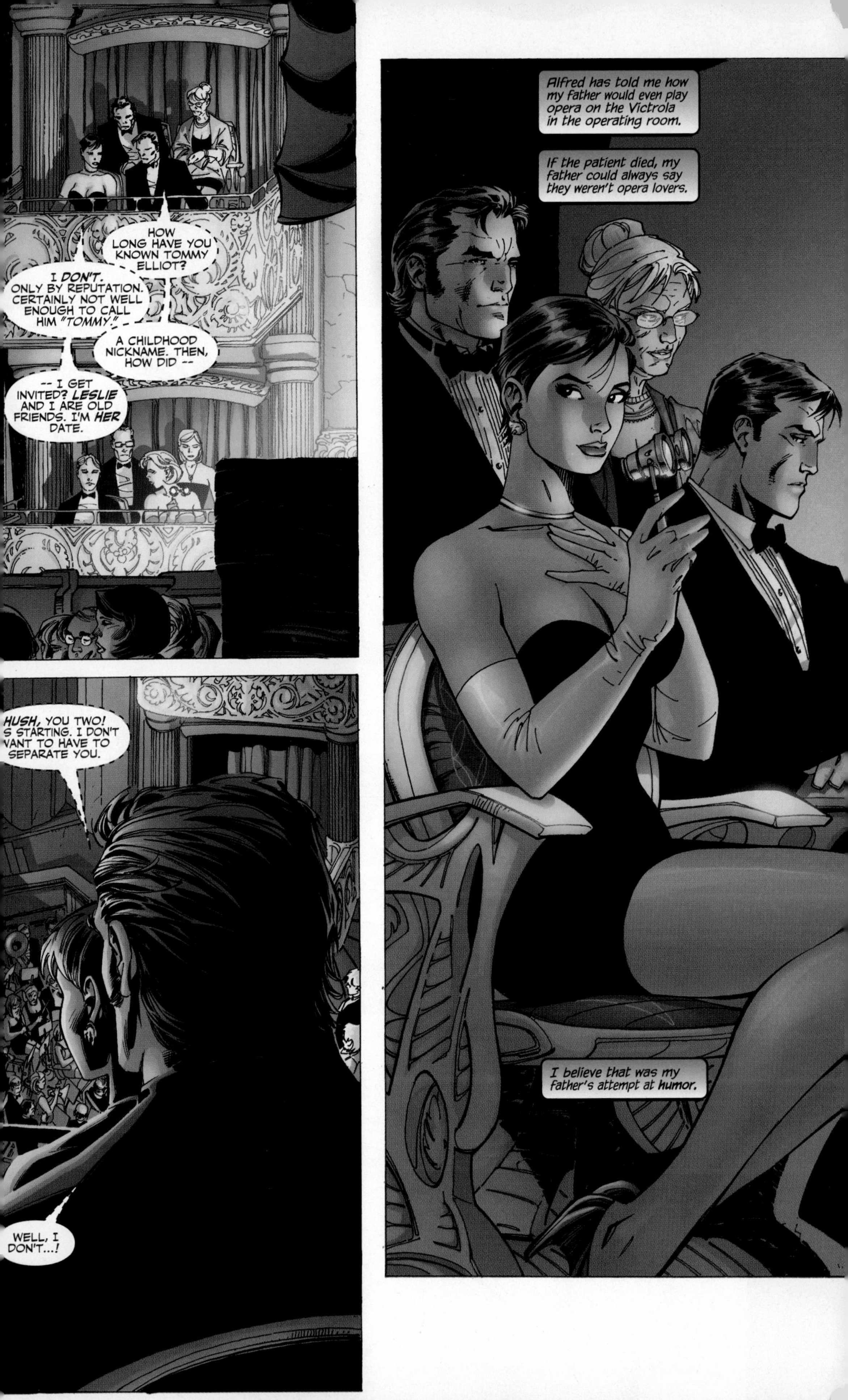

HOW LONG HAVE YOU KNOWN TOMMY ELLIOT?
I DON'T. ONLY BY REPUTATION. CERTAINLY NOT WELL ENOUGH TO CALL HIM "TOMMY."
A CHILDHOOD NICKNAME. THEN, HOW DID --
-- I GET INVITED? LESLIE AND I ARE OLD FRIENDS. I'M HER DATE.
HUSH, YOU TWO! S STARTING. I DON'T VANT TO HAVE TO SEPARATE YOU.
WELL, I DON'T...!
Alfred has told me how my father would even play opera on the Victrola in the operating room.
If the patient died, my father could always say they weren't opera lovers.
I believe that was my father's attempt at humor.

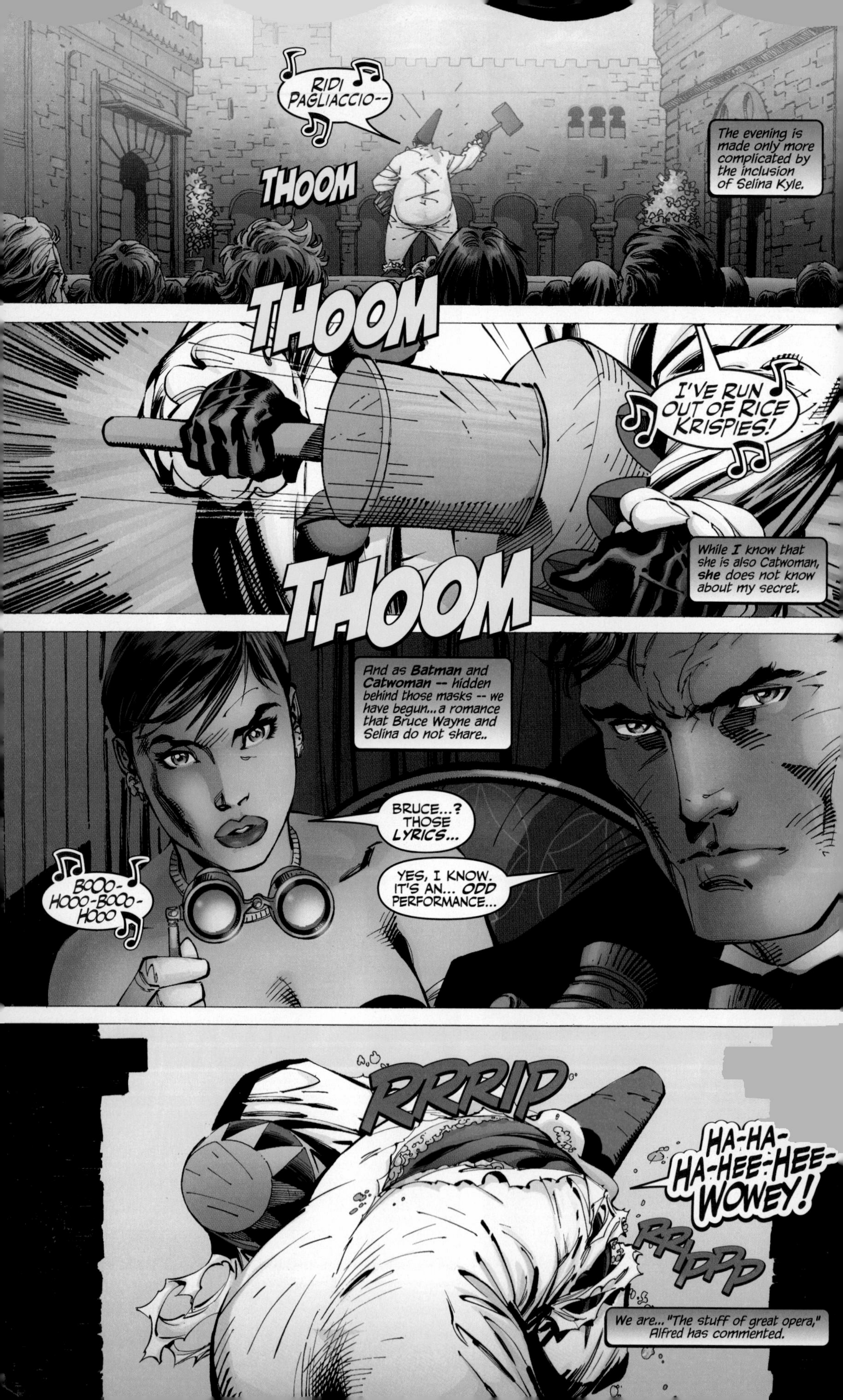
RIDI PAGLIACCIO--
THOOM
The evening is made only more complicated by the inclusion of Selina Kyle.
THOOM
I'VE RUN OUT OF RICE KRISPIES!
THOOM
While I know that she is also Catwoman, she does not know about my secret.
And as Batman and Catwoman -- hidden behind those masks -- we have begun...a romance that Bruce Wayne and Selina do not share..
BRUCE...? THOSE LYRICS...
YES, I KNOW. IT'S AN... ODD PERFORMANCE...
BOOO-HOOO-BOOO-HOOO
RRRIP
HA-HA-HA-HEE-HEE-WOWEY!
RRRIPPP
We are..."The stuff of great opera," Alfred has commented.

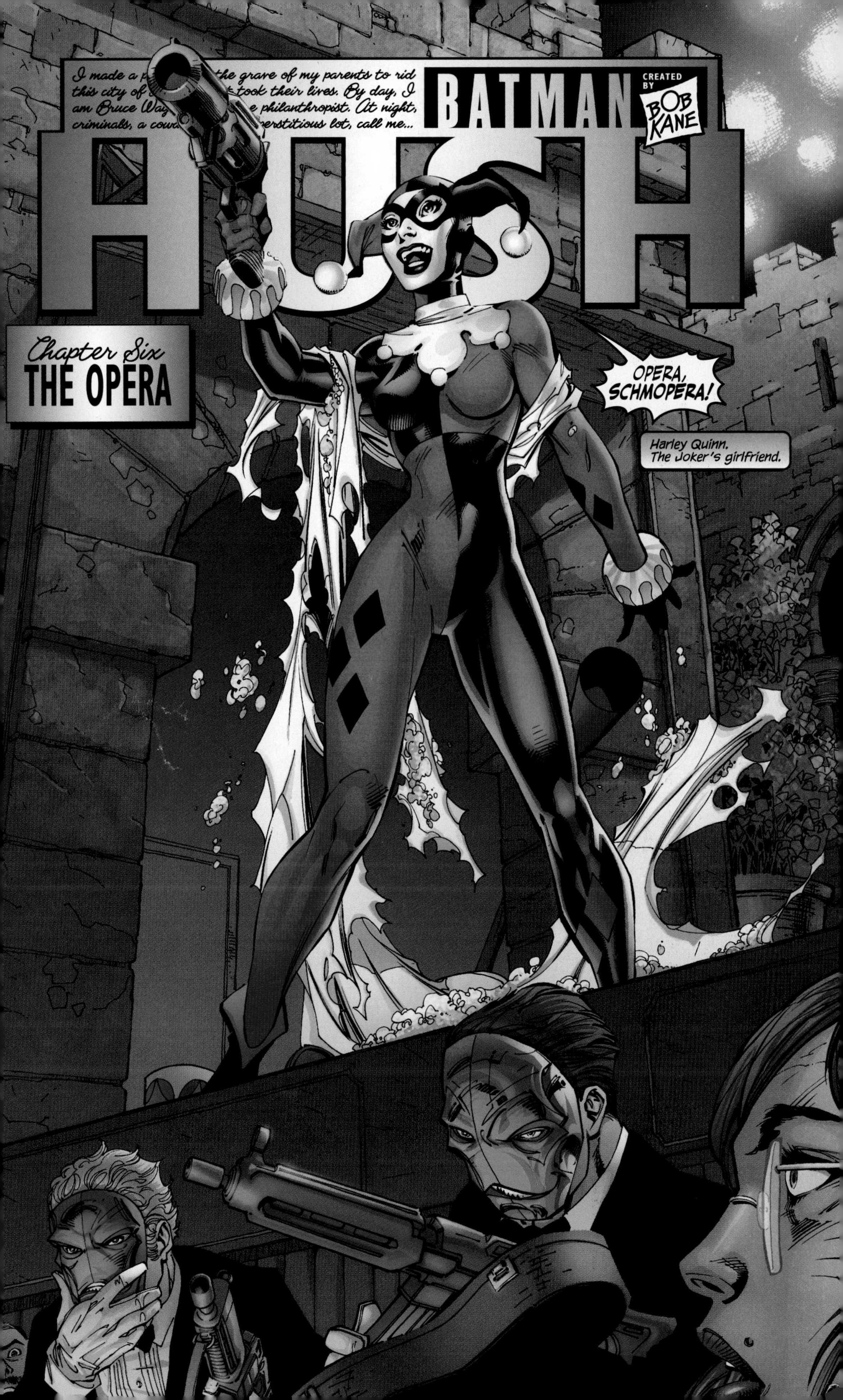

BATMAN
CREATED BY BOB KANE
HUSH
Chapter Six
THE OPERA
OPERA, SCHMOPERA!
Harley Quinn. The Joker's girlfriend.

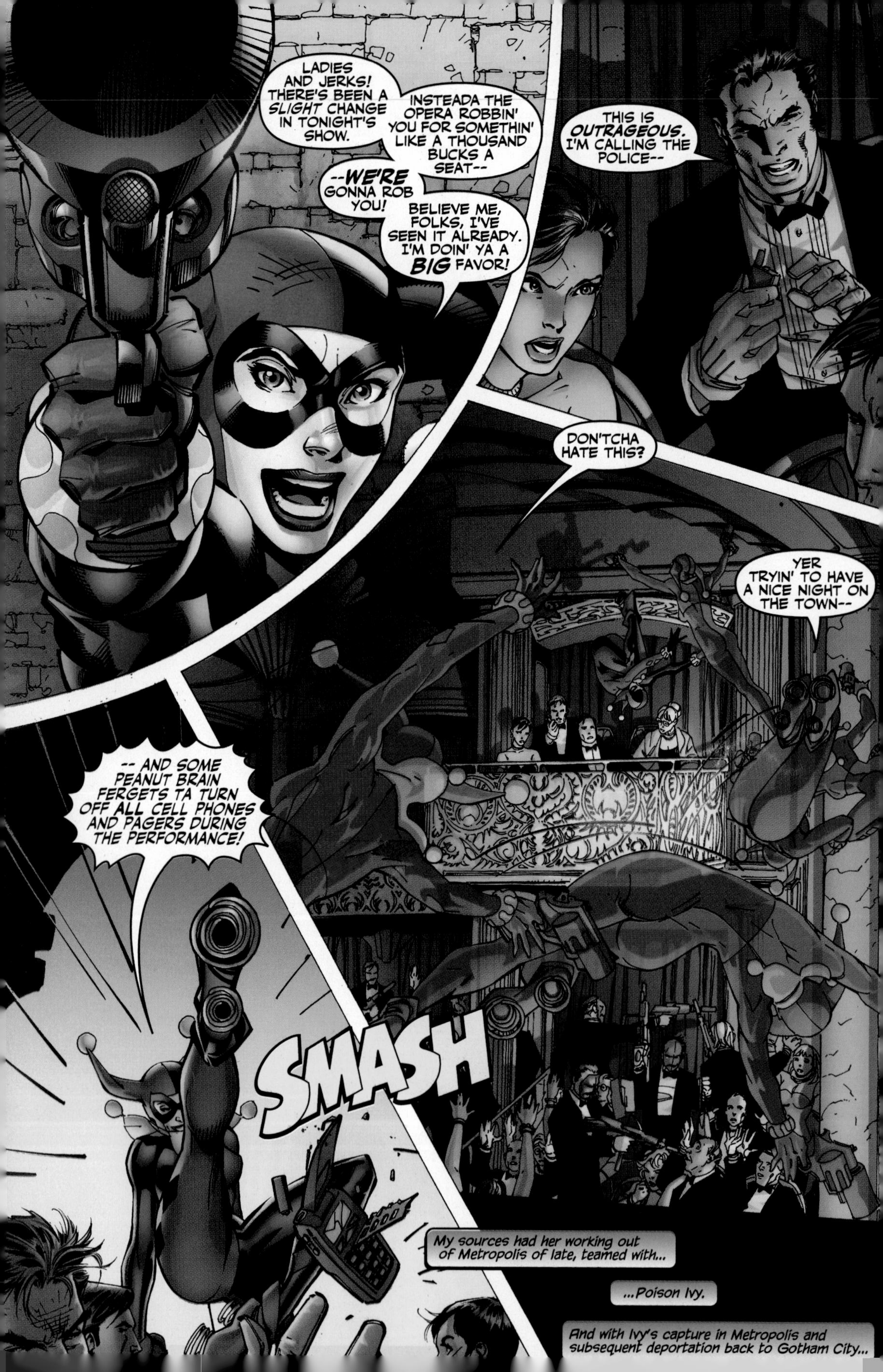
LADIES AND JERKS! THERE'S BEEN A SLIGHT CHANGE IN TONIGHT'S SHOW.
INSTEADA THE OPERA ROBBIN' YOU FOR SOMETHIN' LIKE A THOUSAND BUCKS A SEAT--
--WE'RE GONNA ROB YOU!
BELIEVE ME, FOLKS, I'VE SEEN IT ALREADY. I'M DOIN' YA A BIG FAVOR!
THIS IS OUTRAGEOUS. I'M CALLING THE POLICE--
DON'TCHA HATE THIS?
YER TRYIN' TO HAVE A NICE NIGHT ON THE TOWN--
-- AND SOME PEANUT BRAIN FERGETS TA TURN OFF ALL CELL PHONES AND PAGERS DURING THE PERFORMANCE!
SMASH
My sources had her working out of Metropolis of late, teamed with...
...Poison Ivy.
And with Ivy's capture in Metropolis and subsequent deportation back to Gotham City...

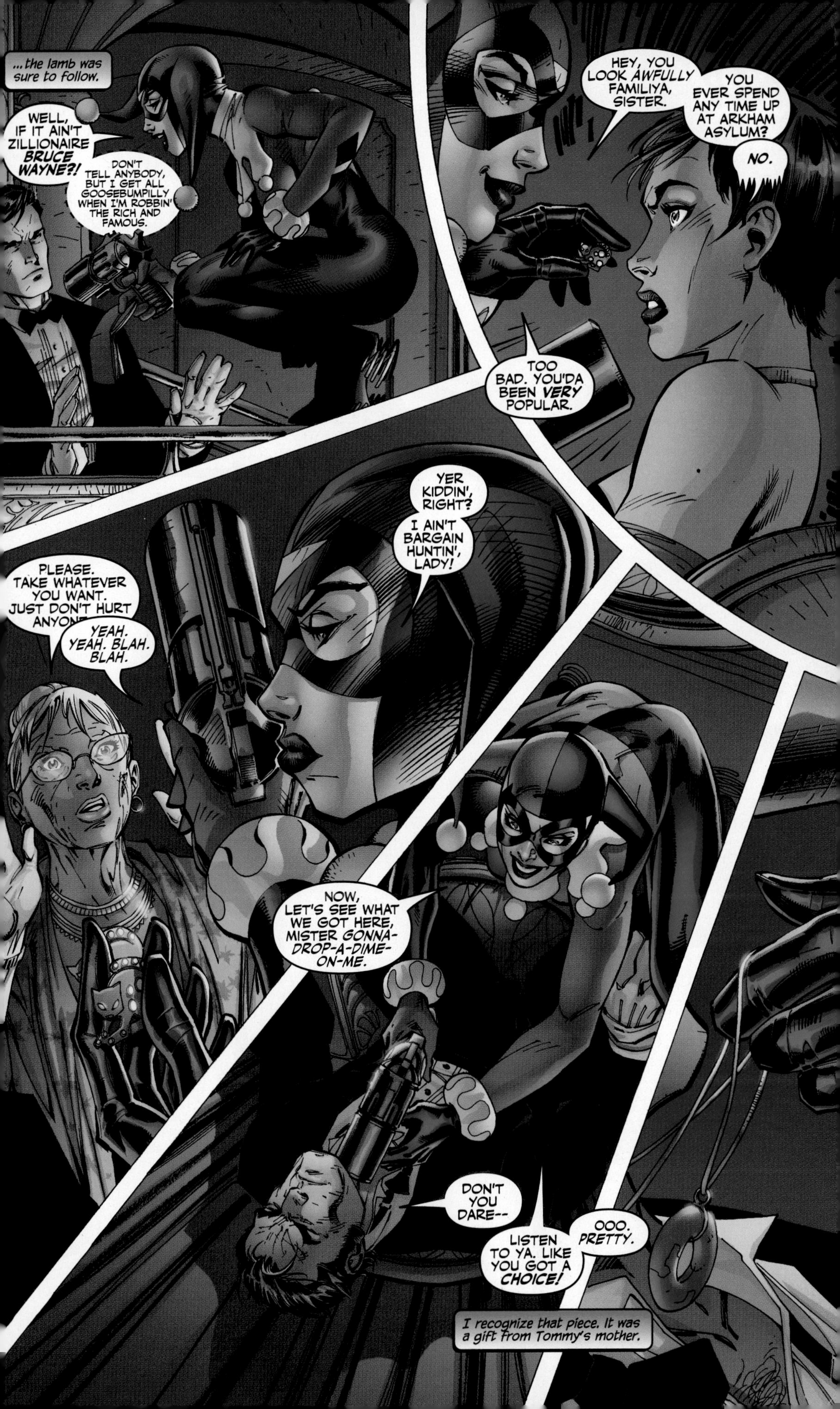
...the lamb was sure to follow.
WELL, IF IT AIN'T ZILLIONAIRE BRUCE WAYNE?!
DON'T TELL ANYBODY, BUT I GET ALL GOOSEBUMPILLY WHEN I'M ROBBIN' THE RICH AND FAMOUS.
HEY, YOU LOOK AWFULLY FAMILIYA, SISTER.
YOU EVER SPEND ANY TIME UP AT ARKHAM ASYLUM?
NO.
TOO BAD. YOU'DA BEEN VERY POPULAR.
PLEASE. TAKE WHATEVER YOU WANT. JUST DON'T HURT ANYON
YEAH. YEAH. BLAH. BLAH.
YER KIDDIN', RIGHT?
I AIN'T BARGAIN HUNTIN', LADY!
NOW, LET'S SEE WHAT WE GOT HERE, MISTER GONNA-DROP-A-DIME-ON-ME.
DON'T YOU DARE--
LISTEN TO YA. LIKE YOU GOT A CHOICE!
OOO. PRETTY.
I recognize that piece. It was a gift from Tommy's mother.

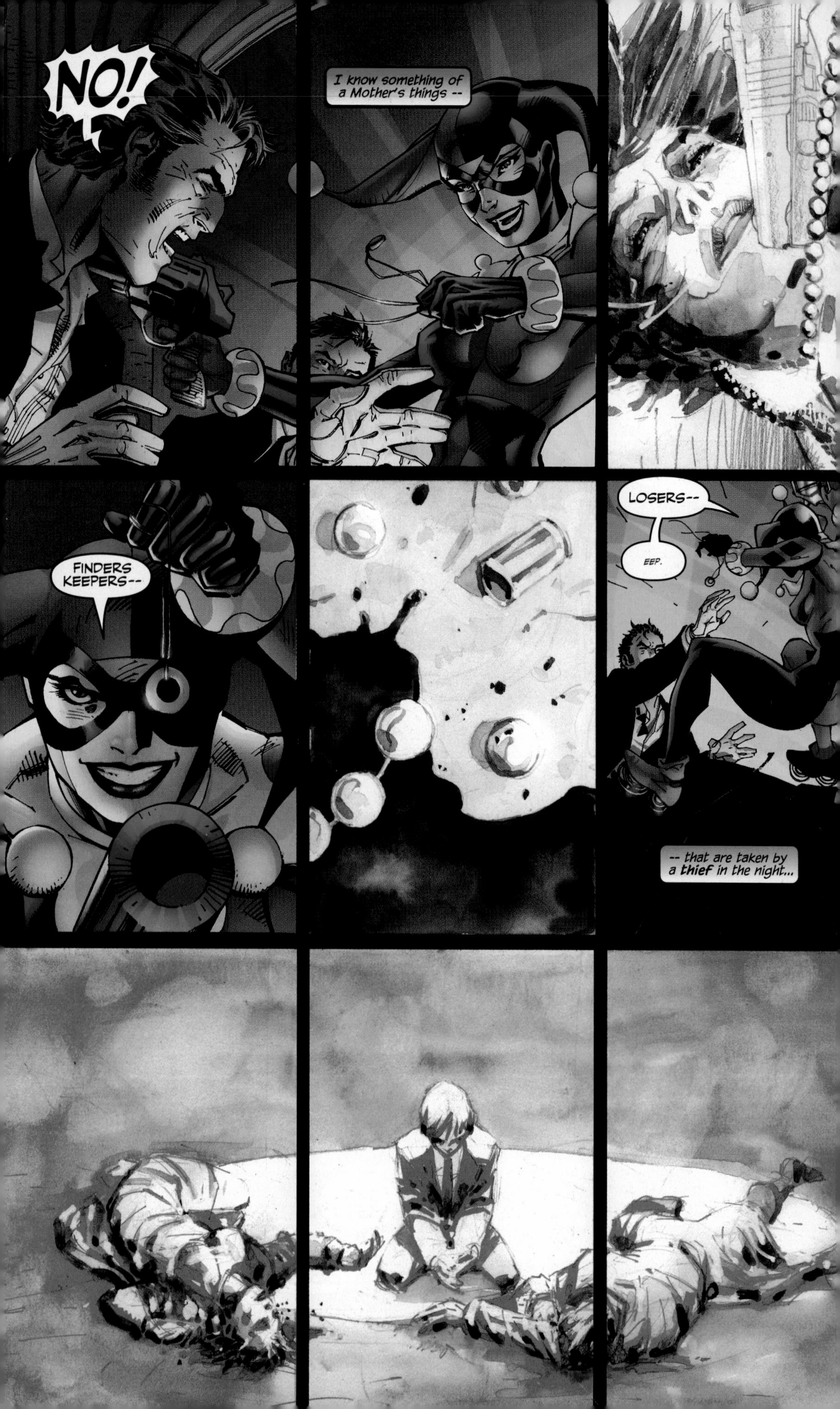
NO!
I know something of a Mother's things --
FINDERS KEEPERS--
LOSERS--
EEP.
-- that are taken by a thief in the night...

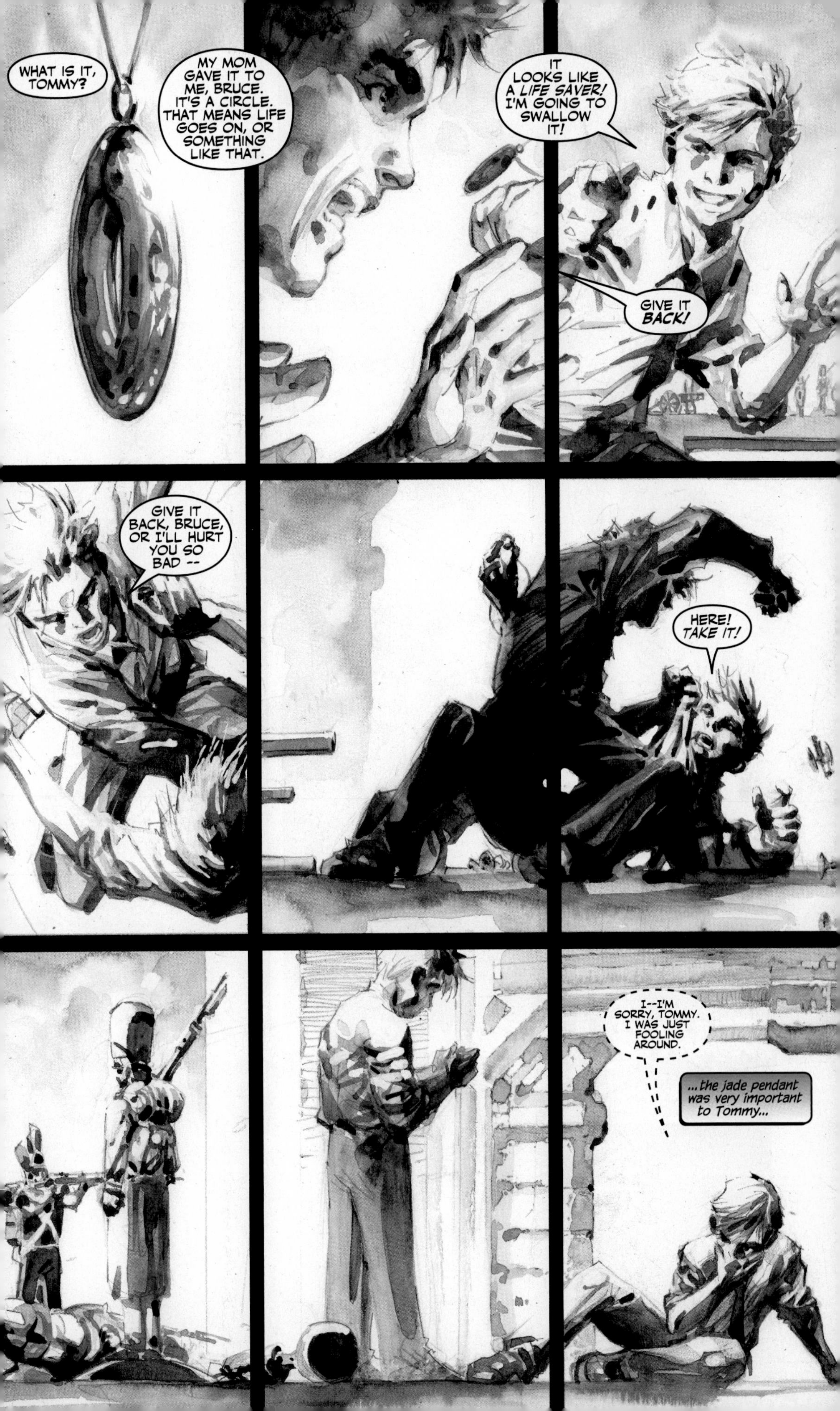
WHAT IS IT, TOMMY?
MY MOM GAVE IT TO ME, BRUCE. IT'S A CIRCLE. THAT MEANS LIFE GOES ON, OR SOMETHING LIKE THAT.
IT LOOKS LIKE A LIFE SAVER! I'M GOING TO SWALLOW IT!
GIVE IT BACK!
GIVE IT BACK, BRUCE, OR I'LL HURT YOU SO BAD --
HERE! TAKE IT!
I--I'M SORRY, TOMMY. I WAS JUST FOOLING AROUND.
...the jade pendant was very important to Tommy...

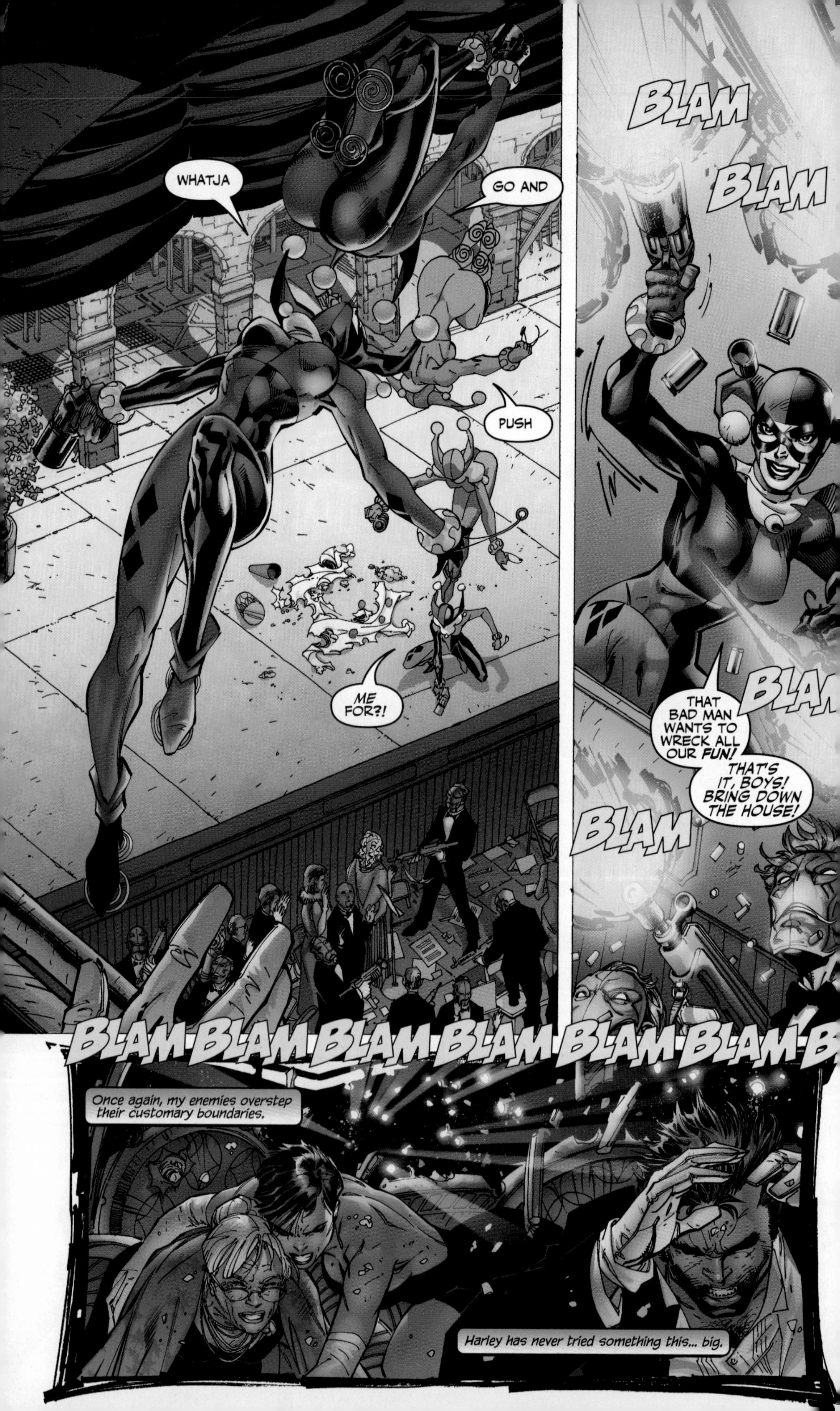
WHATJA
GO AND
PUSH
ME FOR?!
BLAM
BLAM
BLAM
THAT BAD MAN WANTS TO WRECK ALL OUR FUN!
THAT'S IT, BOYS! BRING DOWN THE HOUSE!
BLAM
BLAM BLAM BLAM BLAM BLAM BLAM
Once again, my enemies overstep their customary boundaries.
Harley has never tried something this... big.

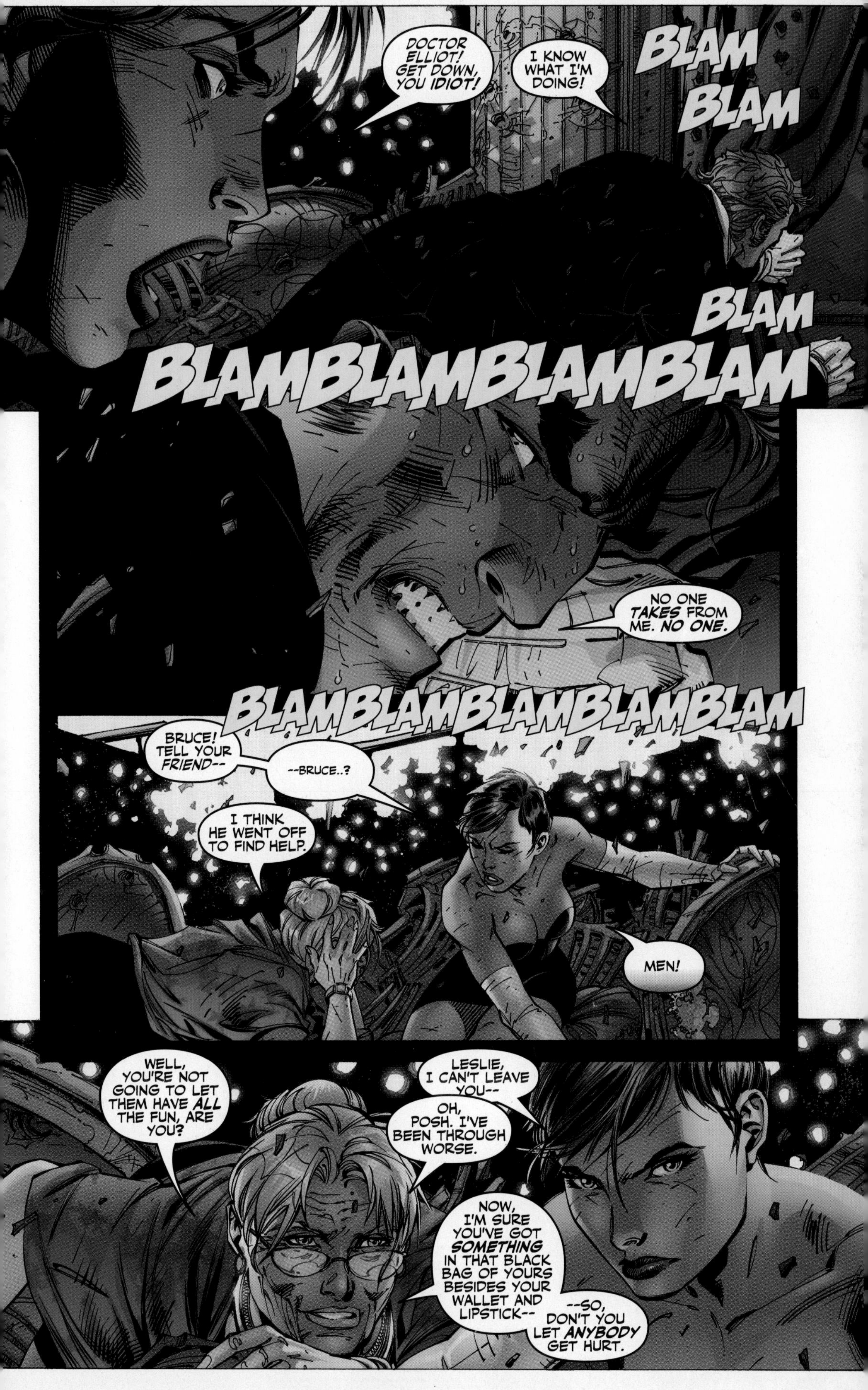
DOCTOR ELLIOT! GET DOWN, YOU IDIOT!
I KNOW WHAT I'M DOING!
BLAM BLAM
BLAM
BLAMBLAMBLAMBLAM
NO ONE TAKES FROM ME. NO ONE.
BLAMBLAMBLAMBLAMBLAM
BRUCE! TELL YOUR FRIEND--
--BRUCE..?
I THINK HE WENT OFF TO FIND HELP.
MEN!
WELL, YOU'RE NOT GOING TO LET THEM HAVE ALL THE FUN, ARE YOU?
LESLIE, I CAN'T LEAVE YOU--
OH, POSH. I'VE BEEN THROUGH WORSE.
NOW, I'M SURE YOU'VE GOT SOMETHING IN THAT BLACK BAG OF YOURS BESIDES YOUR WALLET AND LIPSTICK--
--SO, DON'T YOU LET ANYBODY GET HURT.

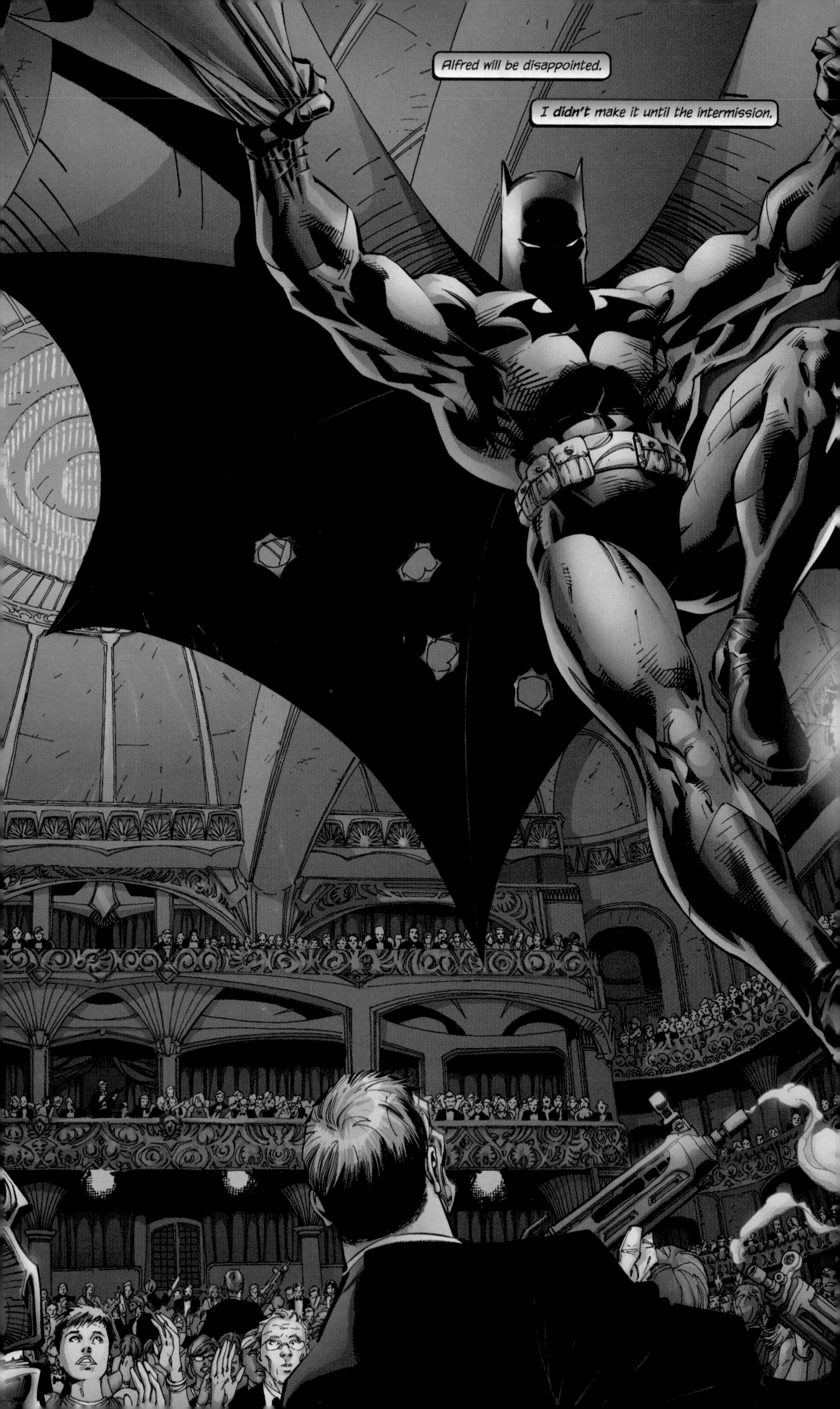
Alfred will be disappointed.
I didn't make it until the intermission.

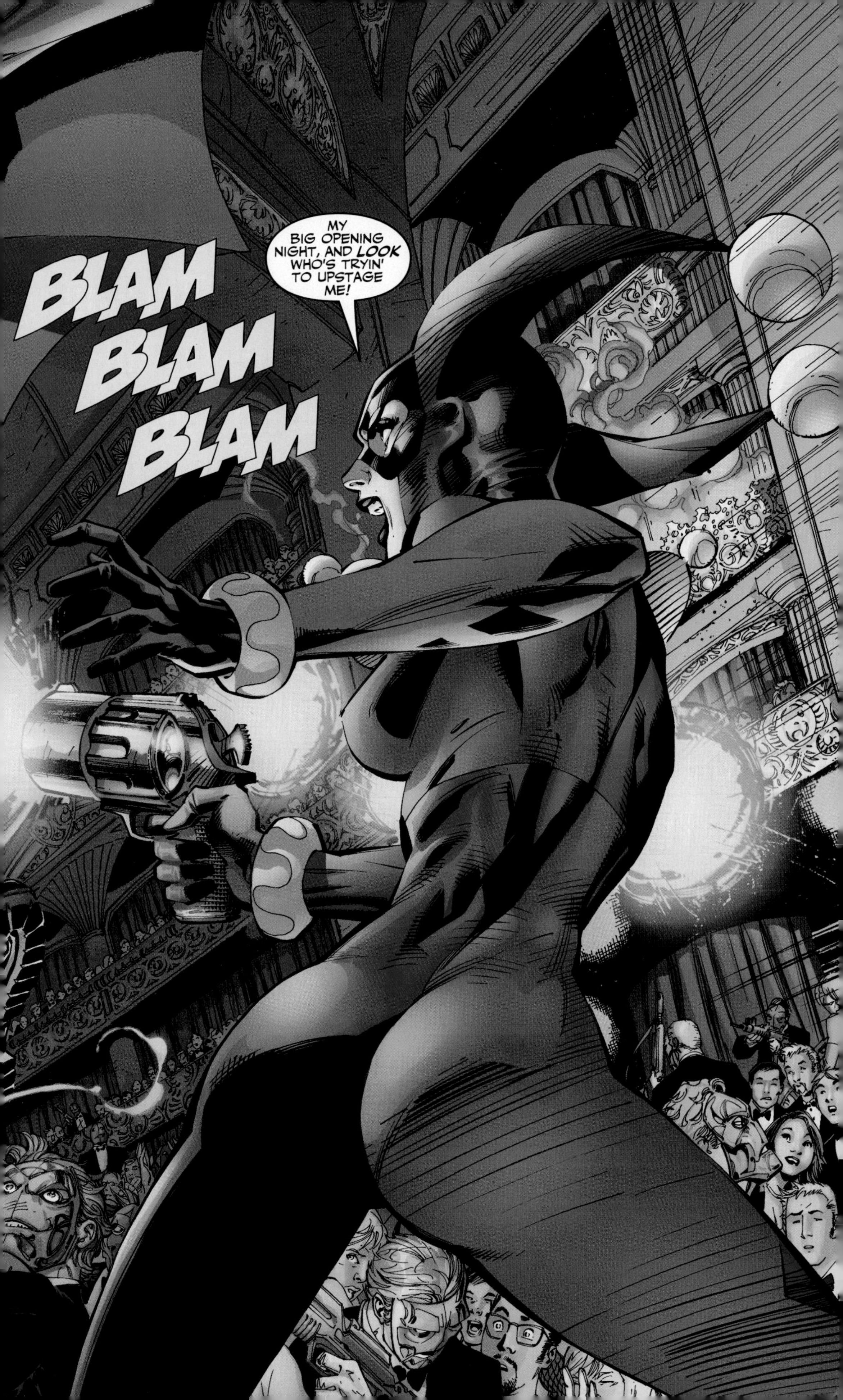
MY BIG OPENING NIGHT, AND LOOK WHO'S TRYIN' TO UPSTAGE ME!
BLAM BLAM BLAM

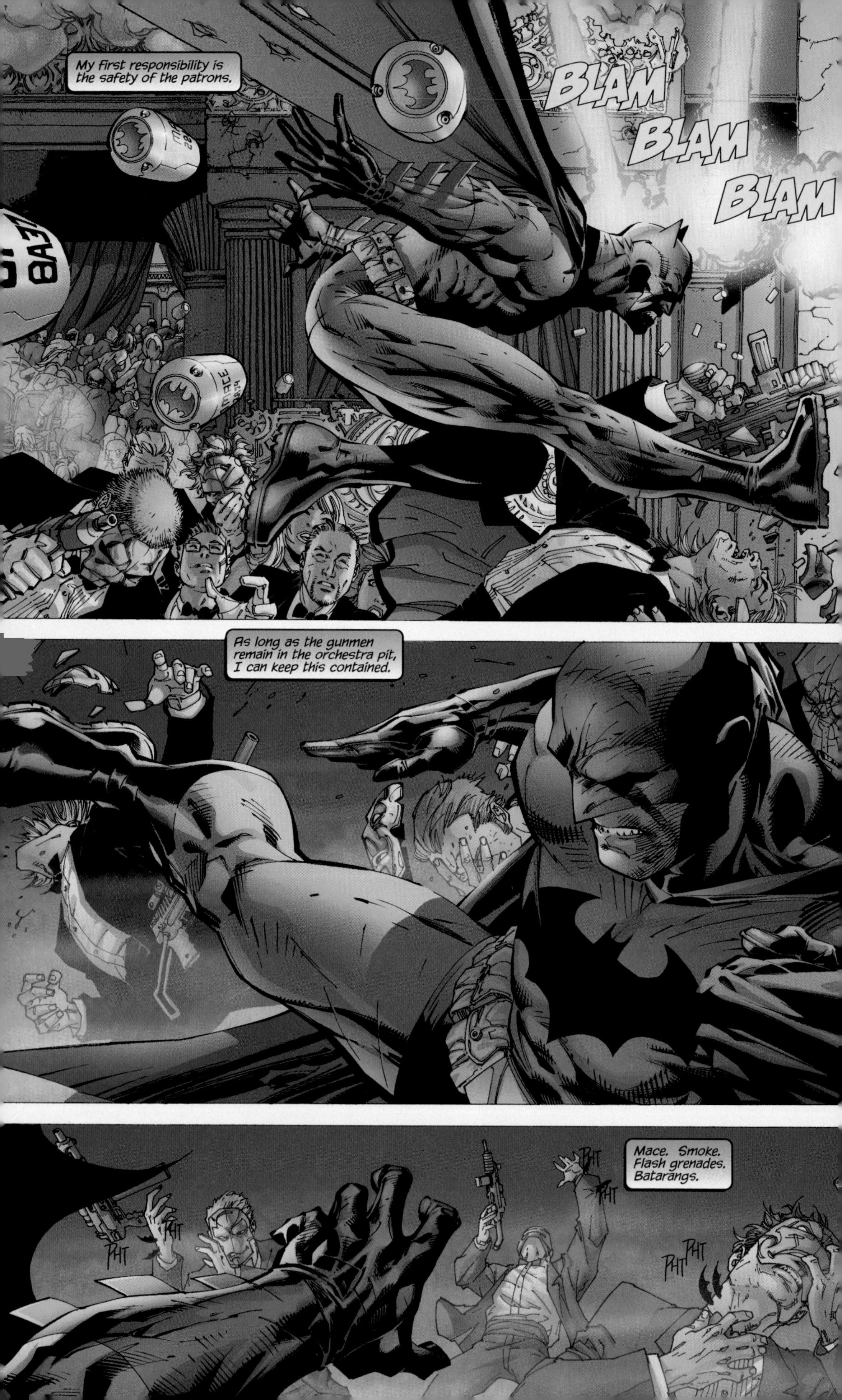
My first responsibility is the safety of the patrons.
BLAM
BLAM
BLAM
As long as the gunmen remain in the orchestra pit, I can keep this contained.
Mace. Smoke. Flash grenades. Batarangs.
PHT
PHT
PHT
PHT
PHT
PHT

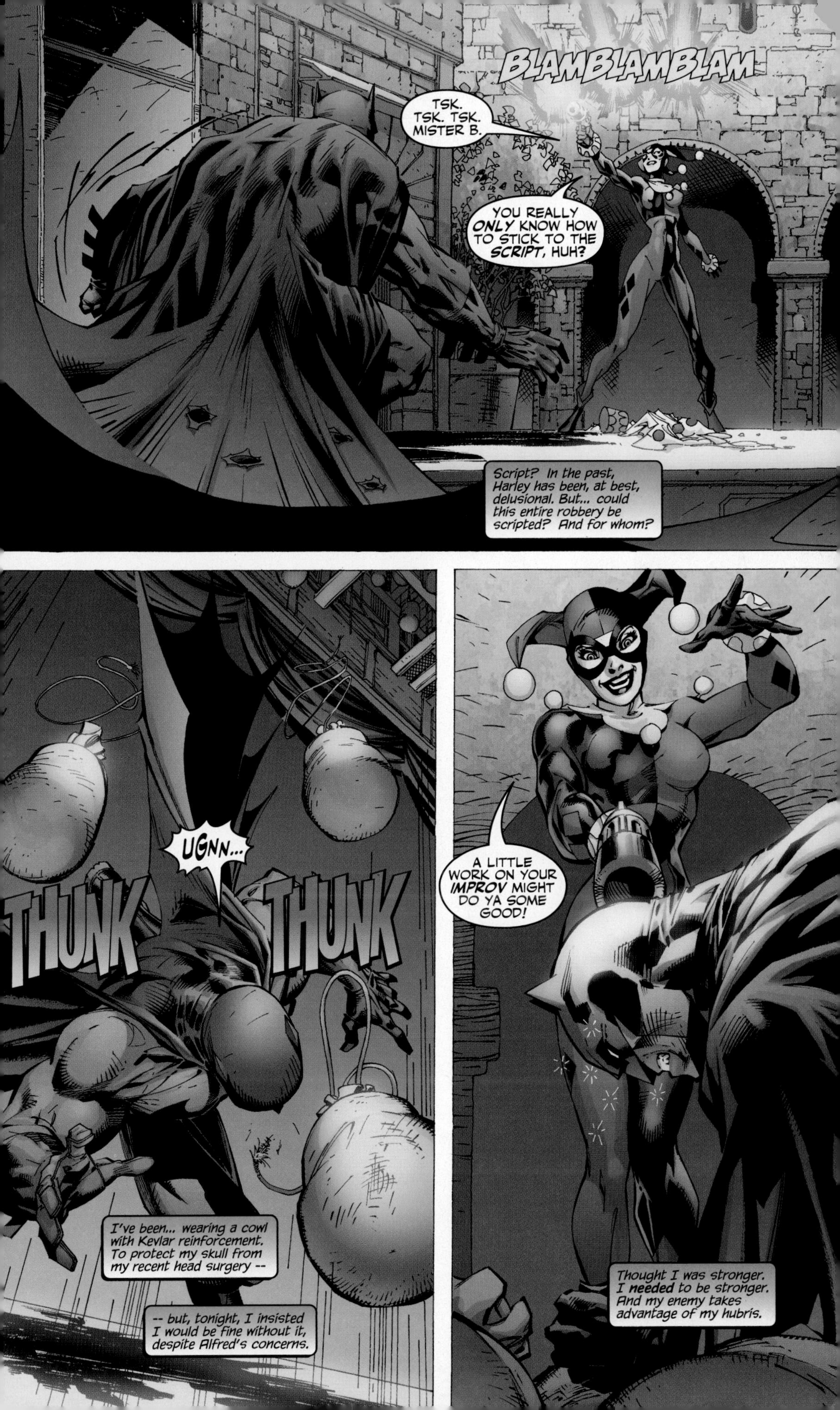
BLAMBLAMBLAM
TSK. TSK. TSK. MISTER B.
YOU REALLY ONLY KNOW HOW TO STICK TO THE SCRIPT, HUH?
Script? In the past, Harley has been, at best, delusional. But... could this entire robbery be scripted? And for whom?
THUNK
UGNN...
THUNK
I've been... wearing a cowl with Kevlar reinforcement. To protect my skull from my recent head surgery --
-- but, tonight, I insisted I would be fine without it, despite Alfred's concerns.
A LITTLE WORK ON YOUR IMPROV MIGHT DO YA SOME GOOD!
Thought I was stronger. I needed to be stronger. And my enemy takes advantage of my hubris.

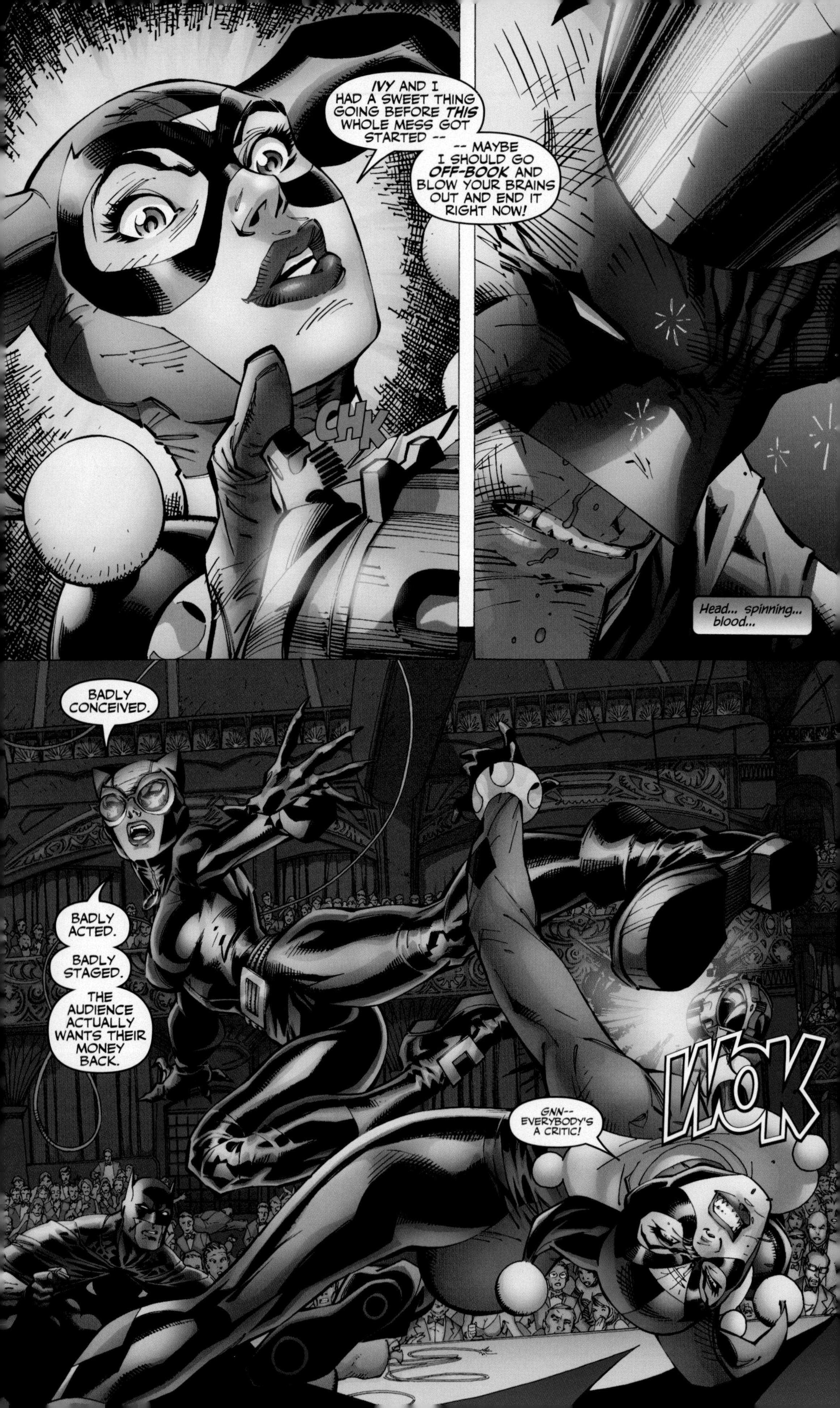
IVY AND I HAD A SWEET THING GOING BEFORE THIS WHOLE MESS GOT STARTED --
-- MAYBE I SHOULD GO OFF-BOOK AND BLOW YOUR BRAINS OUT AND END IT RIGHT NOW!
CHK
Head... spinning... blood...
BADLY CONCEIVED.
BADLY ACTED.
BADLY STAGED.
THE AUDIENCE ACTUALLY WANTS THEIR MONEY BACK.
WOK
GNN-- EVERYBODY'S A CRITIC!

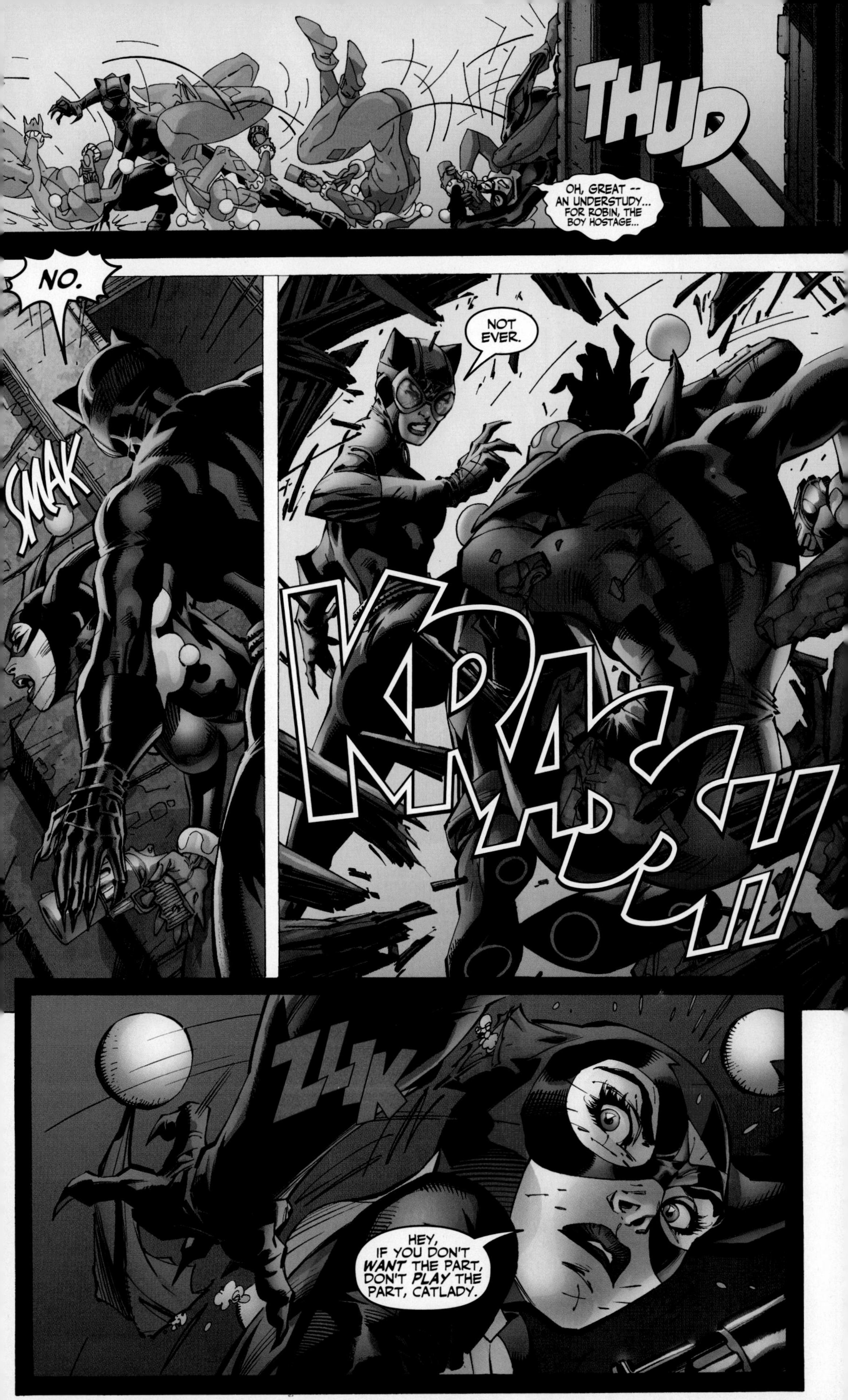
THUD
OH, GREAT -- AN UNDERSTUDY... FOR ROBIN, THE BOY HOSTAGE...
NO.
SMAK
NOT EVER.
KRAKKH
ZZIK
HEY, IF YOU DON'T *WANT* THE PART, DON'T *PLAY* THE PART, CATLADY.

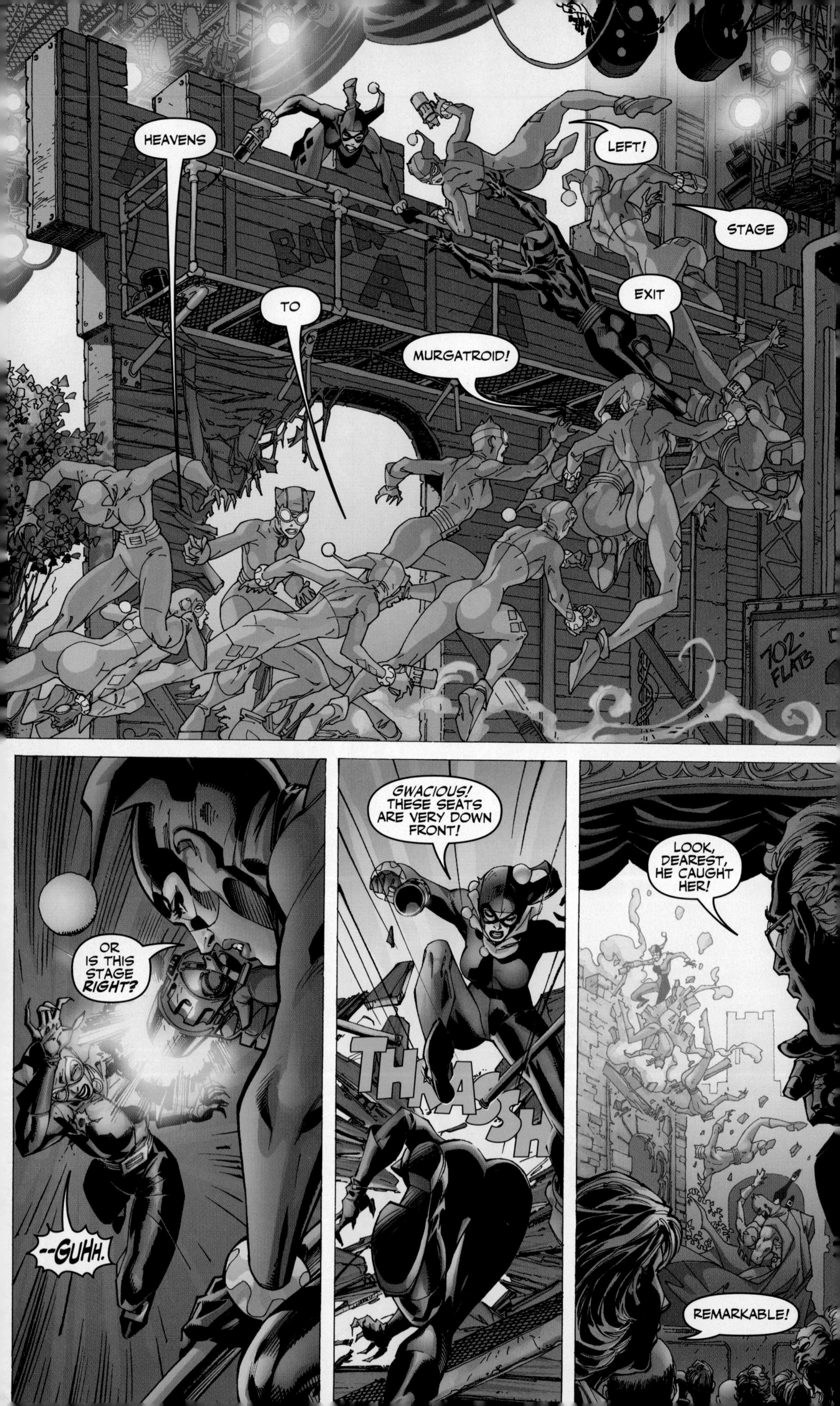

HEAVENS
TO
MURGATROID!
LEFT!
STAGE
EXIT
OR IS THIS STAGE RIGHT?
--GUHH.
GWACIOUS! THESE SEATS ARE VERY DOWN FRONT!
THRASH
LOOK, DEAREST, HE CAUGHT HER!
REMARKABLE!

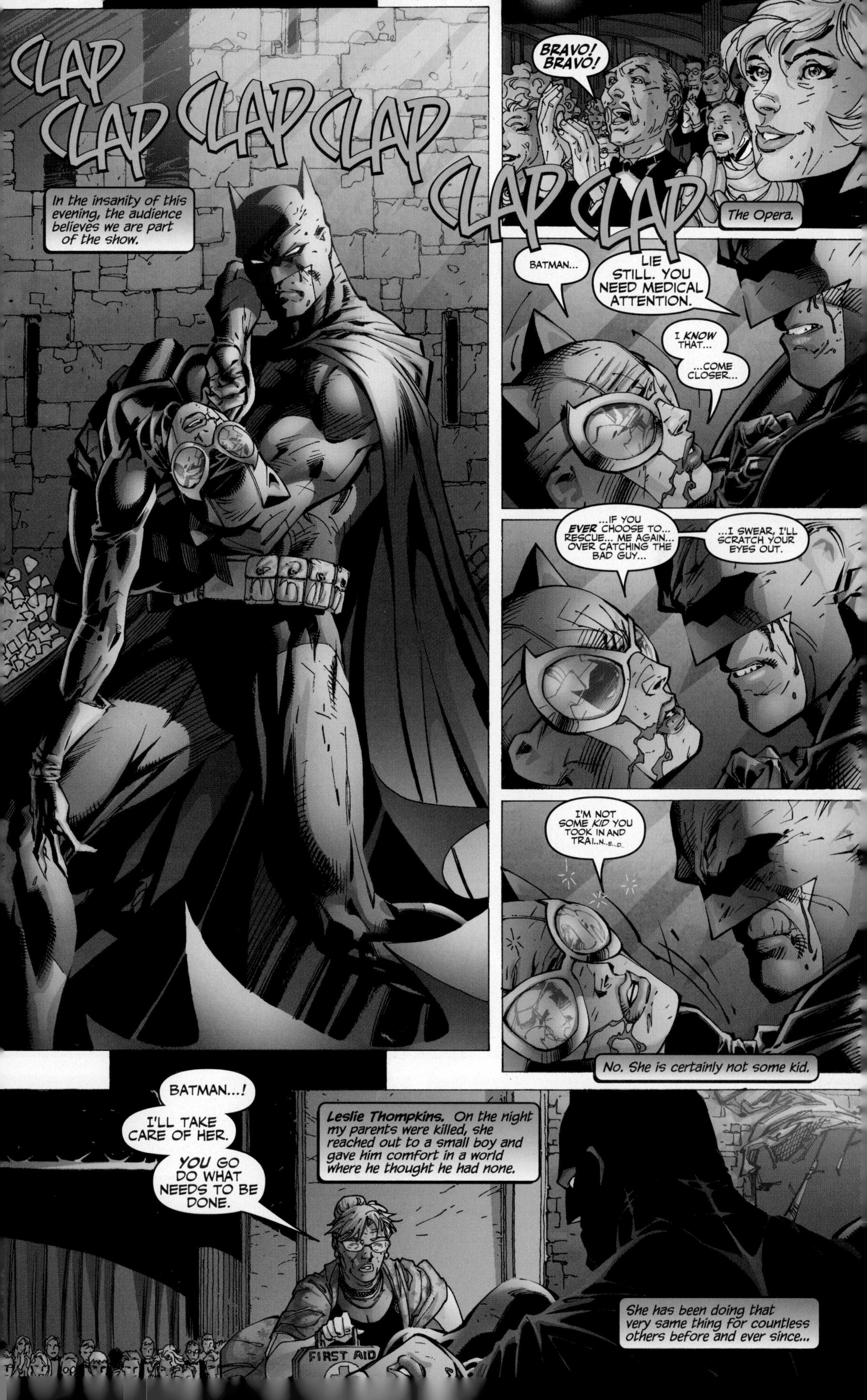
CLAP CLAP CLAP CLAP CLAP CLAP
In the insanity of this evening, the audience believes we are part of the show.
BRAVO! BRAVO!
The Opera.
BATMAN...
LIE STILL. YOU NEED MEDICAL ATTENTION.
I KNOW THAT...
...COME CLOSER...
...IF YOU EVER CHOOSE TO... RESCUE... ME AGAIN... OVER CATCHING THE BAD GUY...
...I SWEAR, I'LL SCRATCH YOUR EYES OUT.
I'M NOT SOME KID YOU TOOK IN AND TRAI..N..E..D.
No. She is certainly not some kid.
BATMAN...!
I'LL TAKE CARE OF HER.
YOU GO DO WHAT NEEDS TO BE DONE.
Leslie Thompkins. On the night my parents were killed, she reached out to a small boy and gave him comfort in a world where he thought he had none.
She has been doing that very same thing for countless others before and ever since...
FIRST AID

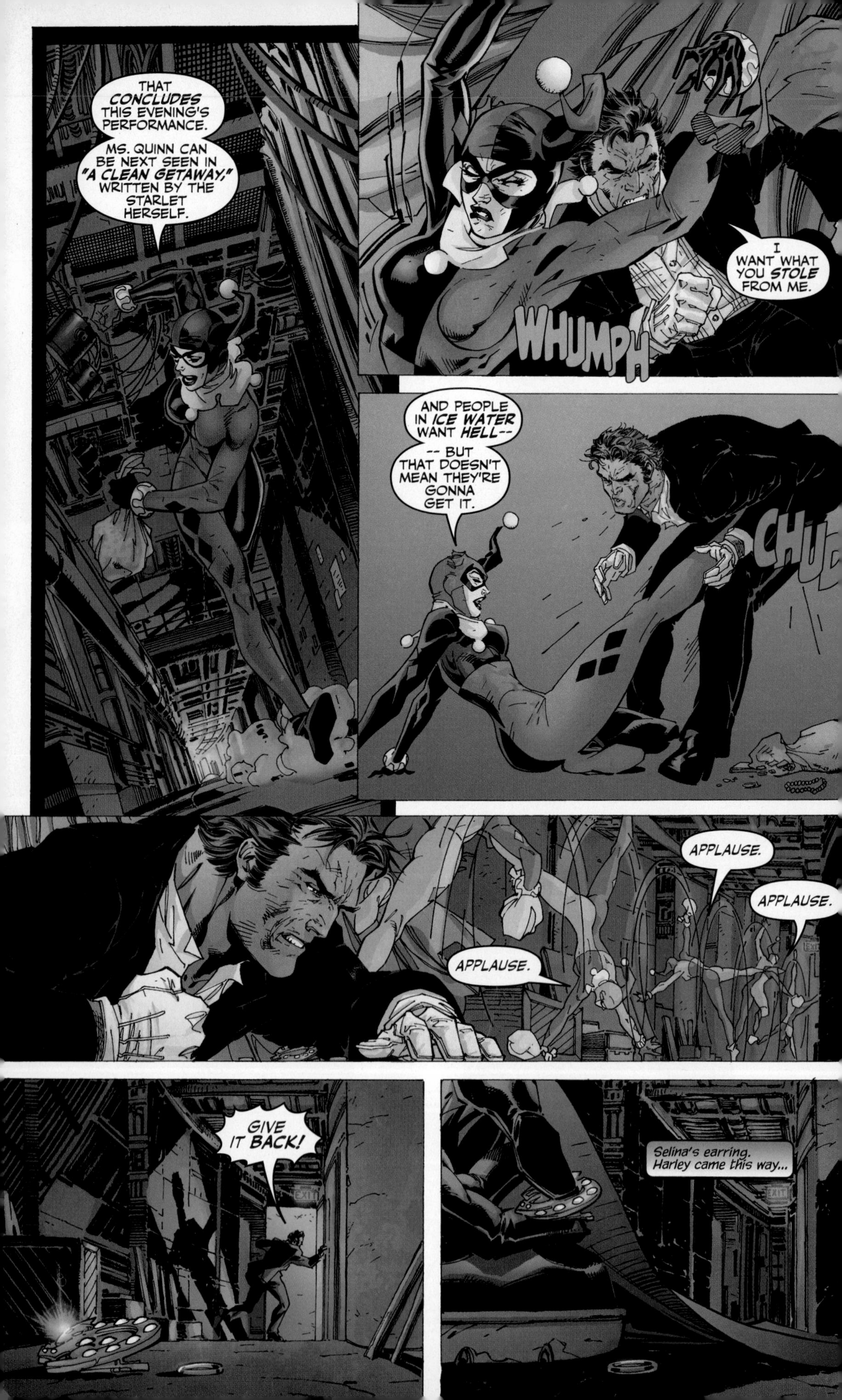
THAT CONCLUDES THIS EVENING'S PERFORMANCE.
MS. QUINN CAN BE NEXT SEEN IN "A CLEAN GETAWAY," WRITTEN BY THE STARLET HERSELF.
I WANT WHAT YOU STOLE FROM ME.
WHUMPH
AND PEOPLE IN ICE WATER WANT HELL--
-- BUT THAT DOESN'T MEAN THEY'RE GONNA GET IT.
CHUD
APPLAUSE.
APPLAUSE.
APPLAUSE.
GIVE IT BACK!
EXIT
Selina's earring. Harley came this way...
EXIT

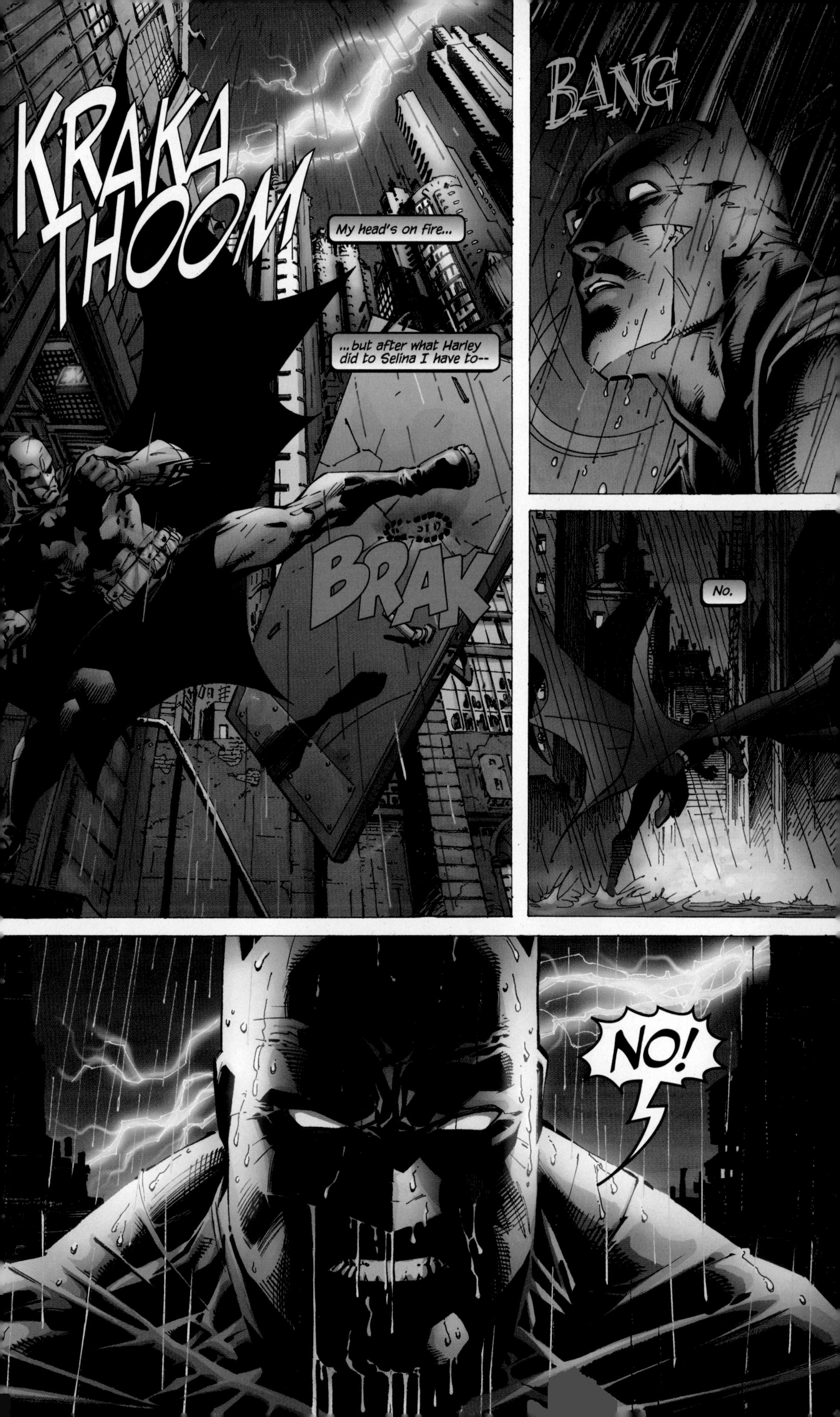
KRAKA THOOM
My head's on fire...
...but after what Harley did to Selina I have to--
BRAK
BANG
No.
NO!

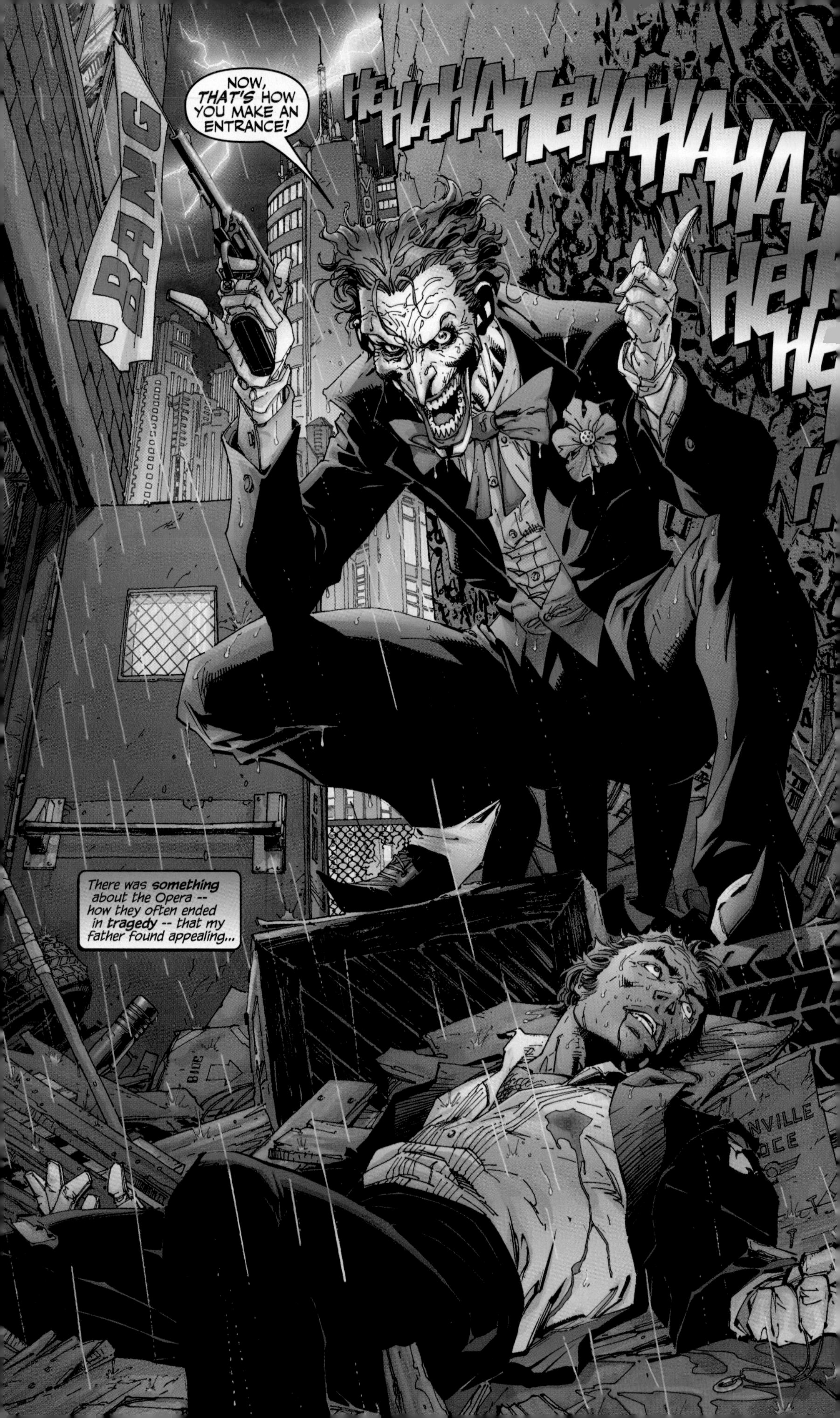
BANG
NOW, THAT'S HOW YOU MAKE AN ENTRANCE!
HEHAHAHAHEHAHAHAHAHA
HA
HEH
HE
There was something about the Opera -- how they often ended in tragedy -- that my father found appealing...

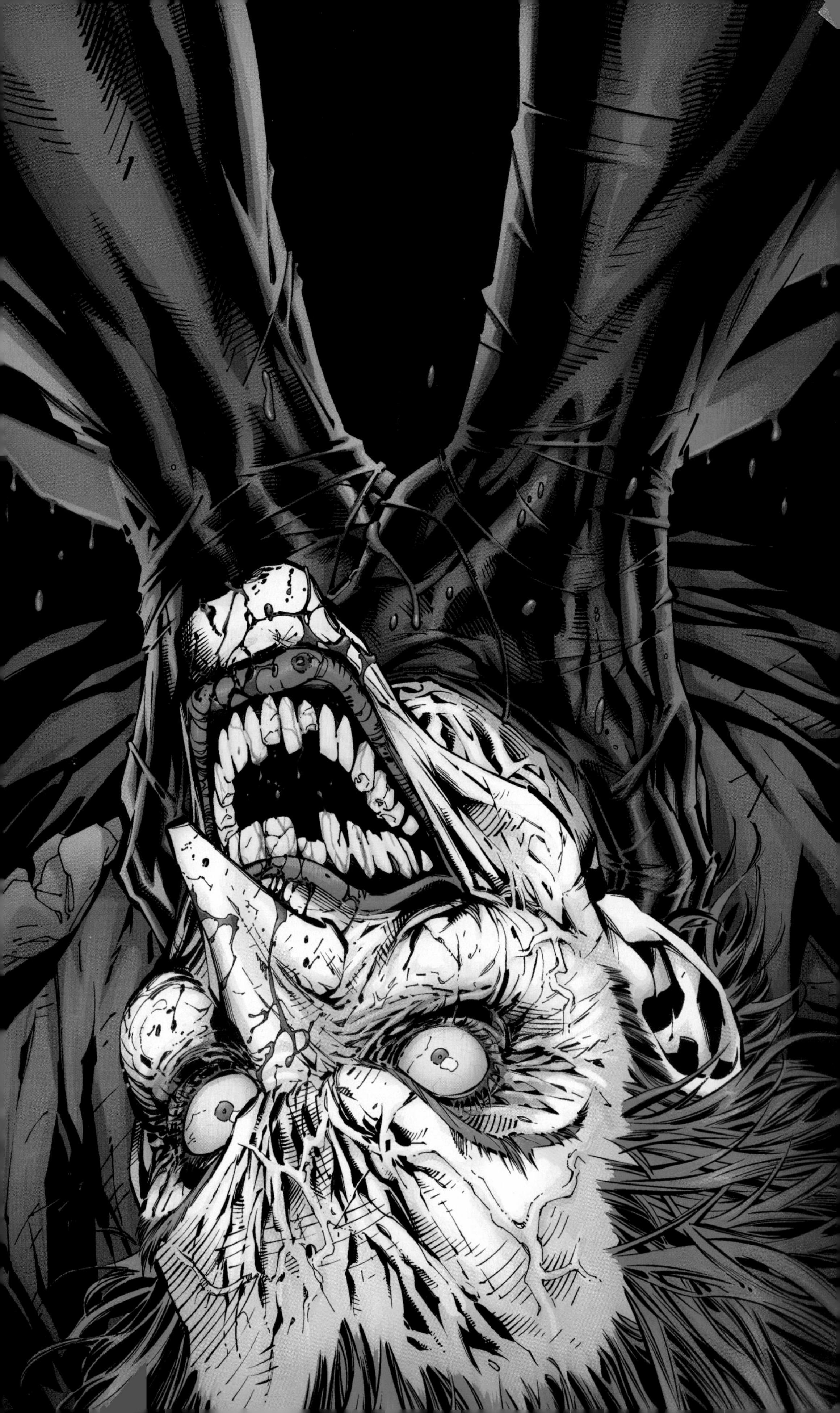

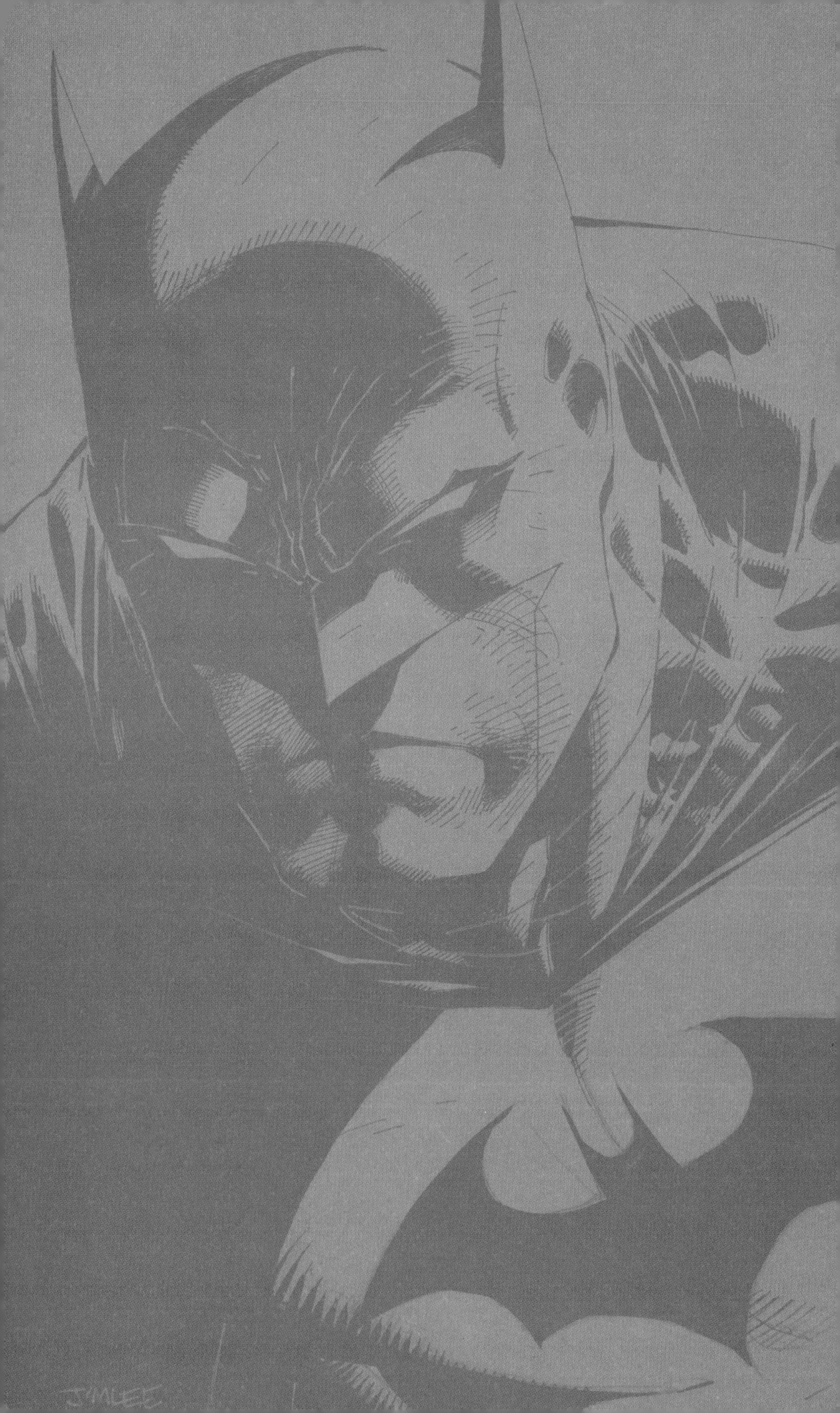

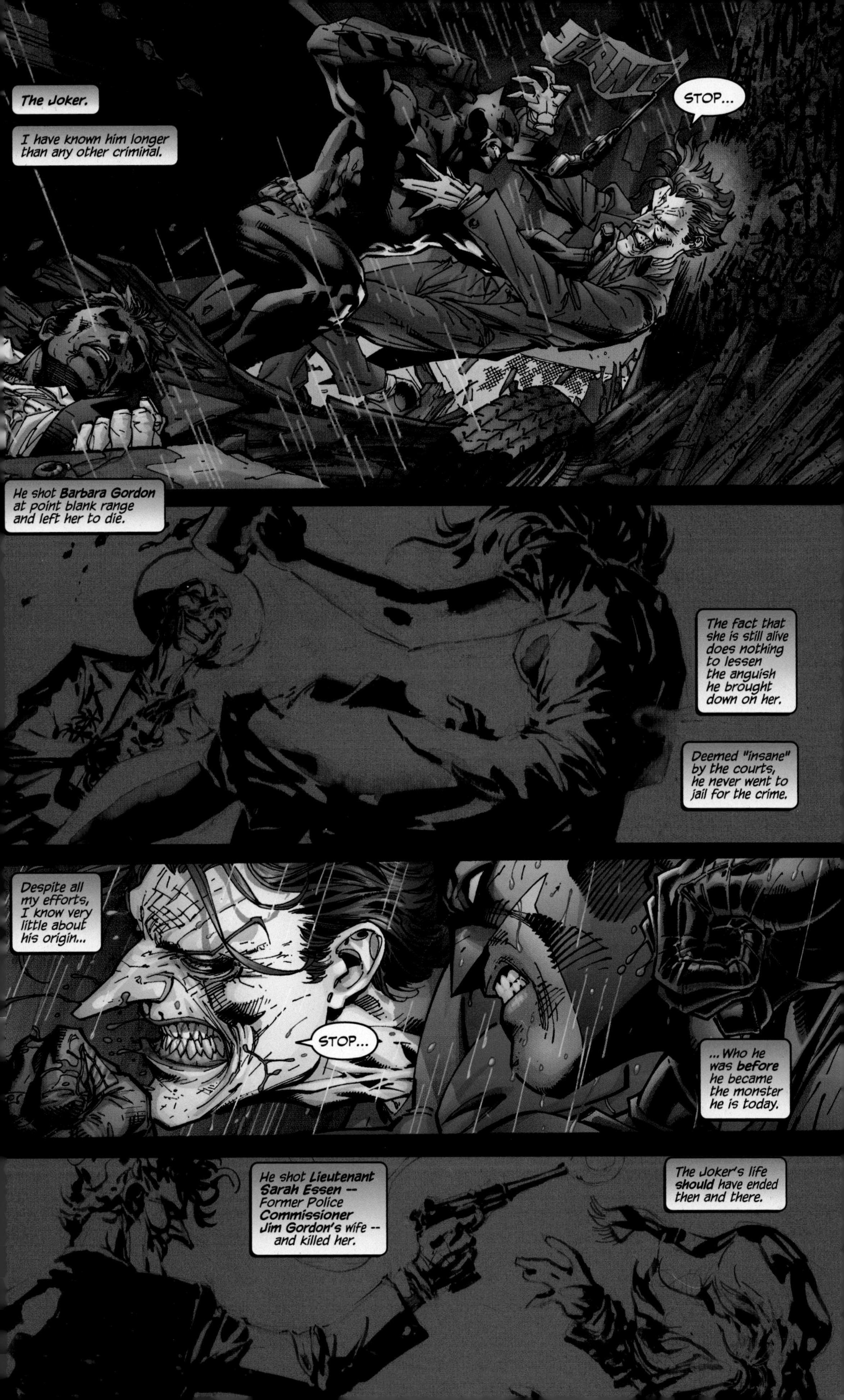
The Joker.
I have known him longer than any other criminal.
STOP...
BANG
He shot Barbara Gordon at point blank range and left her to die.
The fact that she is still alive does nothing to lessen the anguish he brought down on her.
Deemed "insane" by the courts, he never went to jail for the crime.
Despite all my efforts, I know very little about his origin...
STOP...
...Who he was before he became the monster he is today.
He shot Lieutenant Sarah Essen -- Former Police Commissioner Jim Gordon's wife -- and killed her.
The Joker's life should have ended then and there.

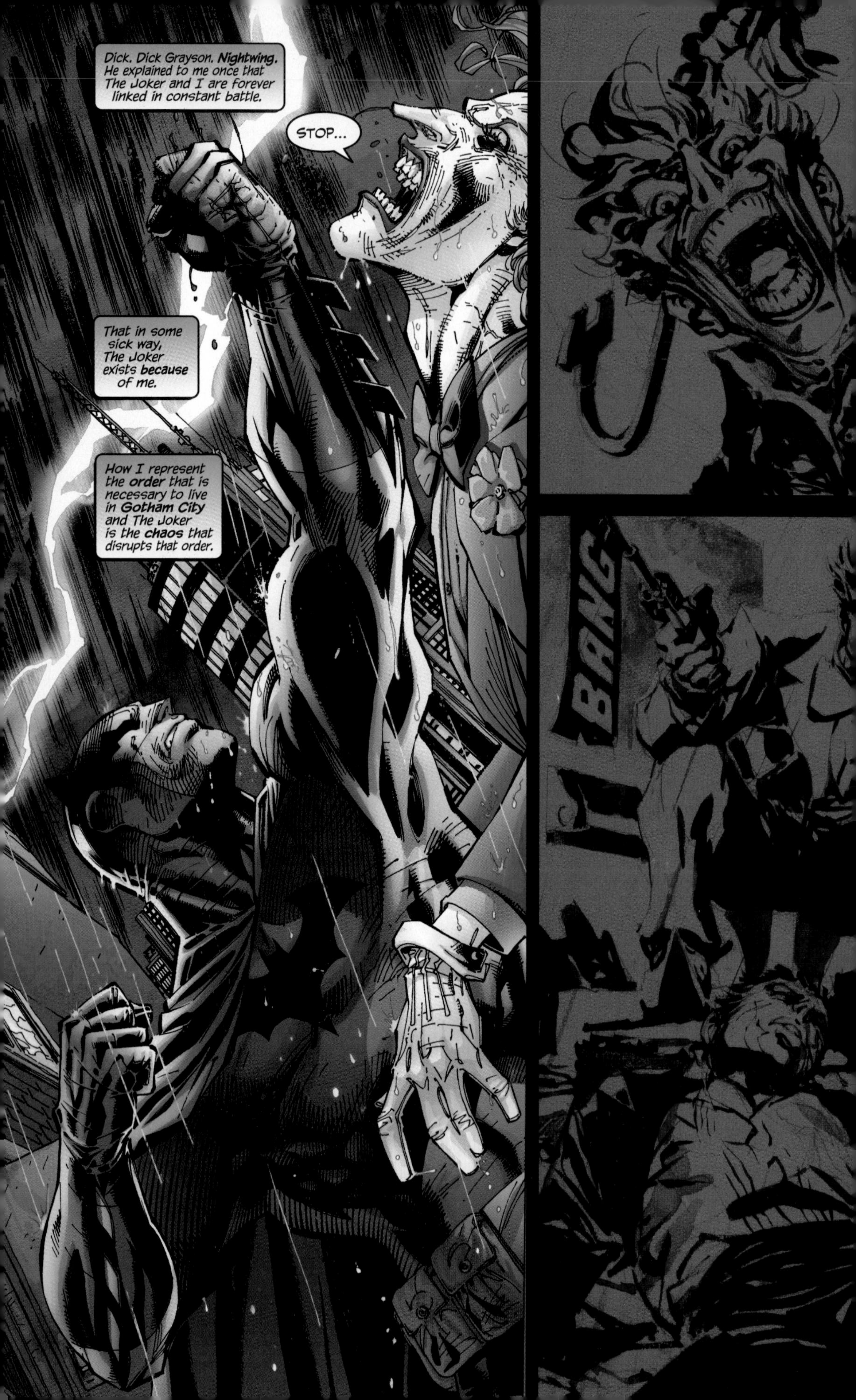
Dick. Dick Grayson. **Nightwing.** He explained to me once that The Joker and I are forever linked in constant battle.
STOP...
That in some sick way, The Joker exists **because** of me.
How I represent the **order** that is necessary to live in **Gotham City** and The Joker is the **chaos** that disrupts that order.
BANG

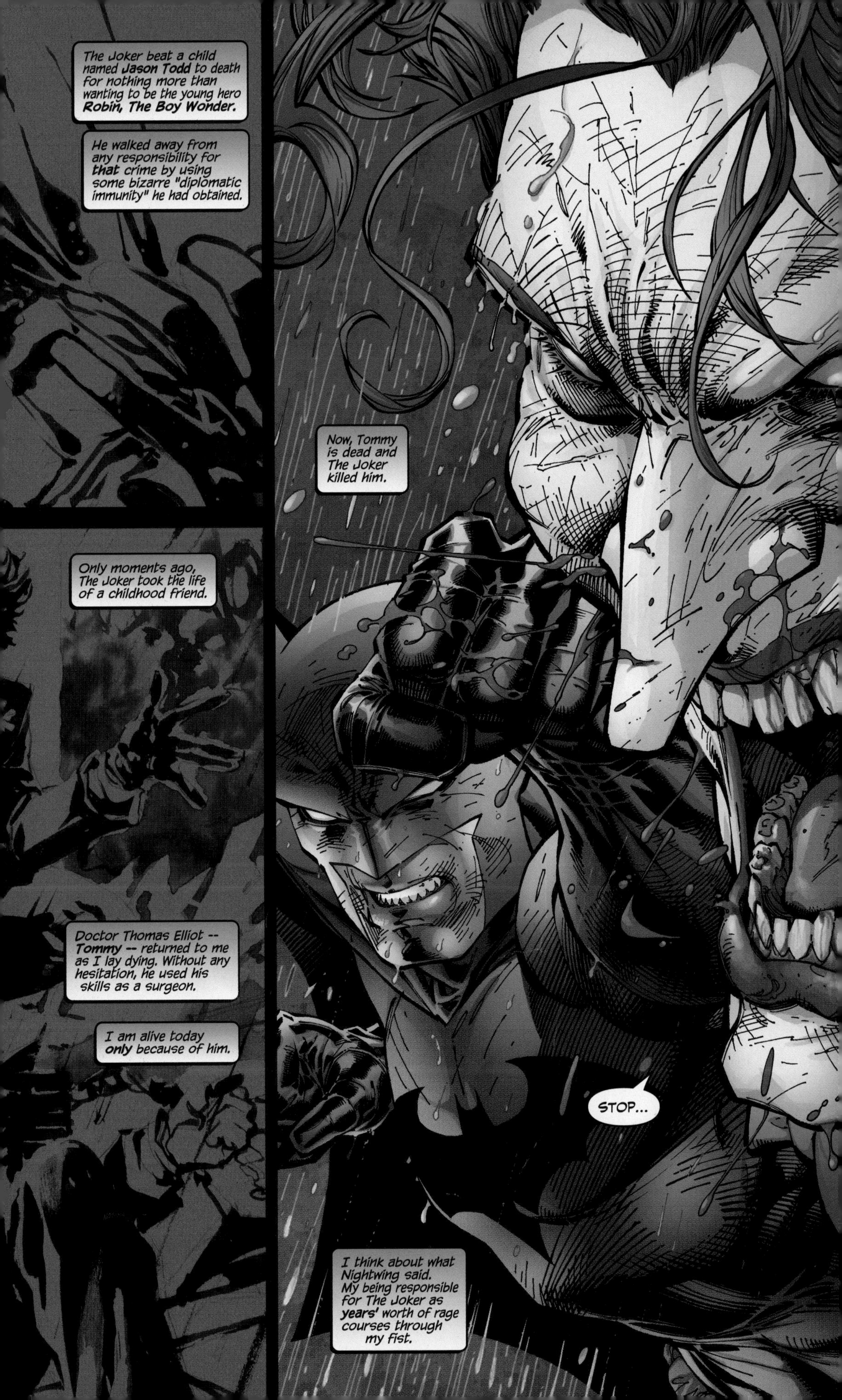
The Joker beat a child named Jason Todd to death for nothing more than wanting to be the young hero Robin, The Boy Wonder.
He walked away from any responsibility for that crime by using some bizarre "diplomatic immunity" he had obtained.
Only moments ago, The Joker took the life of a childhood friend.
Doctor Thomas Elliot -- Tommy -- returned to me as I lay dying. Without any hesitation, he used his skills as a surgeon.
I am alive today only because of him.
Now, Tommy is dead and The Joker killed him.
STOP...
I think about what Nightwing said. My being responsible for The Joker as years' worth of rage courses through my fist.

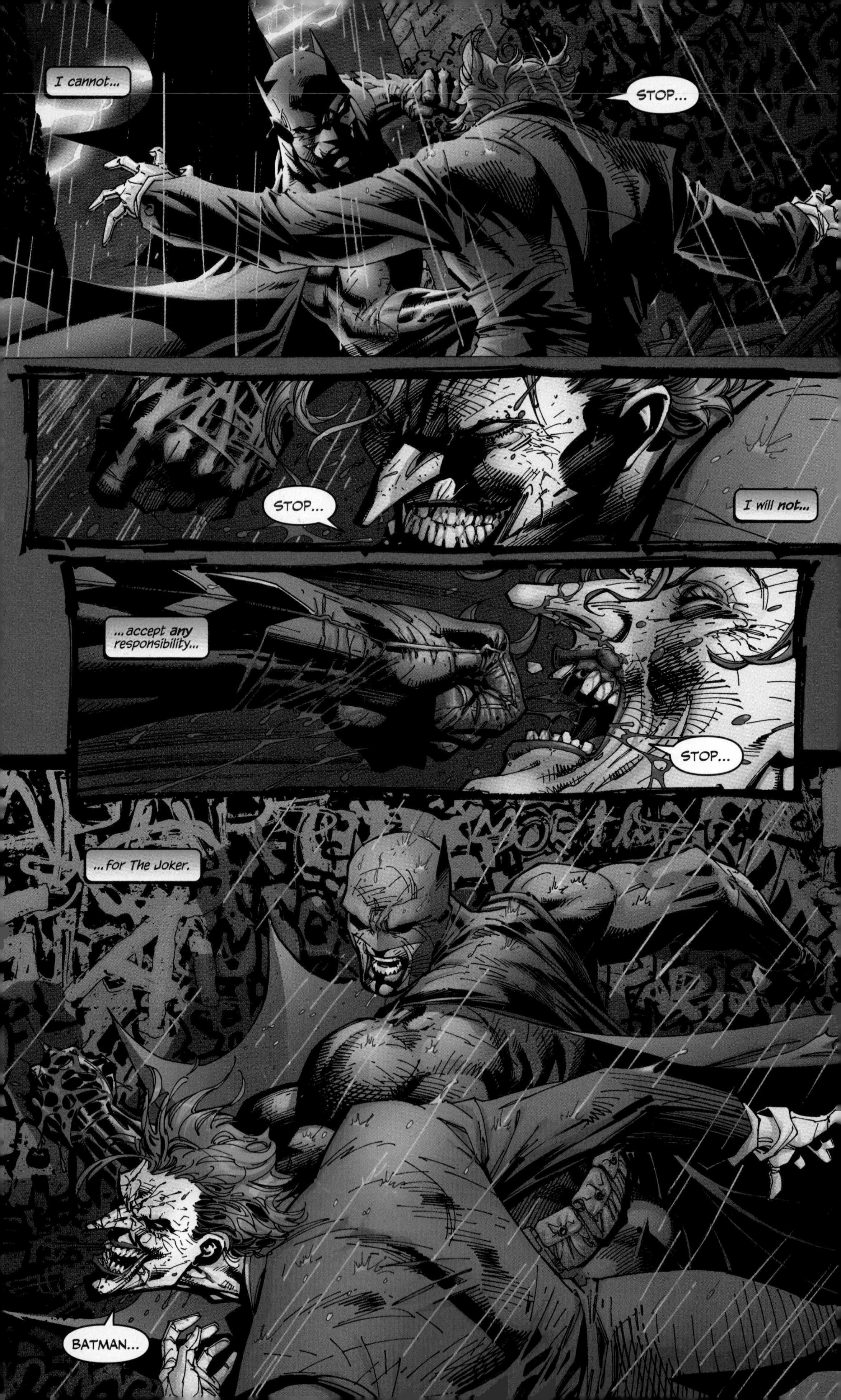
I cannot...
STOP...
STOP...
I will not...
...accept any responsibility...
STOP...
...for The Joker.
BATMAN...

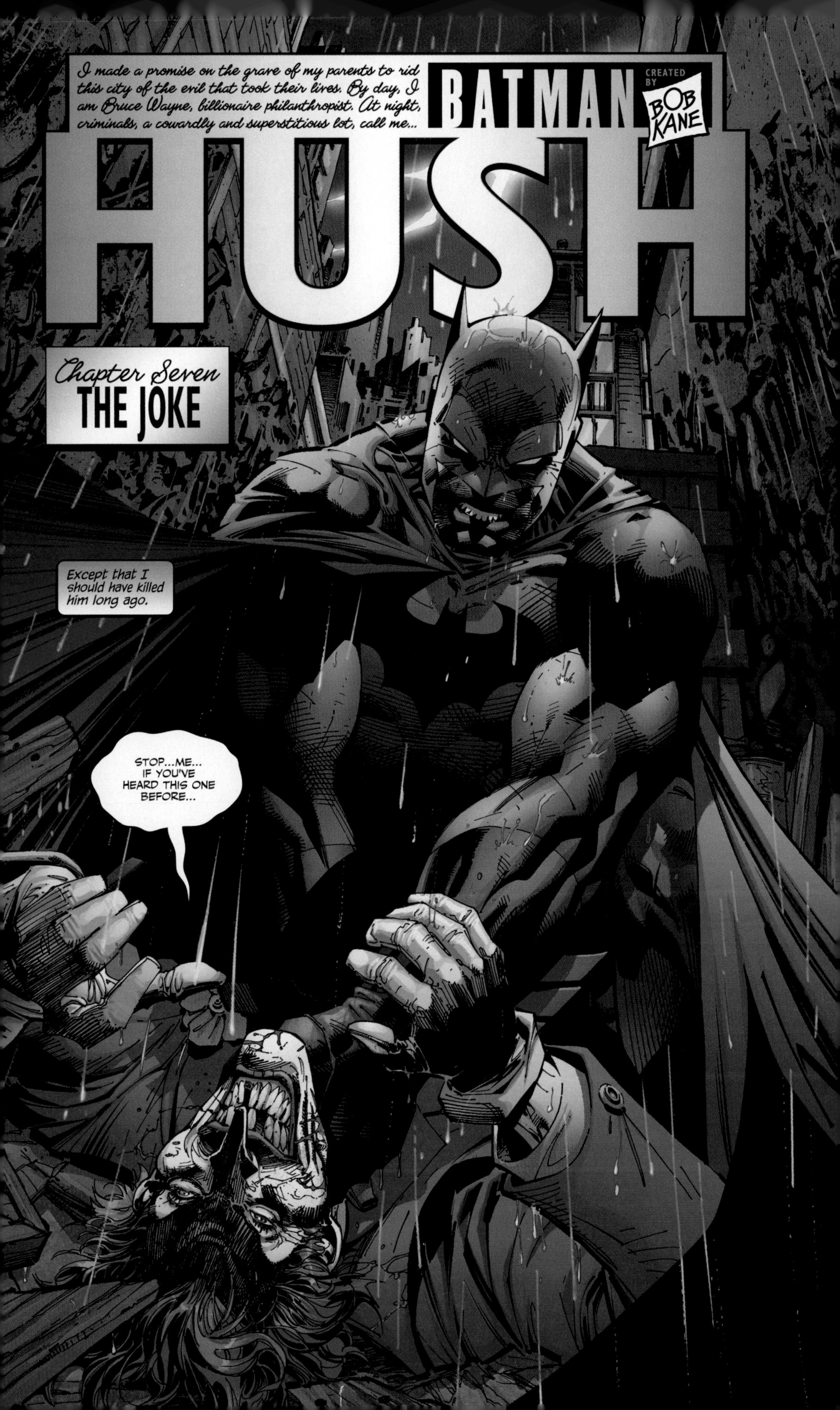

I made a promise on the grave of my parents to rid this city of the evil that took their lives. By day, I am Bruce Wayne, billionaire philanthropist. At night, criminals, a cowardly and superstitious lot, call me...
BATMAN
CREATED BY BOB KANE
HUSH
Chapter Seven
THE JOKE
Except that I should have killed him long ago.
STOP...ME... IF YOU'VE HEARD THIS ONE BEFORE...

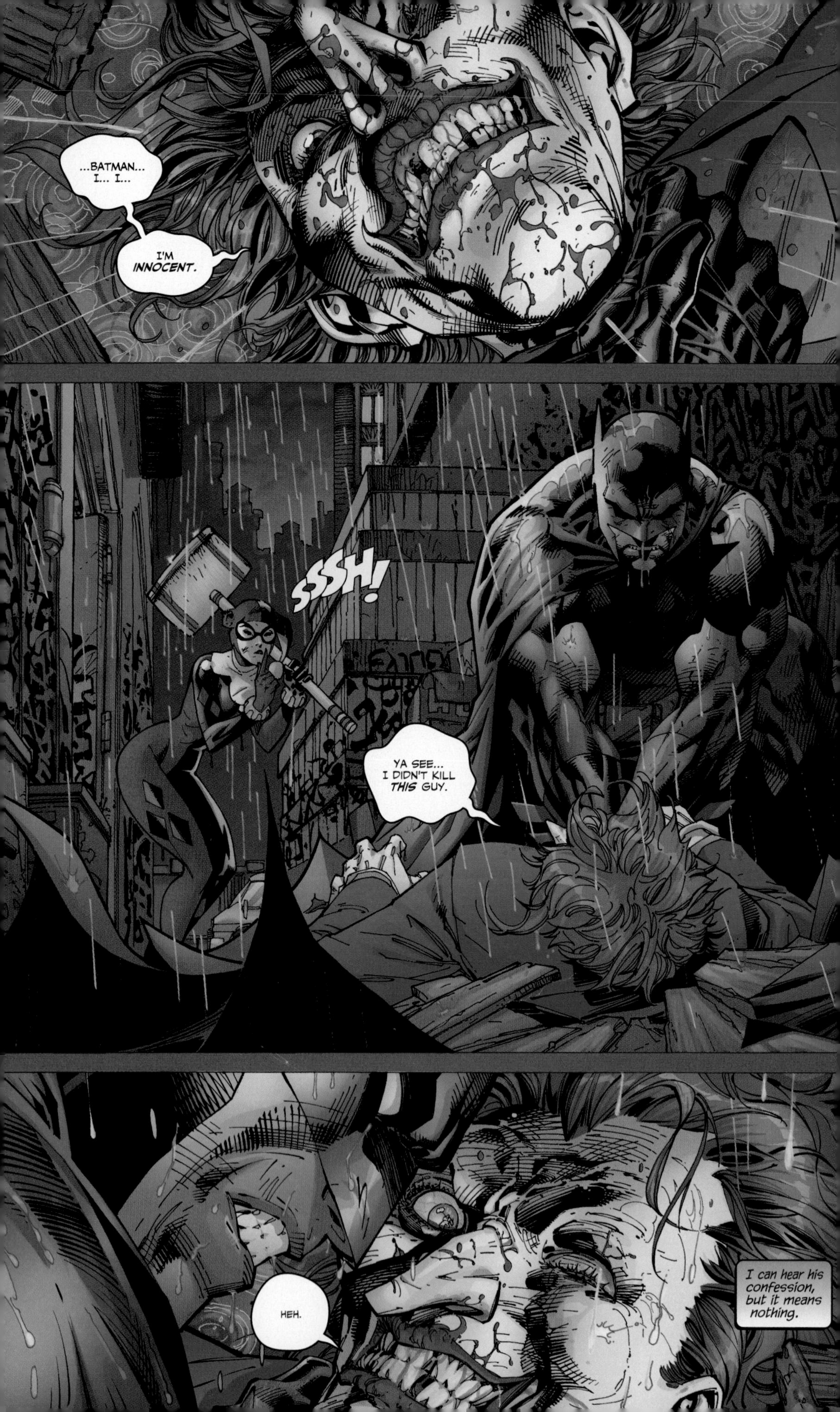

...BATMAN... I... I...
I'M INNOCENT.
SSSH!
YA SEE... I DIDN'T KILL THIS GUY.
I can hear his confession, but it means nothing.
HEH.

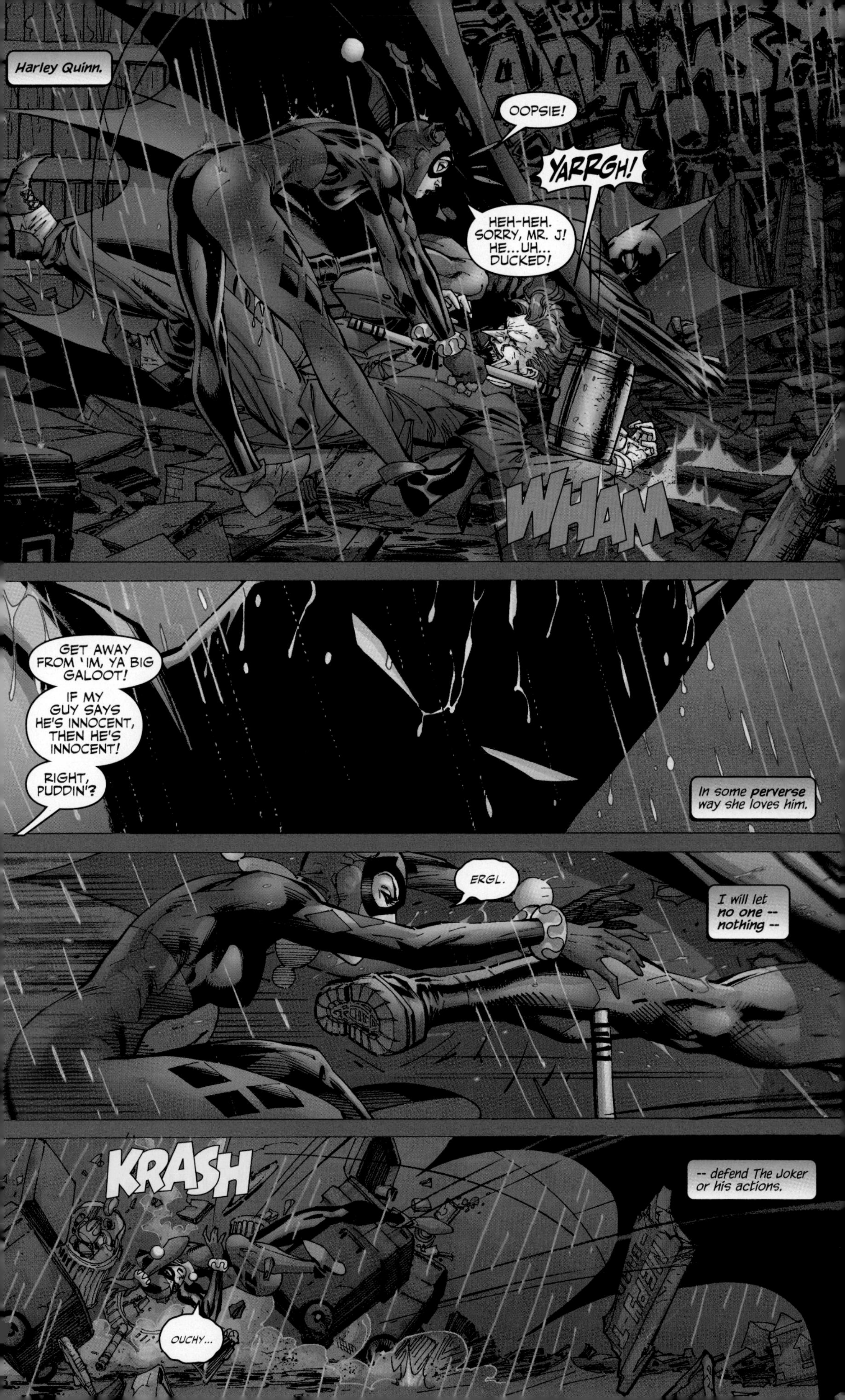
Harley Quinn.
OOPSIE!
YARRGH!
HEH-HEH. SORRY, MR. J! HE...UH... DUCKED!
WHAM
GET AWAY FROM 'IM, YA BIG GALOOT!
IF MY GUY SAYS HE'S INNOCENT, THEN HE'S INNOCENT!
RIGHT, PUDDIN'?
In some perverse way she loves him.
ERGL.
I will let no one -- nothing --
KRASH
-- defend The Joker or his actions.
OUCHY...

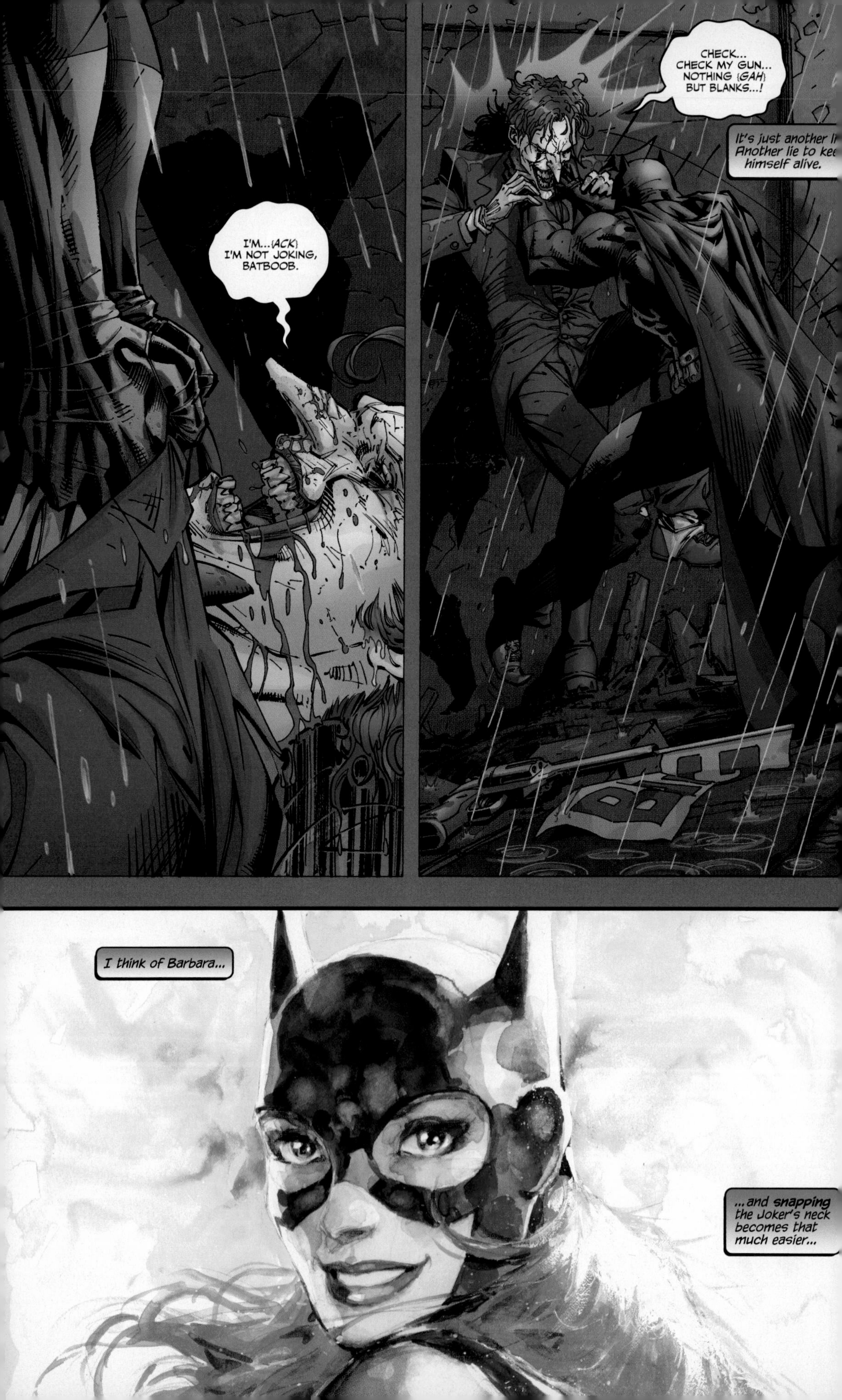
I'M...{ACK} I'M NOT JOKING, BATBOOB.
CHECK... CHECK MY GUN... NOTHING {GAH} BUT BLANKS...!
It's just another li
Another lie to kee
himself alive.
I think of Barbara...
...and snapping the Joker's neck becomes that much easier...

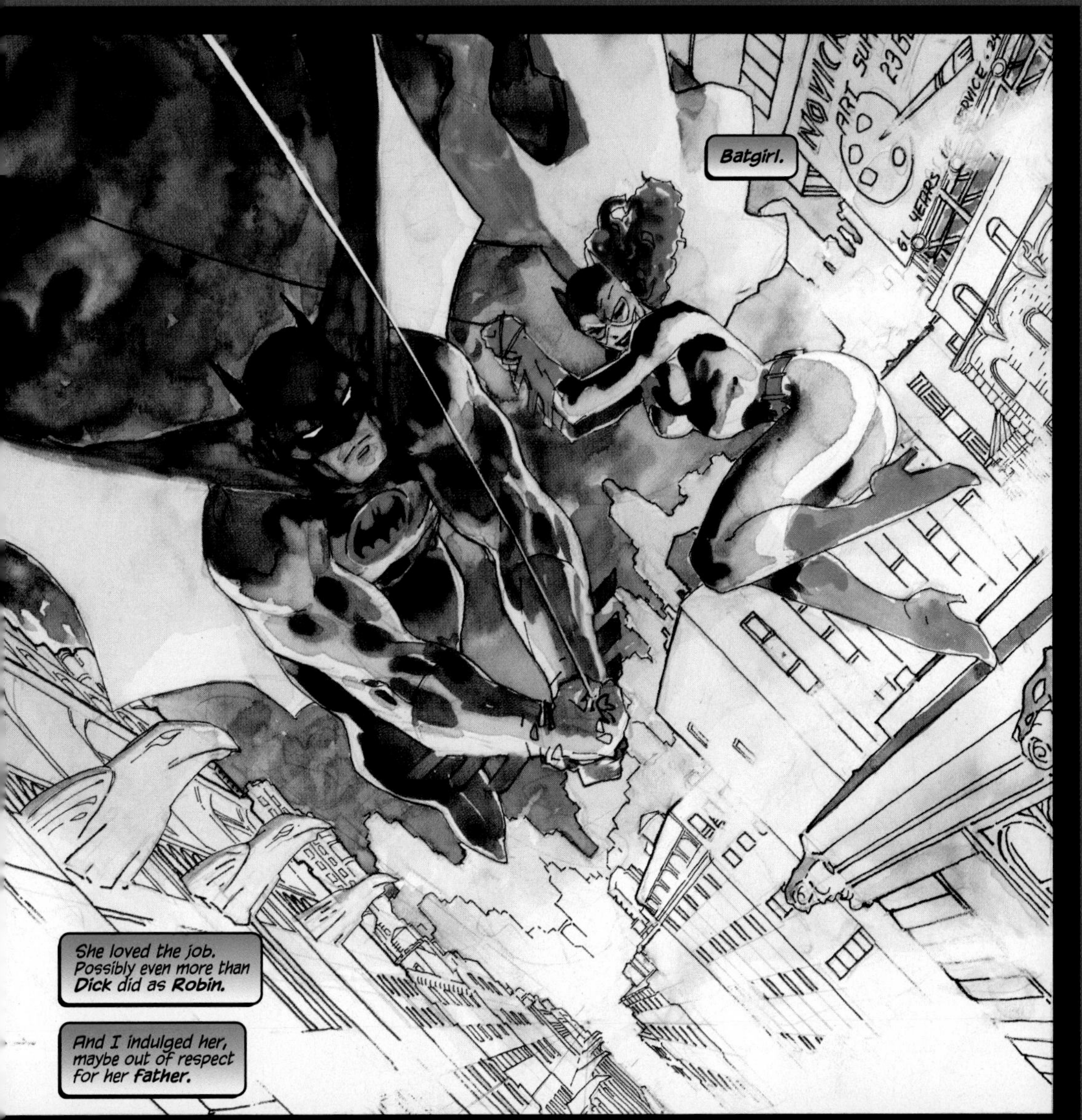
Batgirl.
She loved the job. Possibly even more than Dick did as Robin.
And I indulged her, maybe out of respect for her father.

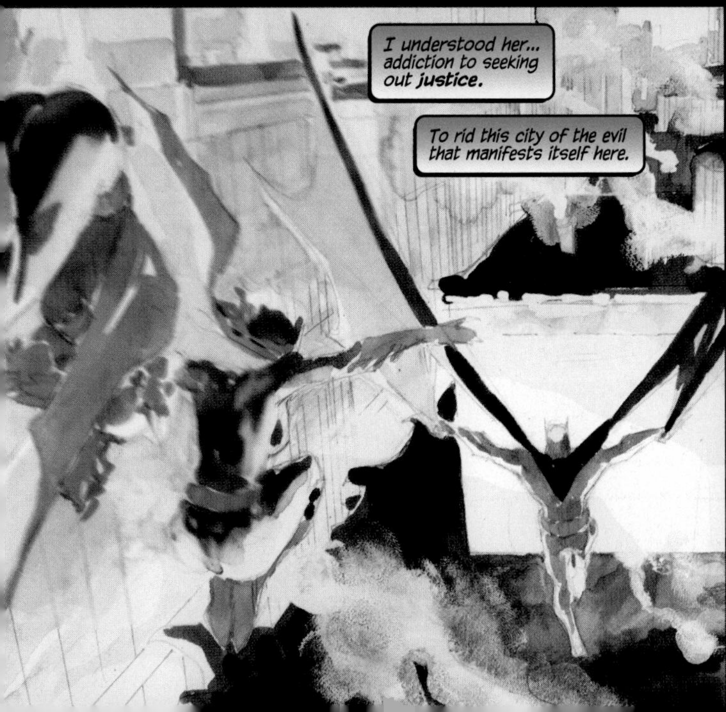
I understood her... addiction to seeking out justice.
To rid this city of the evil that manifests itself here.

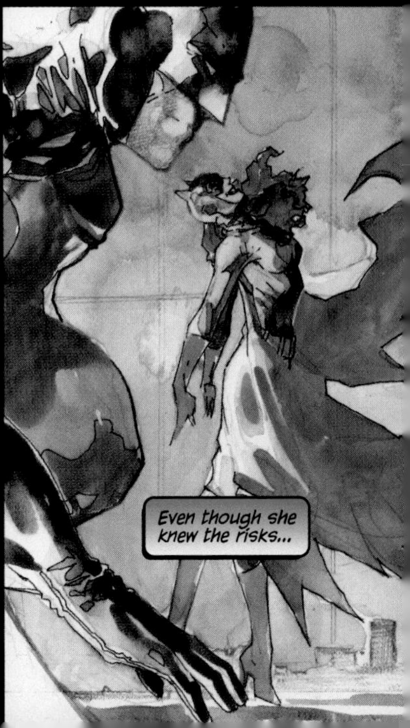
Even though she knew the risks...

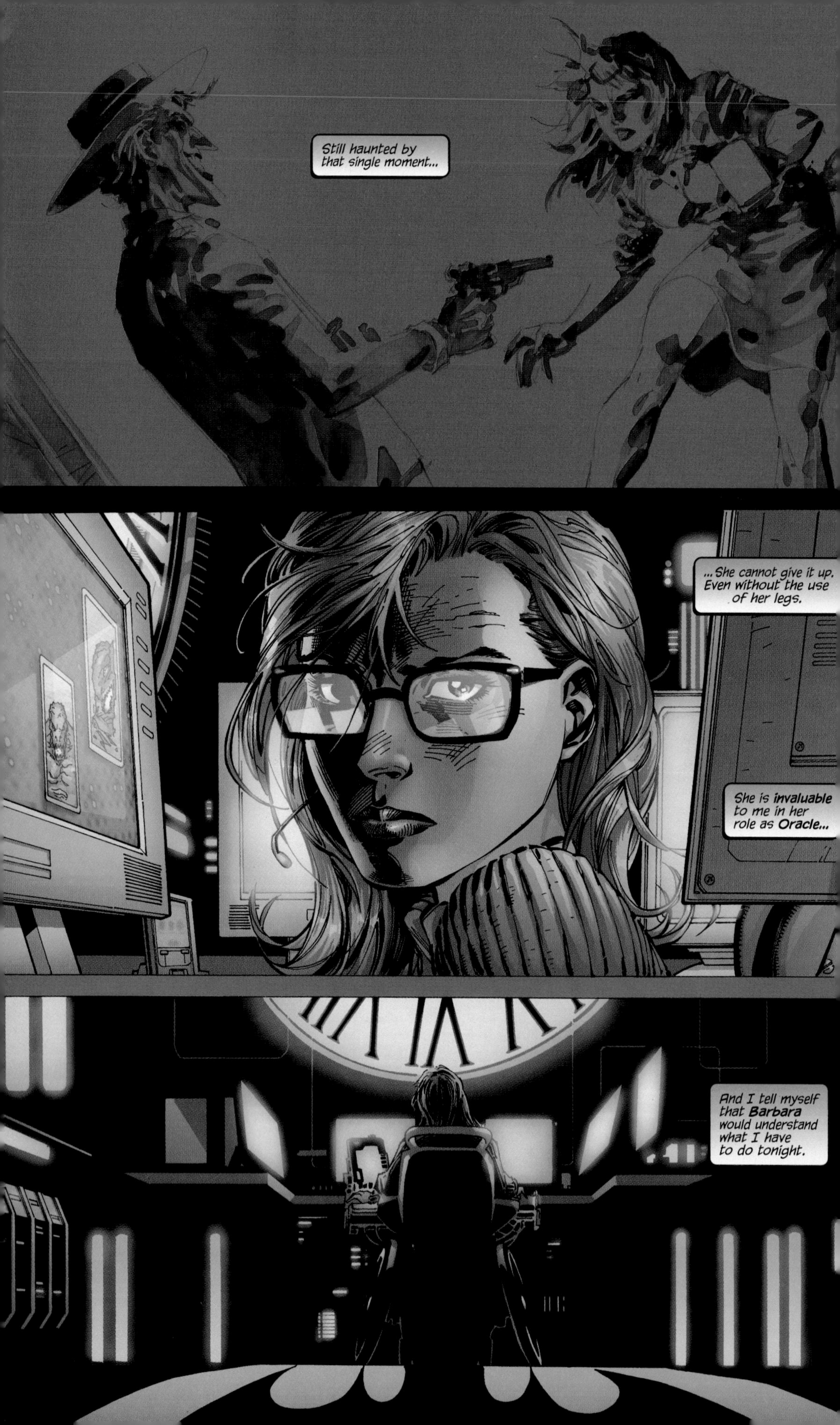

Still haunted by that single moment...
...She cannot give it up. Even without the use of her legs.
She is **invaluable** to me in her role as **Oracle**...
And I tell myself that **Barbara** would understand what I have to do tonight.

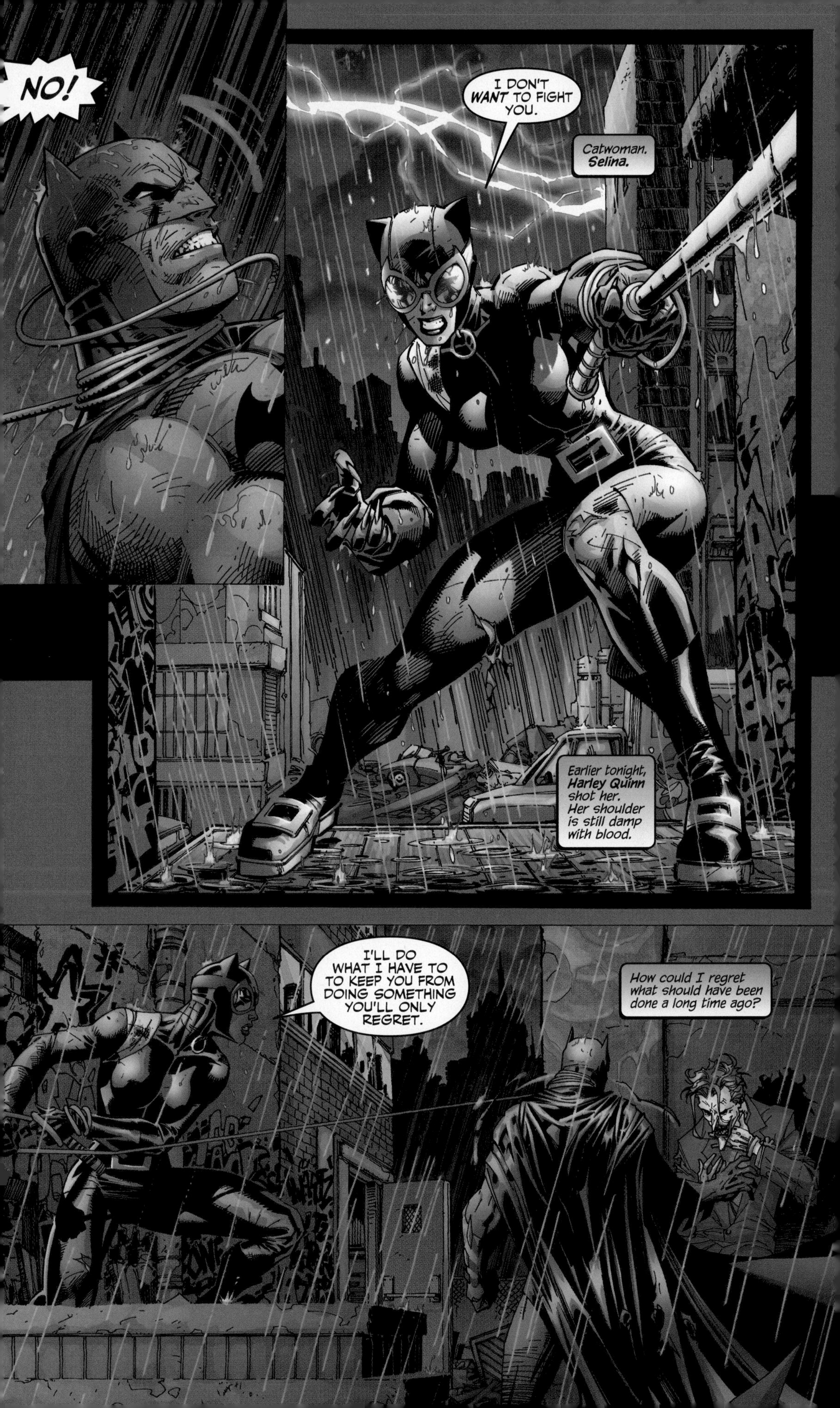
NO!
I DON'T WANT TO FIGHT YOU.
Catwoman. Selina.
Earlier tonight, Harley Quinn shot her. Her shoulder is still damp with blood.
I'LL DO WHAT I HAVE TO TO KEEP YOU FROM DOING SOMETHING YOU'LL ONLY REGRET.
How could I regret what should have been done a long time ago?

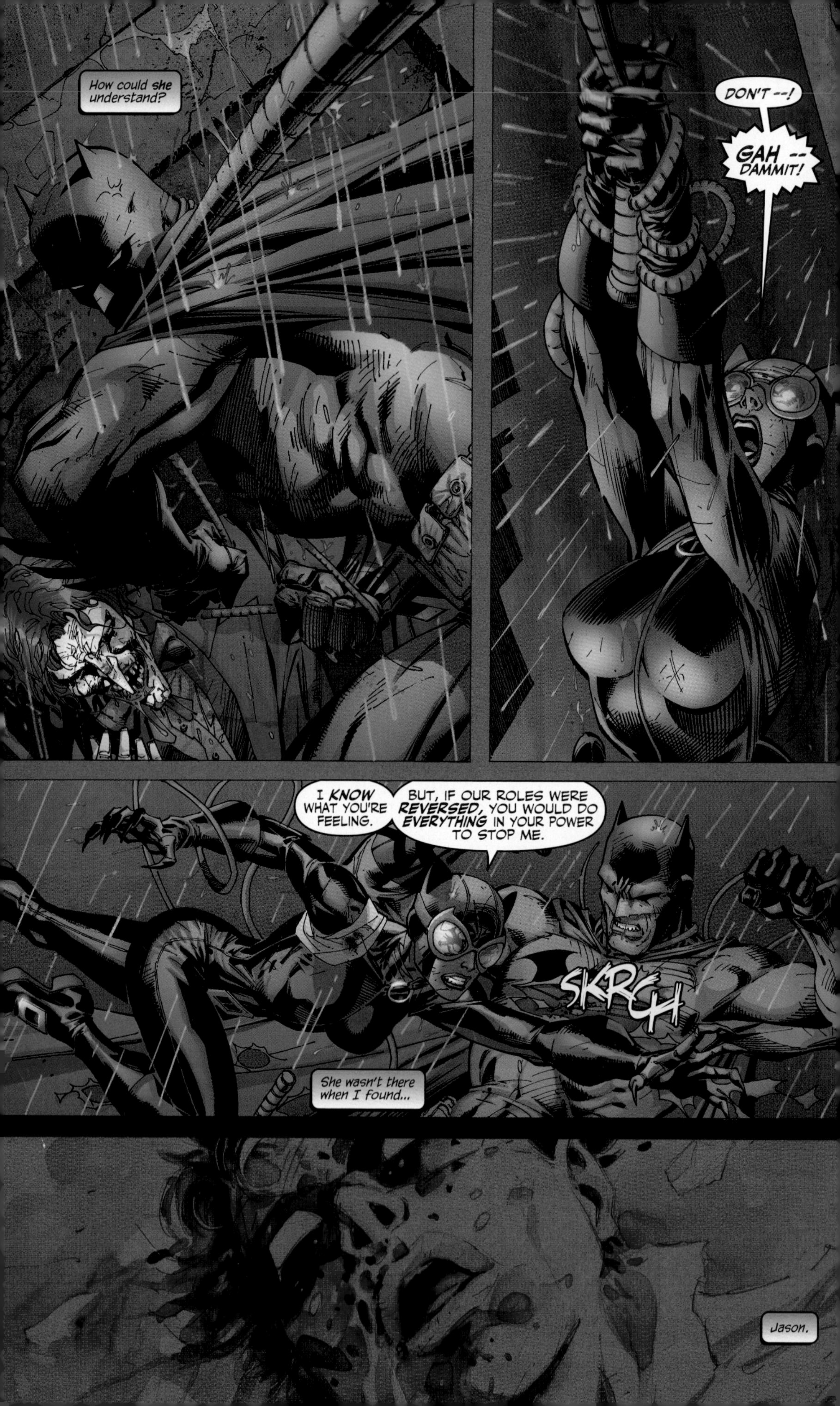
How could she understand?
DON'T --!
GAH -- DAMMIT!
I KNOW WHAT YOU'RE FEELING.
BUT, IF OUR ROLES WERE REVERSED, YOU WOULD DO EVERYTHING IN YOUR POWER TO STOP ME.
SKRCH
She wasn't there when I found...
Jason.

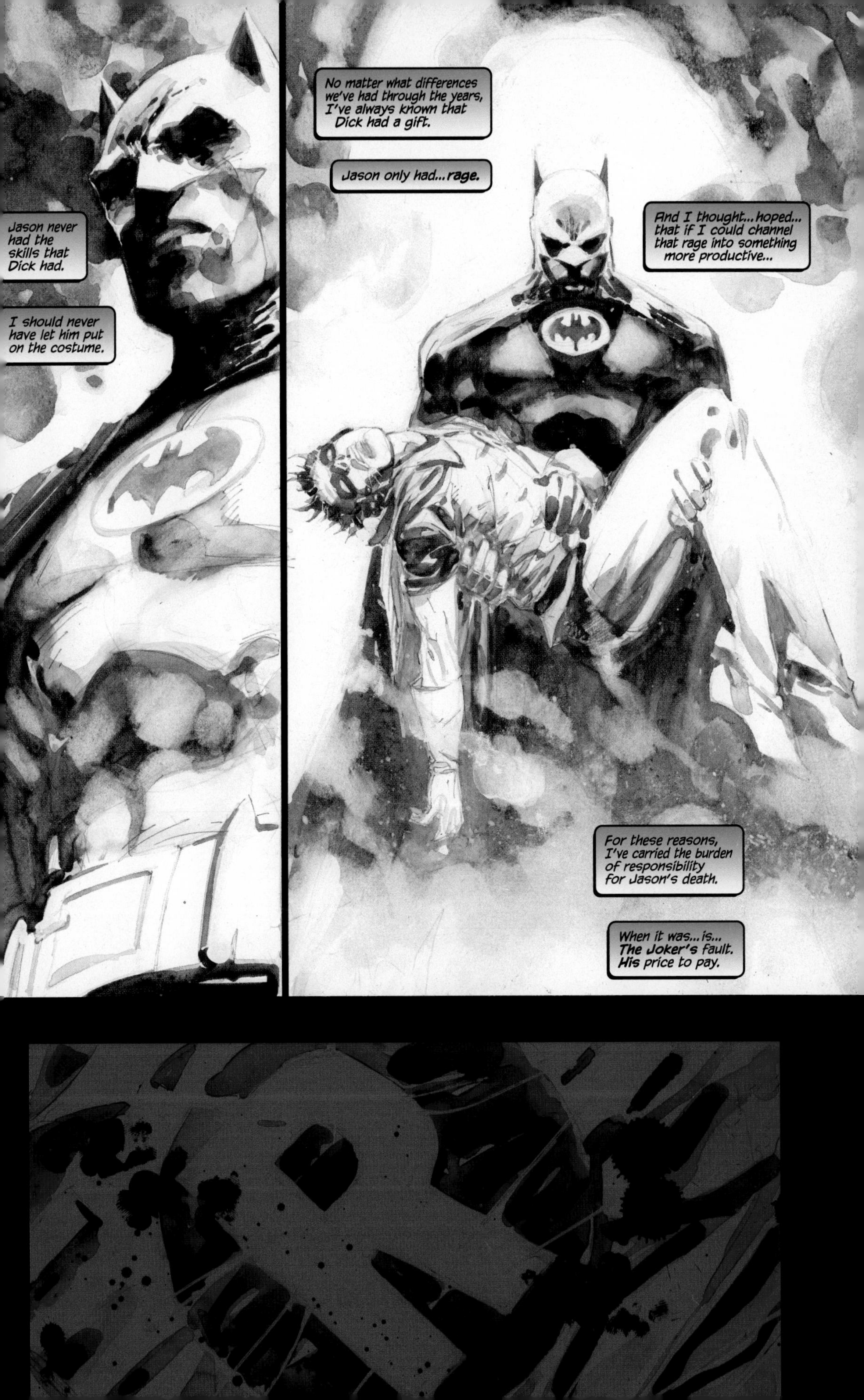
Jason never had the skills that Dick had.
I should never have let him put on the costume.
No matter what differences we've had through the years, I've always known that Dick had a gift.
Jason only had...rage.
And I thought...hoped... that if I could channel that rage into something more productive...
For these reasons, I've carried the burden of responsibility for Jason's death.
When it was...is... The Joker's fault. His price to pay.

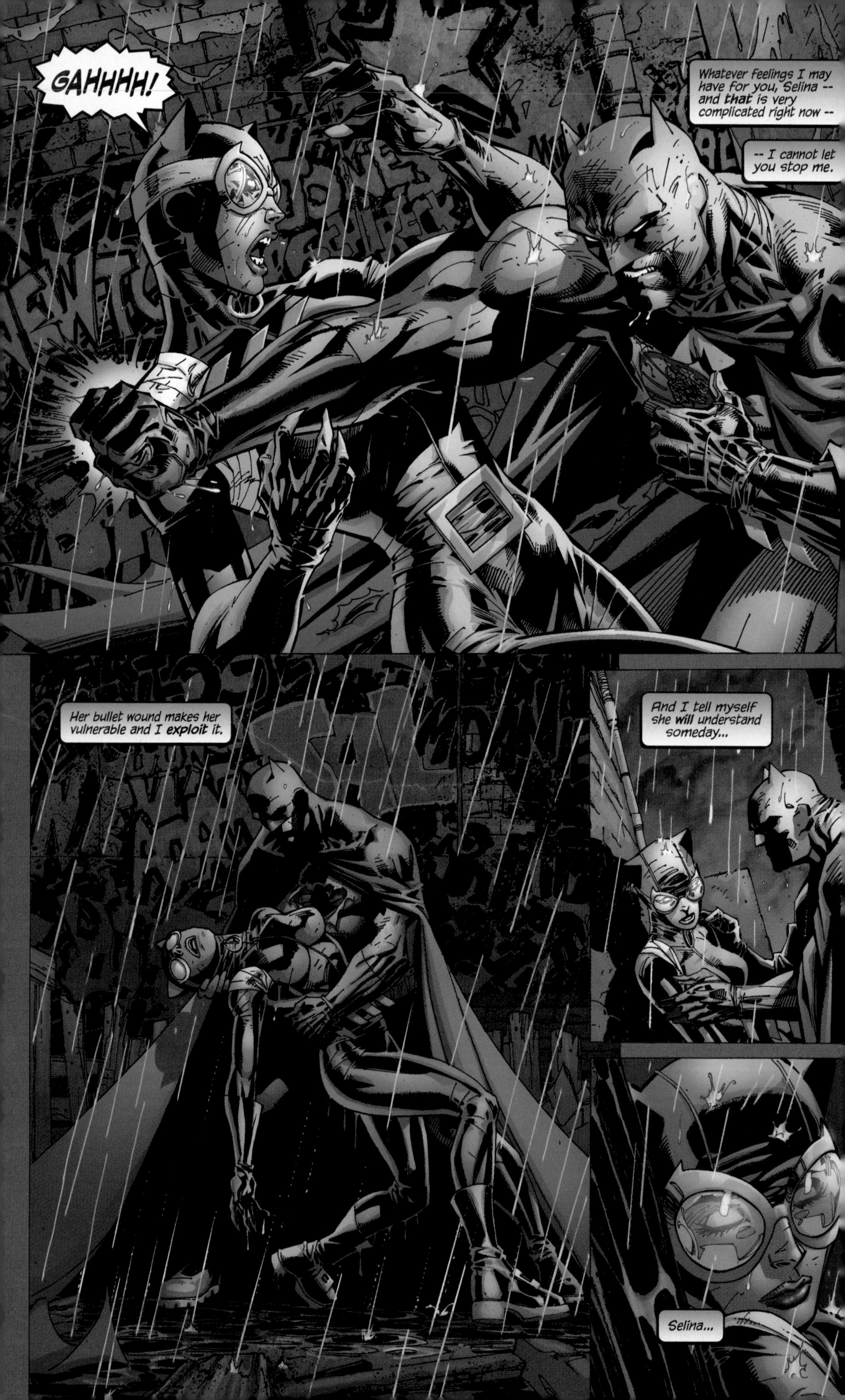
GAHHHH!
Whatever feelings I may have for you, Selina -- and that is very complicated right now --
-- I cannot let you stop me.
Her bullet wound makes her vulnerable and I exploit it.
And I tell myself she will understand someday...
Selina...

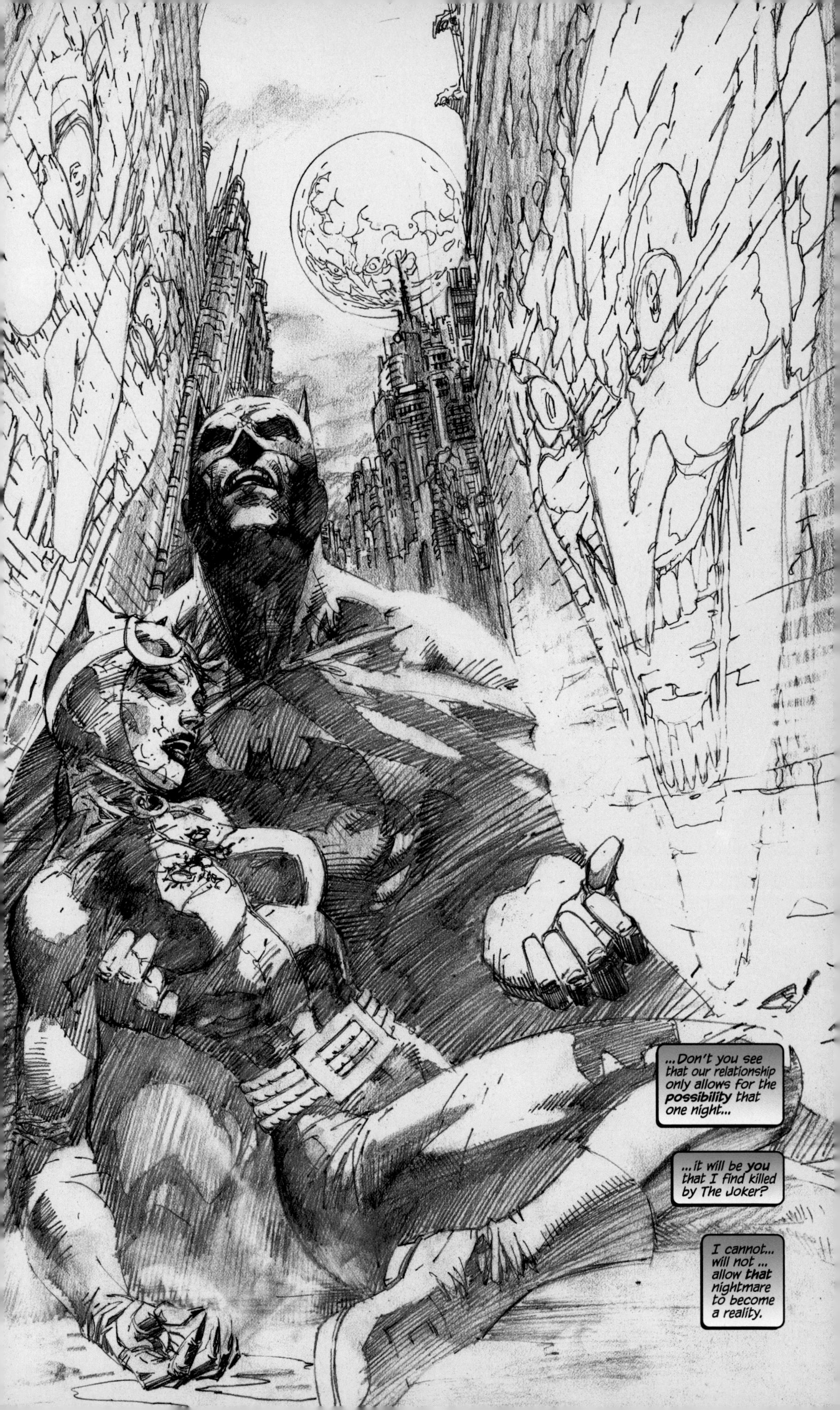
...Don't you see that our relationship only allows for the **possibility** that one night...
...it will be **you** that I find killed by The Joker?
I cannot... will not ... allow **that** nightmare to become a reality.

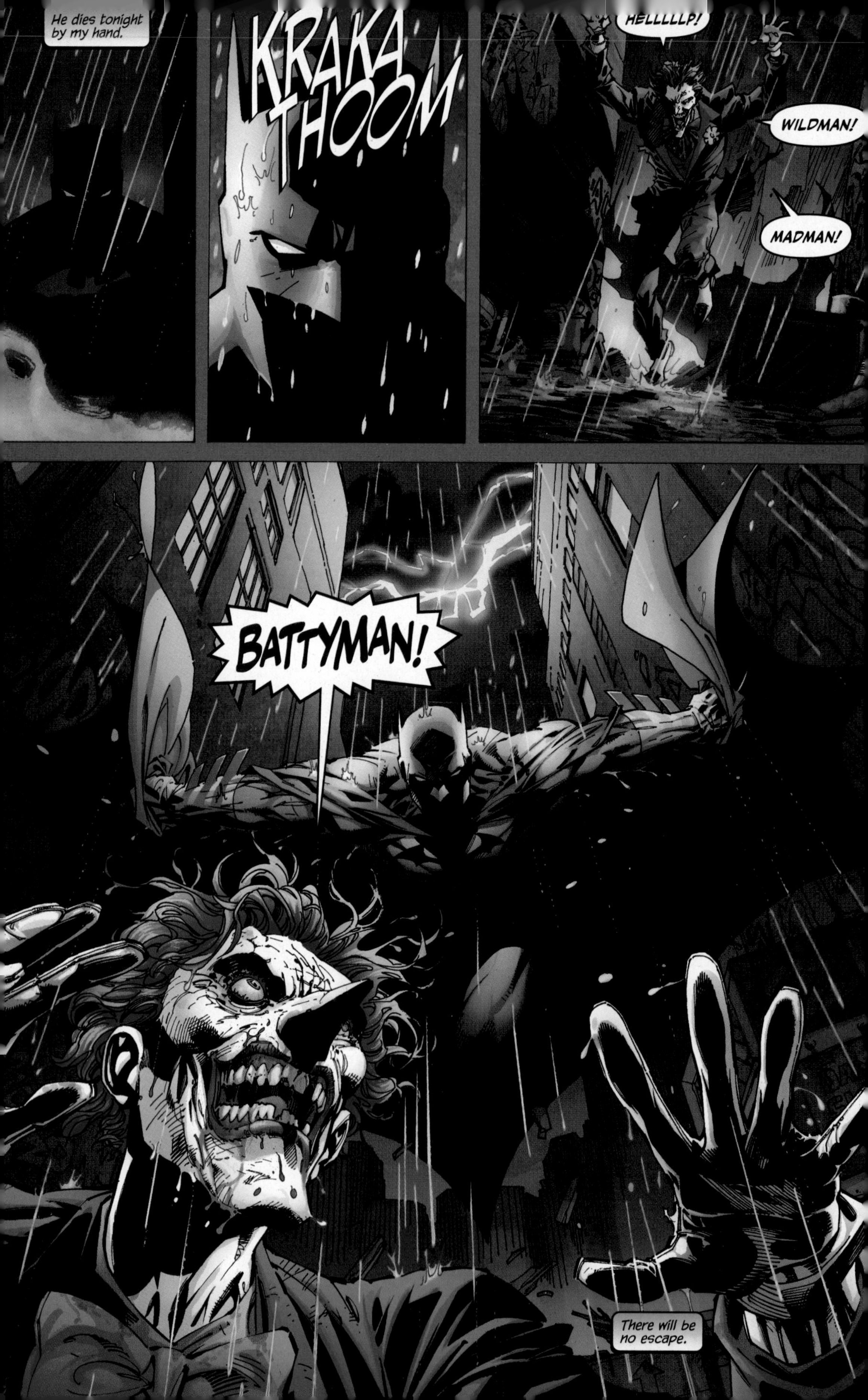
He dies tonight by my hand.
KRAKA THOOM
HELLLLLLP!
WILDMAN!
MADMAN!
BATTYMAN!
There will be no escape.

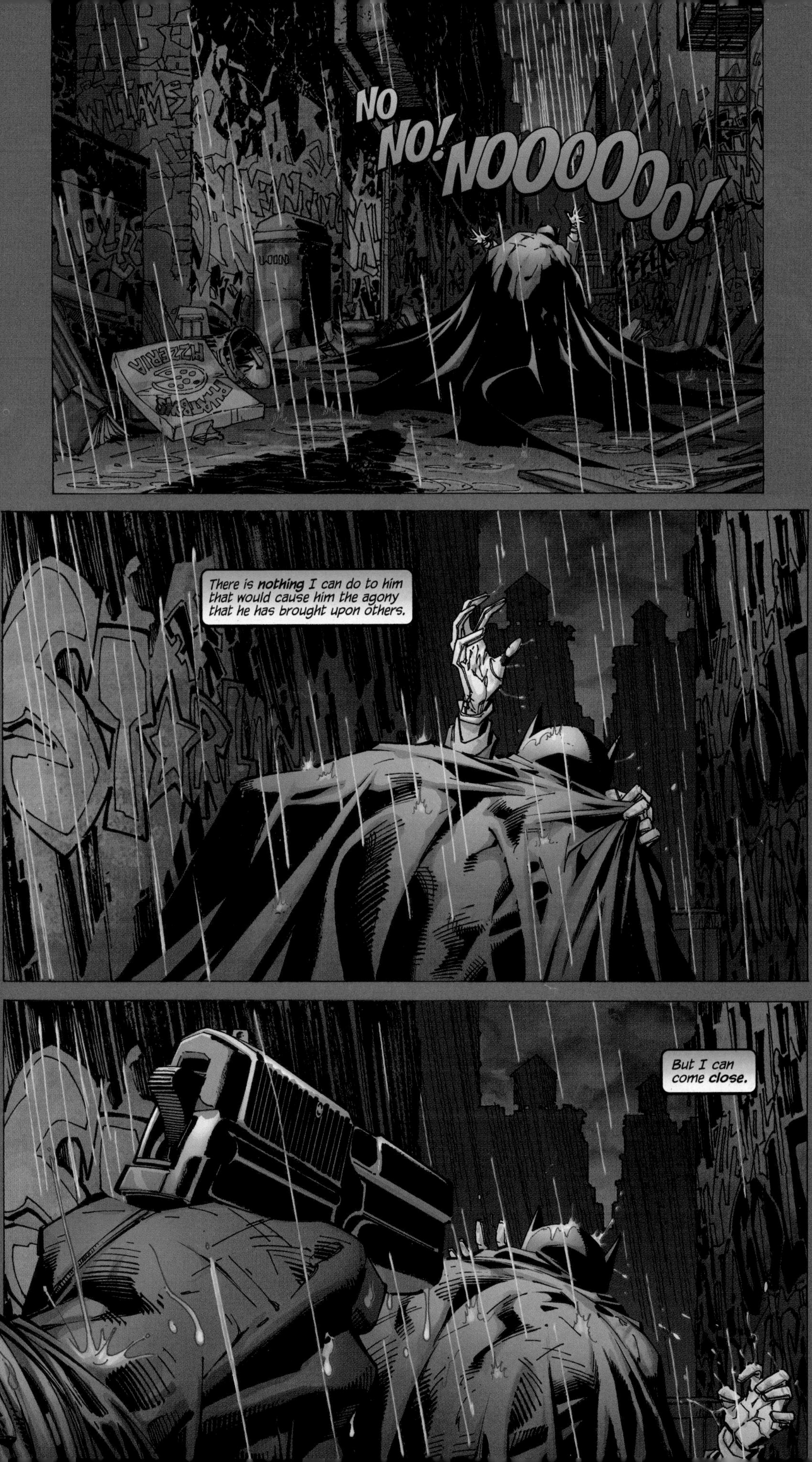
NO NO! NOOOOOOO!
There is nothing I can do to him that would cause him the agony that he has brought upon others.
But I can come close.

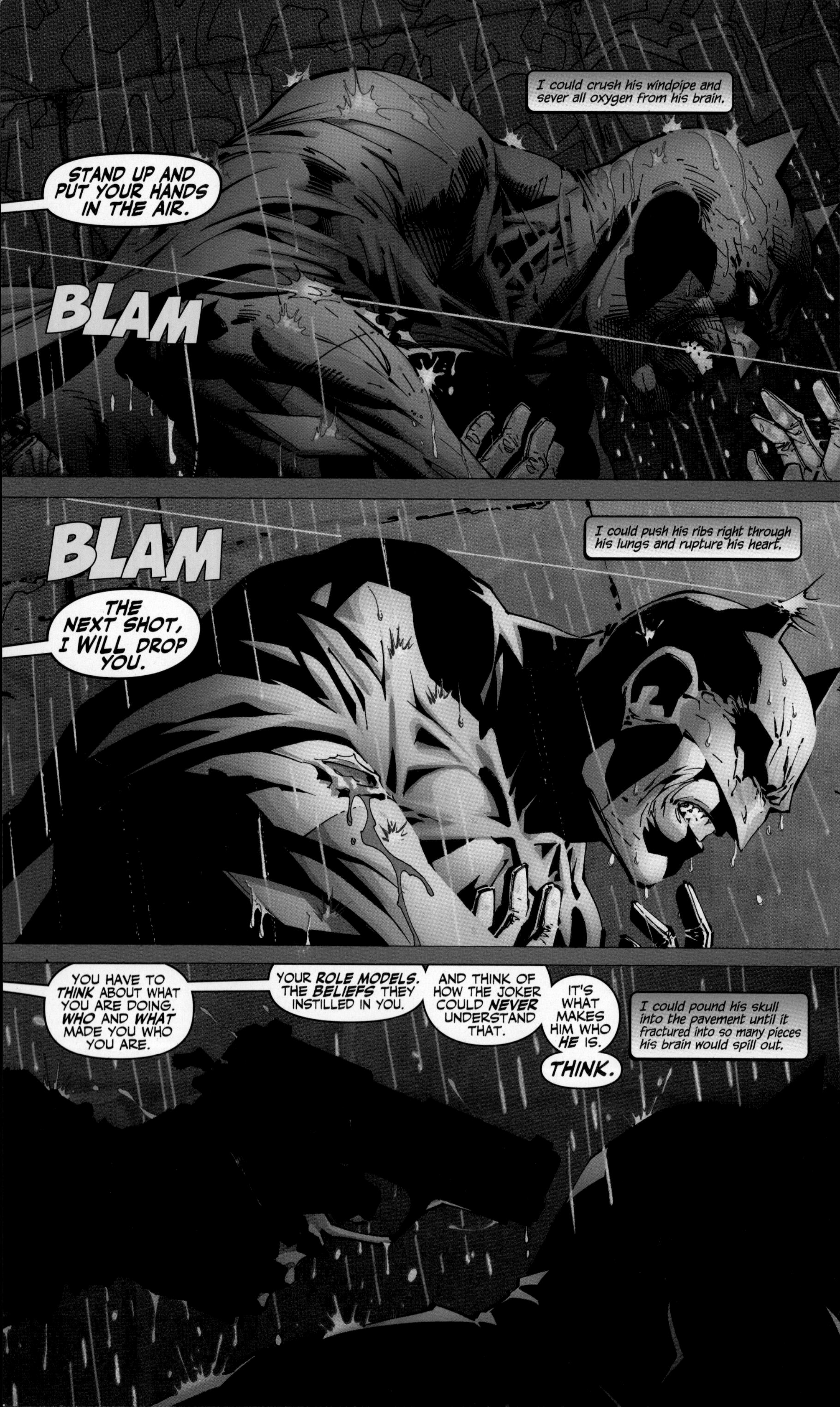

I could crush his windpipe and sever all oxygen from his brain.
STAND UP AND PUT YOUR HANDS IN THE AIR.
BLAM
BLAM
I could push his ribs right through his lungs and rupture his heart.
THE NEXT SHOT, I WILL DROP YOU.
YOU HAVE TO THINK ABOUT WHAT YOU ARE DOING. WHO AND WHAT MADE YOU WHO YOU ARE.
YOUR ROLE MODELS. THE BELIEFS THEY INSTILLED IN YOU.
AND THINK OF HOW THE JOKER COULD NEVER UNDERSTAND THAT.
IT'S WHAT MAKES HIM WHO HE IS.
THINK.
I could pound his skull into the pavement until it fractured into so many pieces his brain would spill out.

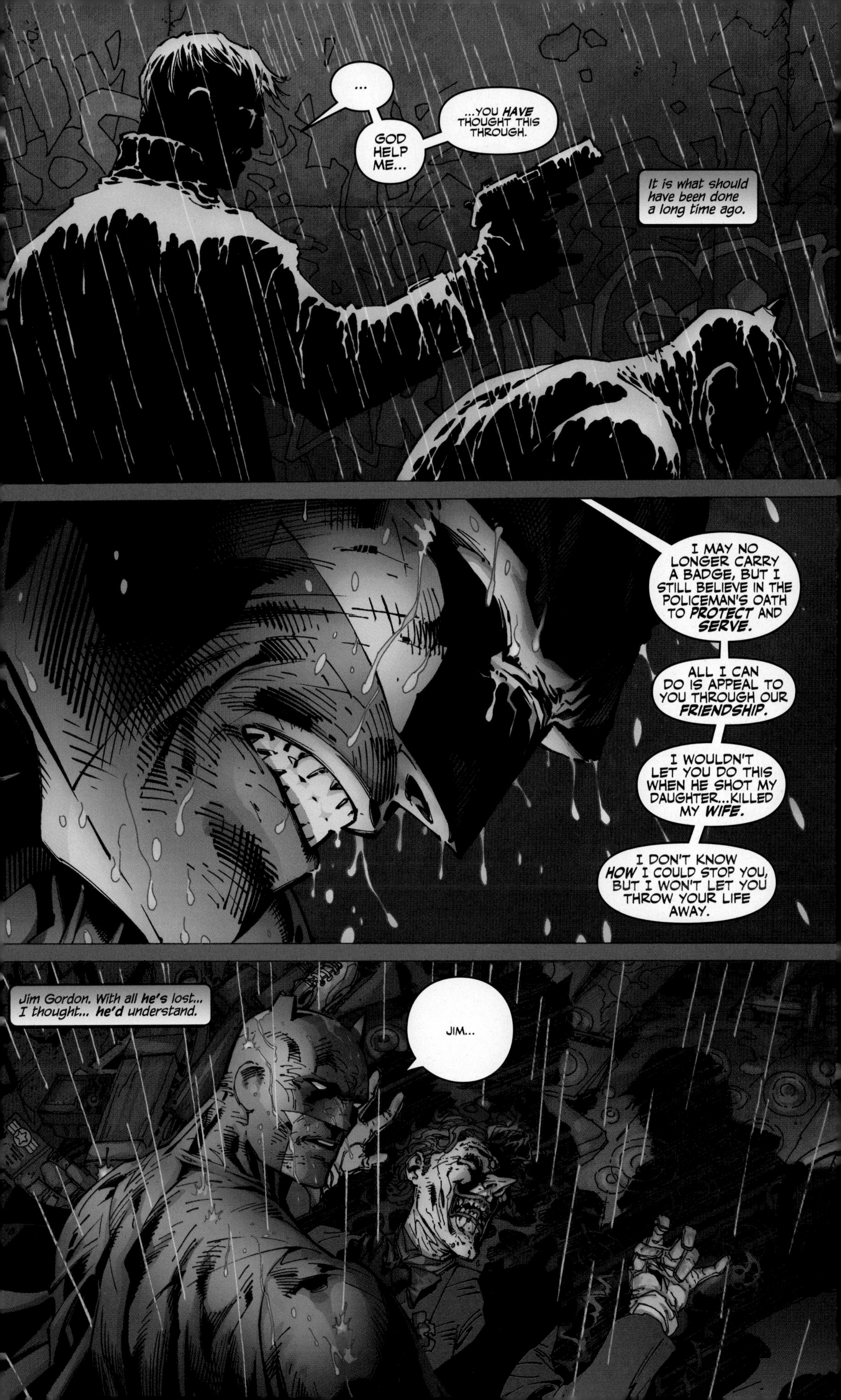
...
GOD HELP ME...
...YOU HAVE THOUGHT THIS THROUGH.
It is what should have been done a long time ago.
I MAY NO LONGER CARRY A BADGE, BUT I STILL BELIEVE IN THE POLICEMAN'S OATH TO PROTECT AND SERVE.
ALL I CAN DO IS APPEAL TO YOU THROUGH OUR FRIENDSHIP.
I WOULDN'T LET YOU DO THIS WHEN HE SHOT MY DAUGHTER...KILLED MY WIFE.
I DON'T KNOW HOW I COULD STOP YOU, BUT I WON'T LET YOU THROW YOUR LIFE AWAY.
Jim Gordon. With all he's lost... I thought... he'd understand.
JIM...

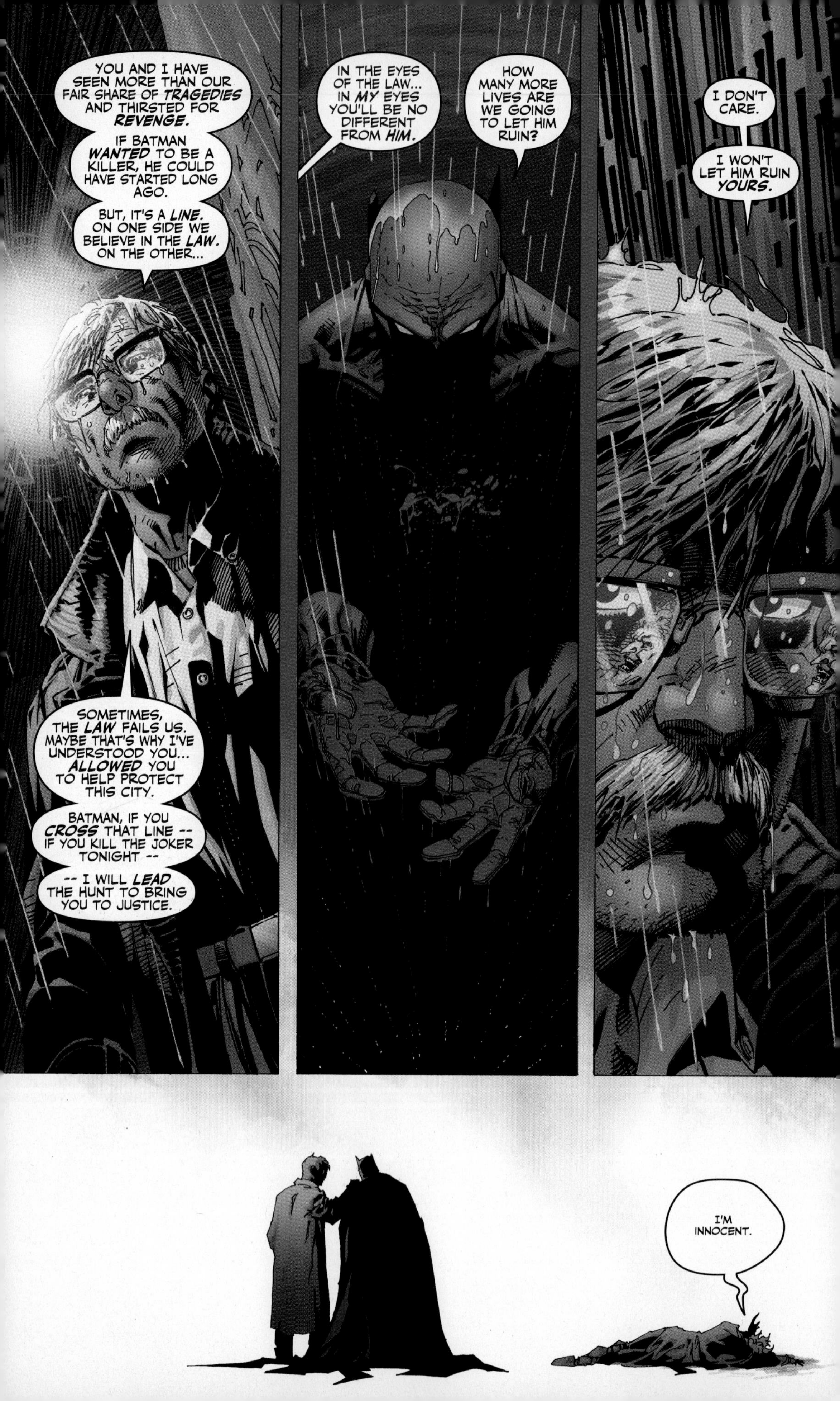
YOU AND I HAVE SEEN MORE THAN OUR FAIR SHARE OF TRAGEDIES AND THIRSTED FOR REVENGE.
IF BATMAN WANTED TO BE A KILLER, HE COULD HAVE STARTED LONG AGO.
BUT, IT'S A LINE. ON ONE SIDE WE BELIEVE IN THE LAW. ON THE OTHER...
SOMETIMES, THE LAW FAILS US. MAYBE THAT'S WHY I'VE UNDERSTOOD YOU... ALLOWED YOU TO HELP PROTECT THIS CITY.
BATMAN, IF YOU CROSS THAT LINE -- IF YOU KILL THE JOKER TONIGHT --
-- I WILL LEAD THE HUNT TO BRING YOU TO JUSTICE.
IN THE EYES OF THE LAW... IN MY EYES YOU'LL BE NO DIFFERENT FROM HIM.
HOW MANY MORE LIVES ARE WE GOING TO LET HIM RUIN?
I DON'T CARE.
I WON'T LET HIM RUIN YOURS.
I'M INNOCENT.

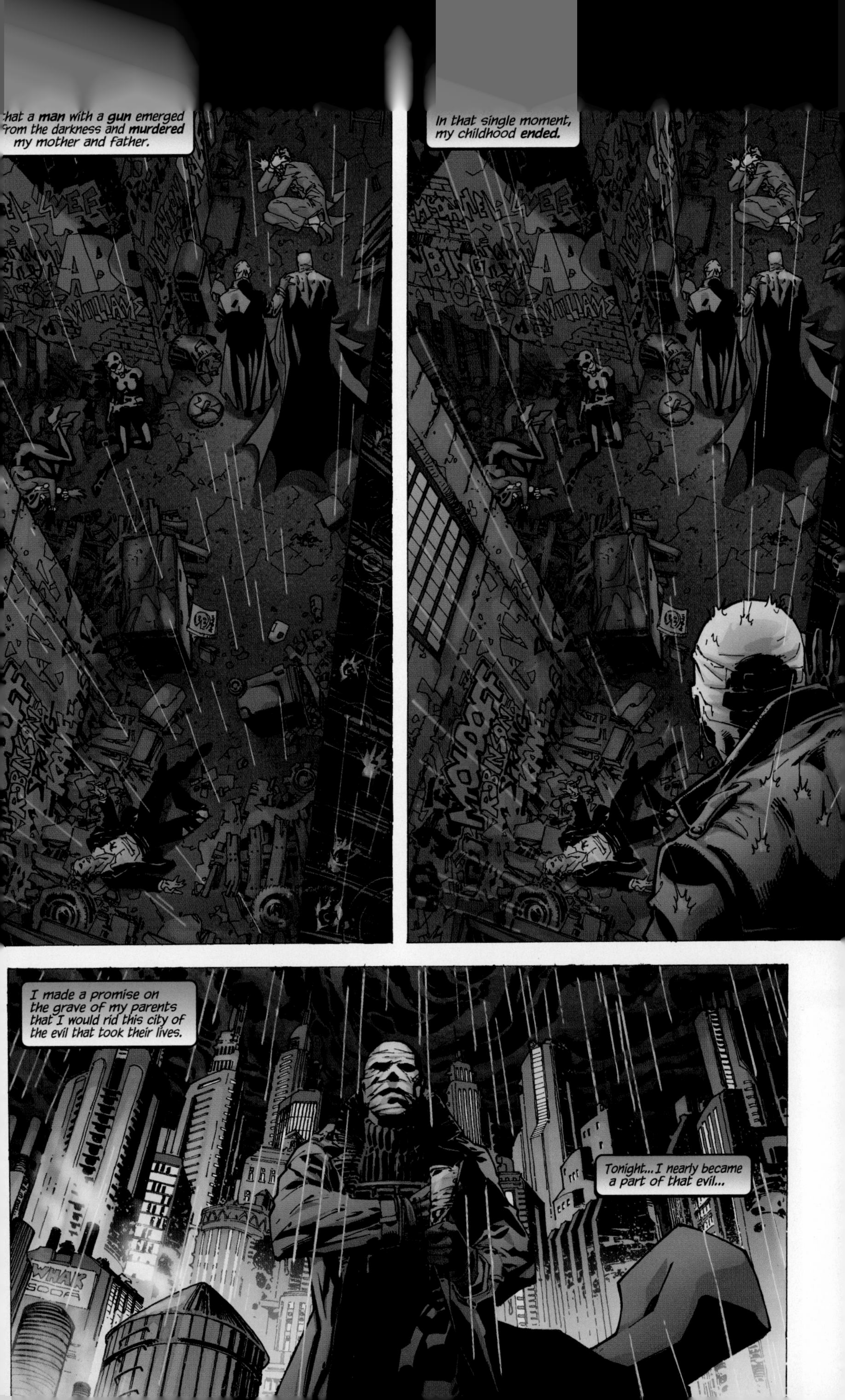
that a man with a gun emerged from the darkness and murdered my mother and father.
In that single moment, my childhood ended.
I made a promise on the grave of my parents that I would rid this city of the evil that took their lives.
Tonight...I nearly became a part of that evil...

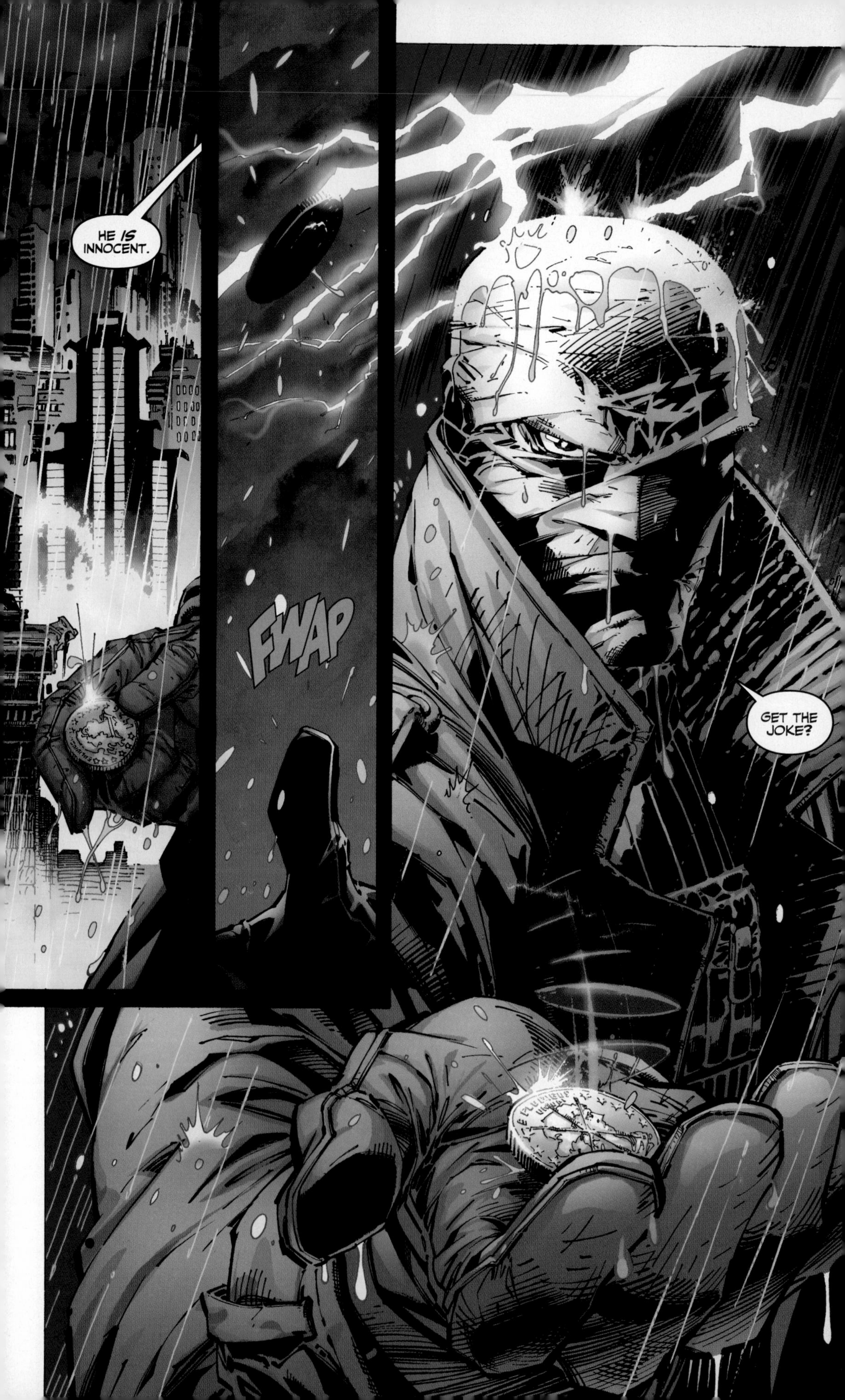
HE IS INNOCENT.
FWAP
GET THE JOKE?

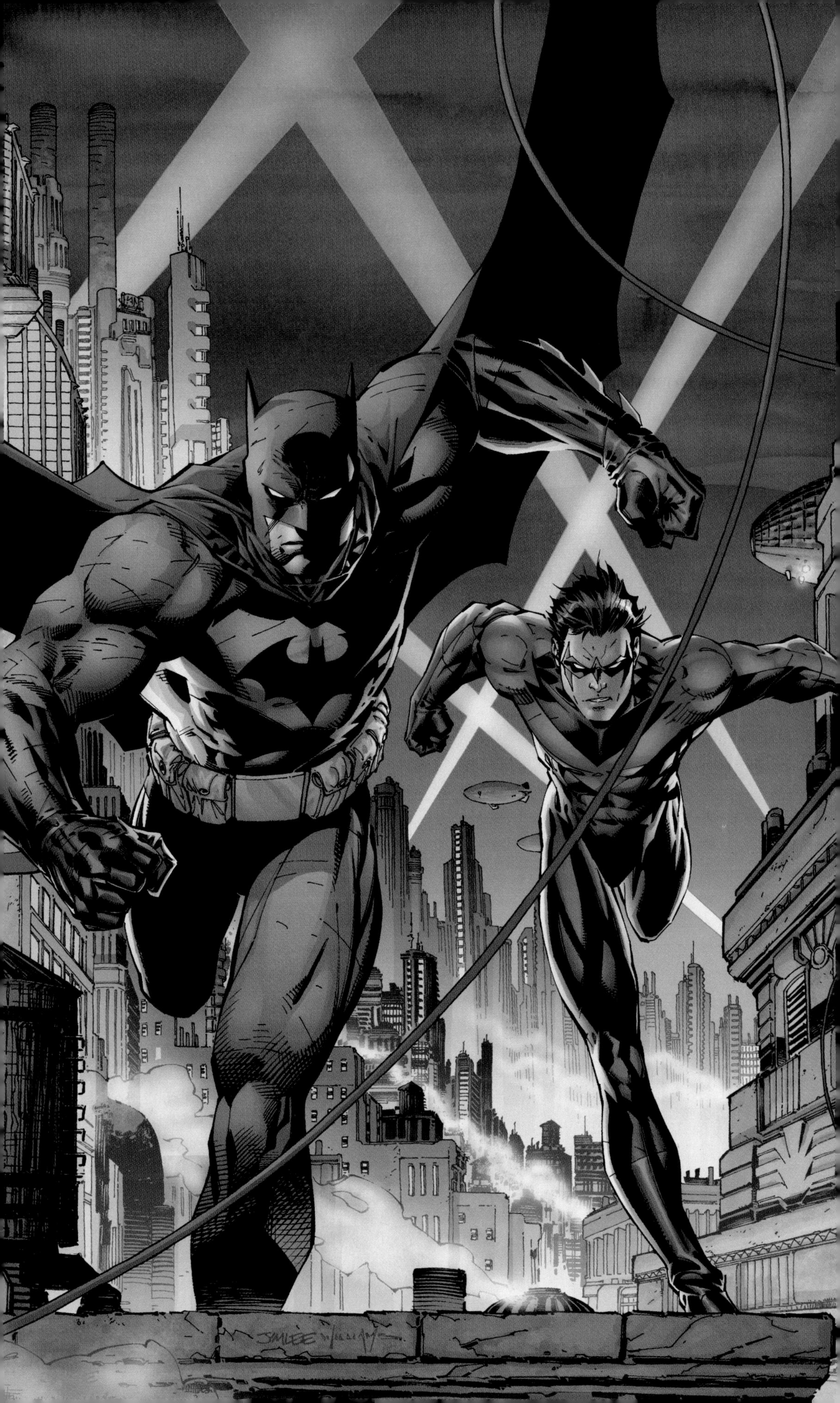

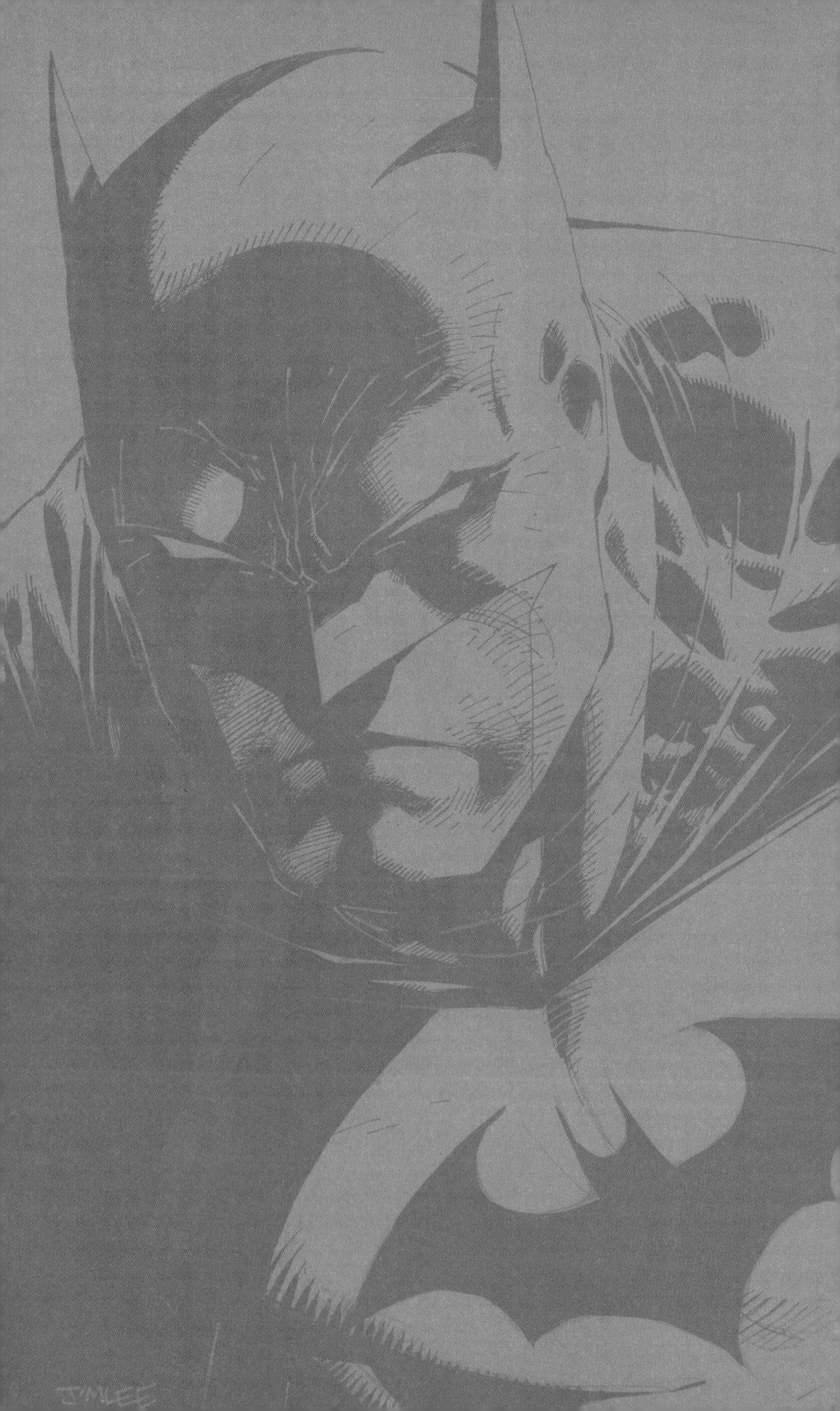

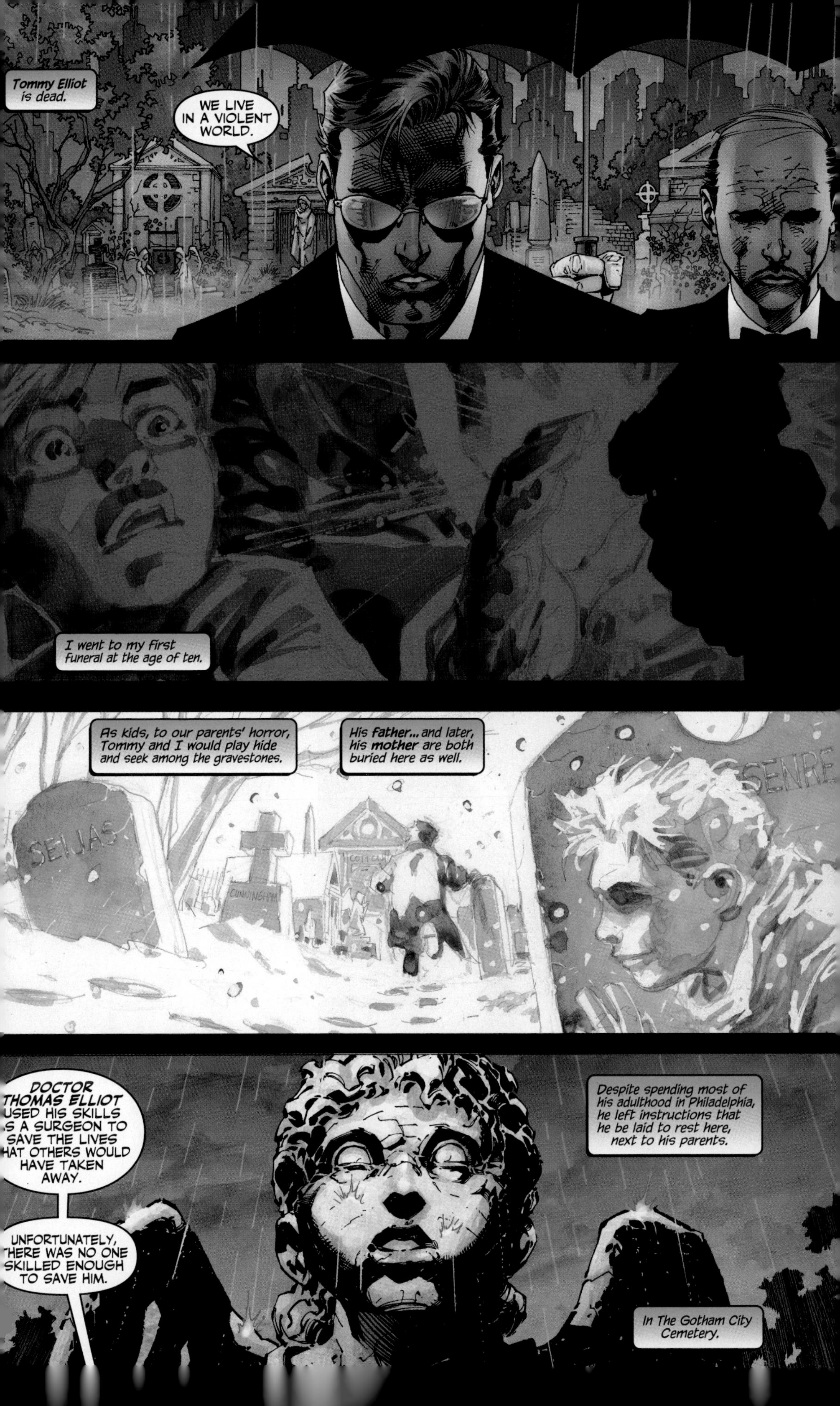

Tommy Elliot is dead.
WE LIVE IN A VIOLENT WORLD.
I went to my first funeral at the age of ten.
As kids, to our parents' horror, Tommy and I would play hide and seek among the gravestones.
His father... and later, his mother are both buried here as well.
SEIJAS
CUNNINGHAM
SENRE
DOCTOR THOMAS ELLIOT USED HIS SKILLS AS A SURGEON TO SAVE THE LIVES THAT OTHERS WOULD HAVE TAKEN AWAY.
UNFORTUNATELY, THERE WAS NO ONE SKILLED ENOUGH TO SAVE HIM.
Despite spending most of his adulthood in Philadelphia, he left instructions that he be laid to rest here, next to his parents.
In The Gotham City Cemetery.

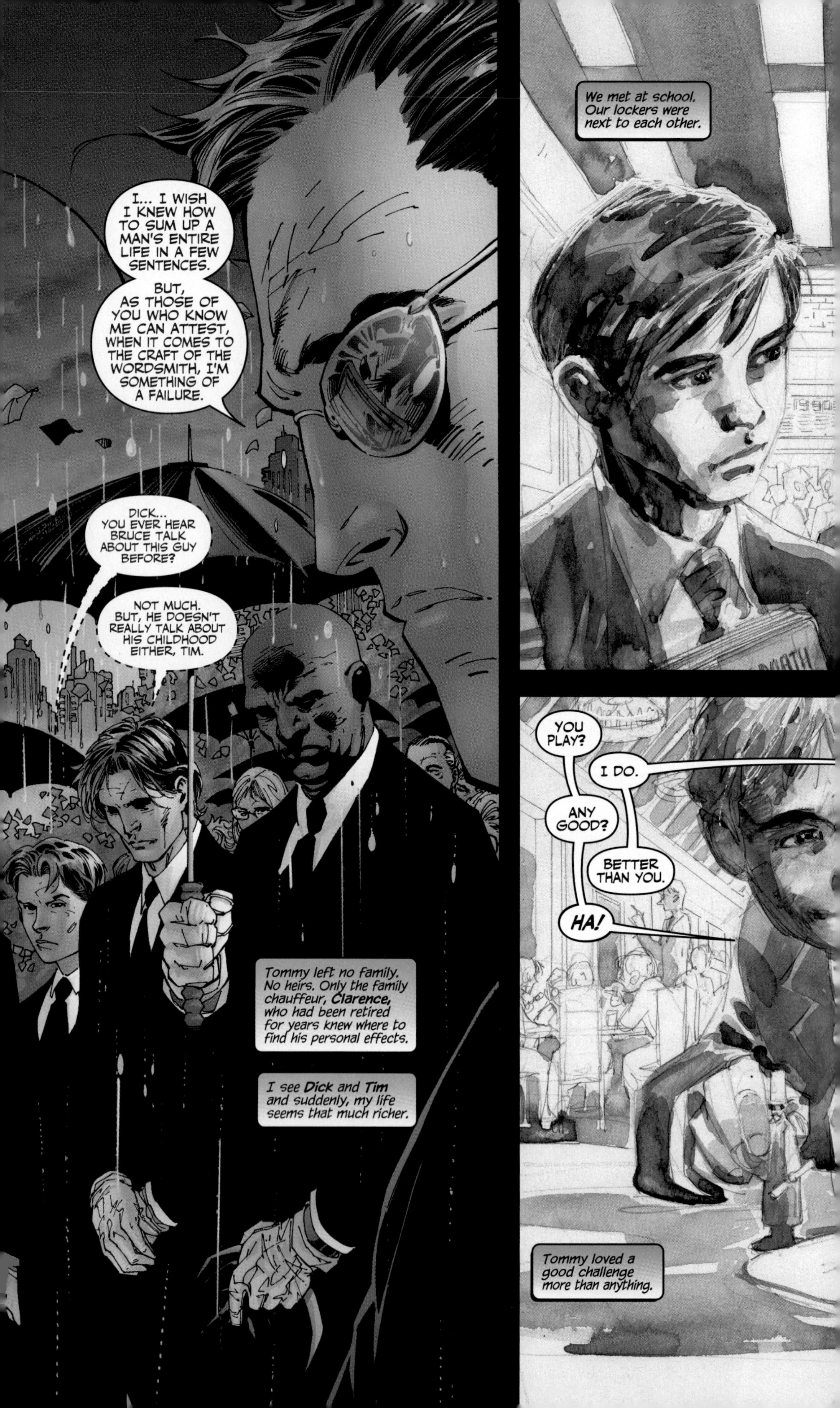
I... I WISH I KNEW HOW TO SUM UP A MAN'S ENTIRE LIFE IN A FEW SENTENCES.
BUT, AS THOSE OF YOU WHO KNOW ME CAN ATTEST, WHEN IT COMES TO THE CRAFT OF THE WORDSMITH, I'M SOMETHING OF A FAILURE.
DICK... YOU EVER HEAR BRUCE TALK ABOUT THIS GUY BEFORE?
NOT MUCH. BUT, HE DOESN'T REALLY TALK ABOUT HIS CHILDHOOD EITHER, TIM.
Tommy left no family. No heirs. Only the family chauffeur, Clarence, who had been retired for years knew where to find his personal effects.
I see Dick and Tim and suddenly, my life seems that much richer.
We met at school. Our lockers were next to each other.
YOU PLAY?
I DO.
ANY GOOD?
BETTER THAN YOU.
HA!
Tommy loved a good challenge more than anything.

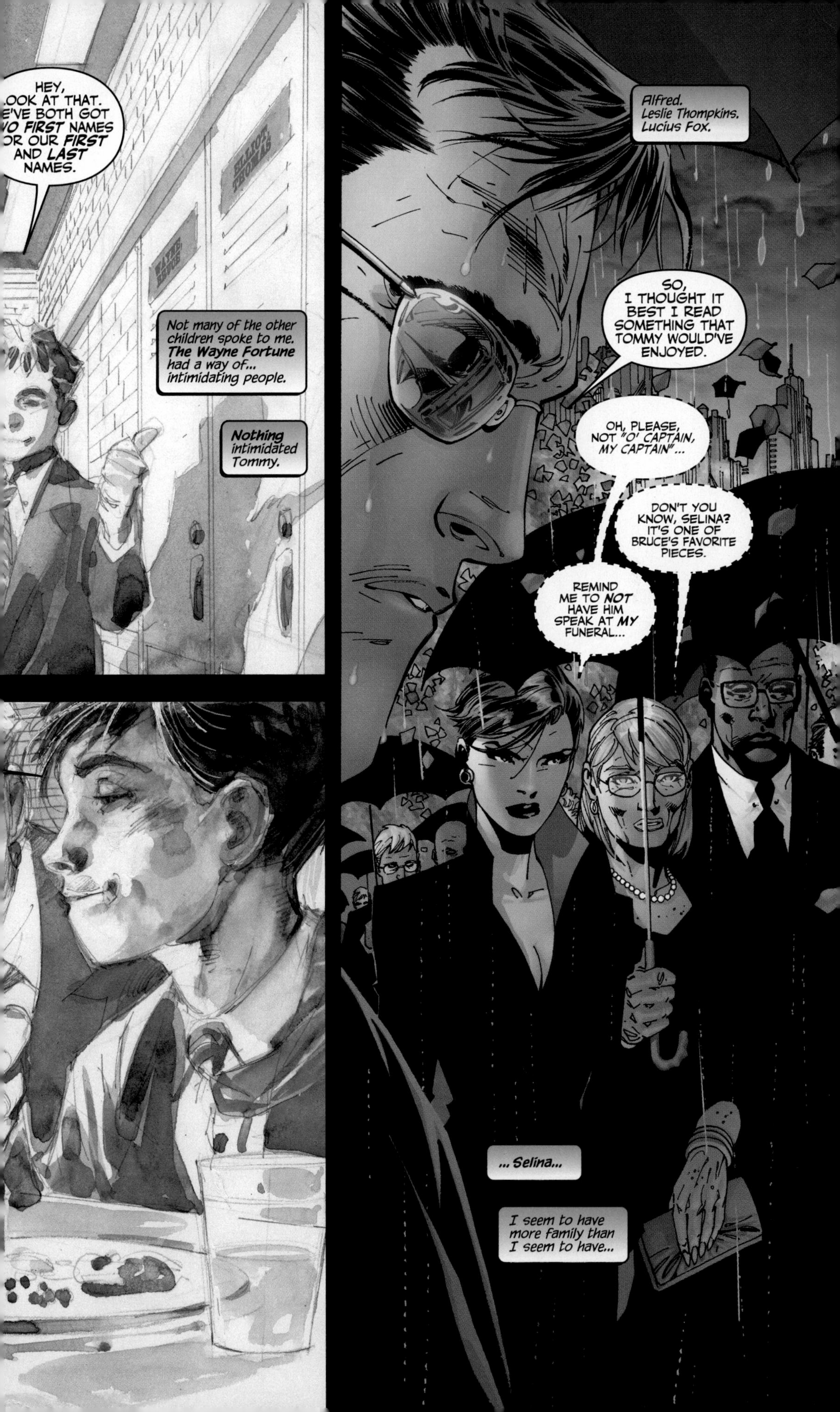
HEY,
OOK AT THAT.
E'VE BOTH GOT
VO FIRST NAMES
OR OUR FIRST
AND LAST
NAMES.
Not many of the other children spoke to me. The Wayne Fortune had a way of... intimidating people.
Nothing intimidated Tommy.
Alfred.
Leslie Thompkins.
Lucius Fox.
SO, I THOUGHT IT BEST I READ SOMETHING THAT TOMMY WOULD'VE ENJOYED.
OH, PLEASE, NOT "O' CAPTAIN, MY CAPTAIN"...
DON'T YOU KNOW, SELINA? IT'S ONE OF BRUCE'S FAVORITE PIECES.
REMIND ME TO NOT HAVE HIM SPEAK AT MY FUNERAL...
...Selina...
I seem to have more family than I seem to have...

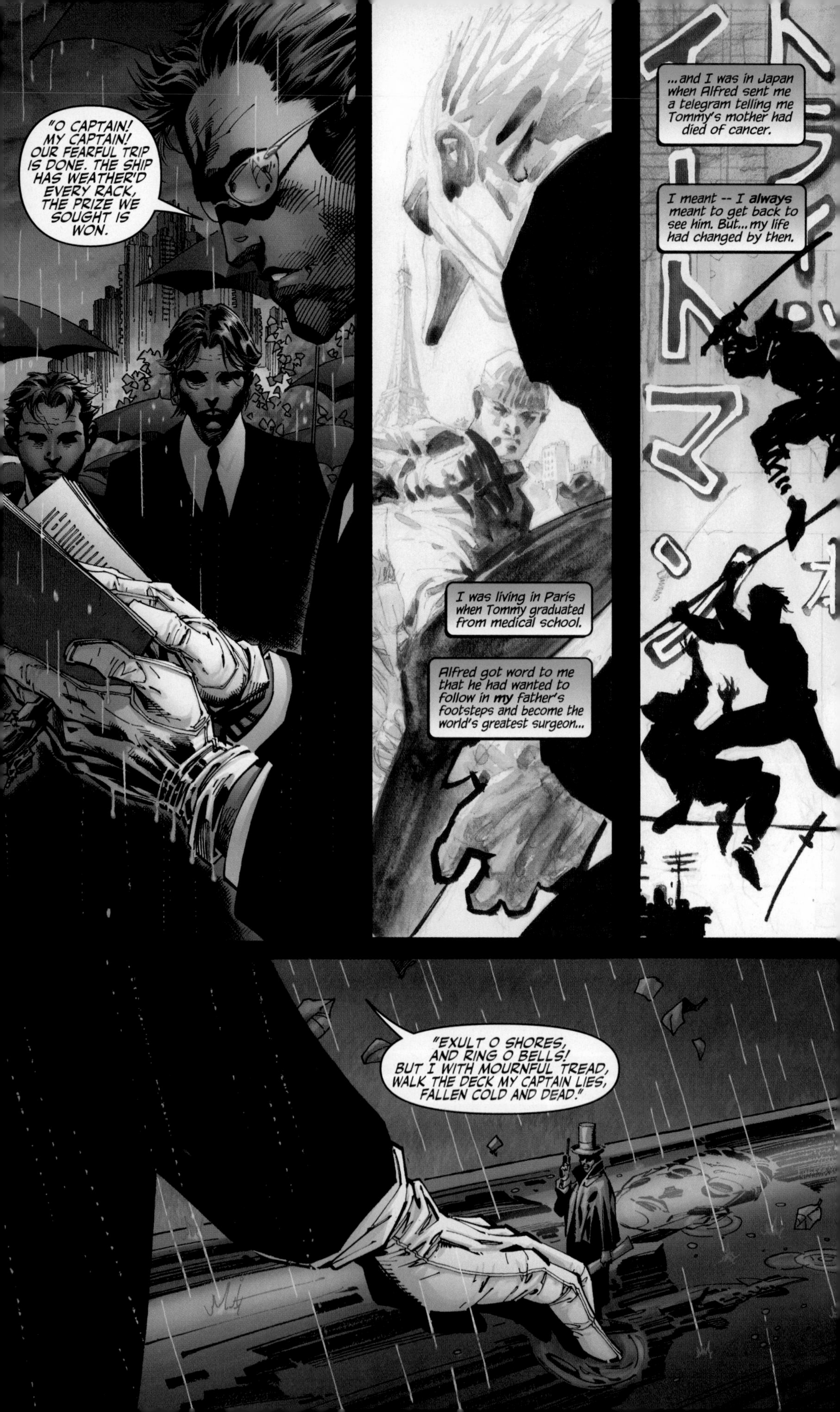
"O CAPTAIN! MY CAPTAIN! OUR FEARFUL TRIP IS DONE. THE SHIP HAS WEATHER'D EVERY RACK, THE PRIZE WE SOUGHT IS WON.
I was living in Paris when Tommy graduated from medical school.
Alfred got word to me that he had wanted to follow in **my** father's footsteps and become the world's greatest surgeon...
...and I was in Japan when Alfred sent me a telegram telling me Tommy's mother had died of cancer.
I meant -- I **always** meant to get back to see him. But...my life had changed by then.
"EXULT O SHORES, AND RING O BELLS! BUT I WITH MOURNFUL TREAD, WALK THE DECK MY CAPTAIN LIES, FALLEN COLD AND DEAD."

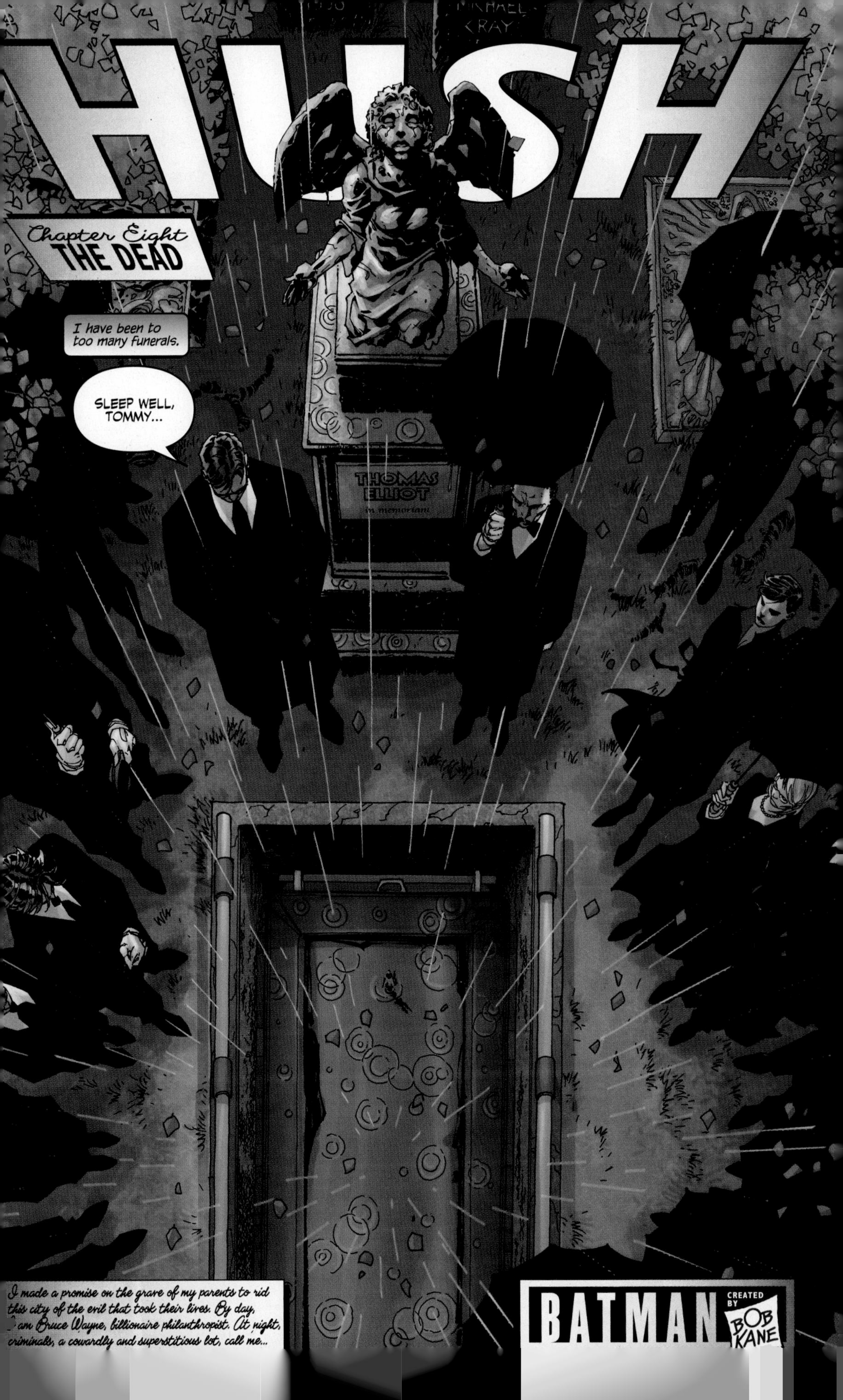
HUSH
Chapter Eight
THE DEAD
I have been to too many funerals.
SLEEP WELL, TOMMY...
THOMAS ELLIOT
in memoriam
I made a promise on the grave of my parents to rid this city of the evil that took their lives. By day, I am Bruce Wayne, billionaire philanthropist. At night, criminals, a cowardly and superstitious lot, call me...
BATMAN
CREATED BY BOB KANE

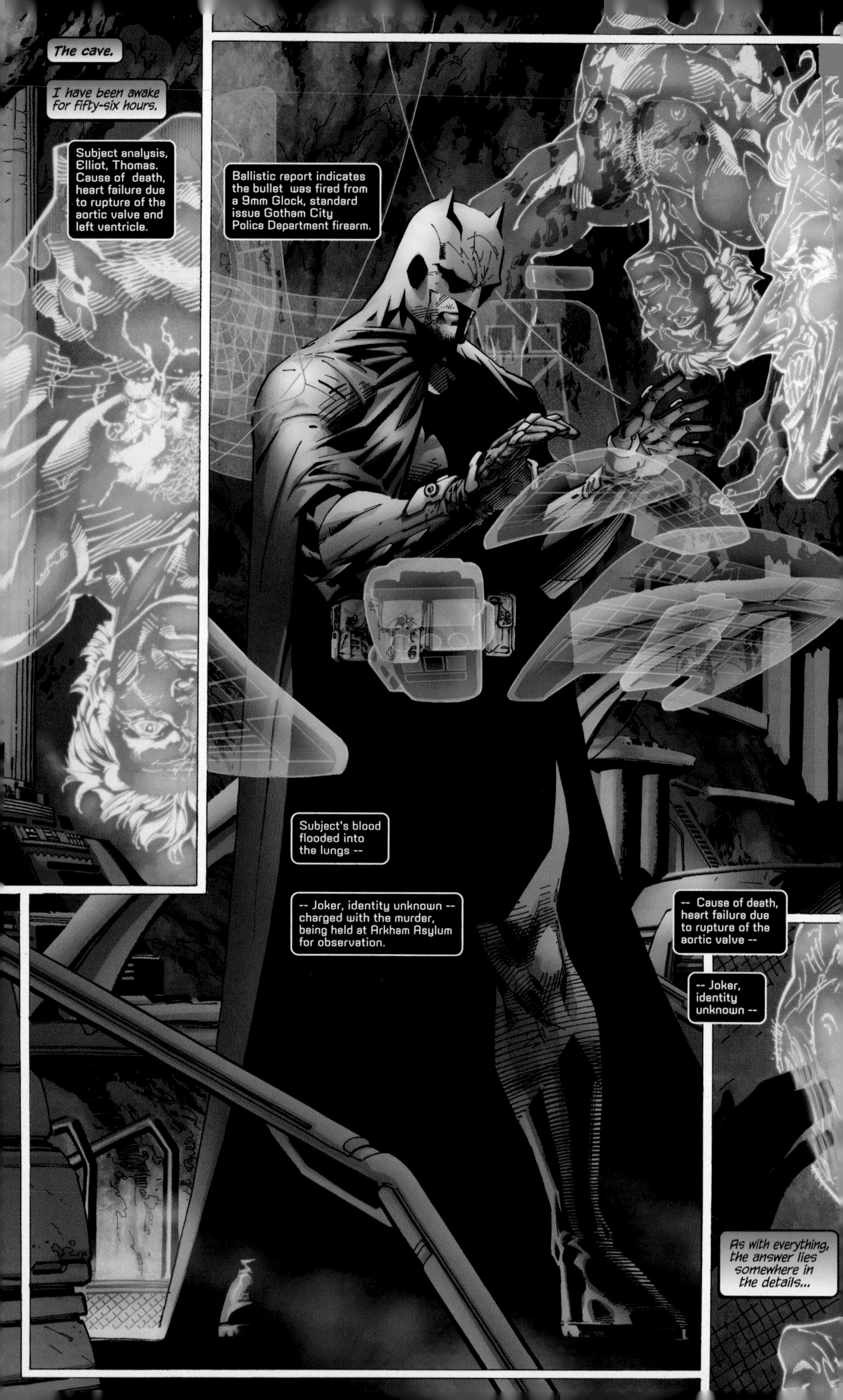
The cave.
I have been awake for fifty-six hours.
Subject analysis, Elliot, Thomas. Cause of death, heart failure due to rupture of the aortic valve and left ventricle.
Ballistic report indicates the bullet was fired from a 9mm Glock, standard issue Gotham City Police Department firearm.
Subject's blood flooded into the lungs --
-- Joker, identity unknown -- charged with the murder, being held at Arkham Asylum for observation.
-- Cause of death, heart failure due to rupture of the aortic valve --
-- Joker, identity unknown --
As with everything, the answer lies somewhere in the details...

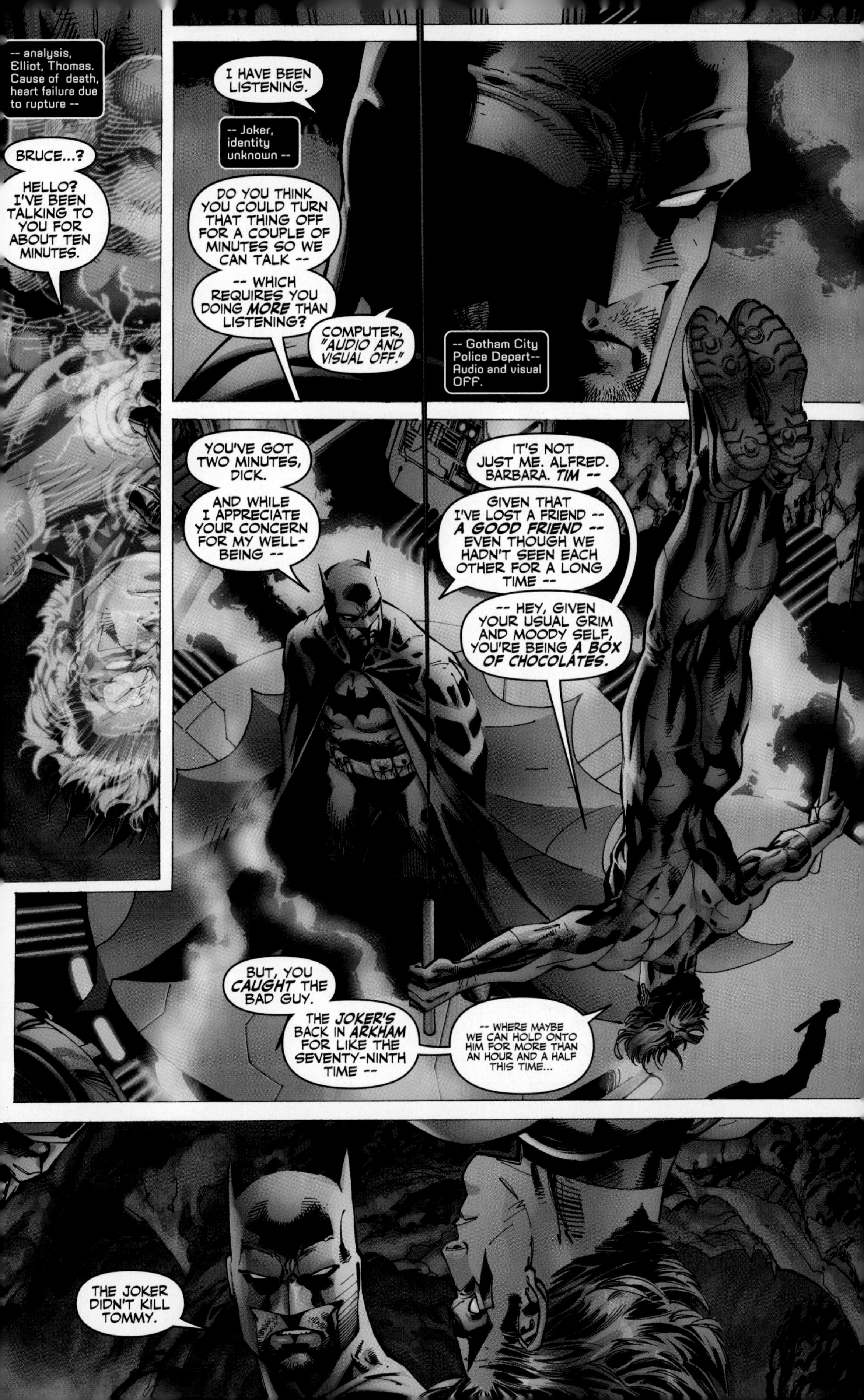
-- analysis, Elliot, Thomas. Cause of death, heart failure due to rupture --
BRUCE...?
HELLO? I'VE BEEN TALKING TO YOU FOR ABOUT TEN MINUTES.
I HAVE BEEN LISTENING.
-- Joker, identity unknown --
DO YOU THINK YOU COULD TURN THAT THING OFF FOR A COUPLE OF MINUTES SO WE CAN TALK --
-- WHICH REQUIRES YOU DOING MORE THAN LISTENING?
COMPUTER, "AUDIO AND VISUAL OFF."
-- Gotham City Police Depart-- Audio and visual OFF.
YOU'VE GOT TWO MINUTES, DICK.
AND WHILE I APPRECIATE YOUR CONCERN FOR MY WELL-BEING --
IT'S NOT JUST ME. ALFRED. BARBARA. TIM --
GIVEN THAT I'VE LOST A FRIEND -- A GOOD FRIEND -- EVEN THOUGH WE HADN'T SEEN EACH OTHER FOR A LONG TIME --
-- HEY, GIVEN YOUR USUAL GRIM AND MOODY SELF, YOU'RE BEING A BOX OF CHOCOLATES.
BUT, YOU CAUGHT THE BAD GUY.
THE JOKER'S BACK IN ARKHAM FOR LIKE THE SEVENTY-NINTH TIME --
-- WHERE MAYBE WE CAN HOLD ONTO HIM FOR MORE THAN AN HOUR AND A HALF THIS TIME...
THE JOKER DIDN'T KILL TOMMY.

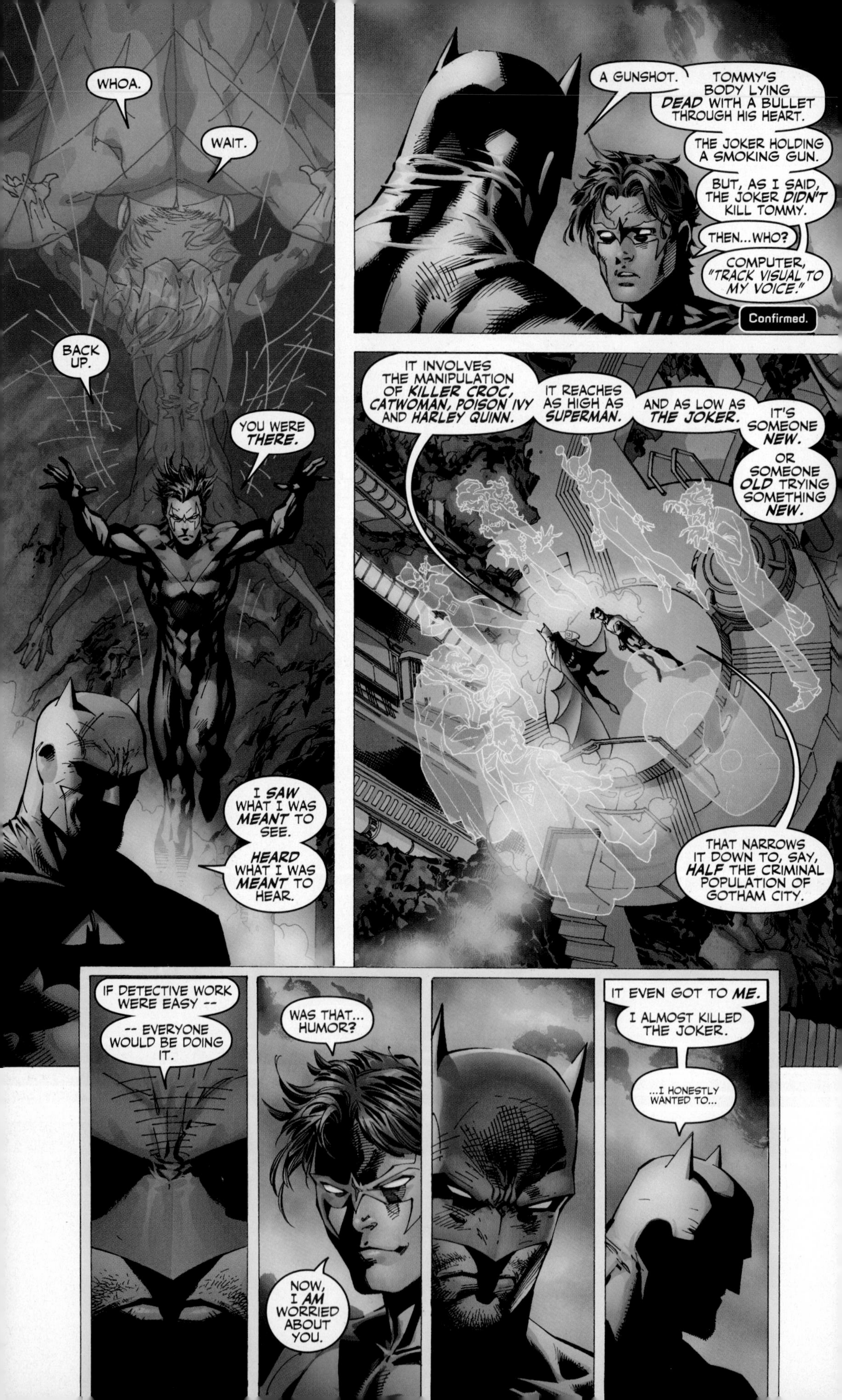
WHOA.
WAIT.
BACK UP.
YOU WERE THERE.
I SAW WHAT I WAS MEANT TO SEE.
HEARD WHAT I WAS MEANT TO HEAR.
A GUNSHOT.
TOMMY'S BODY LYING DEAD WITH A BULLET THROUGH HIS HEART.
THE JOKER HOLDING A SMOKING GUN.
BUT, AS I SAID, THE JOKER DIDN'T KILL TOMMY.
THEN...WHO?
COMPUTER, "TRACK VISUAL TO MY VOICE."
Confirmed.
IT INVOLVES THE MANIPULATION OF KILLER CROC, CATWOMAN, POISON IVY AND HARLEY QUINN.
IT REACHES AS HIGH AS SUPERMAN.
AND AS LOW AS THE JOKER.
IT'S SOMEONE NEW.
OR SOMEONE OLD TRYING SOMETHING NEW.
THAT NARROWS IT DOWN TO, SAY, HALF THE CRIMINAL POPULATION OF GOTHAM CITY.
IF DETECTIVE WORK WERE EASY --
-- EVERYONE WOULD BE DOING IT.
WAS THAT... HUMOR?
NOW, I AM WORRIED ABOUT YOU.
IT EVEN GOT TO ME.
I ALMOST KILLED THE JOKER.
...I HONESTLY WANTED TO...

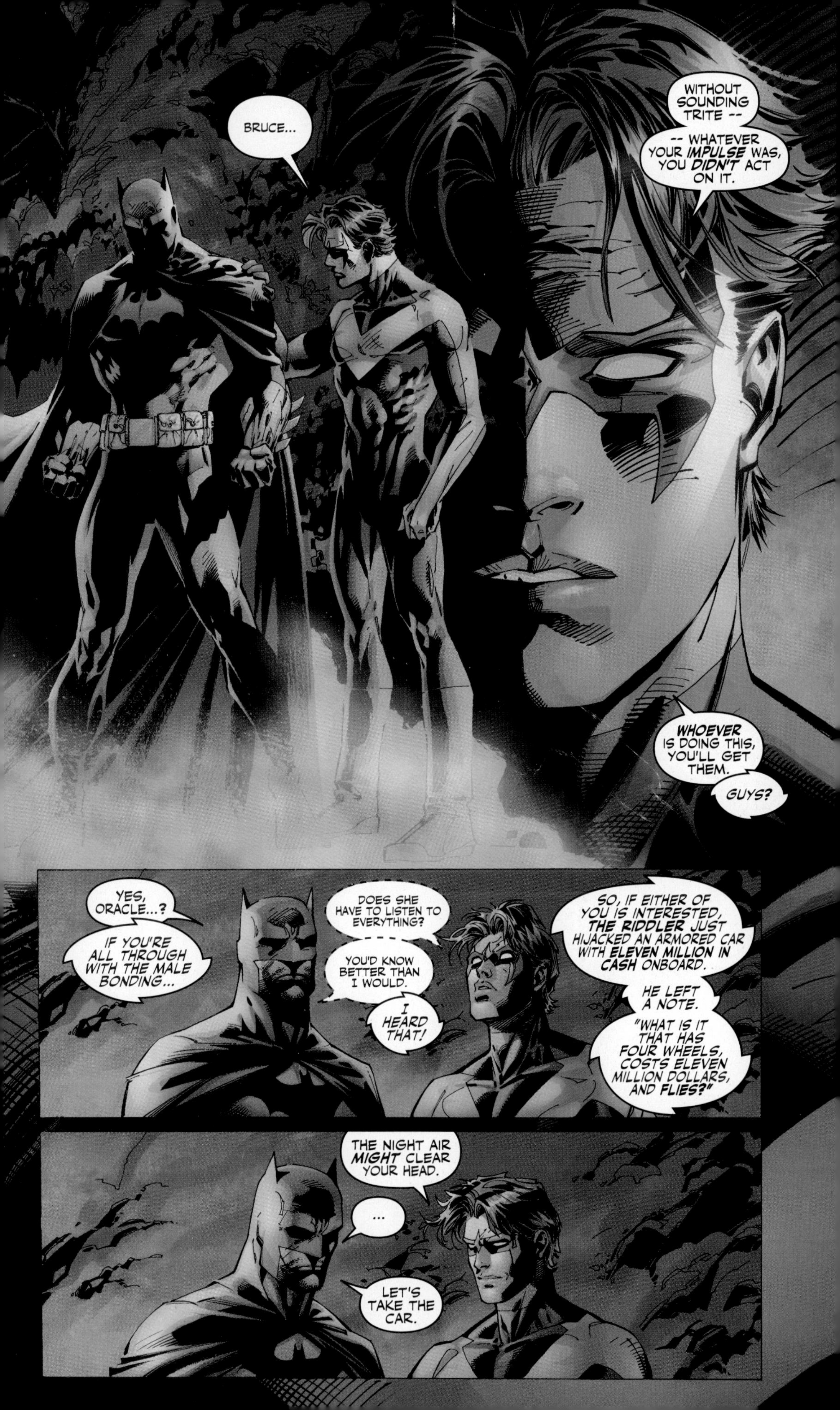
BRUCE...
WITHOUT SOUNDING TRITE --
-- WHATEVER YOUR IMPULSE WAS, YOU DIDN'T ACT ON IT.
WHOEVER IS DOING THIS, YOU'LL GET THEM.
GUYS?
YES, ORACLE...?
IF YOU'RE ALL THROUGH WITH THE MALE BONDING...
DOES SHE HAVE TO LISTEN TO EVERYTHING?
YOU'D KNOW BETTER THAN I WOULD.
I HEARD THAT!
SO, IF EITHER OF YOU IS INTERESTED, THE RIDDLER JUST HIJACKED AN ARMORED CAR WITH ELEVEN MILLION IN CASH ONBOARD.
HE LEFT A NOTE.
"WHAT IS IT THAT HAS FOUR WHEELS, COSTS ELEVEN MILLION DOLLARS, AND FLIES?"
THE NIGHT AIR MIGHT CLEAR YOUR HEAD.
...
LET'S TAKE THE CAR.

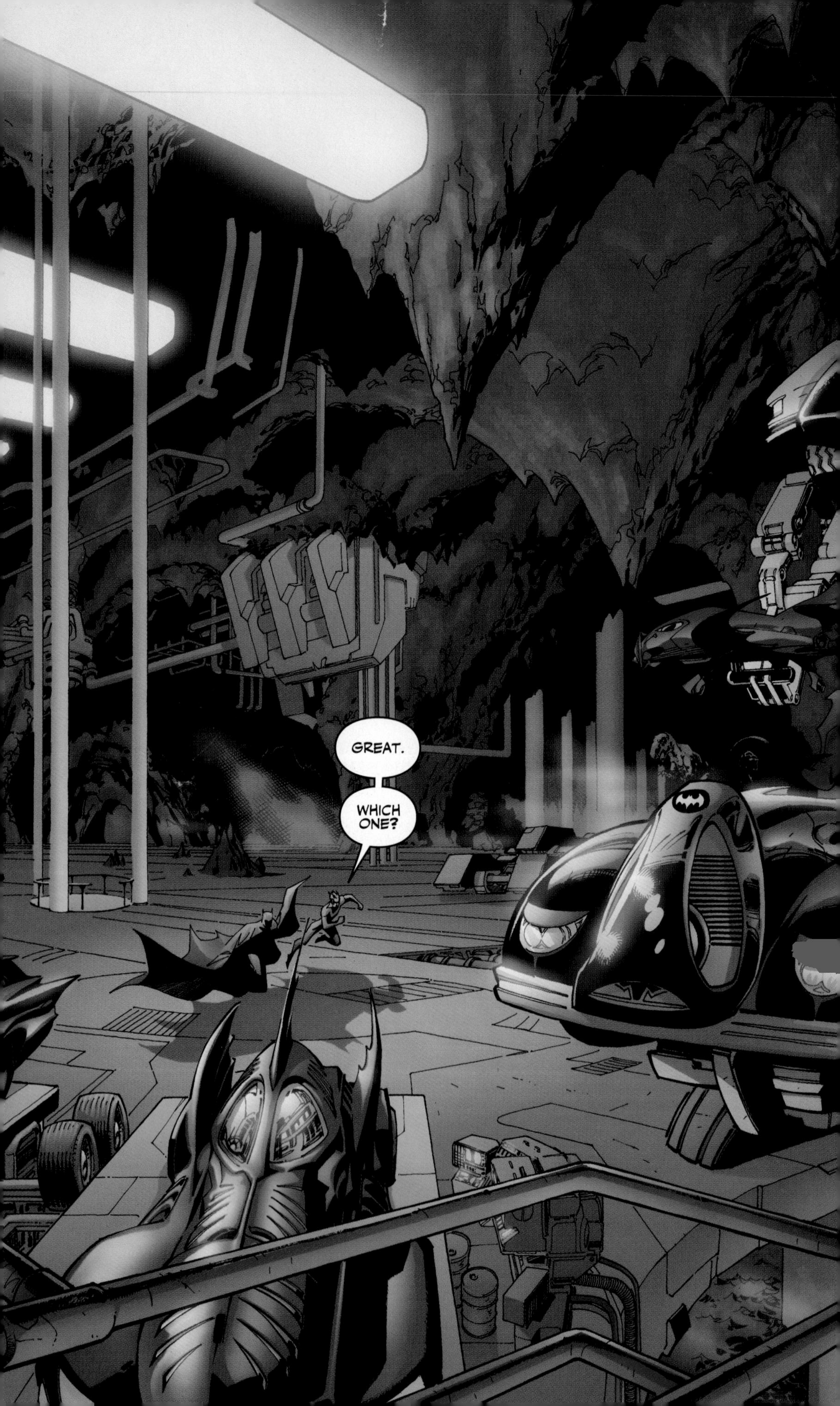
GREAT.
WHICH ONE?

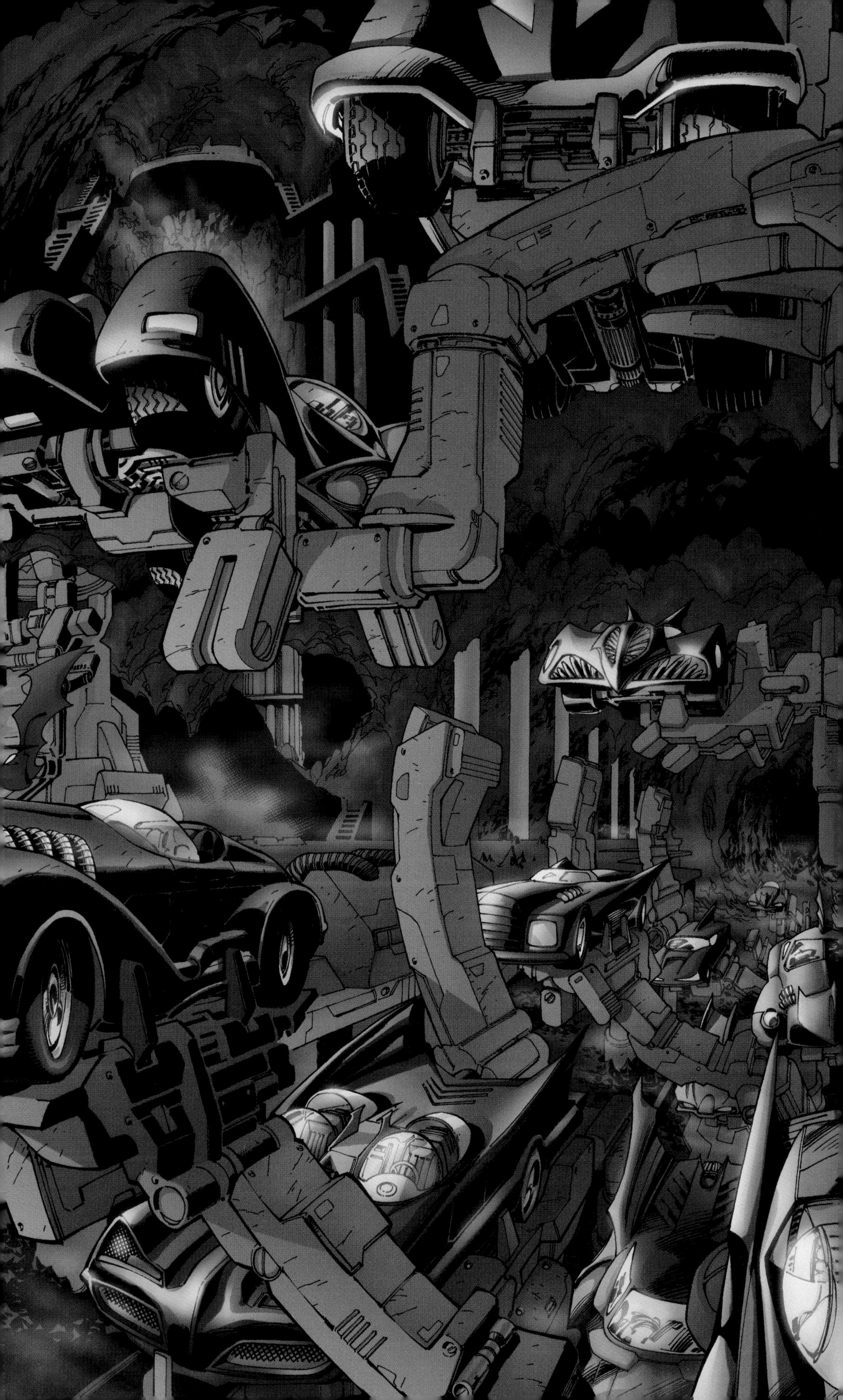

THROOOM

SO. WORD *UNDER* THE STREET IS YOU'RE SEEING CATWOMAN.

ANY *TRUTH* IN THAT?

GOTHAM CITY 14 MILES

SKREEEEEEE

HONK HONK

SHELDON PARK EXIT A STREET

APARO EXPRESSWAY

WELCOME TO GOTHAM CITY

I TAKE IT BY YOUR *SILENCE*...

...IT *IS* TRUE!

Dick always spoke to me without fear. No matter what else has happened to us through the years --

-- he has earned that right.

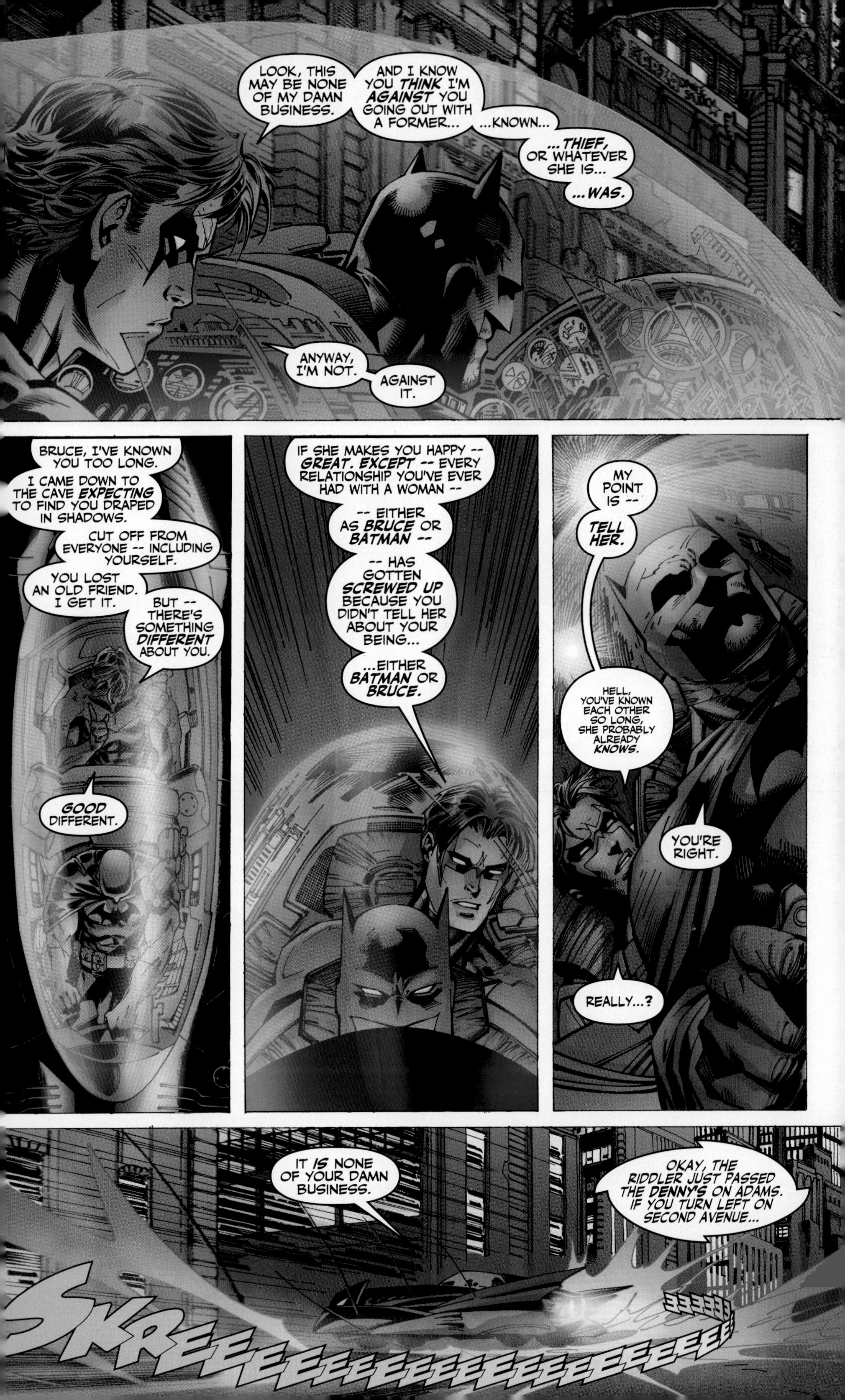
LOOK, THIS MAY BE NONE OF MY DAMN BUSINESS.
AND I KNOW YOU THINK I'M AGAINST YOU GOING OUT WITH A FORMER...
...KNOWN...
...THIEF, OR WHATEVER SHE IS...
...WAS.
ANYWAY, I'M NOT.
AGAINST IT.
BRUCE, I'VE KNOWN YOU TOO LONG.
I CAME DOWN TO THE CAVE EXPECTING TO FIND YOU DRAPED IN SHADOWS.
CUT OFF FROM EVERYONE -- INCLUDING YOURSELF.
YOU LOST AN OLD FRIEND. I GET IT.
BUT -- THERE'S SOMETHING DIFFERENT ABOUT YOU.
GOOD DIFFERENT.
IF SHE MAKES YOU HAPPY -- GREAT. EXCEPT -- EVERY RELATIONSHIP YOU'VE EVER HAD WITH A WOMAN --
-- EITHER AS BRUCE OR BATMAN --
-- HAS GOTTEN SCREWED UP BECAUSE YOU DIDN'T TELL HER ABOUT YOUR BEING...
...EITHER BATMAN OR BRUCE.
MY POINT IS --
TELL HER.
HELL, YOU'VE KNOWN EACH OTHER SO LONG, SHE PROBABLY ALREADY KNOWS.
YOU'RE RIGHT.
REALLY...?
IT IS NONE OF YOUR DAMN BUSINESS.
OKAY, THE RIDDLER JUST PASSED THE DENNY'S ON ADAMS. IF YOU TURN LEFT ON SECOND AVENUE...
SKREEEEEEEEEEEEEEEEEEEEEEEEEEEEE

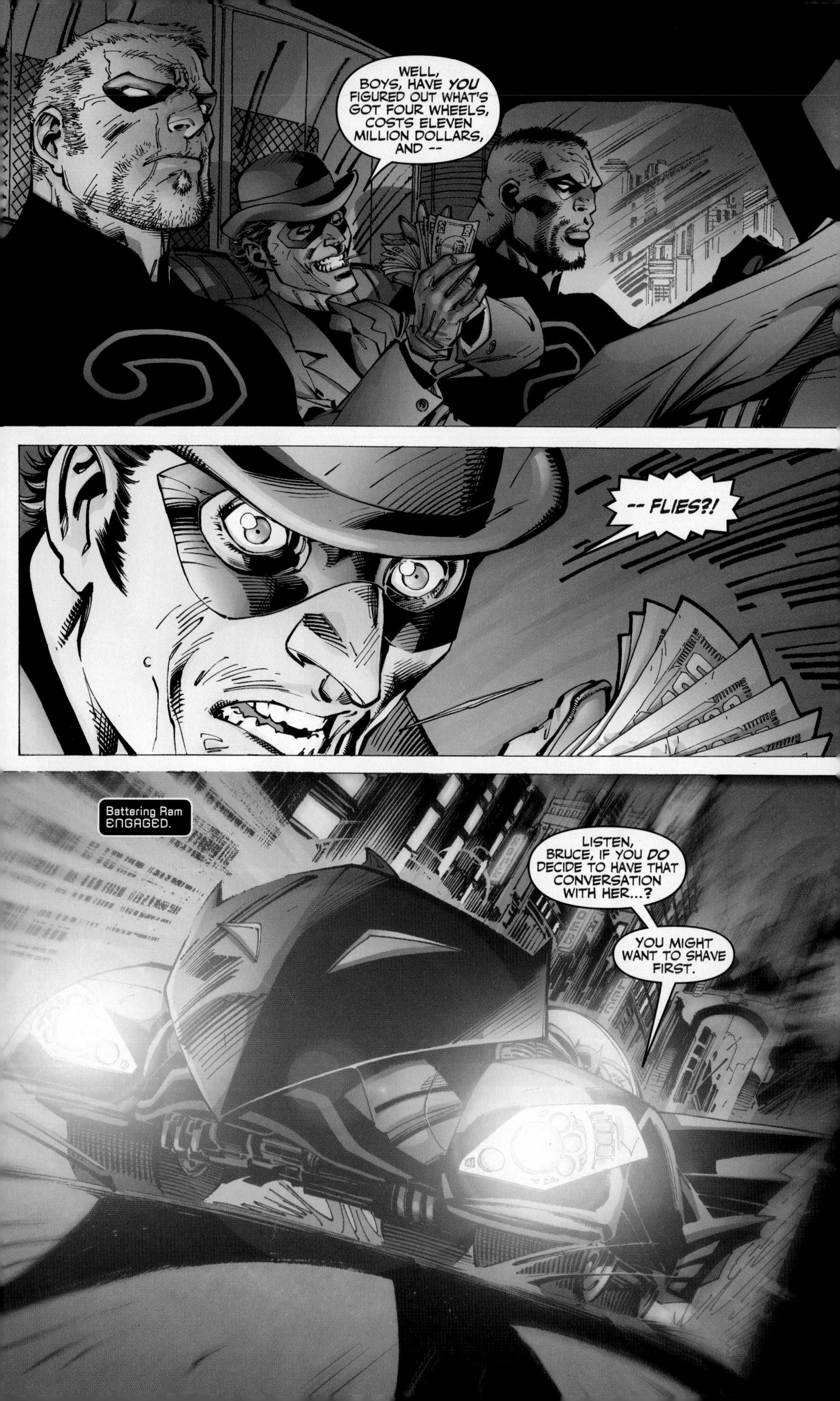
WELL, BOYS, HAVE YOU FIGURED OUT WHAT'S GOT FOUR WHEELS, COSTS ELEVEN MILLION DOLLARS, AND --
-- FLIES?!
Battering Ram ENGAGED.
LISTEN, BRUCE, IF YOU DO DECIDE TO HAVE THAT CONVERSATION WITH HER...?
YOU MIGHT WANT TO SHAVE FIRST.

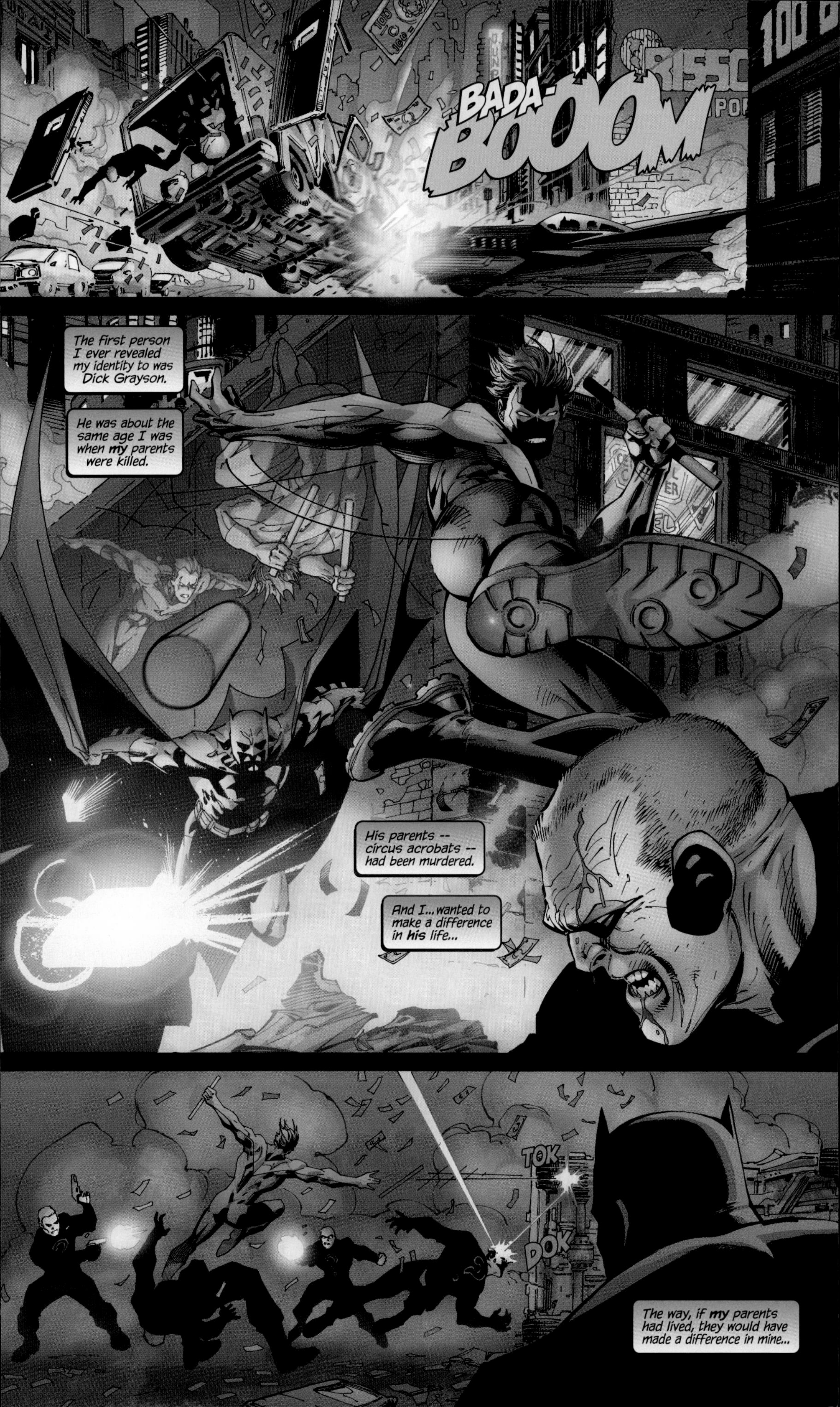
BADA-BOOOM
The first person I ever revealed my identity to was Dick Grayson.
He was about the same age I was when **my** parents were killed.
His parents -- circus acrobats -- had been murdered.
And I...wanted to make a difference in **his** life...
TOK
DOK
The way, if **my** parents had lived, they would have made a difference in mine...

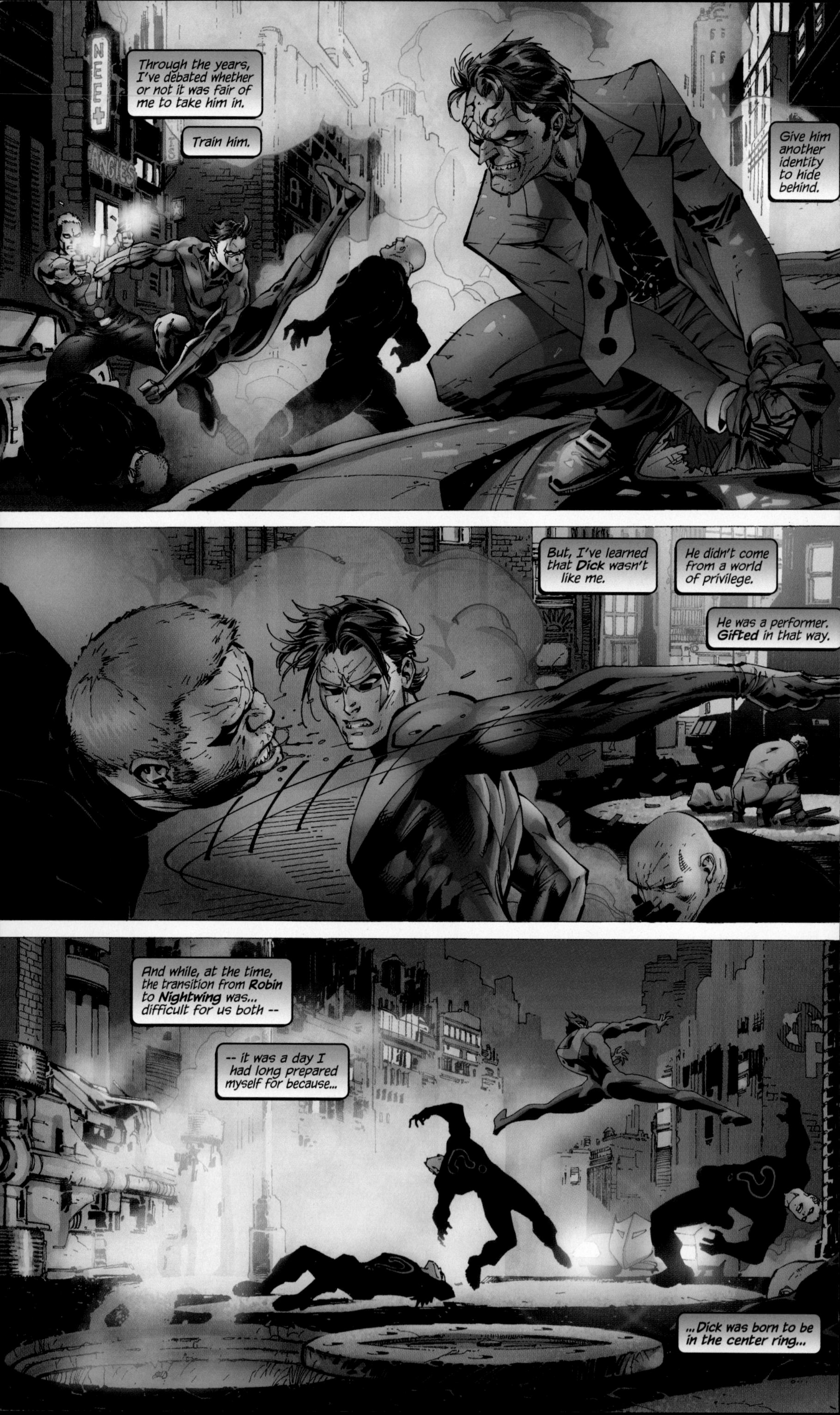
Through the years, I've debated whether or not it was fair of me to take him in.
Train him.
Give him another identity to hide behind.
But, I've learned that Dick wasn't like me.
He didn't come from a world of privilege.
He was a performer. Gifted in that way.
And while, at the time, the transition from Robin to Nightwing was... difficult for us both --
-- it was a day I had long prepared myself for because...
...Dick was born to be in the center ring...

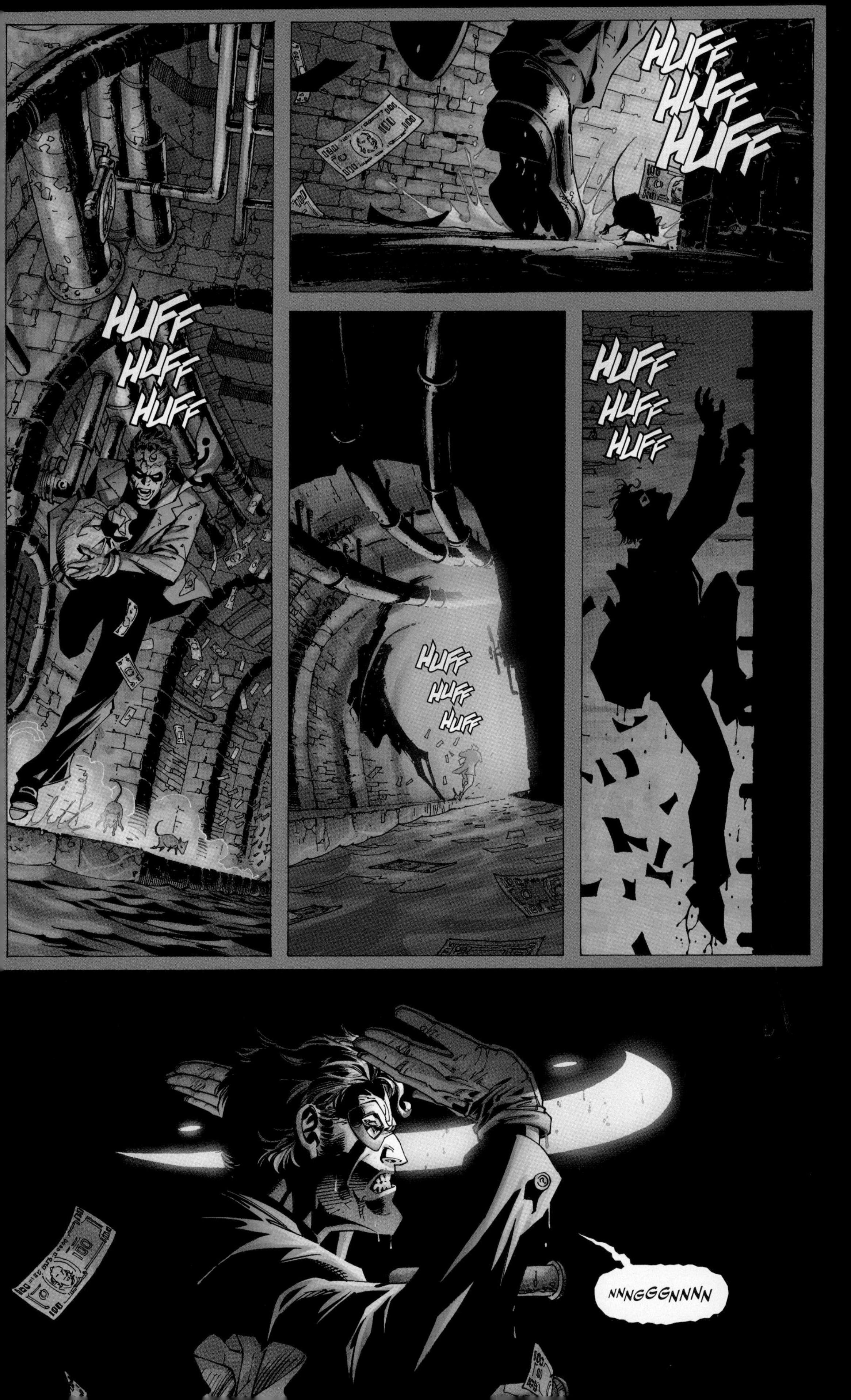
HUFF HUFF HUFF
HUFF HUFF HUFF
HUFF HUFF HUFF
HUFF HUFF HUFF
NNNGGGNNNN

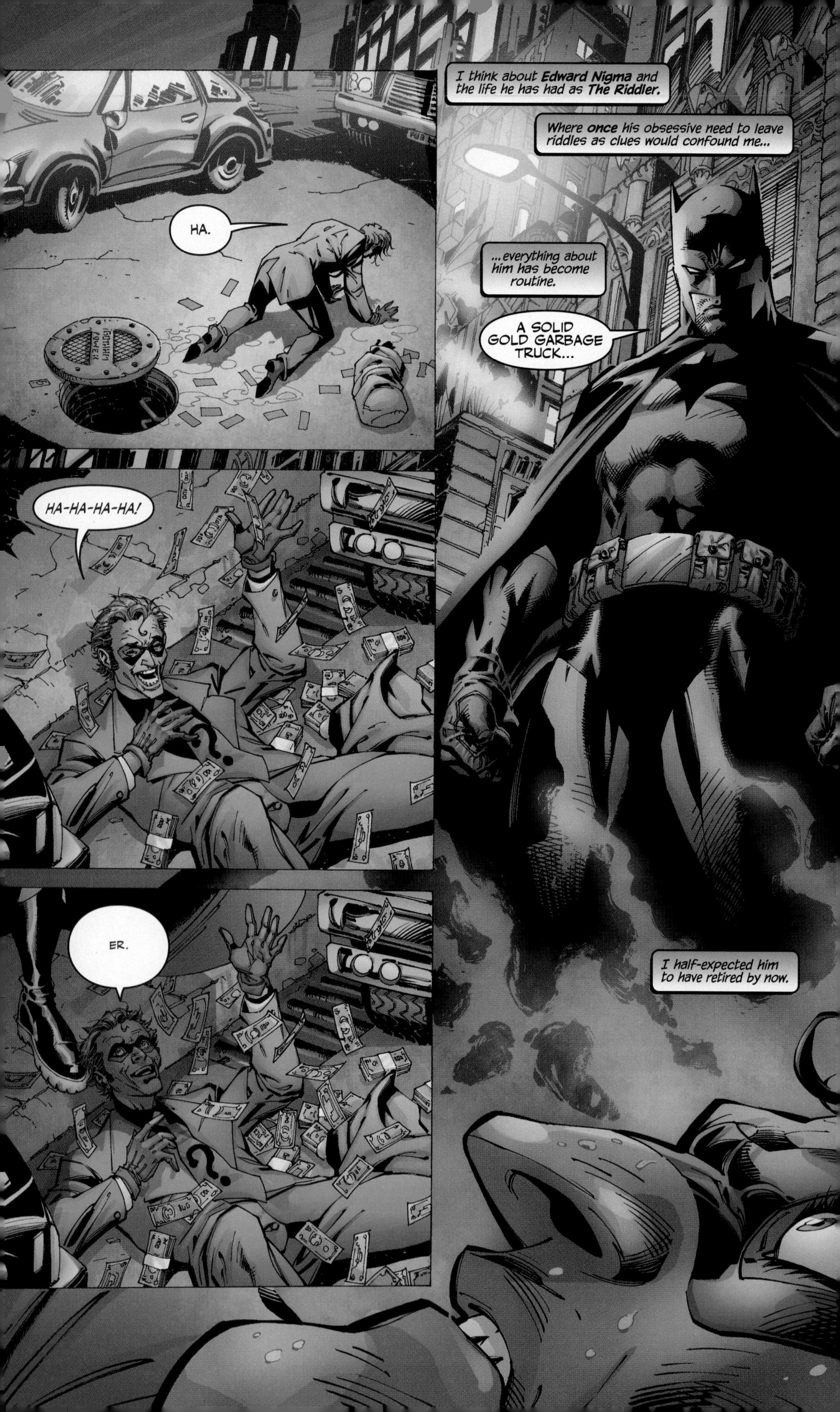
HA.
I think about Edward Nigma and the life he has had as The Riddler.
Where once his obsessive need to leave riddles as clues would confound me...
...everything about him has become routine.
A SOLID GOLD GARBAGE TRUCK...
HA-HA-HA-HA!
ER.
I half-expected him to have retired by now.

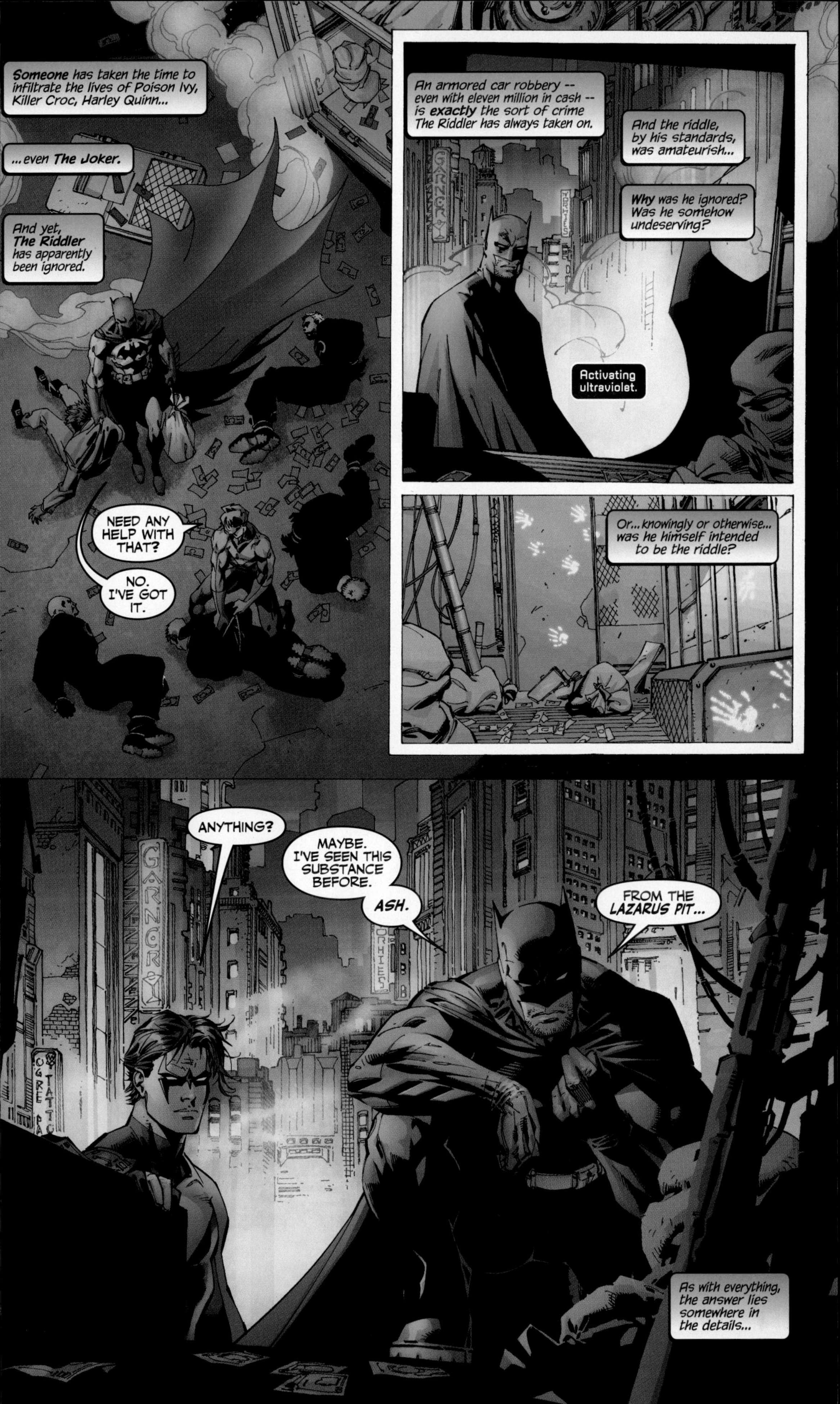

Someone has taken the time to infiltrate the lives of Poison Ivy, Killer Croc, Harley Quinn...
...even The Joker.
And yet, The Riddler has apparently been ignored.
NEED ANY HELP WITH THAT?
NO. I'VE GOT IT.
An armored car robbery -- even with eleven million in cash -- is exactly the sort of crime The Riddler has always taken on.
And the riddle, by his standards, was amateurish...
Why was he ignored? Was he somehow undeserving?
Activating ultraviolet.
Or...knowingly or otherwise... was he himself intended to be the riddle?
ANYTHING?
MAYBE. I'VE SEEN THIS SUBSTANCE BEFORE.
ASH.
FROM THE LAZARUS PIT...
As with everything, the answer lies somewhere in the details...

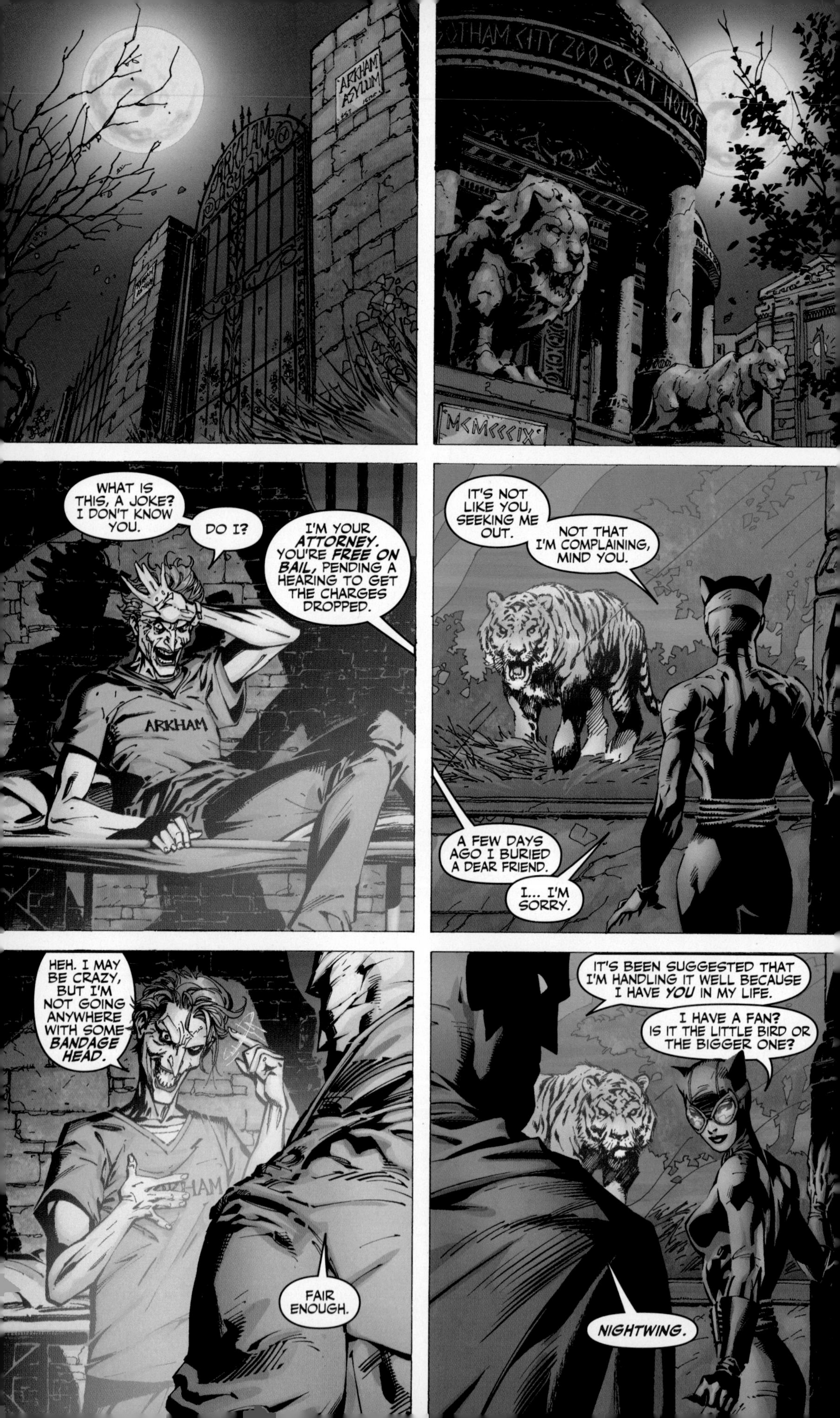
ARKHAM ASYLUM
ARKHAM ASYLUM
GOTHAM CITY ZOO · CAT HOUSE
MCMCCCIX
WHAT IS THIS, A JOKE? I DON'T KNOW YOU.
DO I?
I'M YOUR ATTORNEY. YOU'RE FREE ON BAIL, PENDING A HEARING TO GET THE CHARGES DROPPED.
ARKHAM
IT'S NOT LIKE YOU, SEEKING ME OUT.
NOT THAT I'M COMPLAINING, MIND YOU.
A FEW DAYS AGO I BURIED A DEAR FRIEND.
I... I'M SORRY.
HEH. I MAY BE CRAZY, BUT I'M NOT GOING ANYWHERE WITH SOME BANDAGE HEAD.
FAIR ENOUGH.
IT'S BEEN SUGGESTED THAT I'M HANDLING IT WELL BECAUSE I HAVE YOU IN MY LIFE.
I HAVE A FAN? IS IT THE LITTLE BIRD OR THE BIGGER ONE?
NIGHTWING.

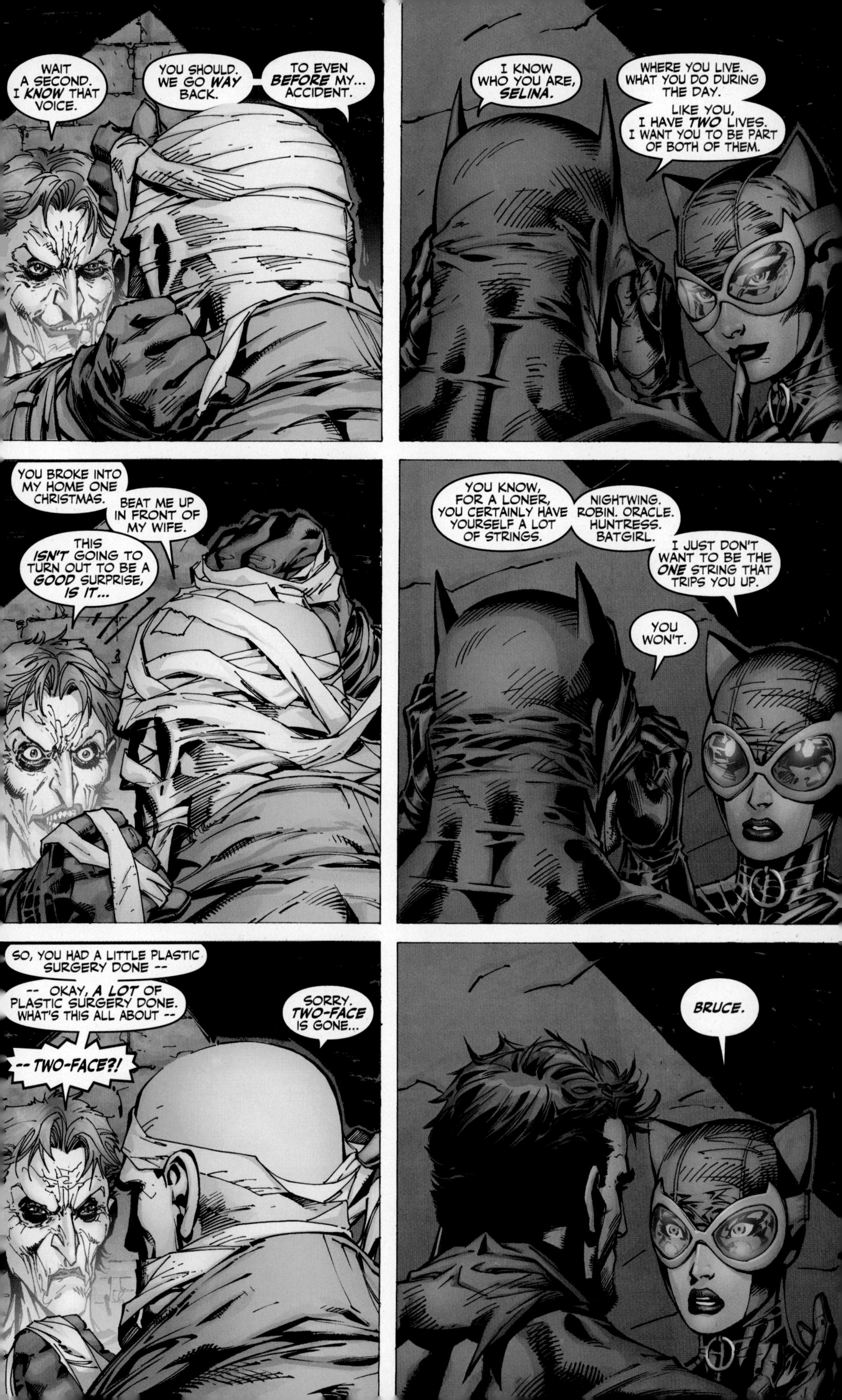
WAIT A SECOND. I KNOW THAT VOICE.
YOU SHOULD. WE GO WAY BACK.
TO EVEN BEFORE MY... ACCIDENT.
I KNOW WHO YOU ARE, SELINA.
WHERE YOU LIVE. WHAT YOU DO DURING THE DAY.
LIKE YOU, I HAVE TWO LIVES. I WANT YOU TO BE PART OF BOTH OF THEM.
YOU BROKE INTO MY HOME ONE CHRISTMAS.
BEAT ME UP IN FRONT OF MY WIFE.
THIS ISN'T GOING TO TURN OUT TO BE A GOOD SURPRISE, IS IT...
YOU KNOW, FOR A LONER, YOU CERTAINLY HAVE YOURSELF A LOT OF STRINGS.
NIGHTWING. ROBIN. ORACLE. HUNTRESS. BATGIRL.
I JUST DON'T WANT TO BE THE ONE STRING THAT TRIPS YOU UP.
YOU WON'T.
SO, YOU HAD A LITTLE PLASTIC SURGERY DONE --
-- OKAY, A LOT OF PLASTIC SURGERY DONE. WHAT'S THIS ALL ABOUT --
-- TWO-FACE?!
SORRY. TWO-FACE IS GONE...
BRUCE.

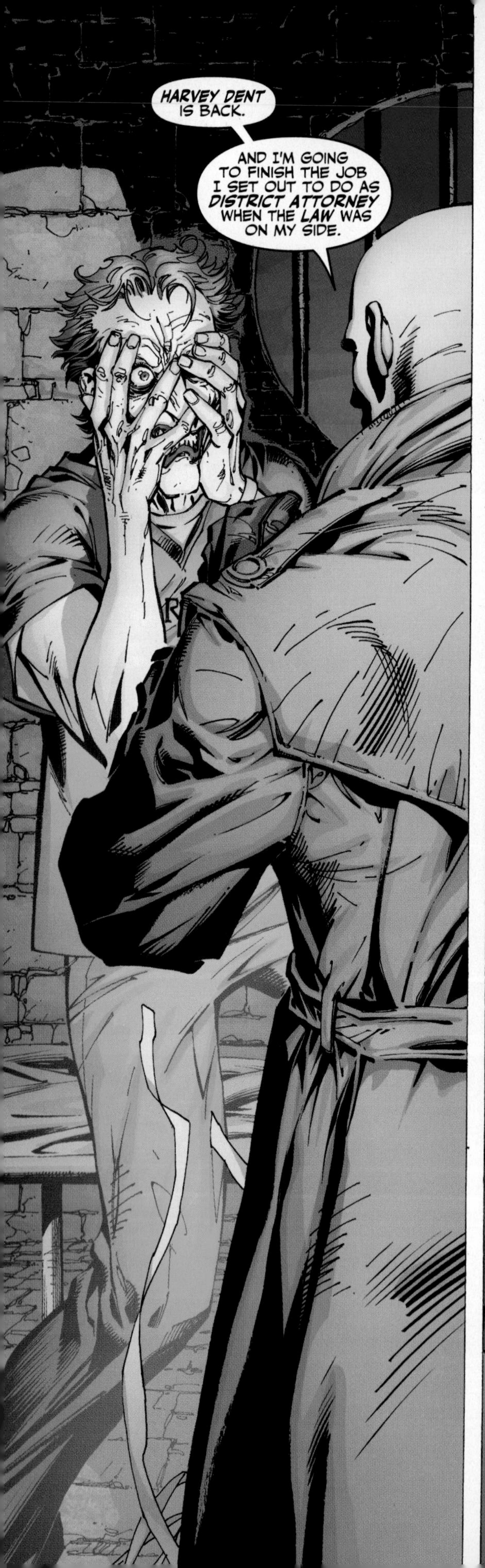
HARVEY DENT IS BACK.
AND I'M GOING TO FINISH THE JOB I SET OUT TO DO AS DISTRICT ATTORNEY WHEN THE LAW WAS ON MY SIDE.

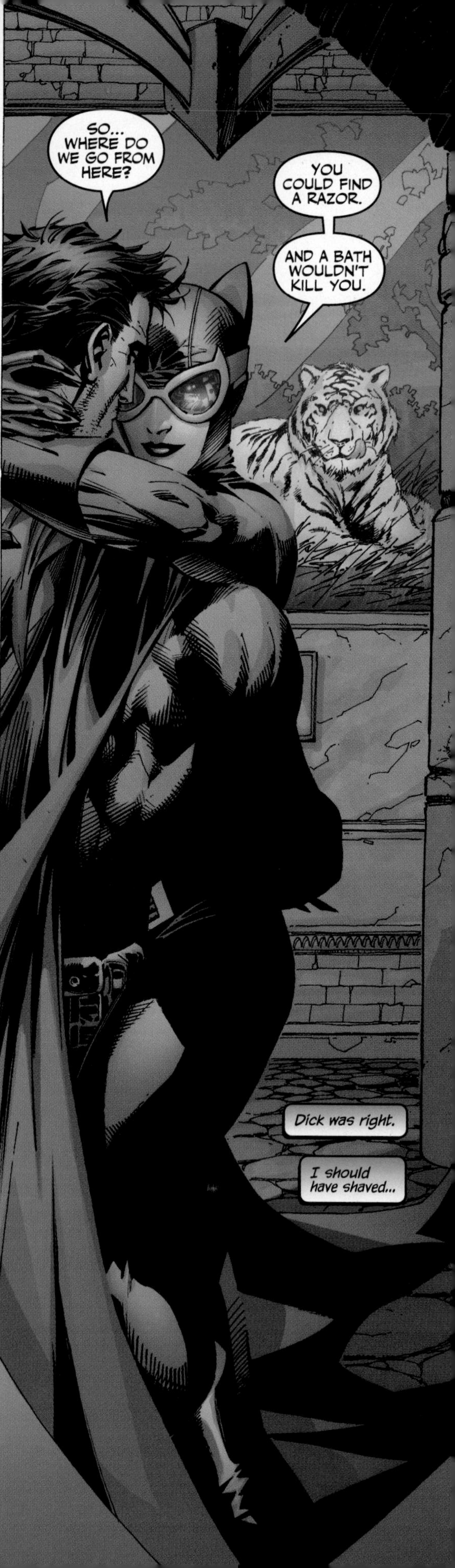
SO... WHERE DO WE GO FROM HERE?
YOU COULD FIND A RAZOR.
AND A BATH WOULDN'T KILL YOU.
Dick was right.
I should have shaved...

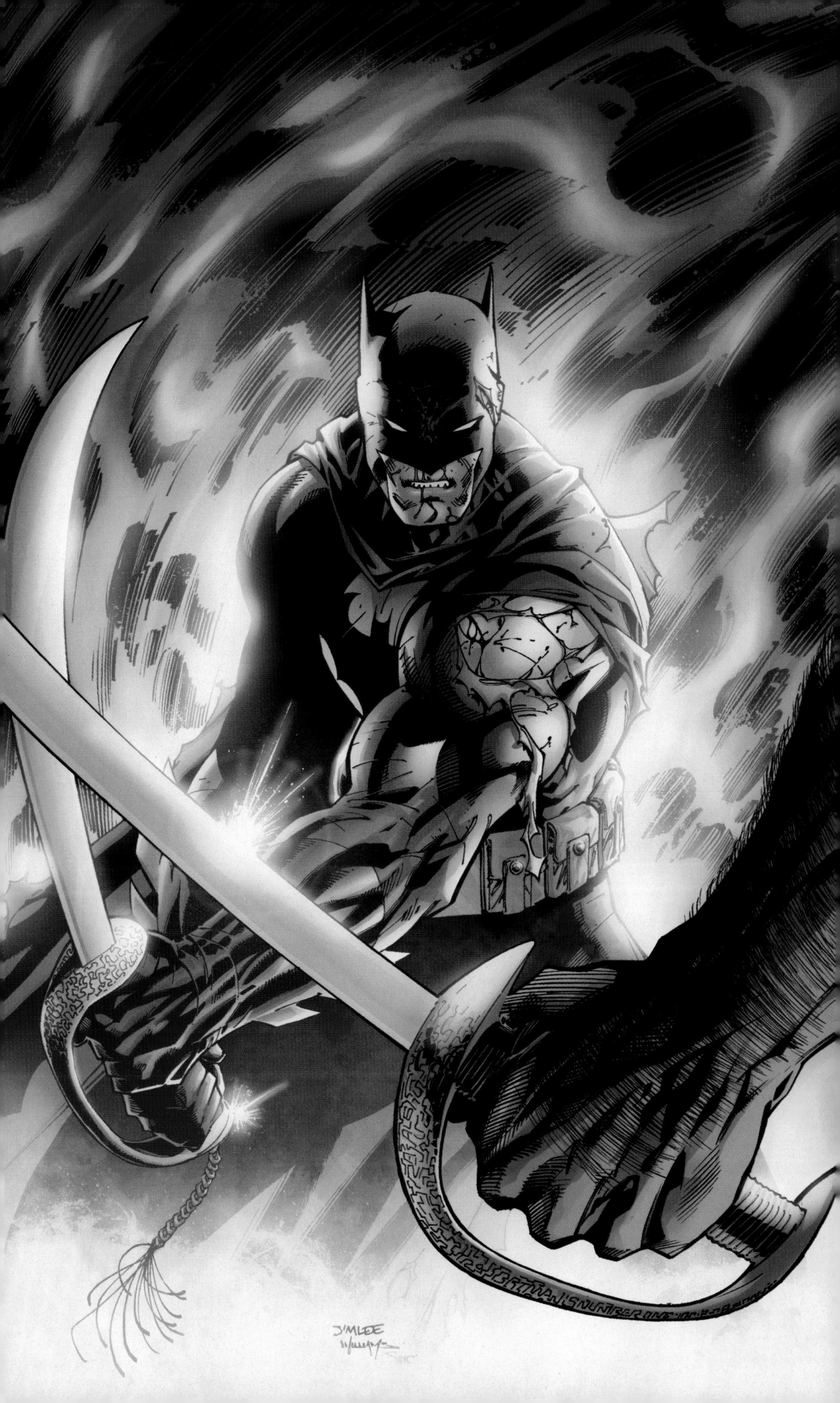

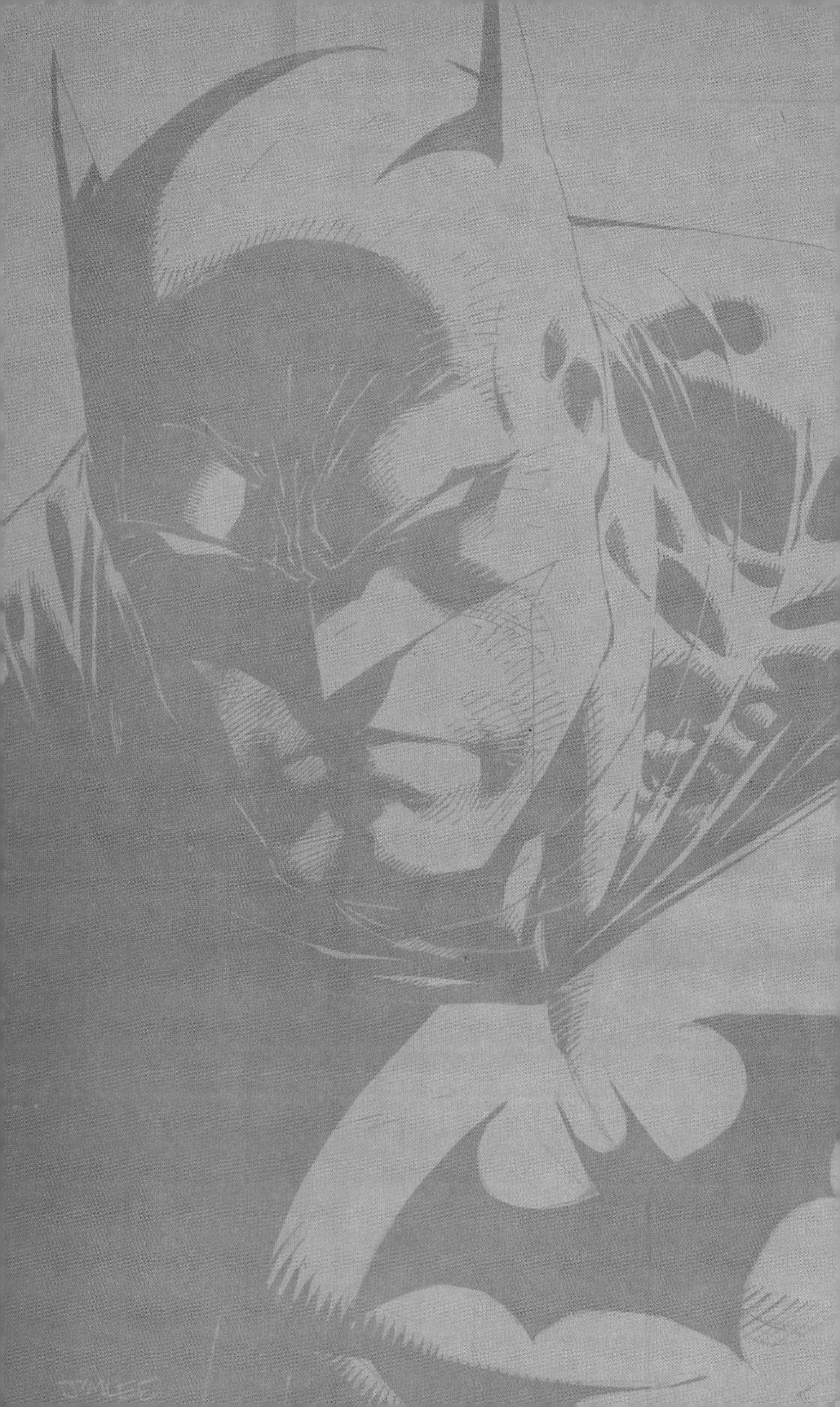

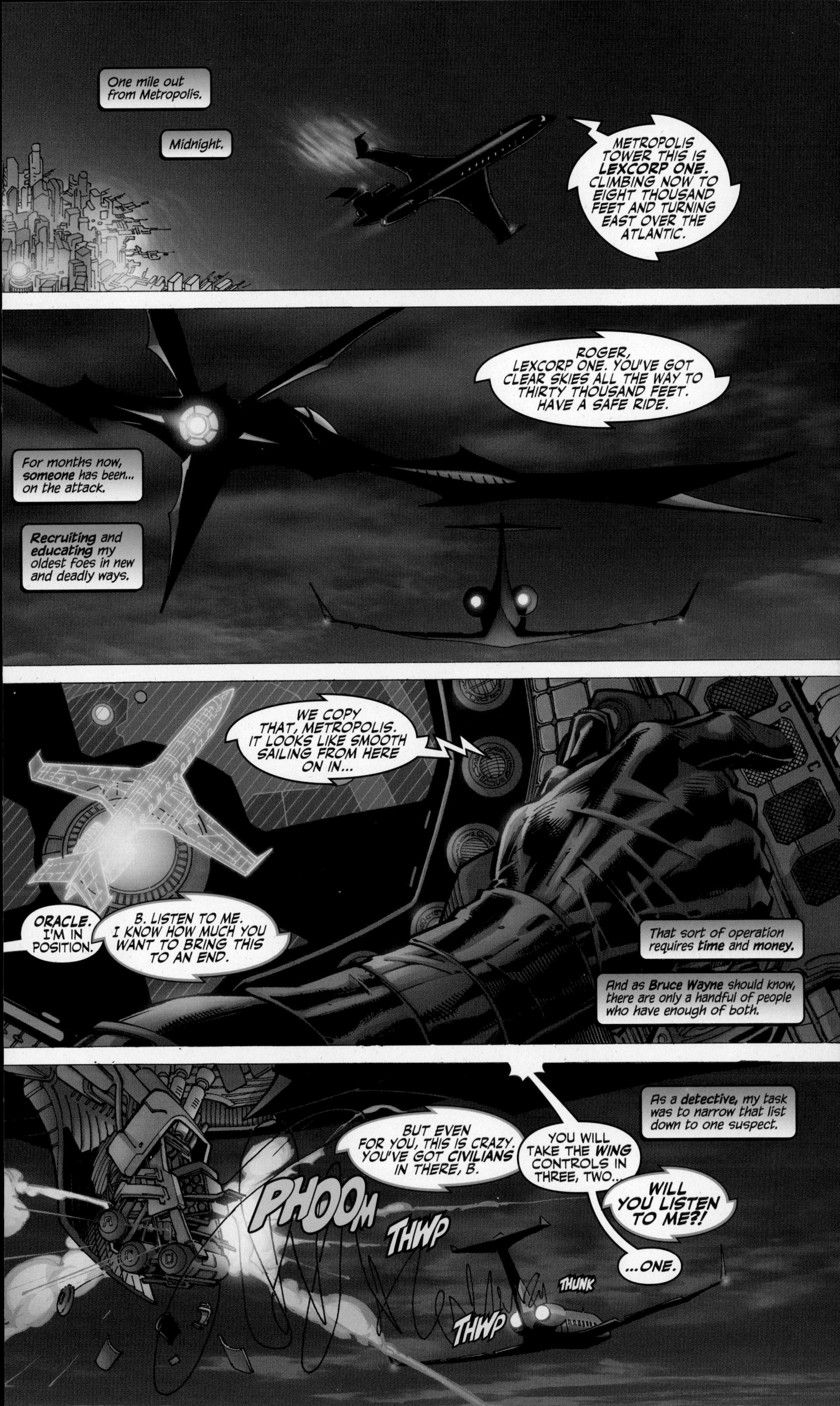
One mile out from Metropolis.
Midnight.
METROPOLIS TOWER THIS IS LEXCORP ONE. CLIMBING NOW TO EIGHT THOUSAND FEET AND TURNING EAST OVER THE ATLANTIC.
ROGER, LEXCORP ONE. YOU'VE GOT CLEAR SKIES ALL THE WAY TO THIRTY THOUSAND FEET. HAVE A SAFE RIDE.
For months now, someone has been... on the attack.
Recruiting and educating my oldest foes in new and deadly ways.
WE COPY THAT, METROPOLIS. IT LOOKS LIKE SMOOTH SAILING FROM HERE ON IN...
ORACLE. I'M IN POSITION.
B. LISTEN TO ME. I KNOW HOW MUCH YOU WANT TO BRING THIS TO AN END.
That sort of operation requires time and money.
And as Bruce Wayne should know, there are only a handful of people who have enough of both.
As a detective, my task was to narrow that list down to one suspect.
BUT EVEN FOR YOU, THIS IS CRAZY. YOU'VE GOT CIVILIANS IN THERE, B.
YOU WILL TAKE THE WING CONTROLS IN THREE, TWO...
WILL YOU LISTEN TO ME?!
PHOOM
THWP
...ONE.
THUNK
THWP

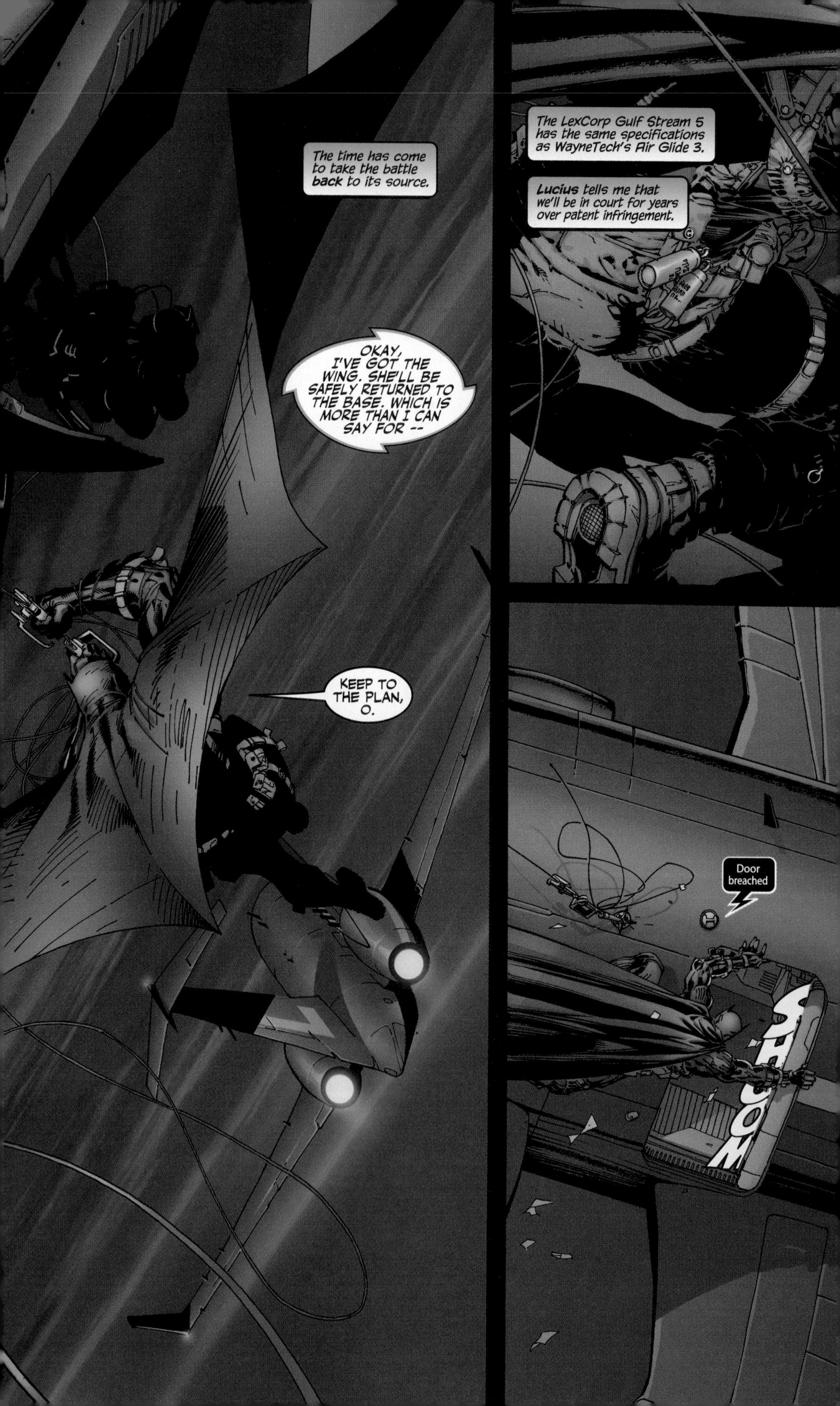
The time has come to take the battle **back** to its source.
OKAY, I'VE GOT THE WING. SHE'LL BE SAFELY RETURNED TO THE BASE. WHICH IS MORE THAN I CAN SAY FOR --
KEEP TO THE PLAN, O.
The LexCorp Gulf Stream 5 has the same specifications as WayneTech's Air Glide 3.
Lucius tells me that we'll be in court for years over patent infringement.
Door breached
SHOOOM

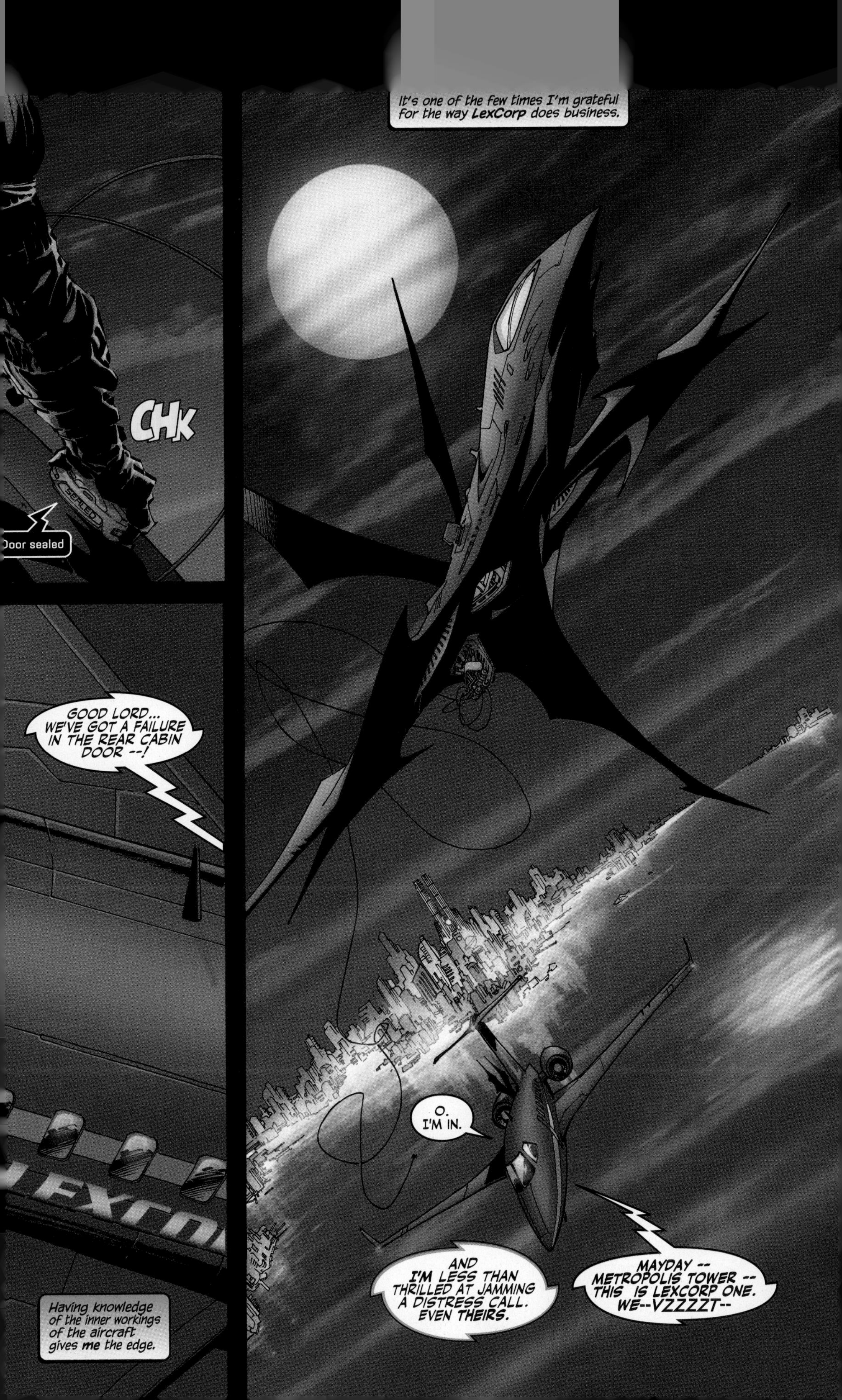
CHK
Door sealed
GOOD LORD... WE'VE GOT A FAILURE IN THE REAR CABIN DOOR --!
Having knowledge of the inner workings of the aircraft gives me the edge.
It's one of the few times I'm grateful for the way LexCorp does business.
O. I'M IN.
MAYDAY -- METROPOLIS TOWER -- THIS IS LEXCORP ONE. WE--VZZZZT--
AND I'M LESS THAN THRILLED AT JAMMING A DISTRESS CALL. EVEN THEIRS.

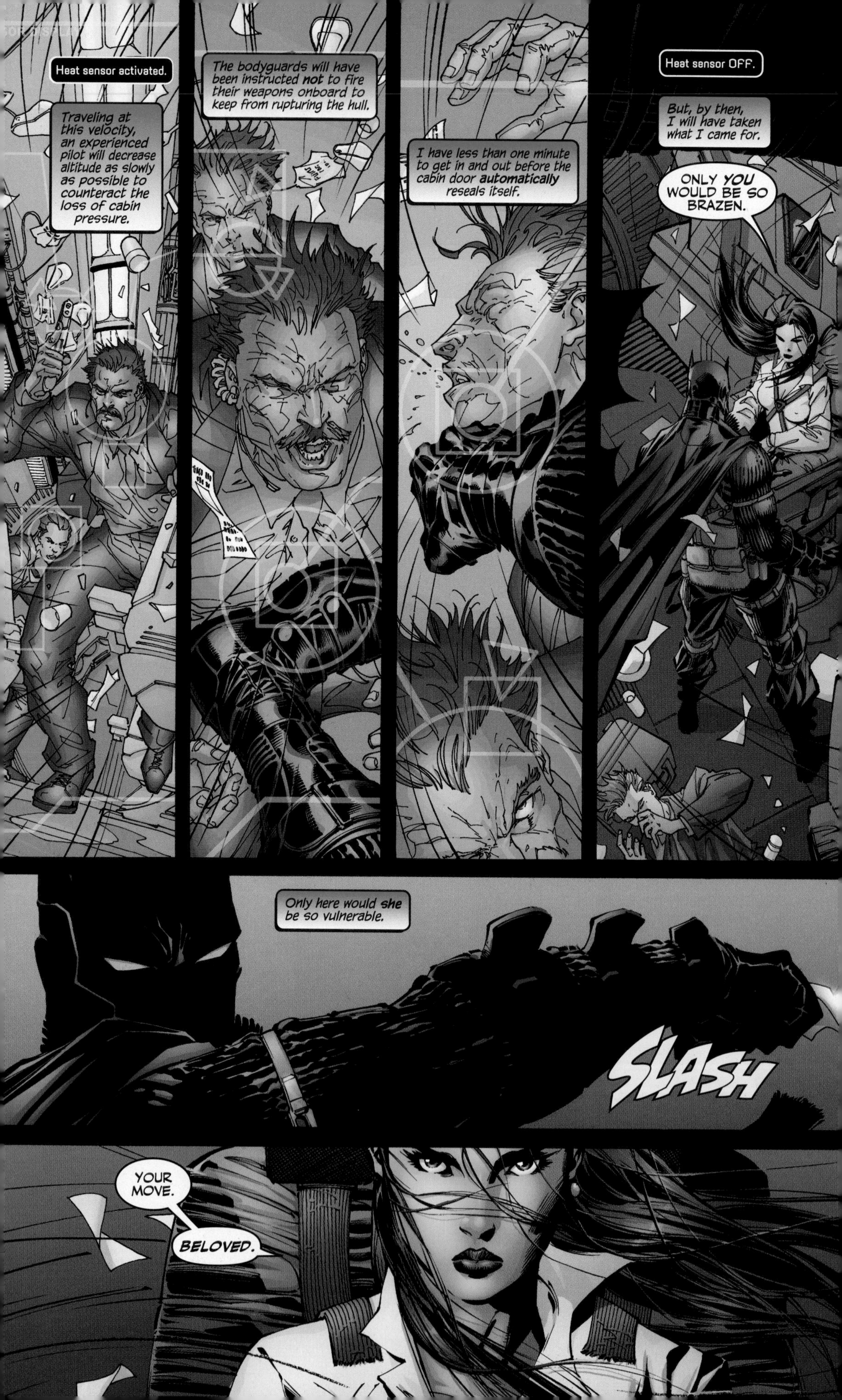
Heat sensor activated.
Traveling at this velocity, an experienced pilot will decrease altitude as slowly as possible to counteract the loss of cabin pressure.
The bodyguards will have been instructed **not** to fire their weapons onboard to keep from rupturing the hull.
I have less than one minute to get in and out before the cabin door **automatically** reseals itself.
Heat sensor OFF.
But, by then, I will have taken what I came for.
ONLY *YOU* WOULD BE SO BRAZEN.
Only here would **she** be so vulnerable.
SLASH
YOUR MOVE.
BELOVED.

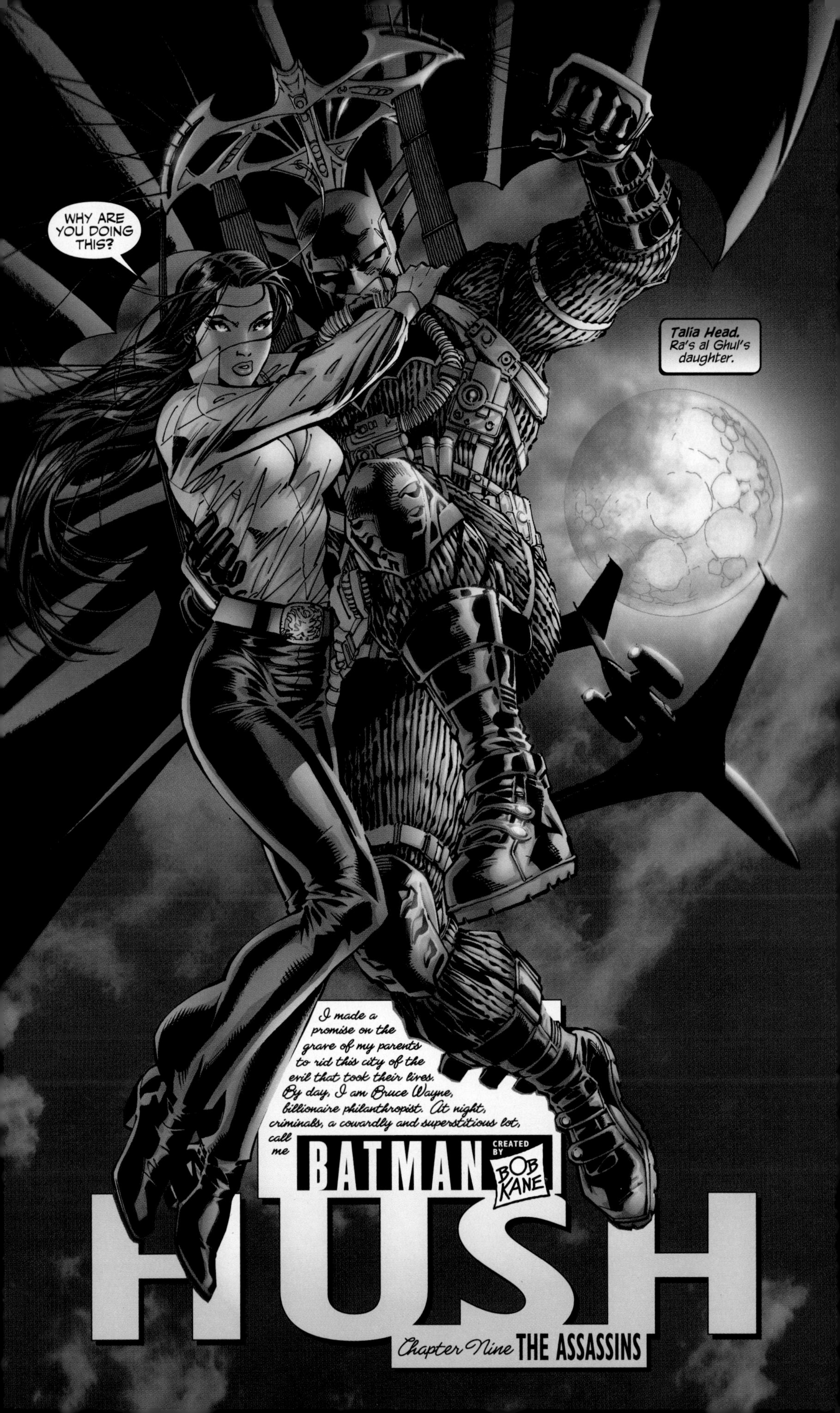

WHY ARE YOU DOING THIS?
Talia Head. Ra's al Ghul's daughter.
I made a promise on the grave of my parents to rid this city of the evil that took their lives. By day, I am Bruce Wayne, billionaire philanthropist. At night, criminals, a cowardly and superstitious lot, call me
BATMAN
CREATED BY BOB KANE
HUSH
Chapter Nine THE ASSASSINS

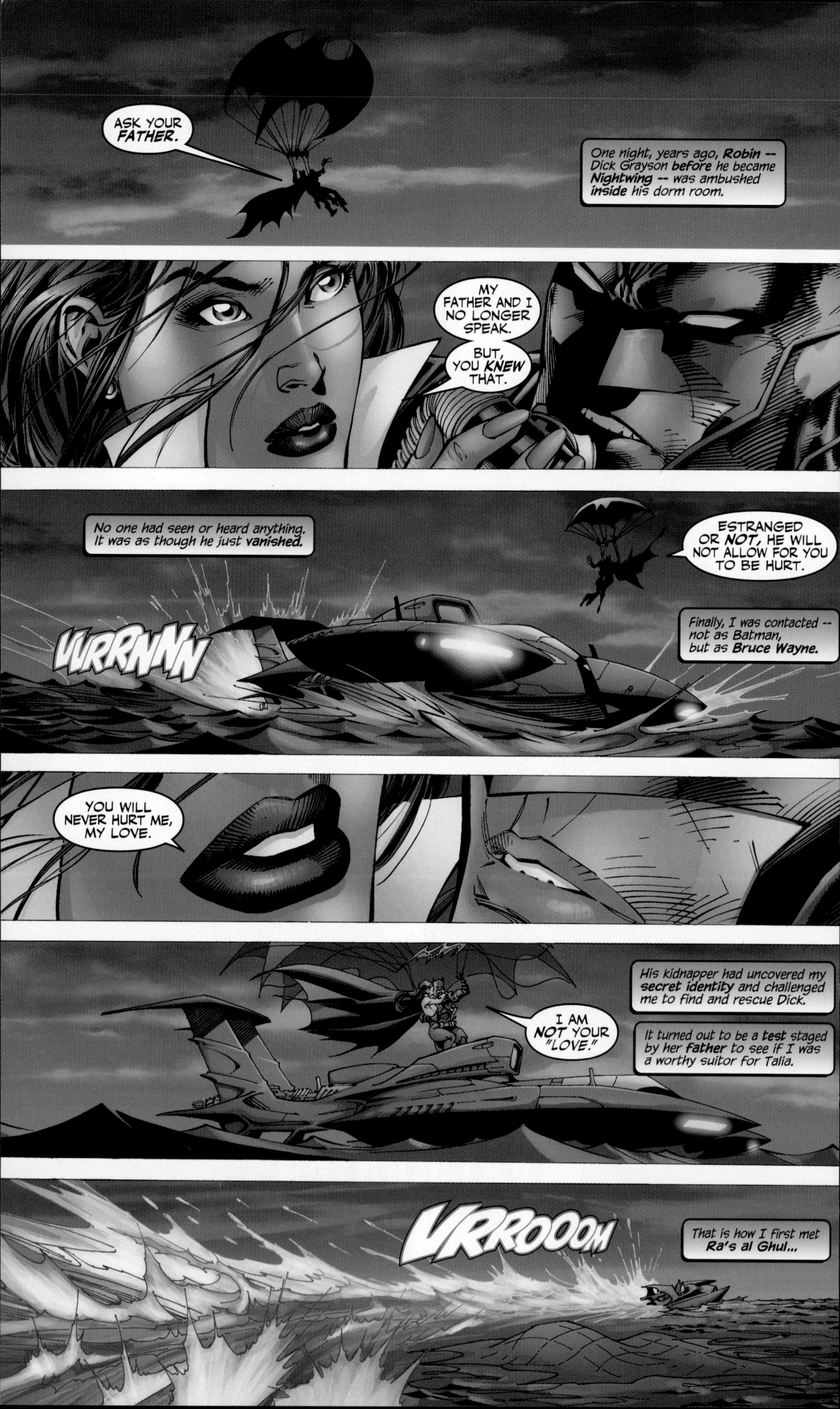
ASK YOUR FATHER.
One night, years ago, Robin -- Dick Grayson before he became Nightwing -- was ambushed inside his dorm room.
MY FATHER AND I NO LONGER SPEAK.
BUT, YOU KNEW THAT.
No one had seen or heard anything. It was as though he just vanished.
ESTRANGED OR NOT, HE WILL NOT ALLOW FOR YOU TO BE HURT.
VVRRNNN
Finally, I was contacted -- not as Batman, but as Bruce Wayne.
YOU WILL NEVER HURT ME, MY LOVE.
His kidnapper had uncovered my secret identity and challenged me to find and rescue Dick.
I AM NOT YOUR "LOVE."
It turned out to be a test staged by her father to see if I was a worthy suitor for Talia.
VRROOOM
That is how I first met Ra's al Ghul...

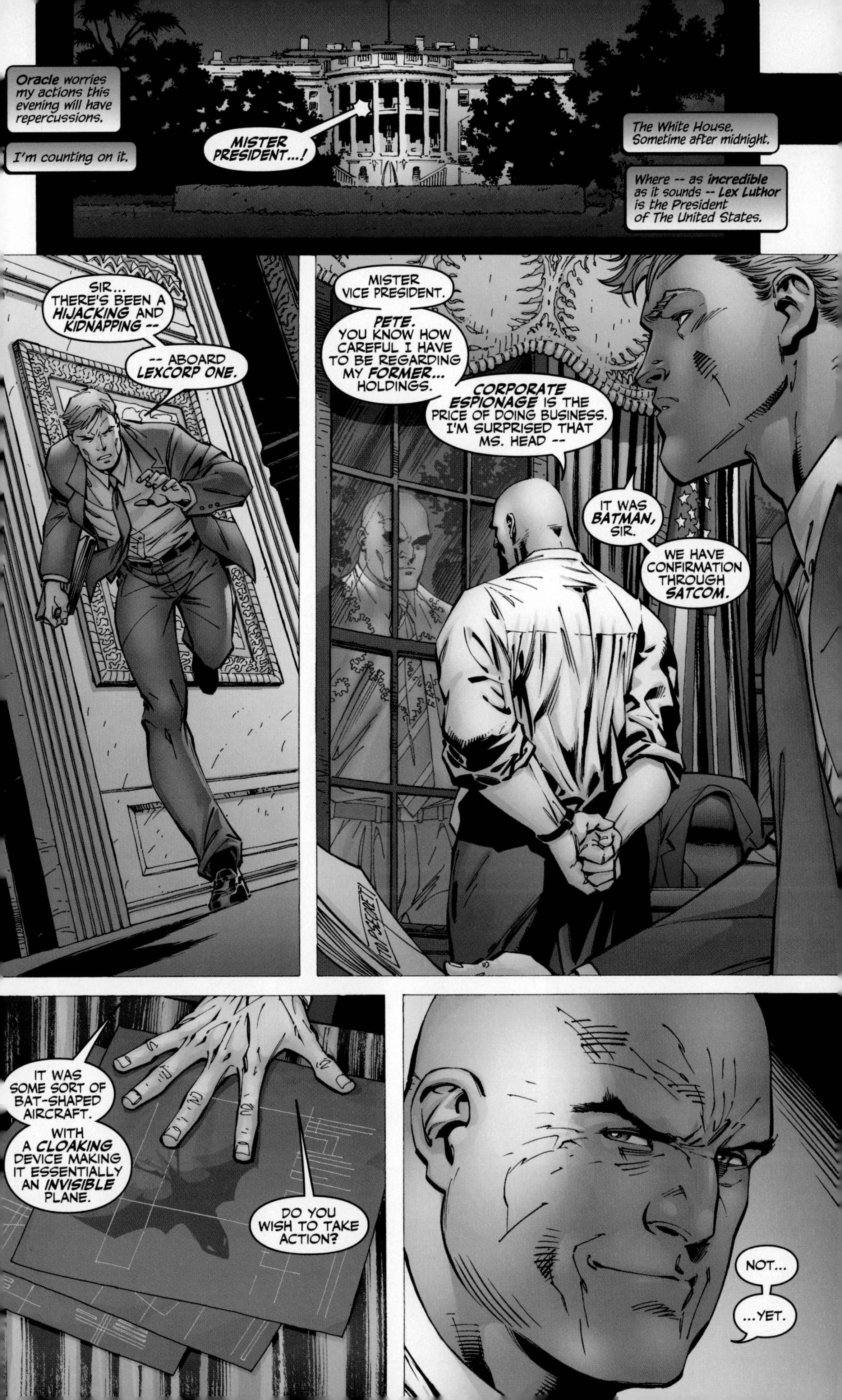

Oracle worries my actions this evening will have repercussions.
I'm counting on it.
MISTER PRESIDENT...!
The White House. Sometime after midnight.
Where -- as incredible as it sounds -- Lex Luthor is the President of The United States.
SIR... THERE'S BEEN A HIJACKING AND KIDNAPPING --
-- ABOARD LEXCORP ONE.
MISTER VICE PRESIDENT.
PETE. YOU KNOW HOW CAREFUL I HAVE TO BE REGARDING MY FORMER... HOLDINGS.
CORPORATE ESPIONAGE IS THE PRICE OF DOING BUSINESS. I'M SURPRISED THAT MS. HEAD --
IT WAS BATMAN, SIR.
WE HAVE CONFIRMATION THROUGH SATCOM.
IT WAS SOME SORT OF BAT-SHAPED AIRCRAFT.
WITH A CLOAKING DEVICE MAKING IT ESSENTIALLY AN INVISIBLE PLANE.
DO YOU WISH TO TAKE ACTION?
NOT...
...YET.

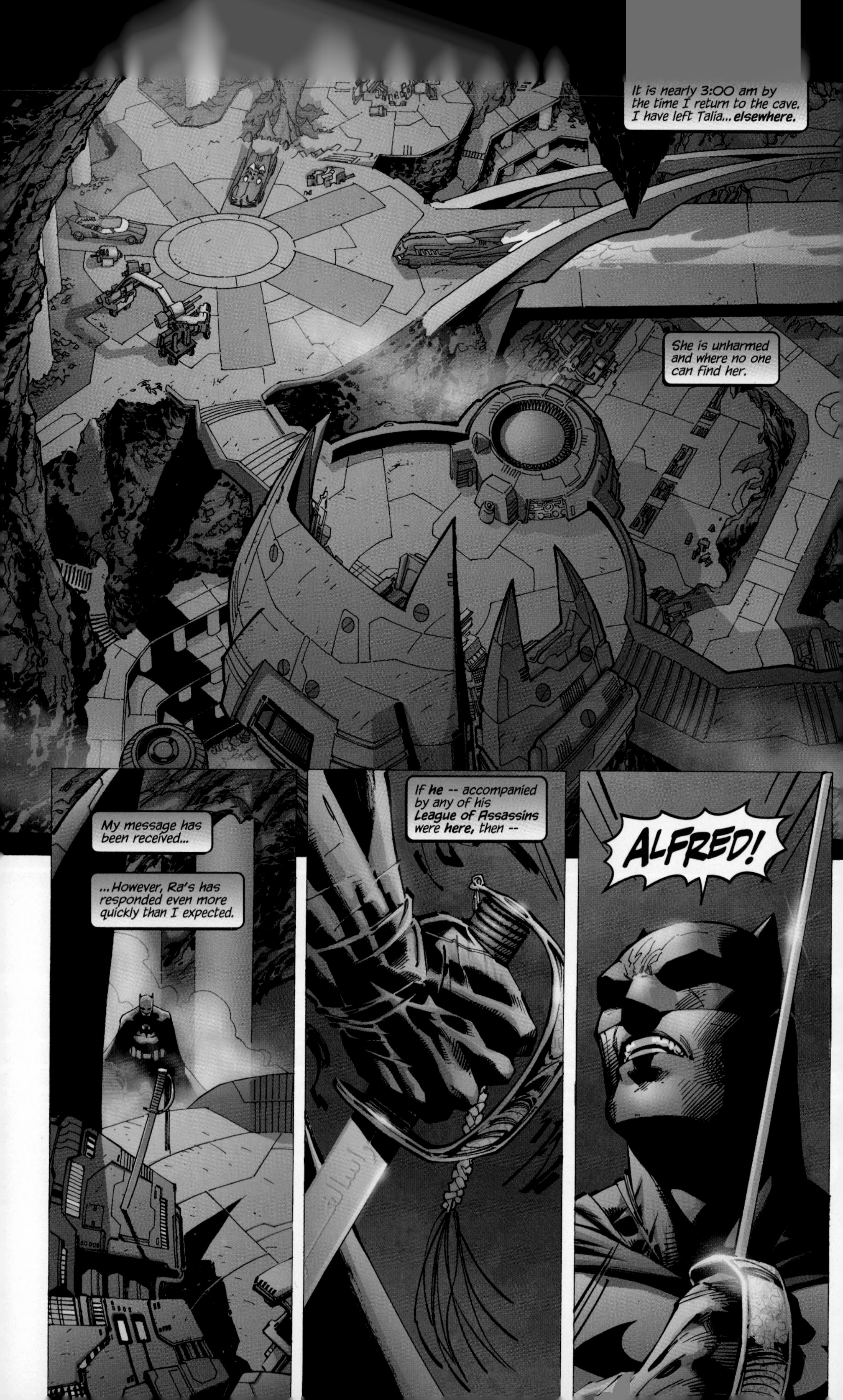

It is nearly 3:00 am by the time I return to the cave. I have left Talia... **elsewhere.**
She is unharmed and where no one can find her.
My message has been received...
...However, Ra's has responded even more quickly than I expected.
If **he** -- accompanied by any of his **League of Assassins** were **here**, then --
ALFRED!

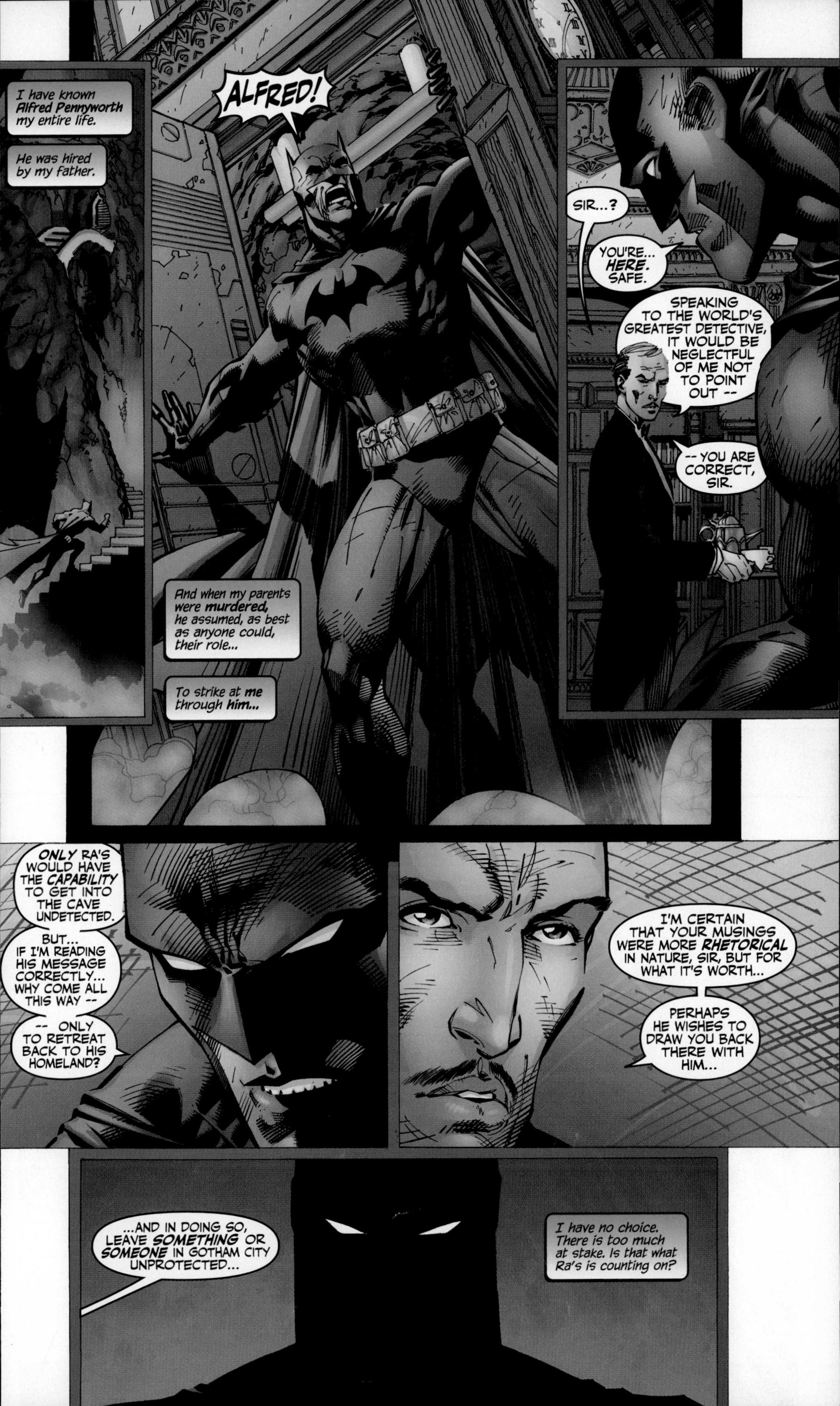

I have known Alfred Pennyworth my entire life.
He was hired by my father.
ALFRED!
And when my parents were murdered, he assumed, as best as anyone could, their role...
To strike at me through him...
SIR...?
YOU'RE... HERE. SAFE.
SPEAKING TO THE WORLD'S GREATEST DETECTIVE, IT WOULD BE NEGLECTFUL OF ME NOT TO POINT OUT --
-- YOU ARE CORRECT, SIR.
ONLY RA'S WOULD HAVE THE CAPABILITY TO GET INTO THE CAVE UNDETECTED.
BUT... IF I'M READING HIS MESSAGE CORRECTLY... WHY COME ALL THIS WAY --
-- ONLY TO RETREAT BACK TO HIS HOMELAND?
I'M CERTAIN THAT YOUR MUSINGS WERE MORE RHETORICAL IN NATURE, SIR, BUT FOR WHAT IT'S WORTH...
PERHAPS HE WISHES TO DRAW YOU BACK THERE WITH HIM...
...AND IN DOING SO, LEAVE SOMETHING OR SOMEONE IN GOTHAM CITY UNPROTECTED...
I have no choice. There is too much at stake. Is that what Ra's is counting on?

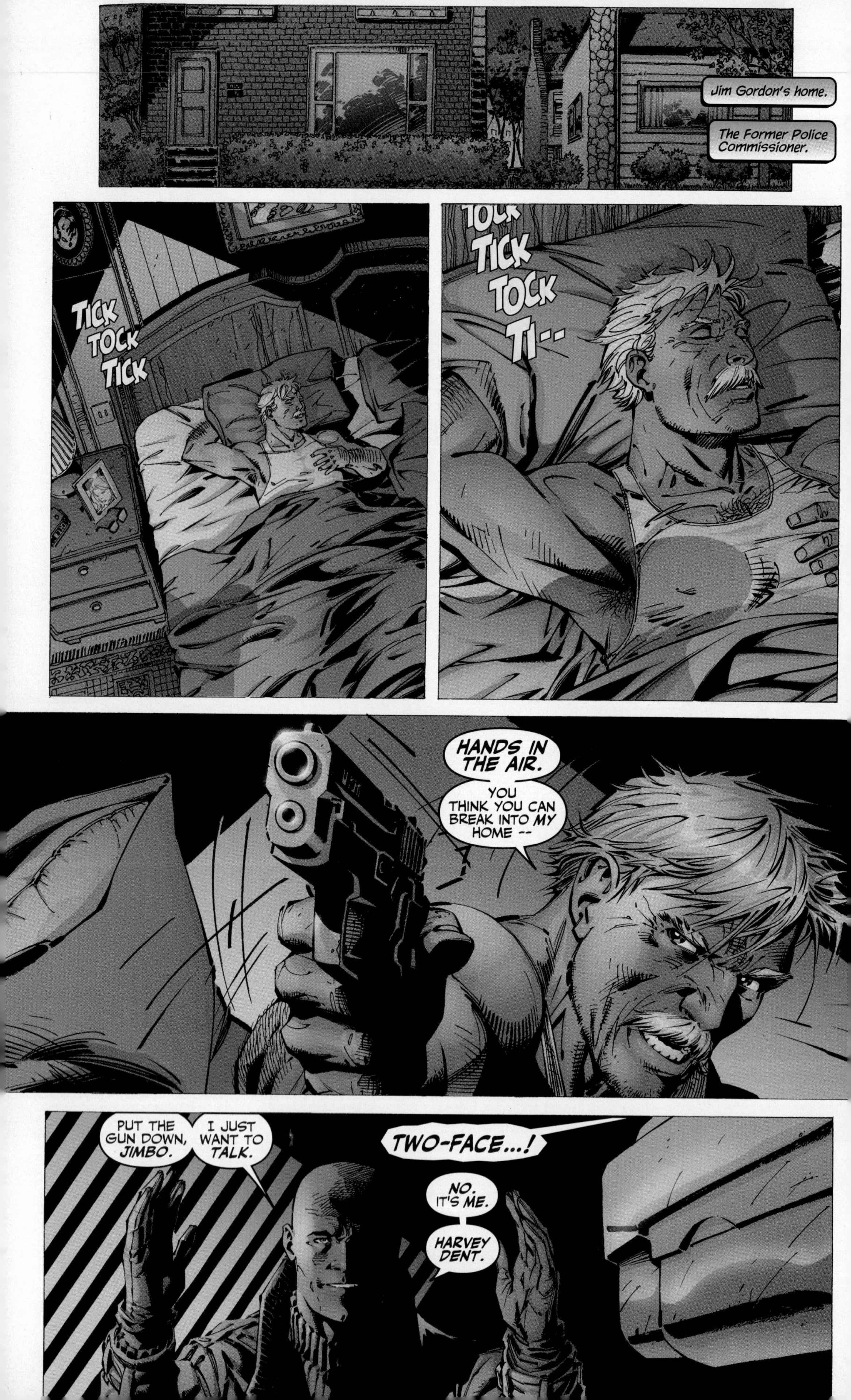

Jim Gordon's home.
The Former Police Commissioner.
TICK TOCK TICK
TOCK TICK TOCK TI--
HANDS IN THE AIR.
YOU THINK YOU CAN BREAK INTO MY HOME --
PUT THE GUN DOWN, JIMBO.
I JUST WANT TO TALK.
TWO-FACE...!
NO. IT'S ME.
HARVEY DENT.

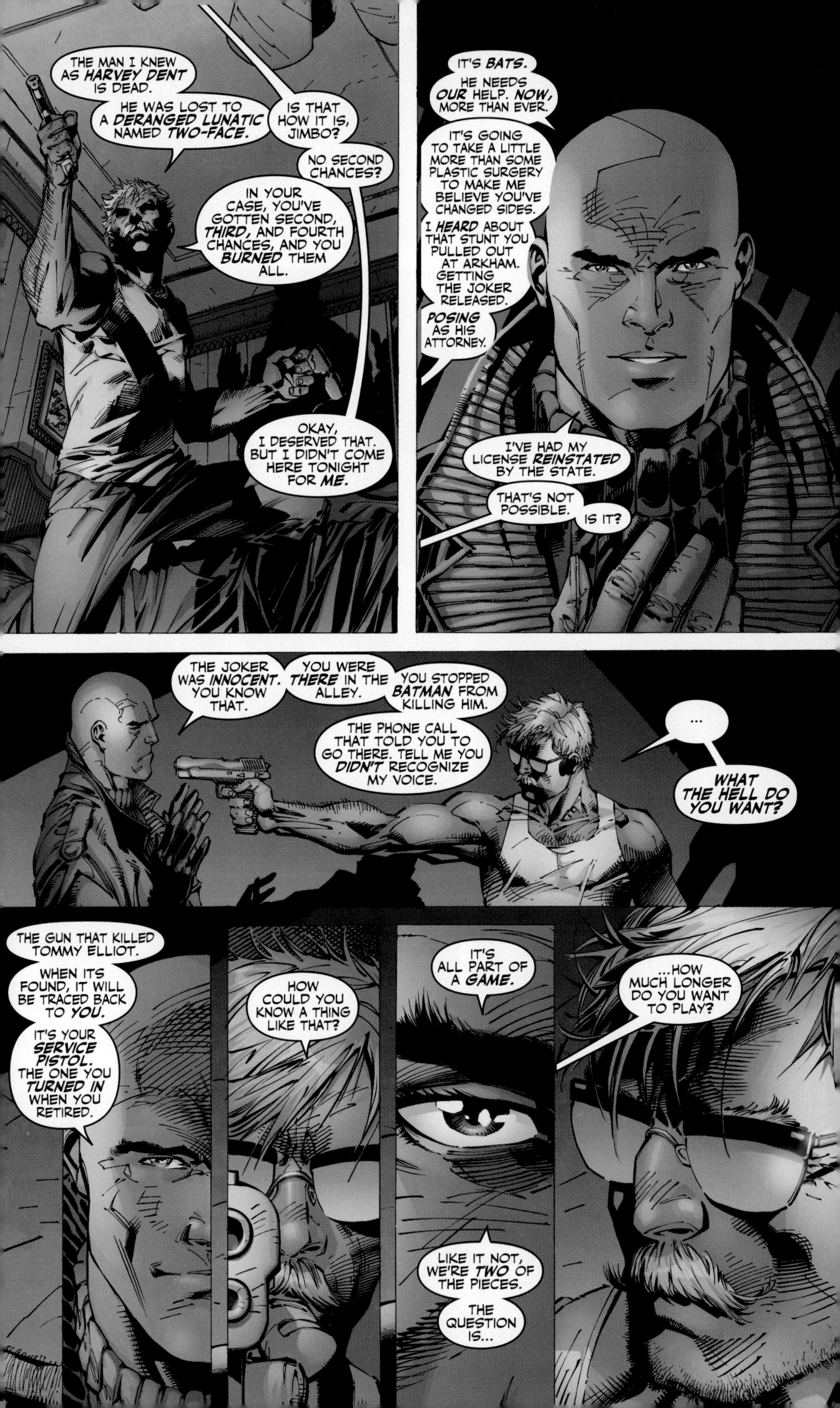
THE MAN I KNEW AS HARVEY DENT IS DEAD.
HE WAS LOST TO A DERANGED LUNATIC NAMED TWO-FACE.
IS THAT HOW IT IS, JIMBO?
NO SECOND CHANCES?
IN YOUR CASE, YOU'VE GOTTEN SECOND, THIRD, AND FOURTH CHANCES, AND YOU BURNED THEM ALL.
OKAY, I DESERVED THAT. BUT I DIDN'T COME HERE TONIGHT FOR ME.
IT'S BATS.
HE NEEDS OUR HELP. NOW, MORE THAN EVER.
IT'S GOING TO TAKE A LITTLE MORE THAN SOME PLASTIC SURGERY TO MAKE ME BELIEVE YOU'VE CHANGED SIDES.
I HEARD ABOUT THAT STUNT YOU PULLED OUT AT ARKHAM. GETTING THE JOKER RELEASED.
POSING AS HIS ATTORNEY.
I'VE HAD MY LICENSE REINSTATED BY THE STATE.
THAT'S NOT POSSIBLE.
IS IT?
THE JOKER WAS INNOCENT. YOU KNOW THAT.
YOU WERE THERE IN THE ALLEY.
YOU STOPPED BATMAN FROM KILLING HIM.
THE PHONE CALL THAT TOLD YOU TO GO THERE. TELL ME YOU DIDN'T RECOGNIZE MY VOICE.
...
WHAT THE HELL DO YOU WANT?
THE GUN THAT KILLED TOMMY ELLIOT.
WHEN ITS FOUND, IT WILL BE TRACED BACK TO YOU.
IT'S YOUR SERVICE PISTOL. THE ONE YOU TURNED IN WHEN YOU RETIRED.
HOW COULD YOU KNOW A THING LIKE THAT?
IT'S ALL PART OF A GAME.
LIKE IT NOT, WE'RE TWO OF THE PIECES.
THE QUESTION IS...
...HOW MUCH LONGER DO YOU WANT TO PLAY?

The camel's bridle on the **hilt** of the sword.

One of my **earliest** encounters with Ra's began with my finding one he had left behind.

It brought me here, to **North Africa**, as it has again.

WHERE IS MY DAUGHTER...

...DETECTIVE?

SAFE.

YOU **THINK** I AM RESPONSIBLE FOR YOUR RECENT...

...MISFORTUNES. THE DEATH OF YOUR FRIEND **THOMAS ELLIOT**, FOR EXAMPLE.

YOU ARE **MISTAKEN**.

YOU HAVE MEANS.

OPPORTUNITY.

AND **KNOWLEDGE** ONLY A **FEW** POSSESS...

...ABOUT MY PERSONAL LIFE.

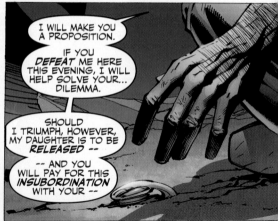

I WILL MAKE YOU A PROPOSITION.

IF YOU **DEFEAT** ME HERE THIS EVENING, I WILL HELP SOLVE YOUR... DILEMMA.

SHOULD I **TRIUMPH**, HOWEVER, MY DAUGHTER IS TO BE **RELEASED** --

-- AND YOU WILL PAY FOR THIS **INSUBORDINATION** WITH YOUR --

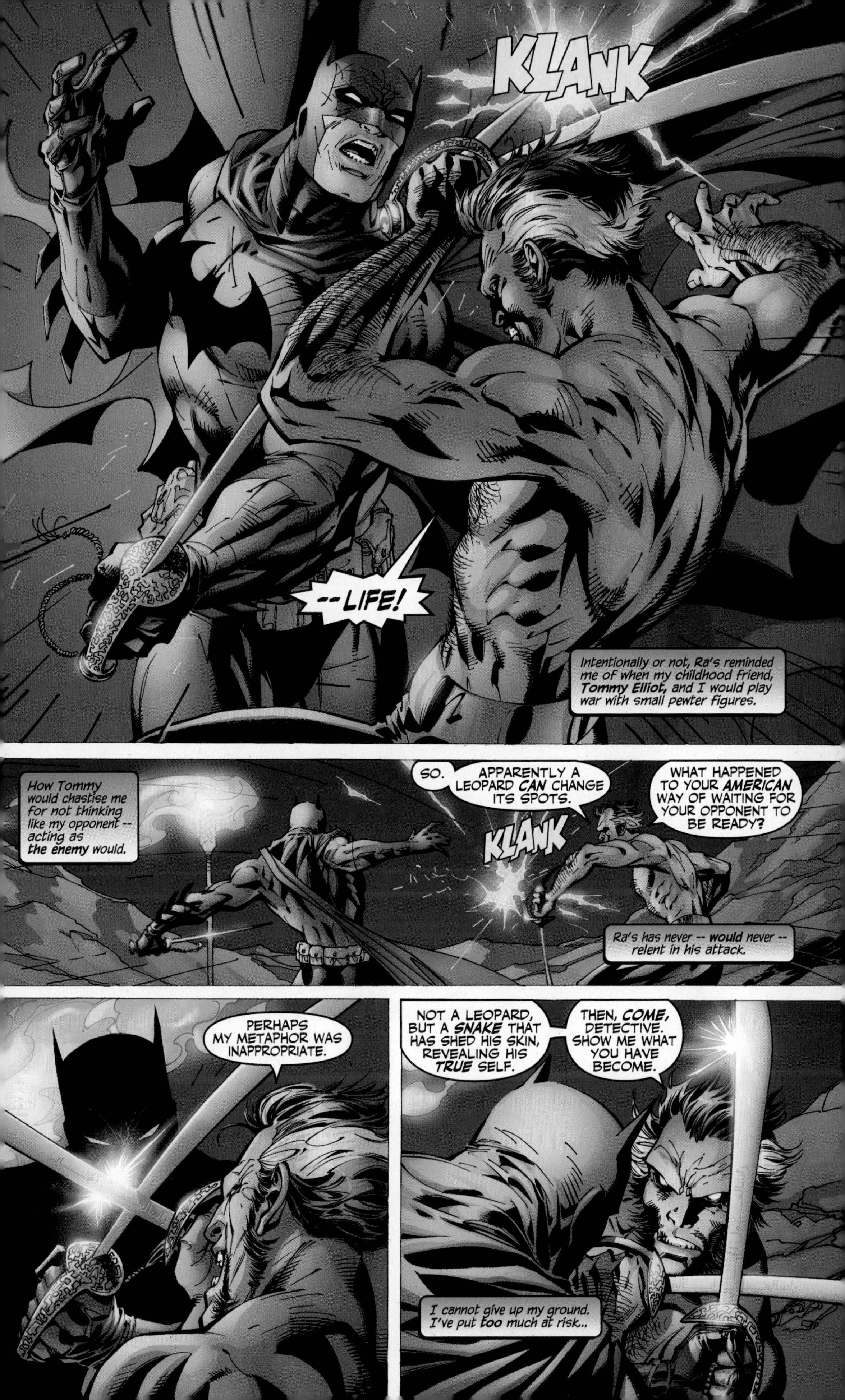
KLANK
--LIFE!
Intentionally or not, Ra's reminded me of when my childhood friend, Tommy Elliot, and I would play war with small pewter figures.
How Tommy would chastise me for not thinking like my opponent -- acting as the enemy would.
SO.
APPARENTLY A LEOPARD CAN CHANGE ITS SPOTS.
WHAT HAPPENED TO YOUR AMERICAN WAY OF WAITING FOR YOUR OPPONENT TO BE READY?
KLANK
Ra's has never -- would never -- relent in his attack.
PERHAPS MY METAPHOR WAS INAPPROPRIATE.
NOT A LEOPARD, BUT A SNAKE THAT HAS SHED HIS SKIN, REVEALING HIS TRUE SELF.
THEN, COME, DETECTIVE. SHOW ME WHAT YOU HAVE BECOME.
I cannot give up my ground. I've put too much at risk...

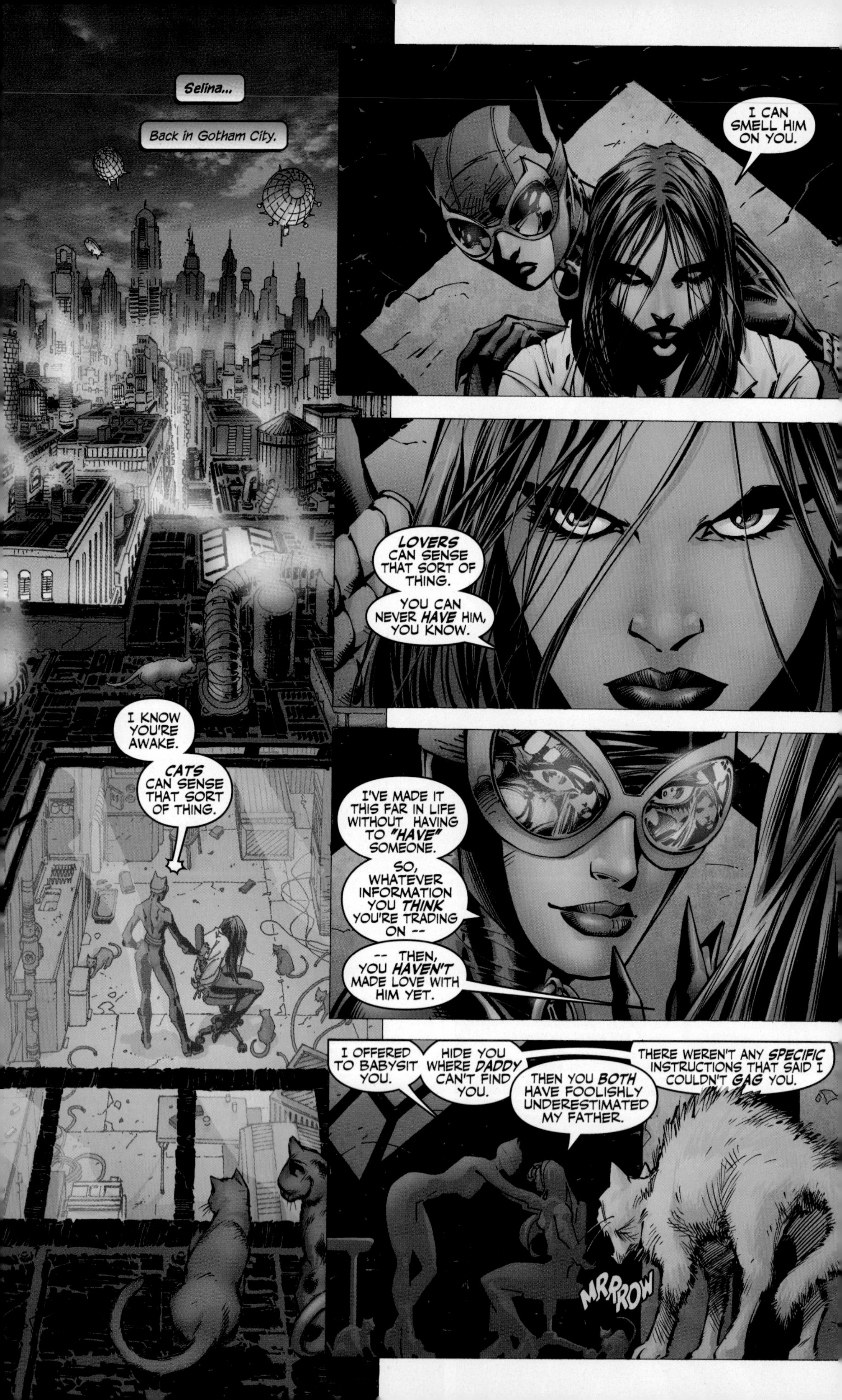
Selina...
Back in Gotham City.
I CAN SMELL HIM ON YOU.
LOVERS CAN SENSE THAT SORT OF THING.
YOU CAN NEVER HAVE HIM, YOU KNOW.
I KNOW YOU'RE AWAKE.
CATS CAN SENSE THAT SORT OF THING.
I'VE MADE IT THIS FAR IN LIFE WITHOUT HAVING TO "HAVE" SOMEONE.
SO, WHATEVER INFORMATION YOU THINK YOU'RE TRADING ON --
-- THEN, YOU HAVEN'T MADE LOVE WITH HIM YET.
I OFFERED TO BABYSIT YOU.
HIDE YOU WHERE DADDY CAN'T FIND YOU.
THEN YOU BOTH HAVE FOOLISHLY UNDERESTIMATED MY FATHER.
THERE WEREN'T ANY SPECIFIC INSTRUCTIONS THAT SAID I COULDN'T GAG YOU.
MRRROW

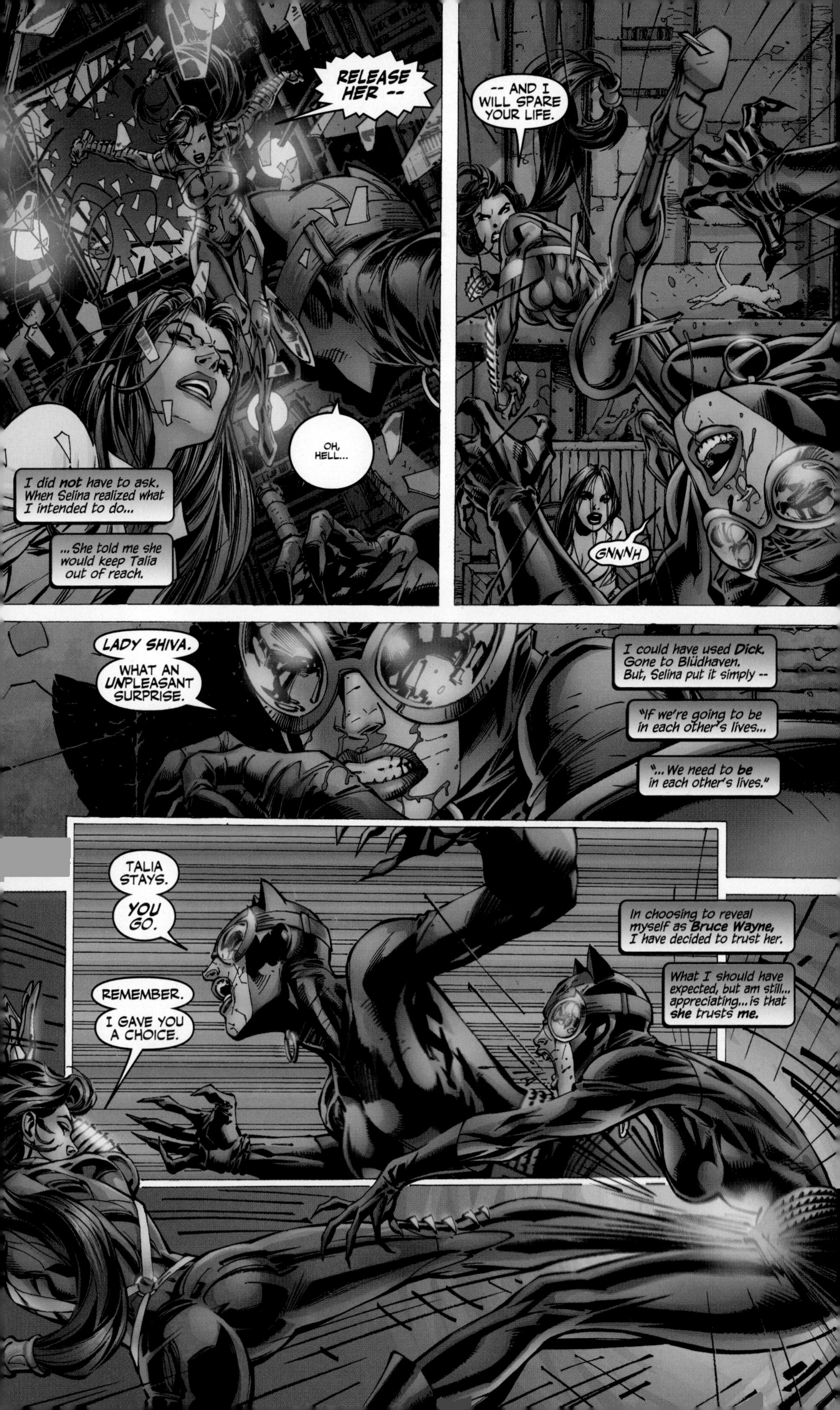

RELEASE HER --
OH, HELL...
I did not have to ask. When Selina realized what I intended to do...
...She told me she would keep Talia out of reach.
-- AND I WILL SPARE YOUR LIFE.
GNNNH
LADY SHIVA. WHAT AN UNPLEASANT SURPRISE.
I could have used Dick. Gone to Blüdhaven. But, Selina put it simply --
"If we're going to be in each other's lives...
"...We need to be in each other's lives."
TALIA STAYS. YOU GO.
REMEMBER. I GAVE YOU A CHOICE.
In choosing to reveal myself as Bruce Wayne, I have decided to trust her.
What I should have expected, but am still... appreciating... is that she trusts me.

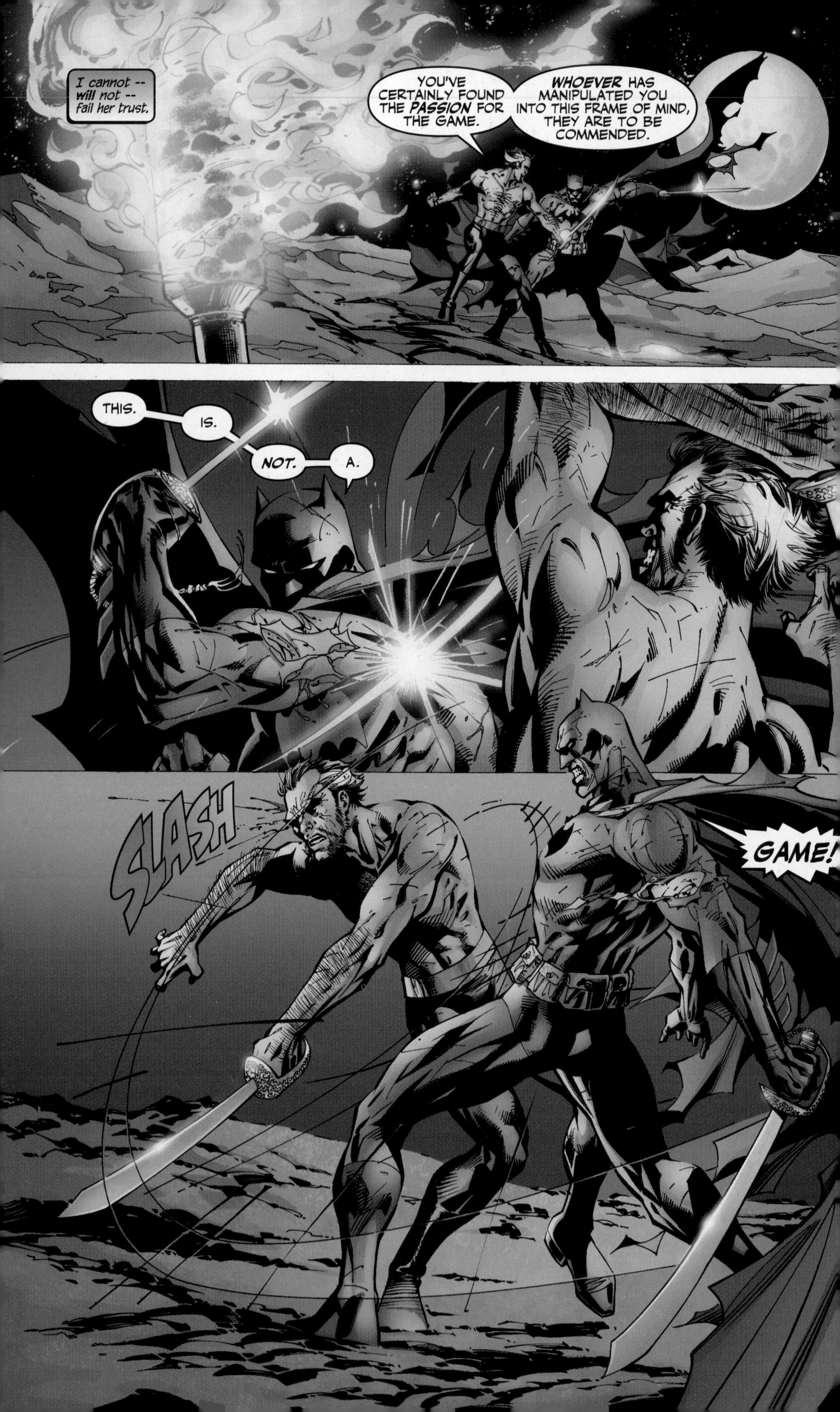
I cannot -- will not -- fail her trust.
YOU'VE CERTAINLY FOUND THE PASSION FOR THE GAME.
WHOEVER HAS MANIPULATED YOU INTO THIS FRAME OF MIND, THEY ARE TO BE COMMENDED.
THIS.
IS.
NOT.
A.
SLASH
GAME!

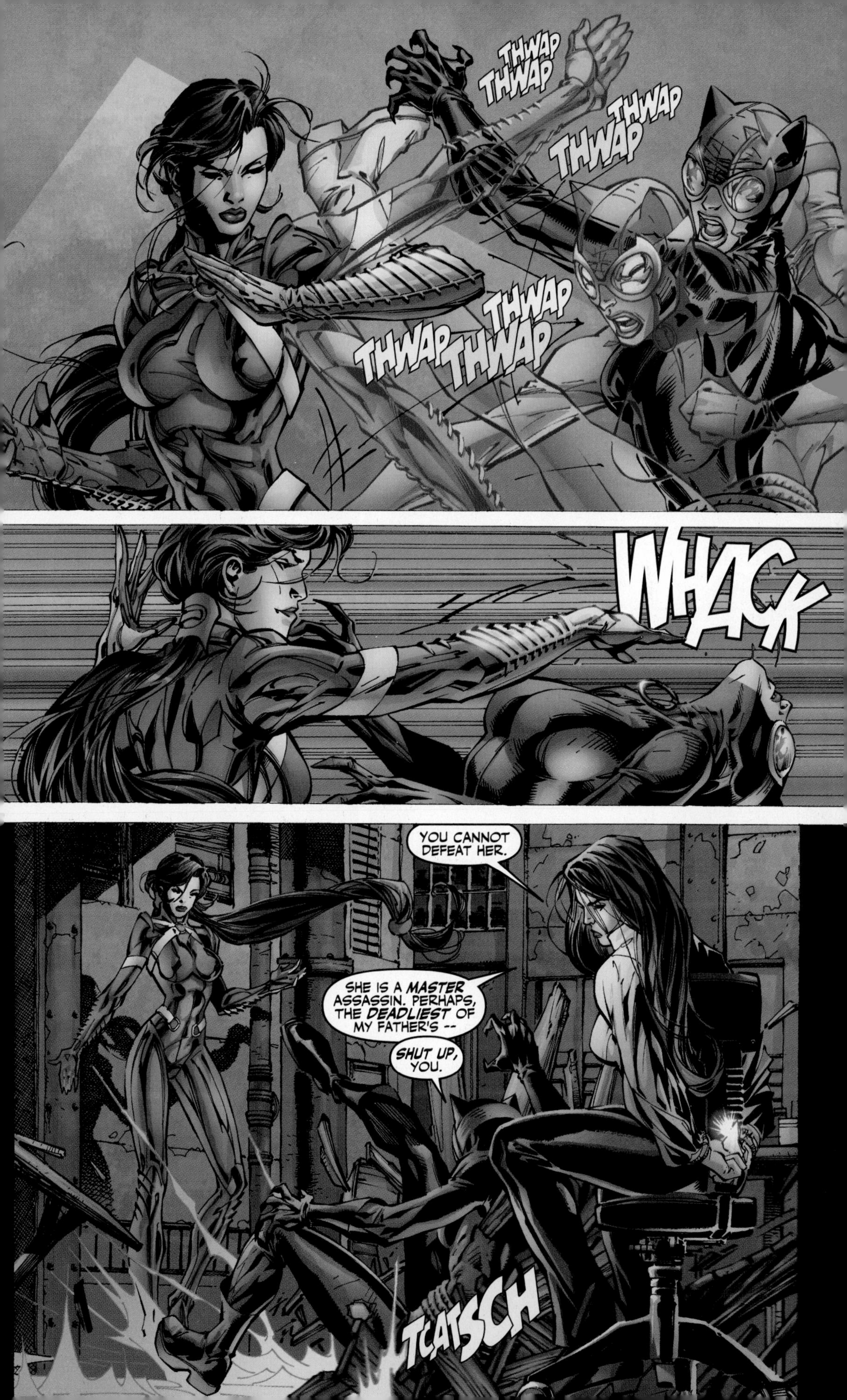
THWAP
THWAP
THWAP
THWAP
THWAP
THWAP
THWAP
WHACK
YOU CANNOT DEFEAT HER.
SHE IS A MASTER ASSASSIN. PERHAPS, THE DEADLIEST OF MY FATHER'S --
SHUT UP, YOU.
TCATSCH

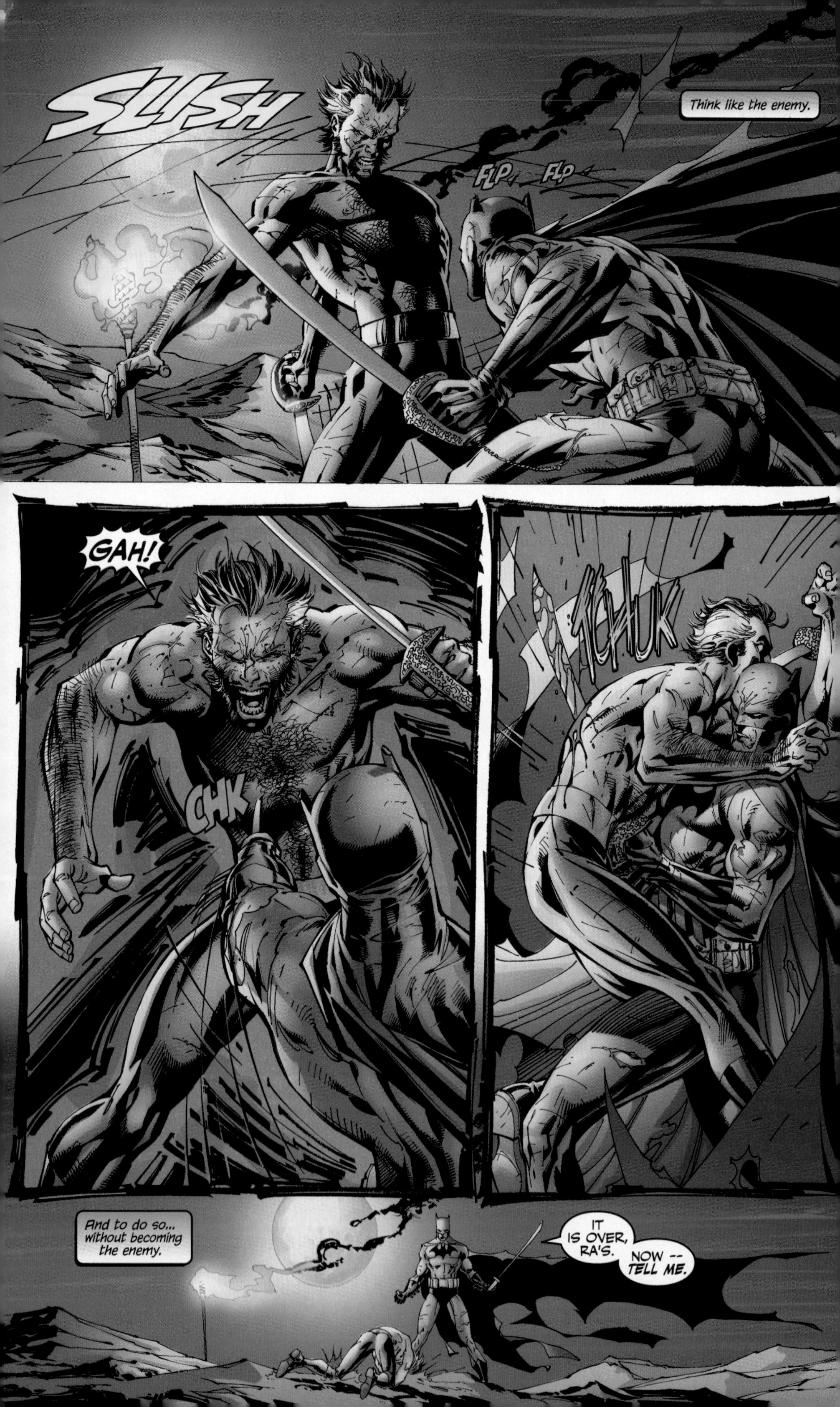

SLISH
Think like the enemy.
FLP
FLP
GAH!
CHK
KCHUK
And to do so... without becoming the enemy.
IT IS OVER, RA'S.
NOW -- TELL ME.

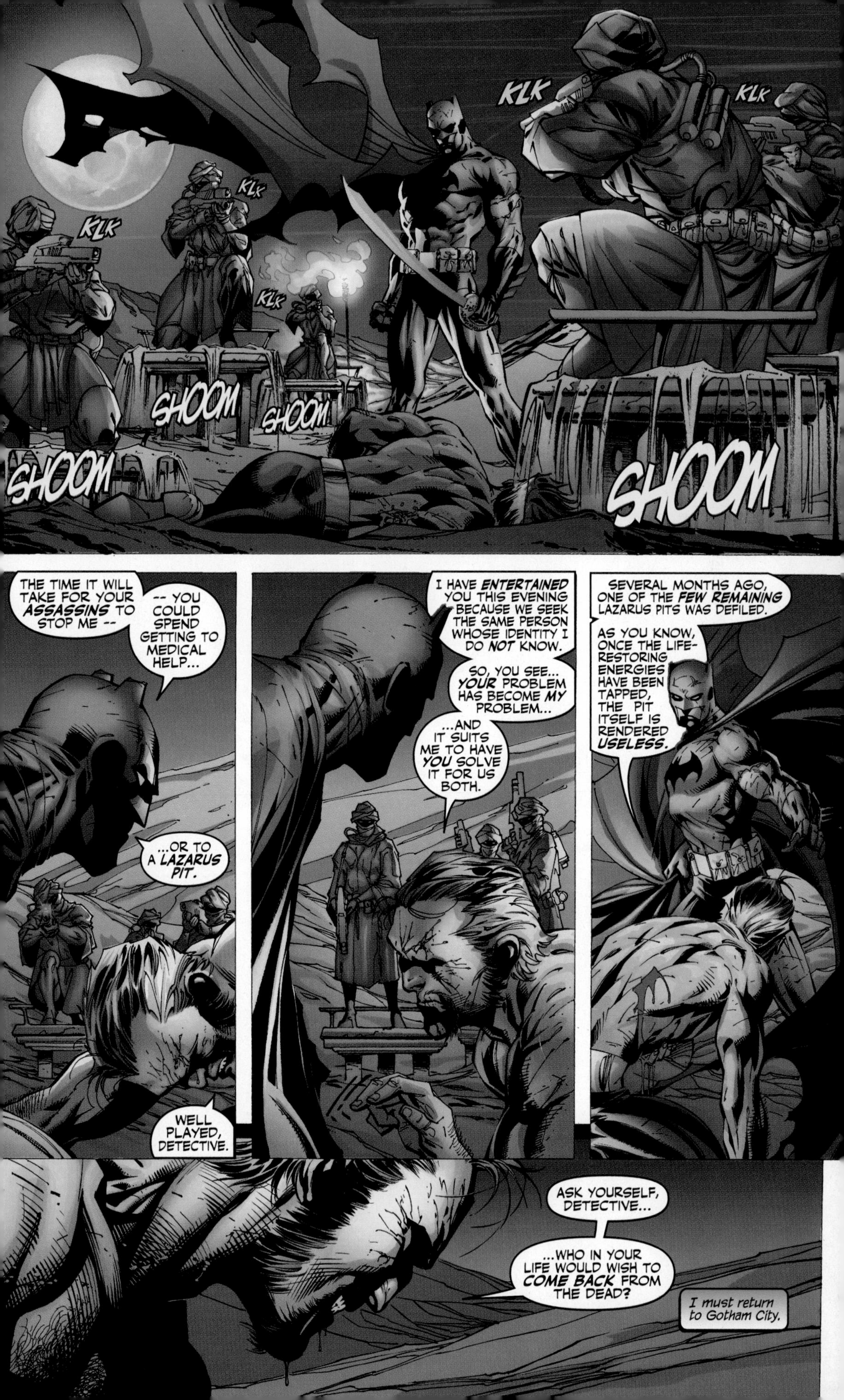

KLK
KLK
KLK
KLK
KLK
SHOOM
SHOOM
SHOOM
SHOOM
THE TIME IT WILL TAKE FOR YOUR ASSASSINS TO STOP ME --
-- YOU COULD SPEND GETTING TO MEDICAL HELP...
...OR TO A LAZARUS PIT.
WELL PLAYED, DETECTIVE.
I HAVE ENTERTAINED YOU THIS EVENING BECAUSE WE SEEK THE SAME PERSON WHOSE IDENTITY I DO NOT KNOW.
SO, YOU SEE... YOUR PROBLEM HAS BECOME MY PROBLEM...
...AND IT SUITS ME TO HAVE YOU SOLVE IT FOR US BOTH.
SEVERAL MONTHS AGO, ONE OF THE FEW REMAINING LAZARUS PITS WAS DEFILED.
AS YOU KNOW, ONCE THE LIFE-RESTORING ENERGIES HAVE BEEN TAPPED, THE PIT ITSELF IS RENDERED USELESS.
ASK YOURSELF, DETECTIVE...
...WHO IN YOUR LIFE WOULD WISH TO COME BACK FROM THE DEAD?
I must return to Gotham City.

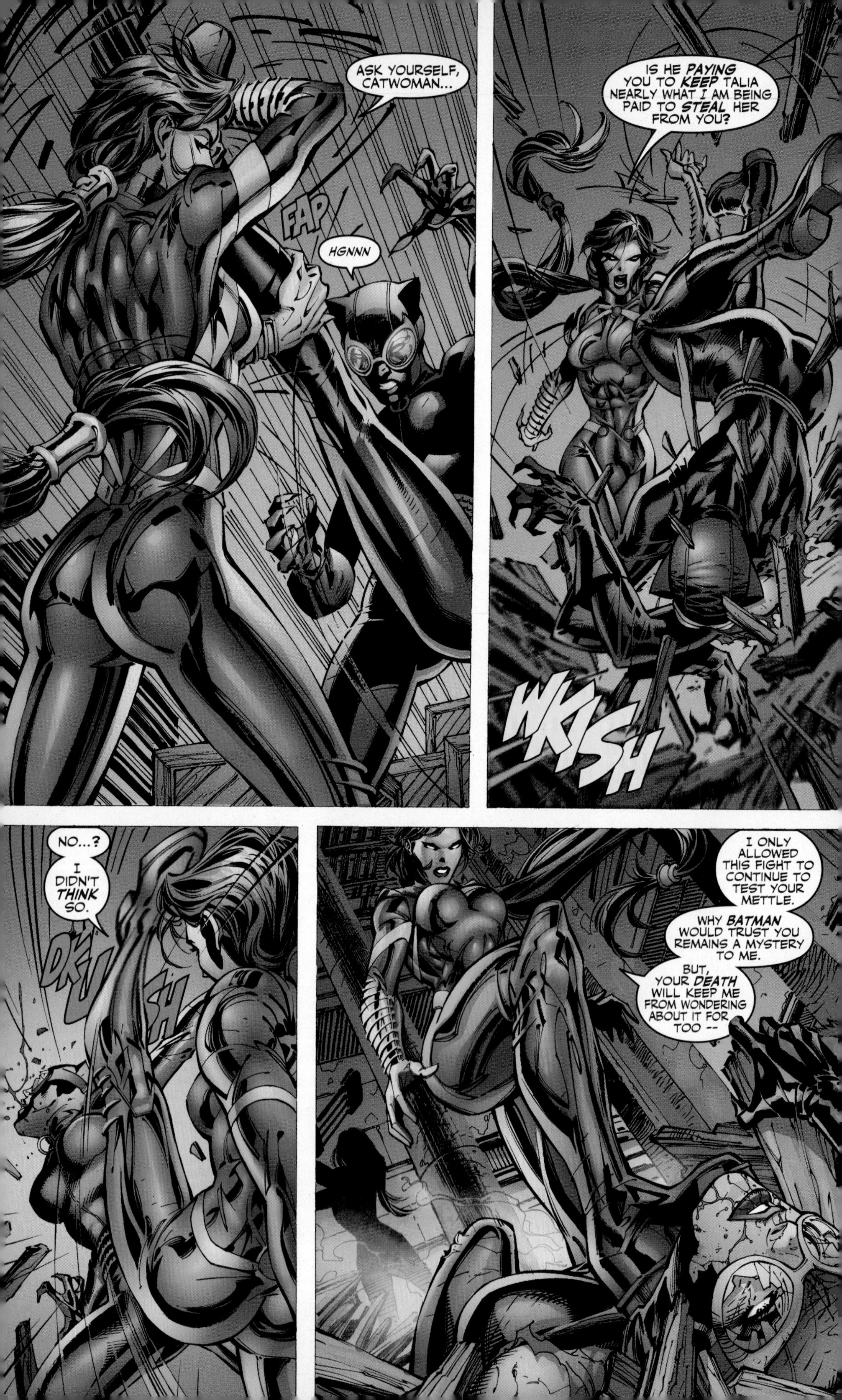
ASK YOURSELF, CATWOMAN...
FAP
HGNNN
IS HE PAYING YOU TO KEEP TALIA NEARLY WHAT I AM BEING PAID TO STEAL HER FROM YOU?
WKISH
NO...?
I DIDN'T THINK SO.
I ONLY ALLOWED THIS FIGHT TO CONTINUE TO TEST YOUR METTLE.
WHY BATMAN WOULD TRUST YOU REMAINS A MYSTERY TO ME.
BUT, YOUR DEATH WILL KEEP ME FROM WONDERING ABOUT IT FOR TOO --

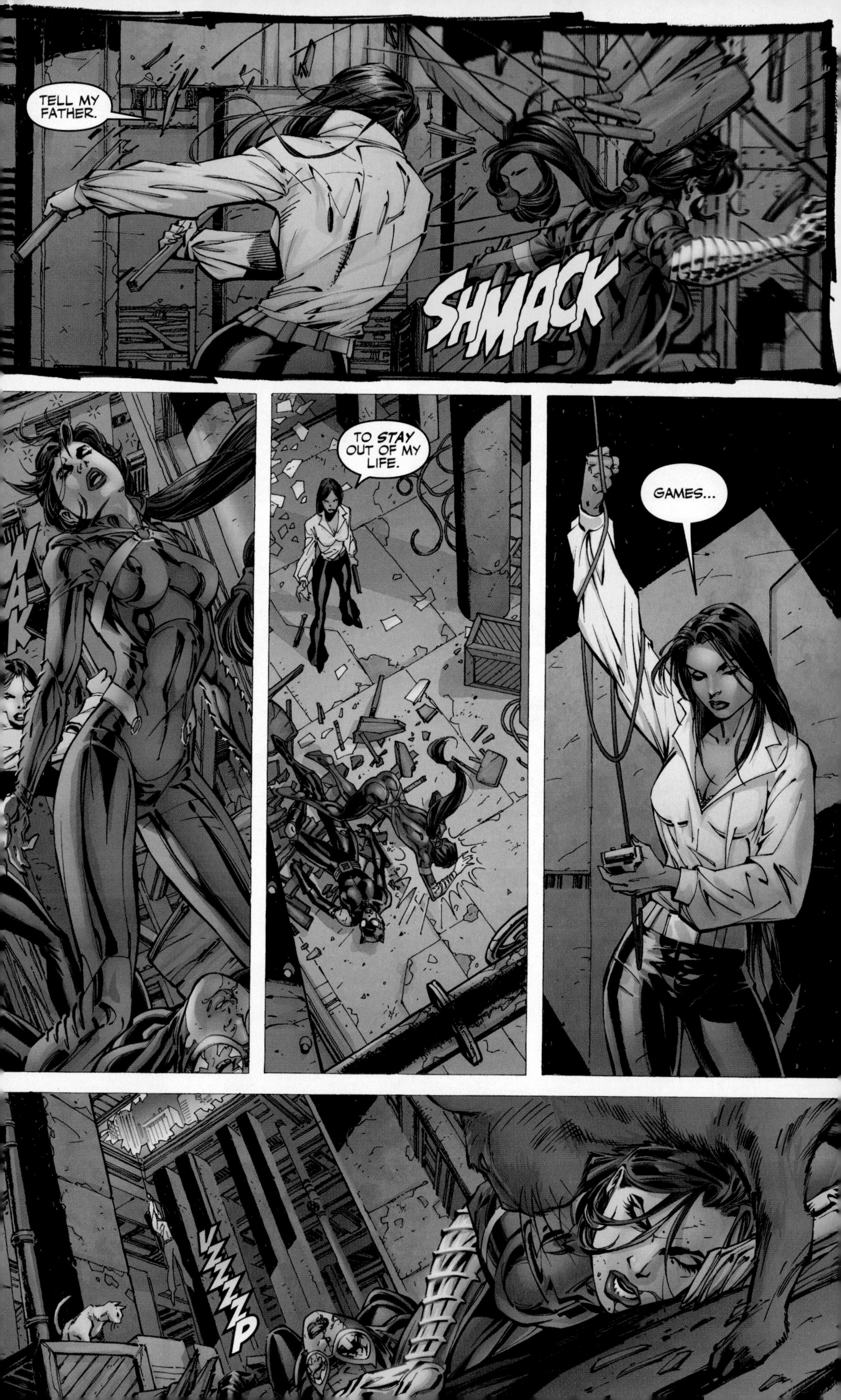
TELL MY FATHER.
SHMACK
WAK
TO STAY OUT OF MY LIFE.
GAMES...
VZZZZP

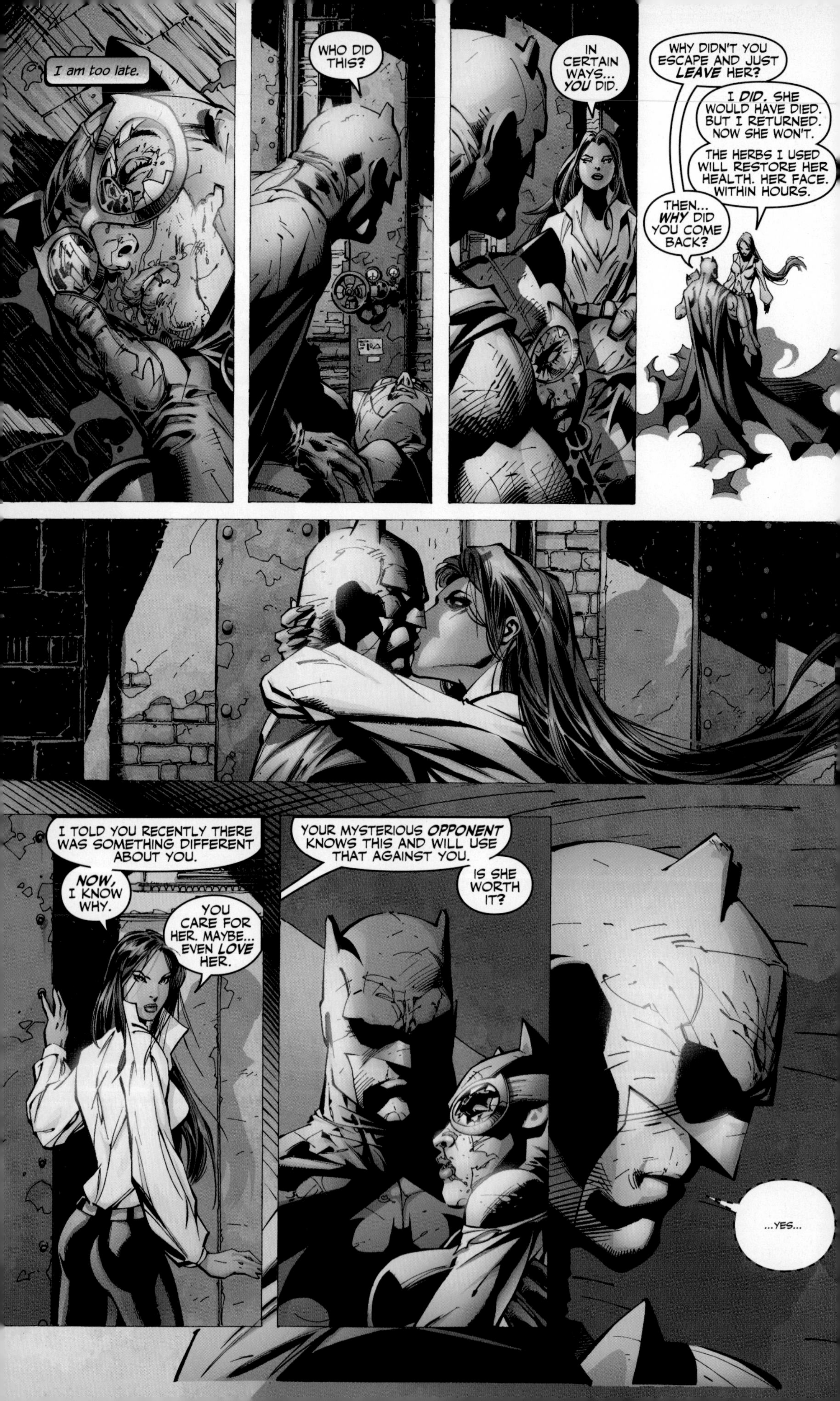
I am too late.
WHO DID THIS?
IN CERTAIN WAYS... YOU DID.
WHY DIDN'T YOU ESCAPE AND JUST LEAVE HER?
I DID. SHE WOULD HAVE DIED. BUT I RETURNED. NOW SHE WON'T.
THE HERBS I USED WILL RESTORE HER HEALTH. HER FACE. WITHIN HOURS.
THEN... WHY DID YOU COME BACK?
I TOLD YOU RECENTLY THERE WAS SOMETHING DIFFERENT ABOUT YOU.
NOW, I KNOW WHY.
YOU CARE FOR HER. MAYBE... EVEN LOVE HER.
YOUR MYSTERIOUS OPPONENT KNOWS THIS AND WILL USE THAT AGAINST YOU.
IS SHE WORTH IT?
...YES...

INTERLUDE

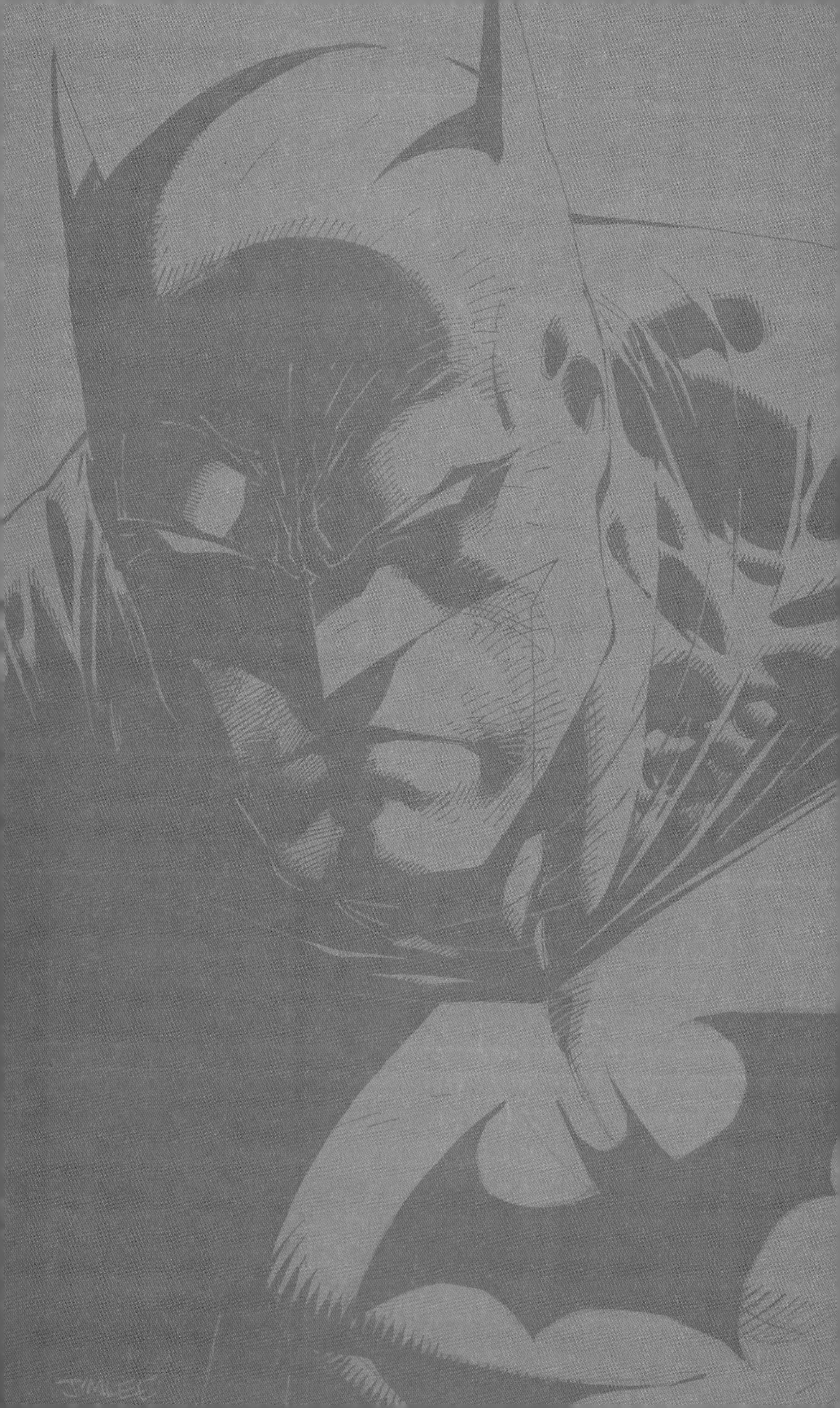

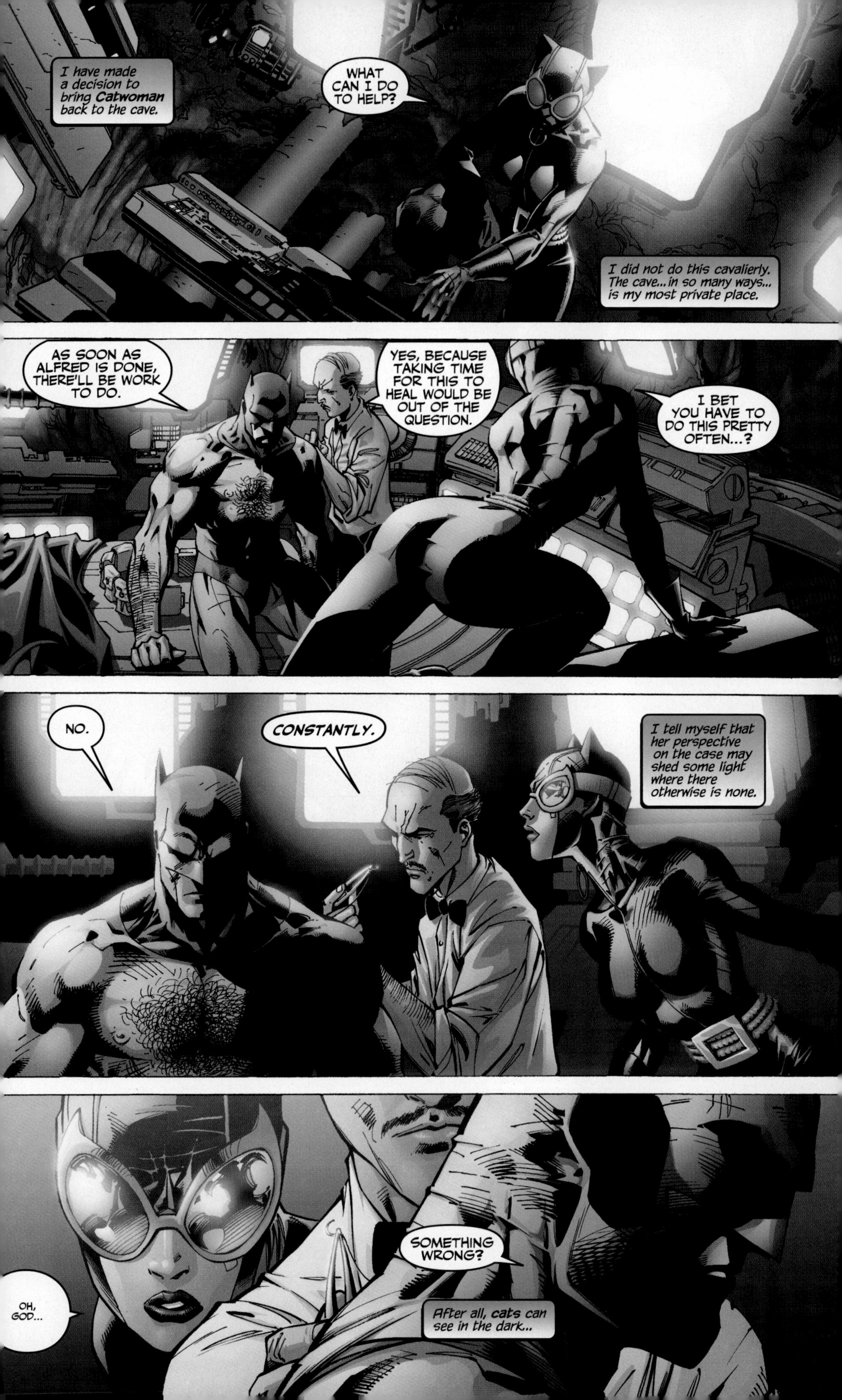
I have made a decision to bring Catwoman back to the cave.
WHAT CAN I DO TO HELP?
I did not do this cavalierly. The cave...in so many ways... is my most private place.
AS SOON AS ALFRED IS DONE, THERE'LL BE WORK TO DO.
YES, BECAUSE TAKING TIME FOR THIS TO HEAL WOULD BE OUT OF THE QUESTION.
I BET YOU HAVE TO DO THIS PRETTY OFTEN...?
NO.
CONSTANTLY.
I tell myself that her perspective on the case may shed some light where there otherwise is none.
SOMETHING WRONG?
OH, GOD...
After all, cats can see in the dark...

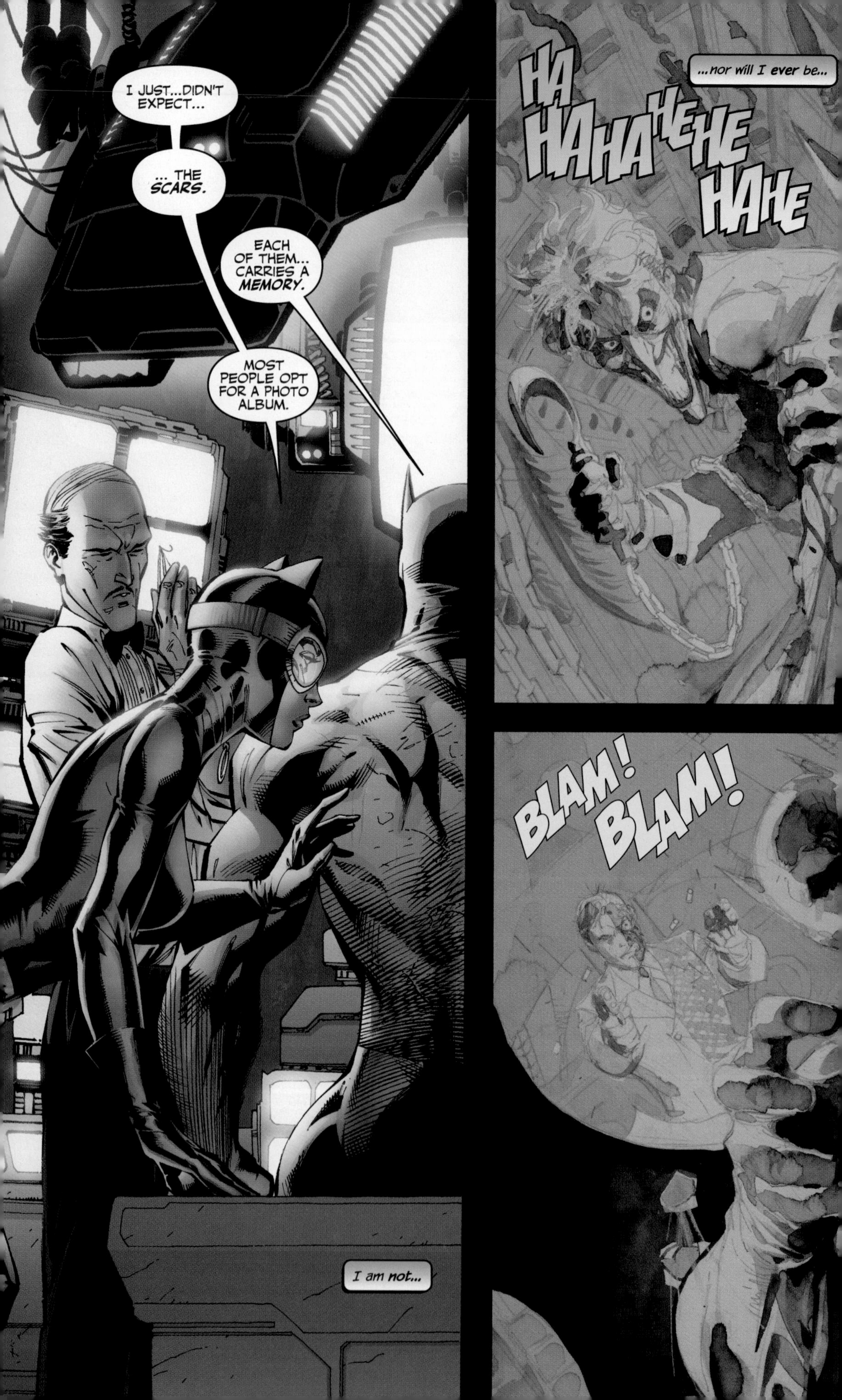
I JUST...DIDN'T EXPECT...
... THE SCARS.
EACH OF THEM... CARRIES A MEMORY.
MOST PEOPLE OPT FOR A PHOTO ALBUM.
I am not...
...nor will I ever be...
HA HAHAHEHE HAHE
BLAM! BLAM!

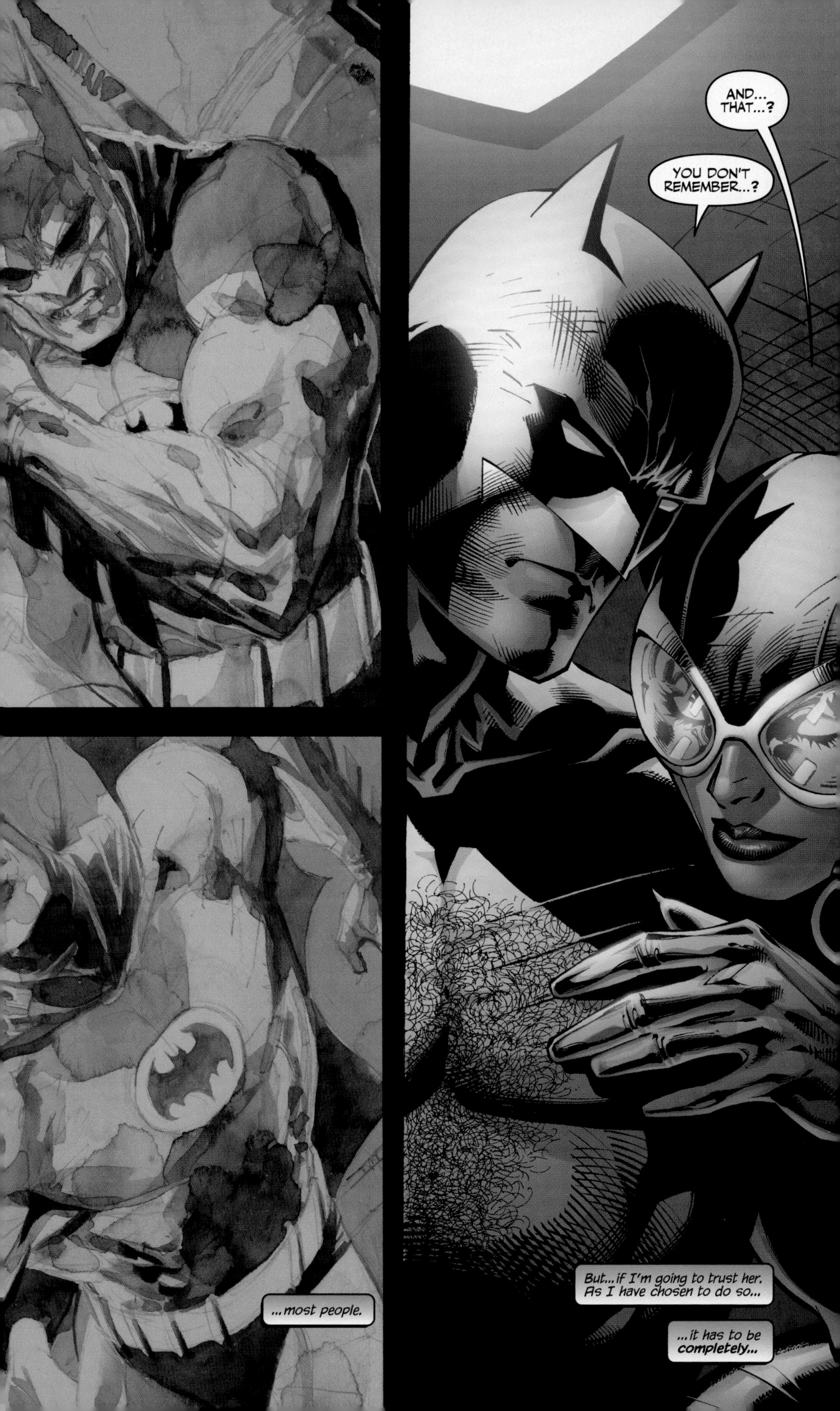
...most people.
AND... THAT...?
YOU DON'T REMEMBER...?
But...if I'm going to trust her. As I have chosen to do so...
...it has to be completely...

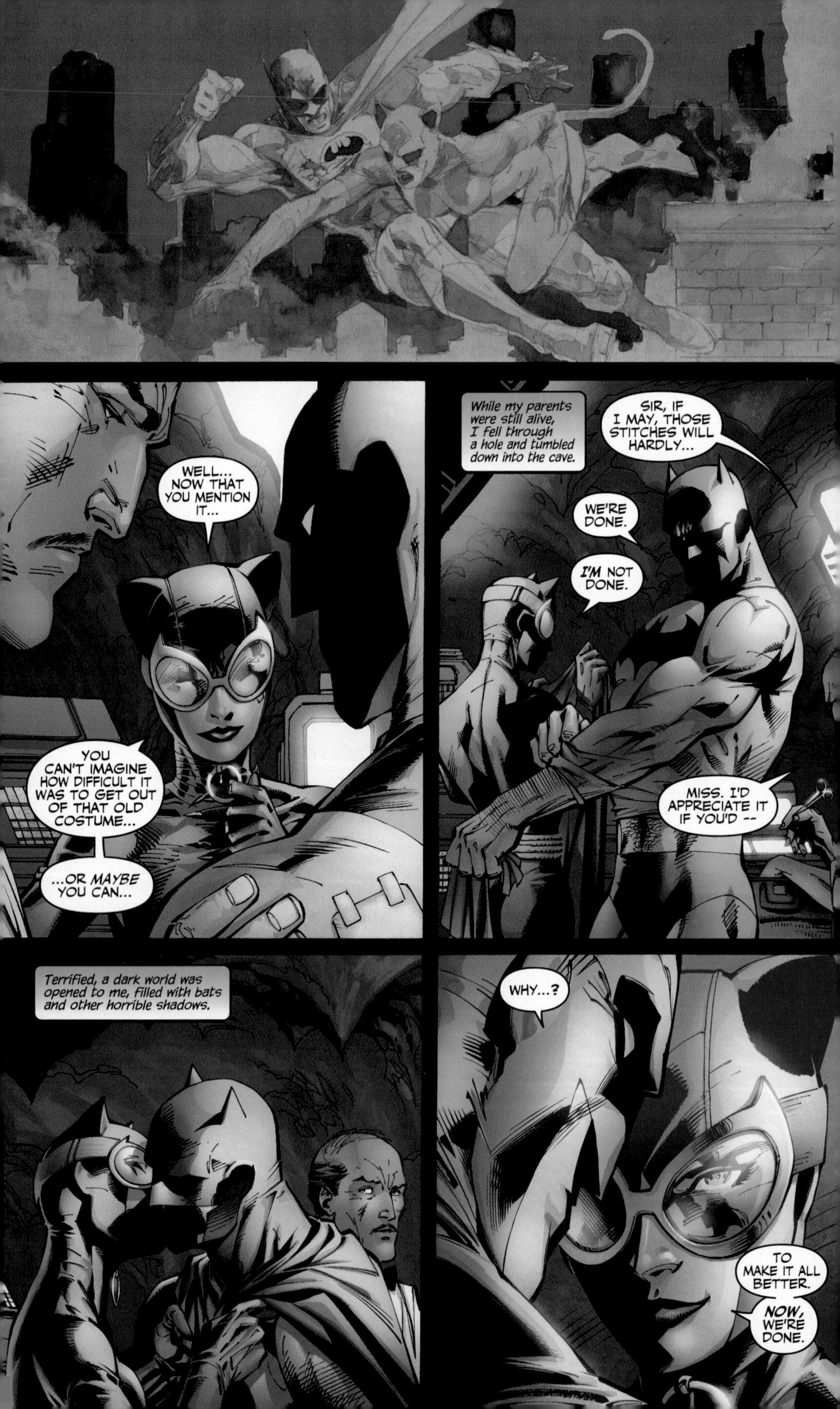
WELL... NOW THAT YOU MENTION IT...
YOU CAN'T IMAGINE HOW DIFFICULT IT WAS TO GET OUT OF THAT OLD COSTUME...
...OR *MAYBE* YOU CAN...
While my parents were still alive, I fell through a hole and tumbled down into the cave.
SIR, IF I MAY, THOSE STITCHES WILL HARDLY...
WE'RE DONE.
I'M NOT DONE.
MISS. I'D APPRECIATE IT IF YOU'D --
Terrified, a dark world was opened to me, filled with bats and other horrible shadows.
WHY...?
TO MAKE IT ALL BETTER.
NOW, WE'RE DONE.

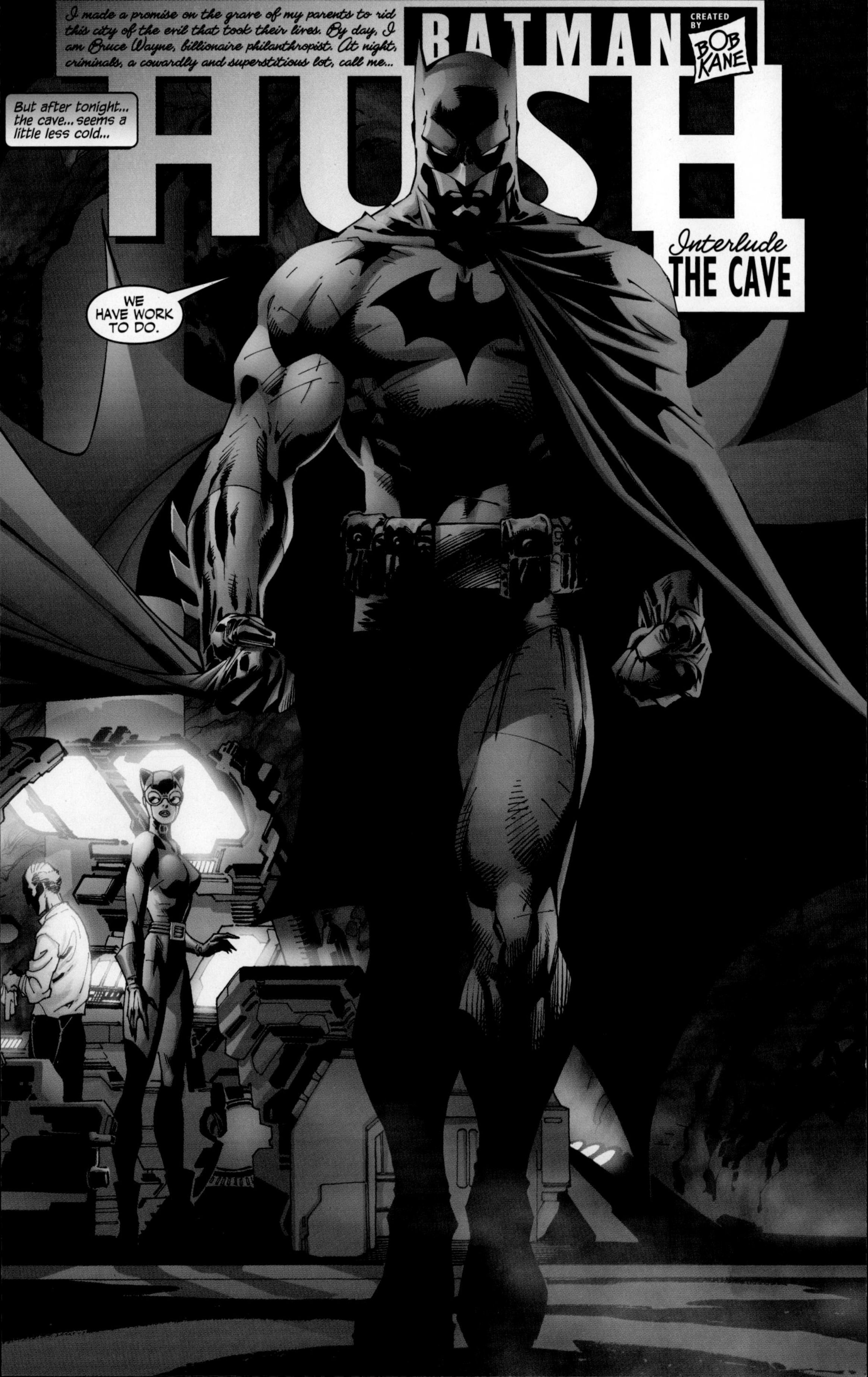
I made a promise on the grave of my parents to rid this city of the evil that took their lives. By day, I am Bruce Wayne, billionaire philanthropist. At night, criminals, a cowardly and superstitious lot, call me...
BATMAN
CREATED BY BOB KANE
HUSH
But after tonight... the cave... seems a little less cold...
Interlude
THE CAVE
WE HAVE WORK TO DO.

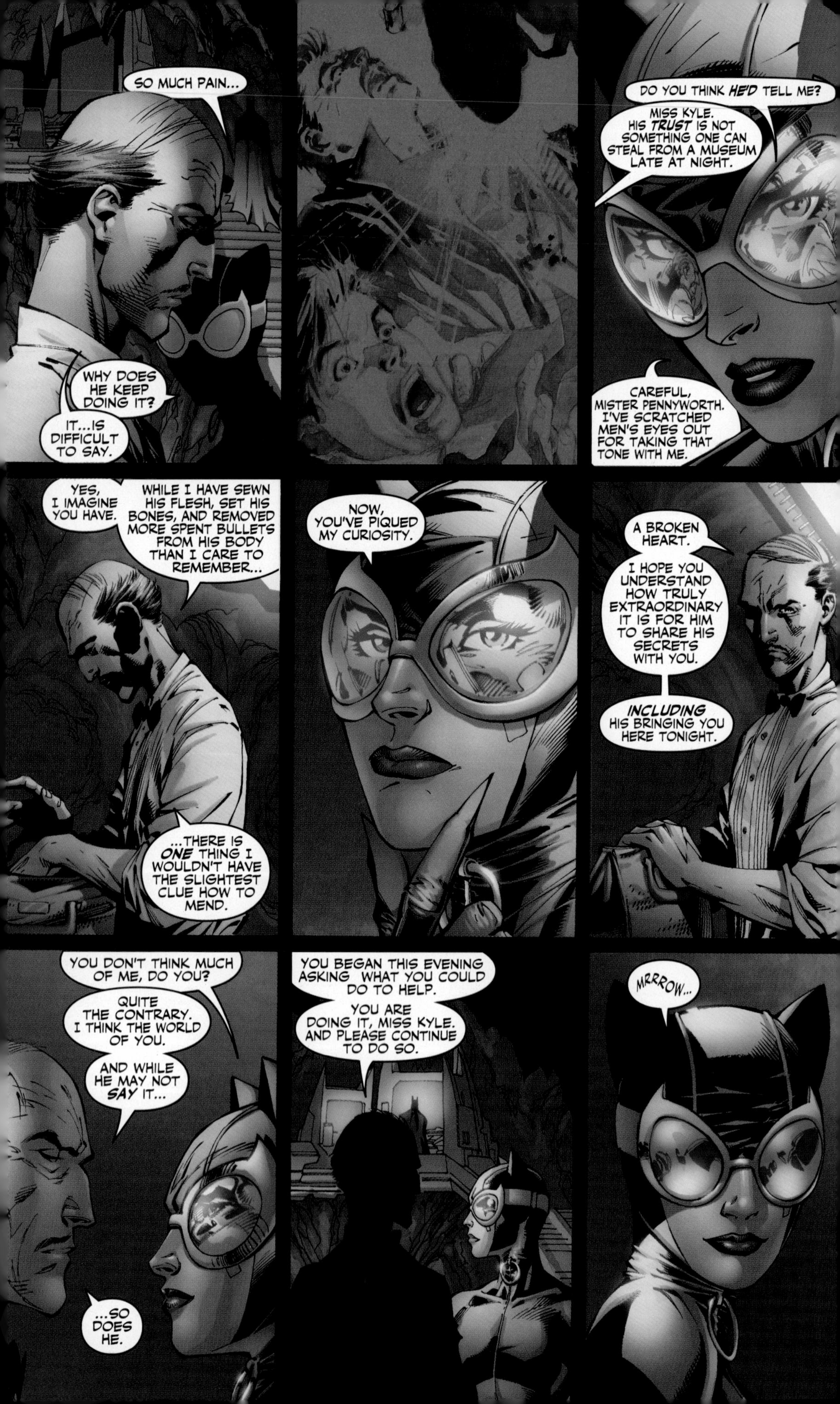
SO MUCH PAIN...
WHY DOES HE KEEP DOING IT?
IT...IS DIFFICULT TO SAY.
DO YOU THINK HE'D TELL ME?
MISS KYLE. HIS TRUST IS NOT SOMETHING ONE CAN STEAL FROM A MUSEUM LATE AT NIGHT.
CAREFUL, MISTER PENNYWORTH. I'VE SCRATCHED MEN'S EYES OUT FOR TAKING THAT TONE WITH ME.
YES, I IMAGINE YOU HAVE.
WHILE I HAVE SEWN HIS FLESH, SET HIS BONES, AND REMOVED MORE SPENT BULLETS FROM HIS BODY THAN I CARE TO REMEMBER...
...THERE IS ONE THING I WOULDN'T HAVE THE SLIGHTEST CLUE HOW TO MEND.
NOW, YOU'VE PIQUED MY CURIOSITY.
A BROKEN HEART.
I HOPE YOU UNDERSTAND HOW TRULY EXTRAORDINARY IT IS FOR HIM TO SHARE HIS SECRETS WITH YOU.
INCLUDING HIS BRINGING YOU HERE TONIGHT.
YOU DON'T THINK MUCH OF ME, DO YOU?
QUITE THE CONTRARY. I THINK THE WORLD OF YOU.
AND WHILE HE MAY NOT SAY IT...
...SO DOES HE.
YOU BEGAN THIS EVENING ASKING WHAT YOU COULD DO TO HELP.
YOU ARE DOING IT, MISS KYLE. AND PLEASE CONTINUE TO DO SO.
MRRROW...

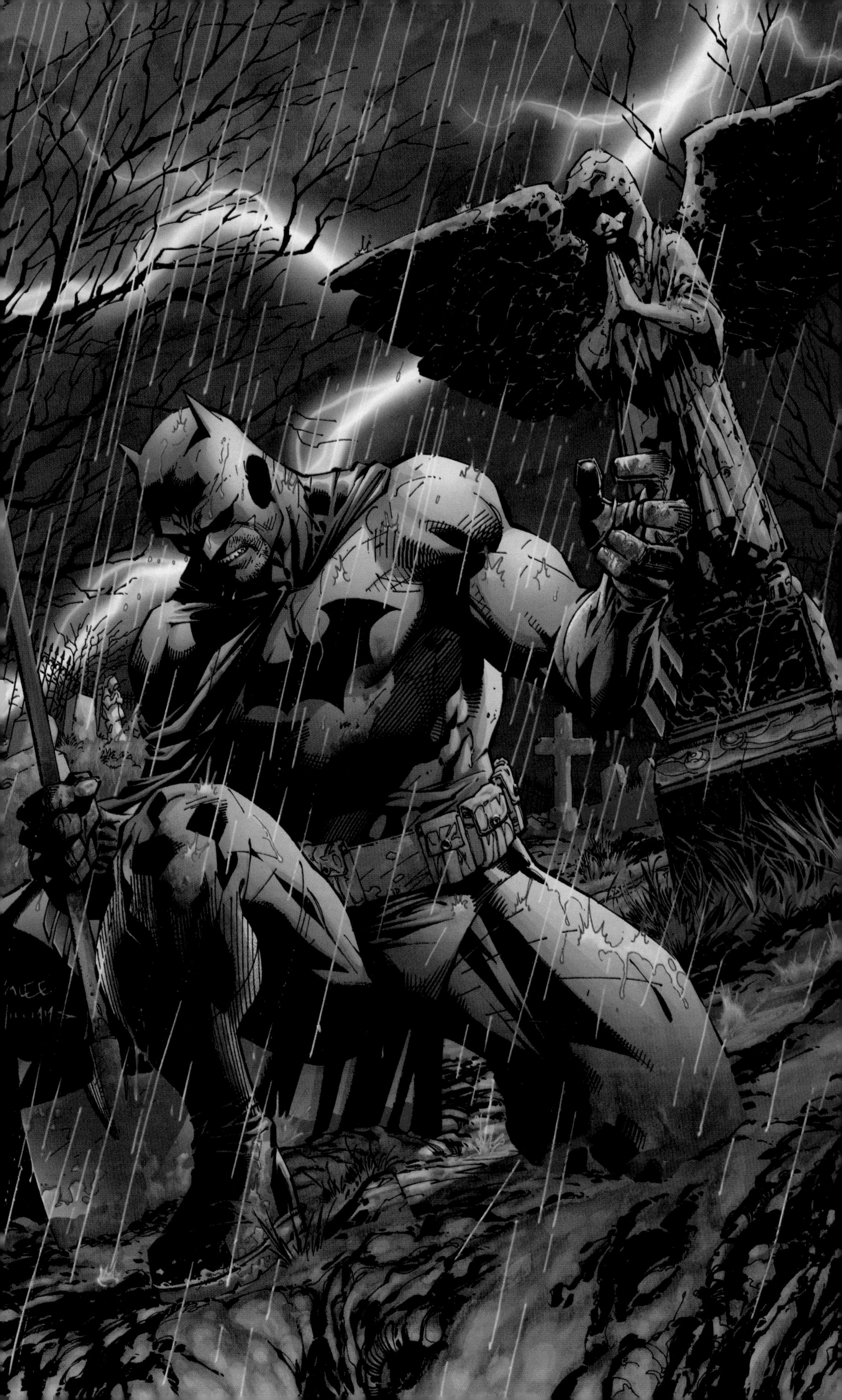

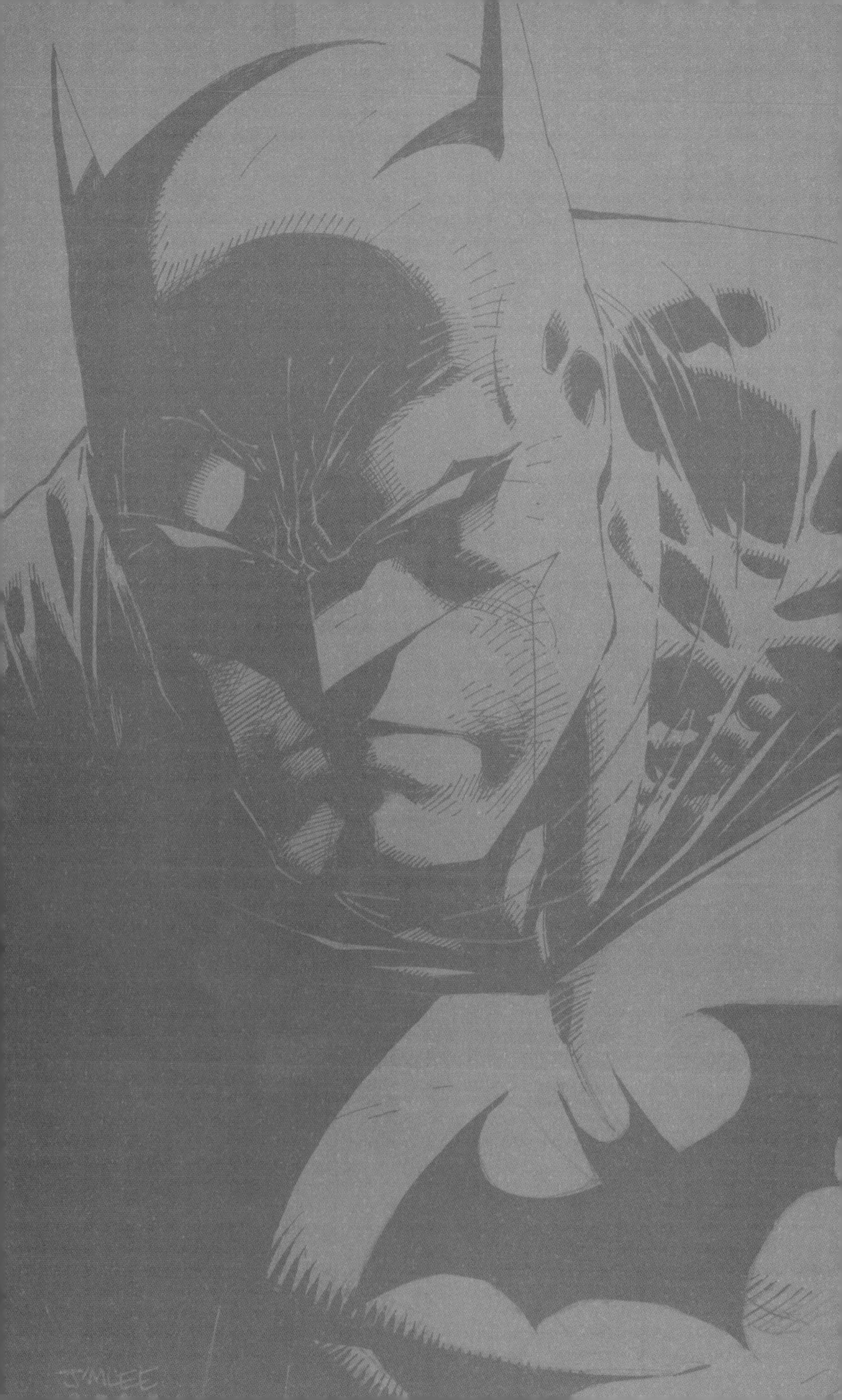

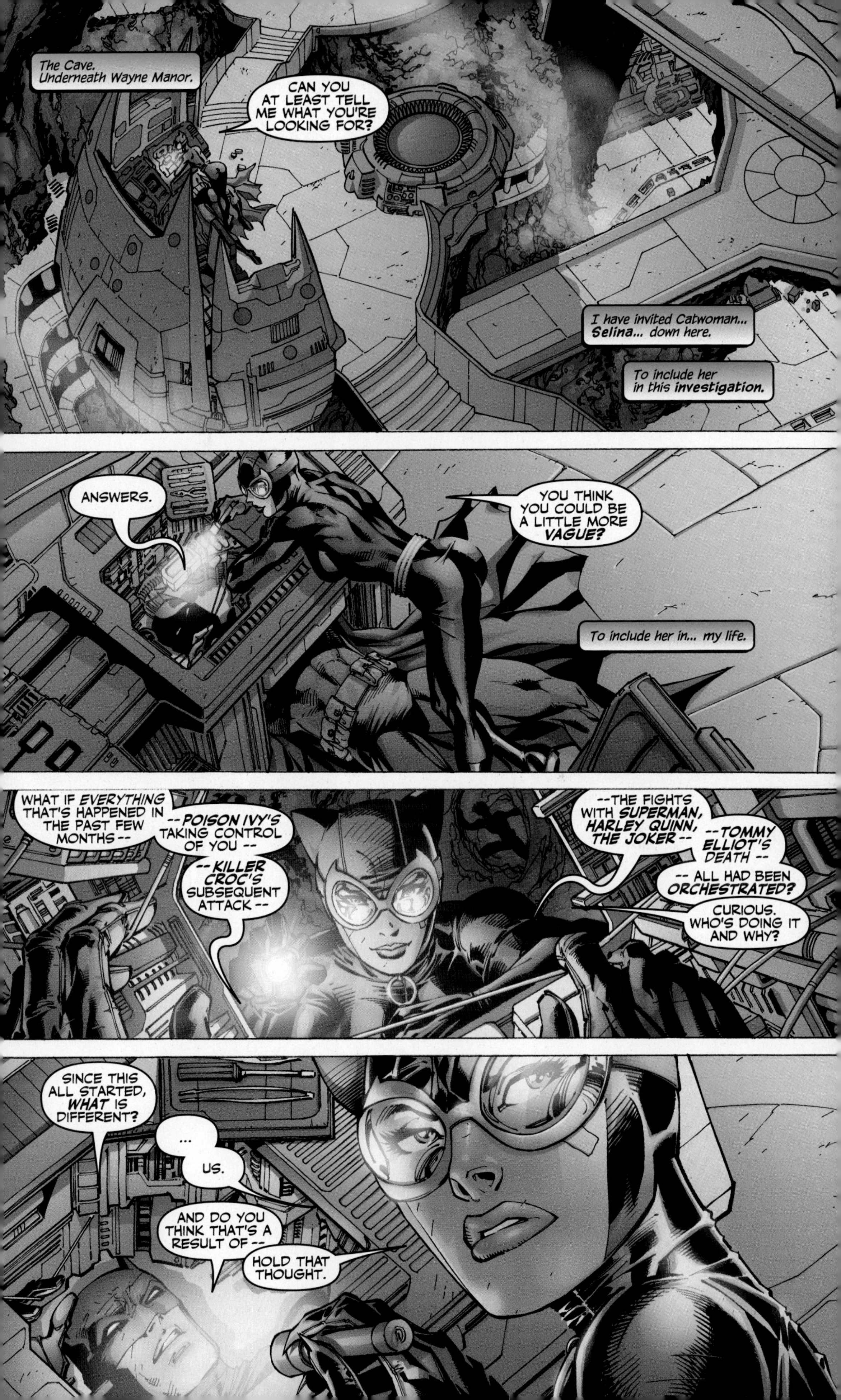

The Cave. Underneath Wayne Manor.
CAN YOU AT LEAST TELL ME WHAT YOU'RE LOOKING FOR?
I have invited Catwoman... Selina... down here.
To include her in this investigation.
ANSWERS.
YOU THINK YOU COULD BE A LITTLE MORE VAGUE?
To include her in... my life.
WHAT IF EVERYTHING THAT'S HAPPENED IN THE PAST FEW MONTHS --
--POISON IVY'S TAKING CONTROL OF YOU --
--KILLER CROC'S SUBSEQUENT ATTACK --
--THE FIGHTS WITH SUPERMAN, HARLEY QUINN, THE JOKER --
--TOMMY ELLIOT'S DEATH --
-- ALL HAD BEEN ORCHESTRATED?
CURIOUS. WHO'S DOING IT AND WHY?
SINCE THIS ALL STARTED, WHAT IS DIFFERENT?
...
US.
AND DO YOU THINK THAT'S A RESULT OF --
HOLD THAT THOUGHT.

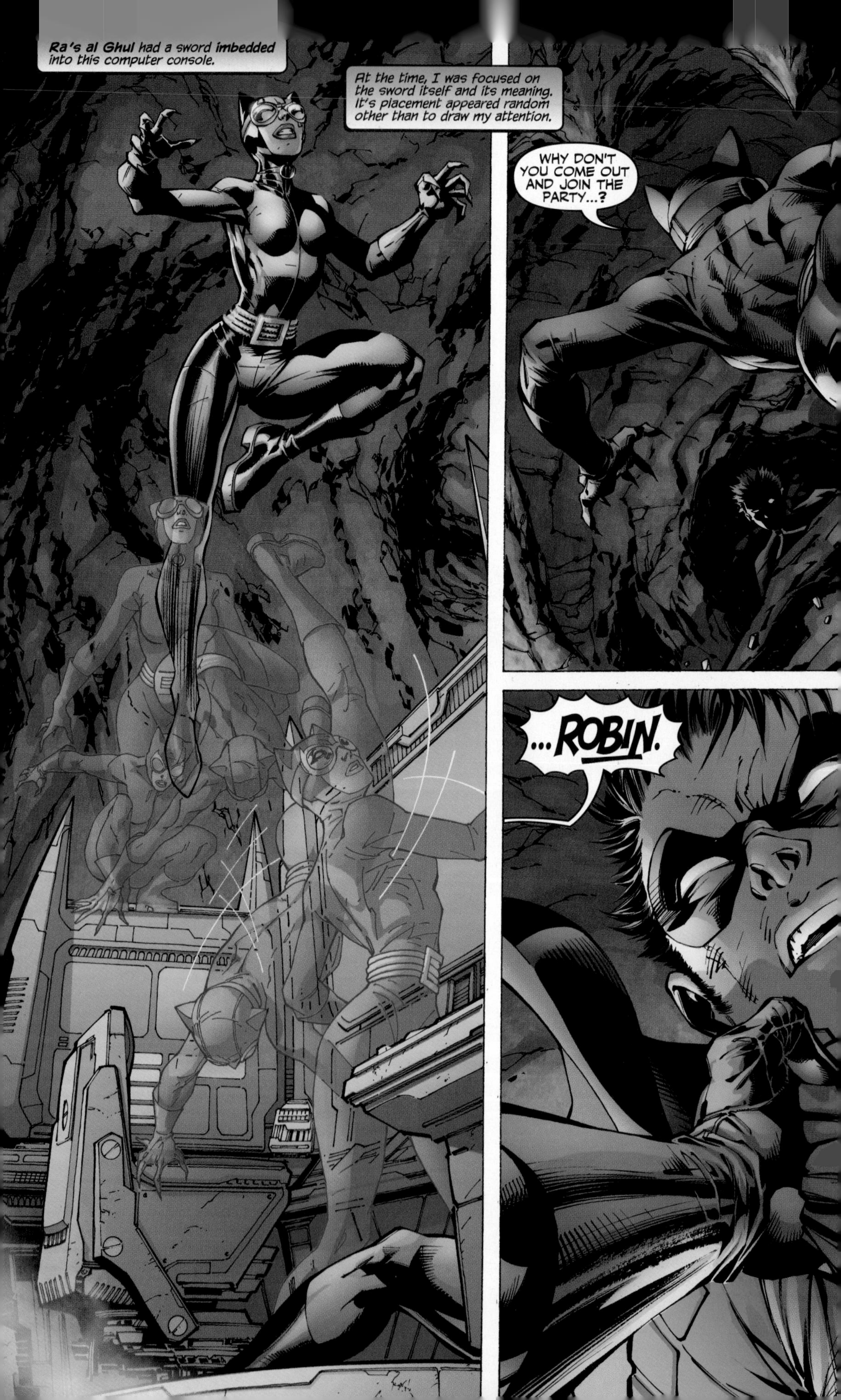
Ra's al Ghul had a sword imbedded into this computer console.
At the time, I was focused on the sword itself and its meaning. It's placement appeared random other than to draw my attention.
WHY DON'T YOU COME OUT AND JOIN THE PARTY...?
...ROBIN.

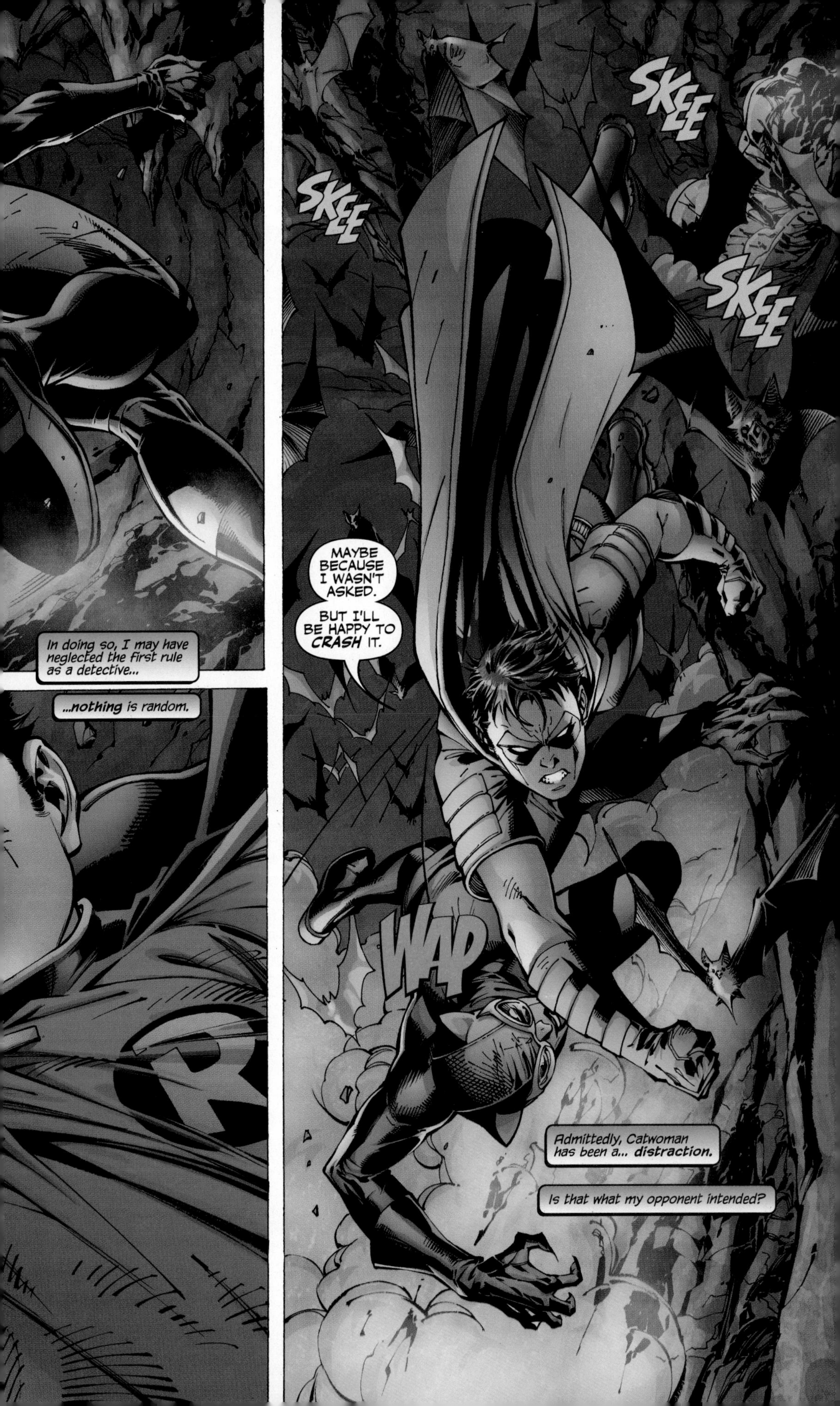
In doing so, I may have neglected the first rule as a detective...
...nothing is random.
SKEE
SKEE
SKEE
MAYBE BECAUSE I WASN'T ASKED.
BUT I'LL BE HAPPY TO CRASH IT.
WAP
Admittedly, Catwoman has been a... distraction.
Is that what my opponent intended?

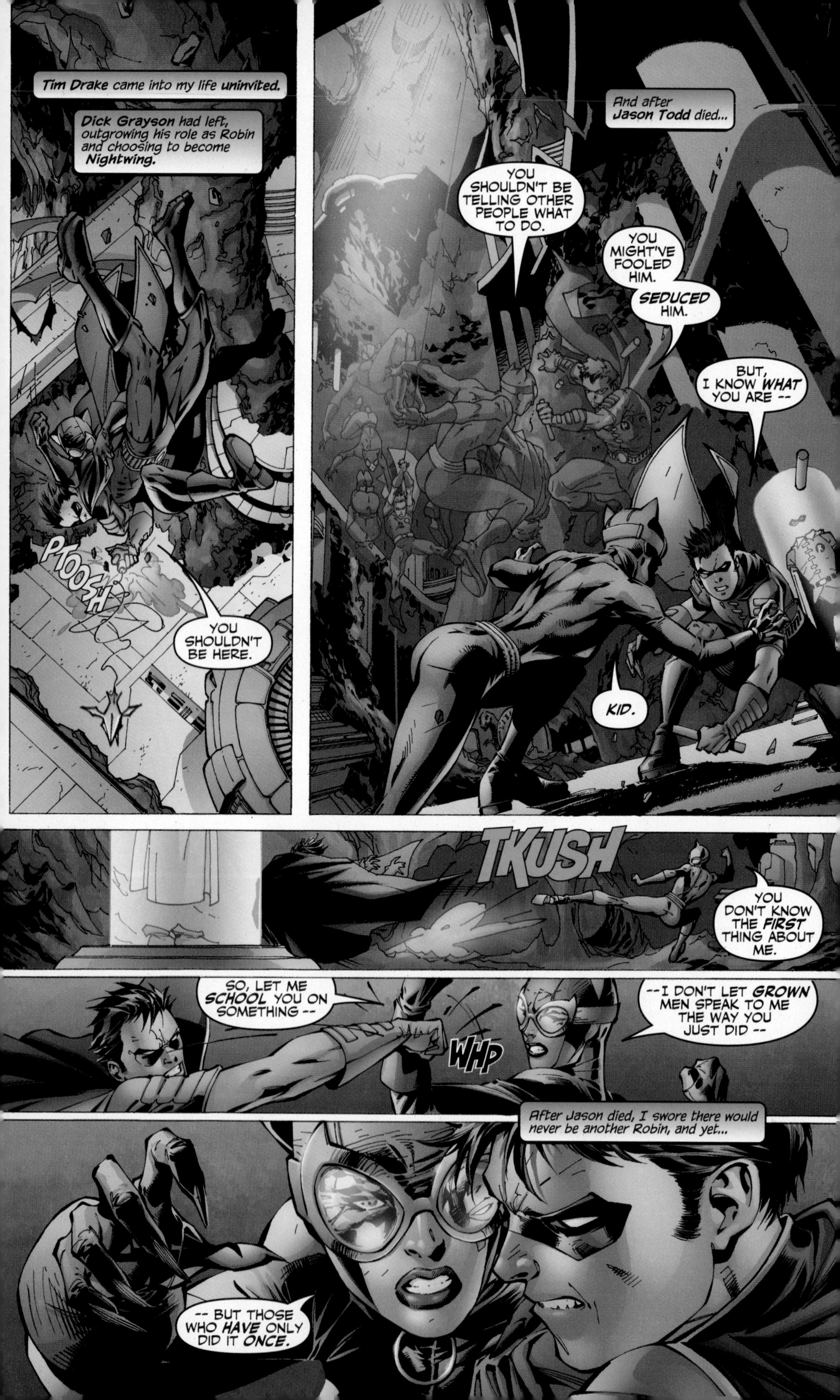

Tim Drake came into my life uninvited.
Dick Grayson had left, outgrowing his role as Robin and choosing to become Nightwing.
PTOOSH
YOU SHOULDN'T BE HERE.
And after Jason Todd died...
YOU SHOULDN'T BE TELLING OTHER PEOPLE WHAT TO DO.
YOU MIGHT'VE FOOLED HIM. SEDUCED HIM.
BUT, I KNOW WHAT YOU ARE --
KID.
TKUSH
YOU DON'T KNOW THE FIRST THING ABOUT ME.
SO, LET ME SCHOOL YOU ON SOMETHING --
WHP
--I DON'T LET GROWN MEN SPEAK TO ME THE WAY YOU JUST DID --
After Jason died, I swore there would never be another Robin, and yet...
-- BUT THOSE WHO HAVE ONLY DID IT ONCE.

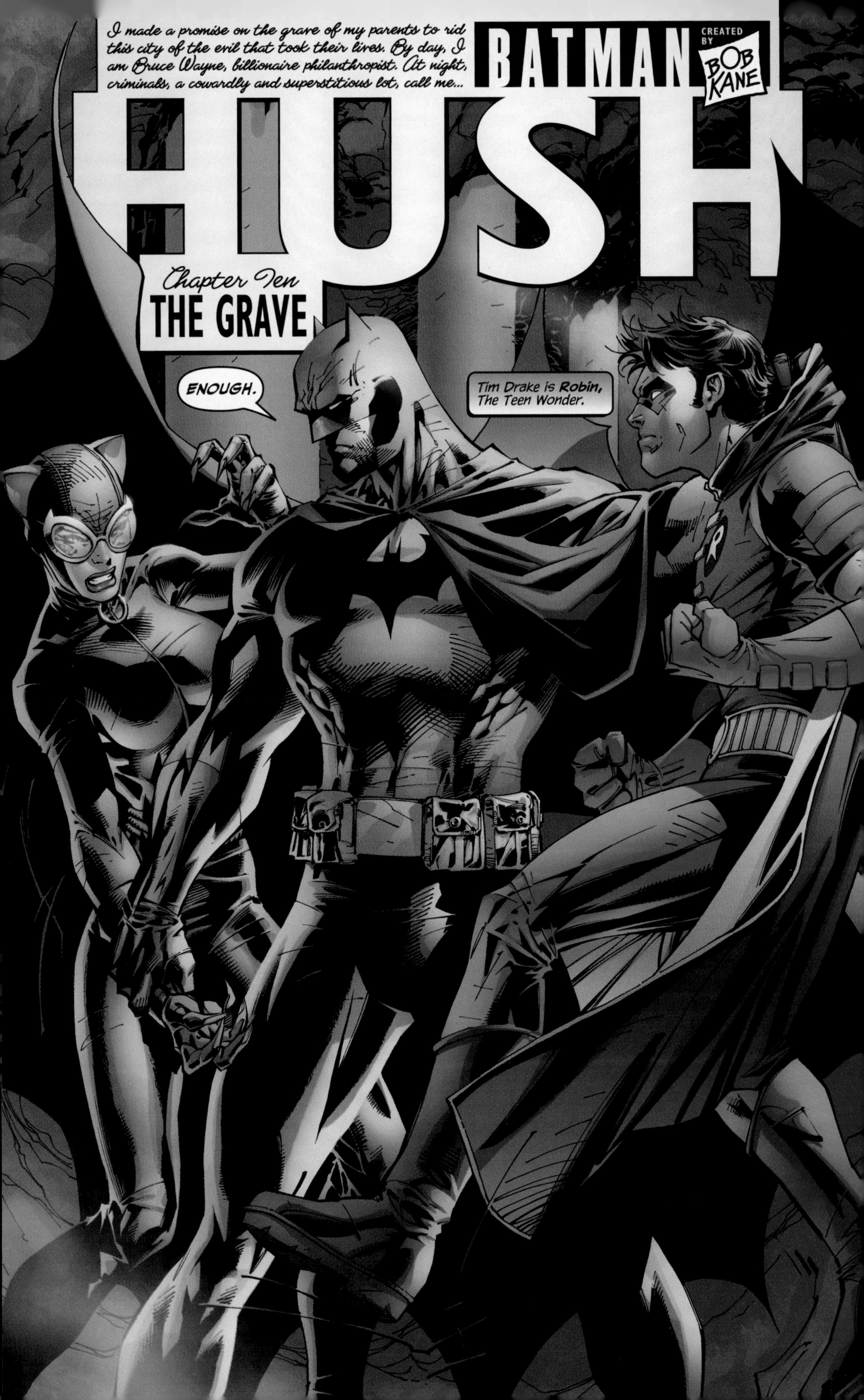
I made a promise on the grave of my parents to rid this city of the evil that took their lives. By day, I am Bruce Wayne, billionaire philanthropist. At night, criminals, a cowardly and superstitious lot, call me...
BATMAN
CREATED BY BOB KANE
HUSH
Chapter Ten
THE GRAVE
ENOUGH.
Tim Drake is Robin, The Teen Wonder.

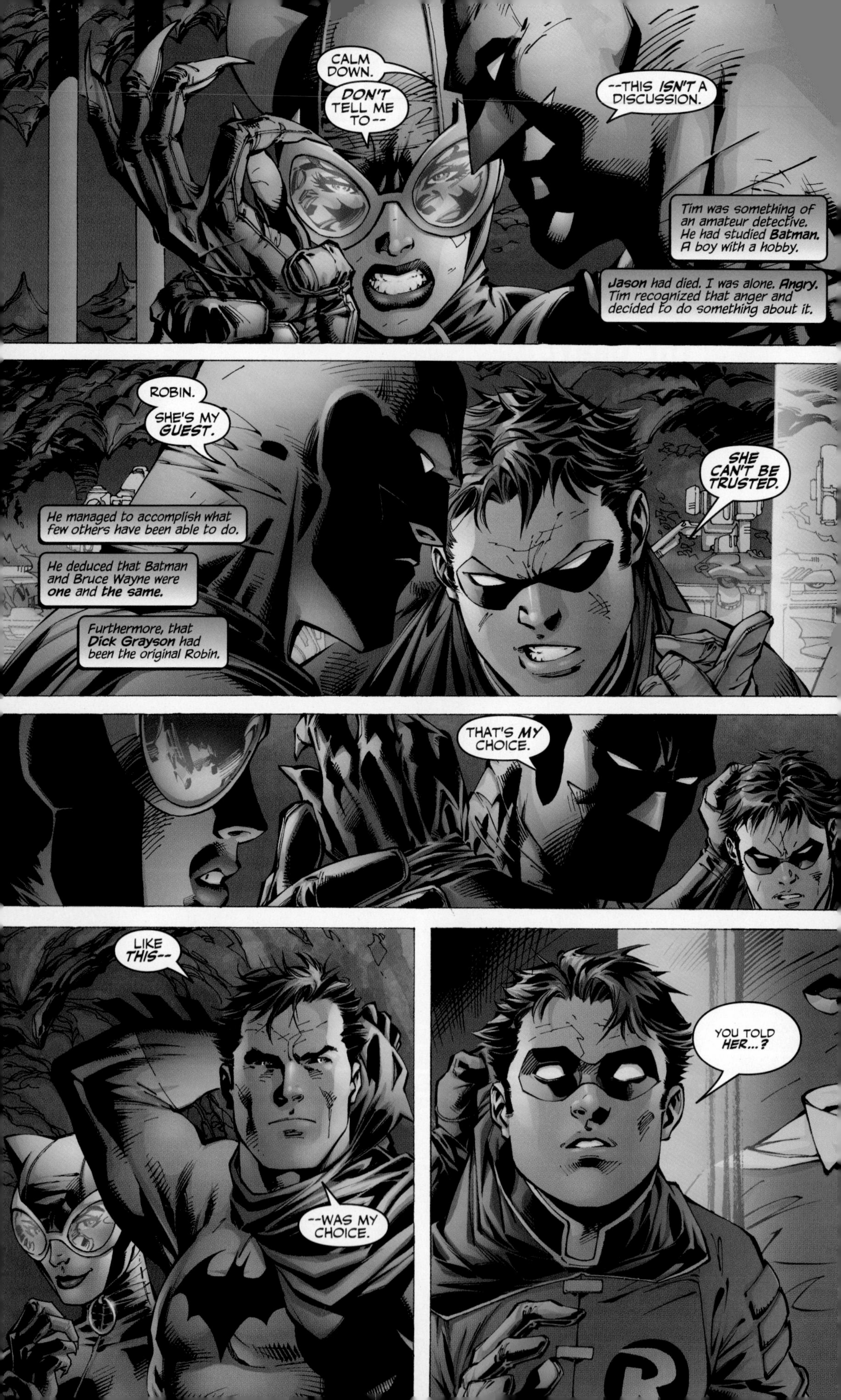

CALM DOWN.
DON'T TELL ME TO--
--THIS ISN'T A DISCUSSION.
Tim was something of an amateur detective. He had studied Batman. A boy with a hobby.
Jason had died. I was alone. Angry. Tim recognized that anger and decided to do something about it.
ROBIN.
SHE'S MY GUEST.
SHE CAN'T BE TRUSTED.
He managed to accomplish what few others have been able to do.
He deduced that Batman and Bruce Wayne were one and the same.
Furthermore, that Dick Grayson had been the original Robin.
THAT'S MY CHOICE.
LIKE THIS--
--WAS MY CHOICE.
YOU TOLD HER...?

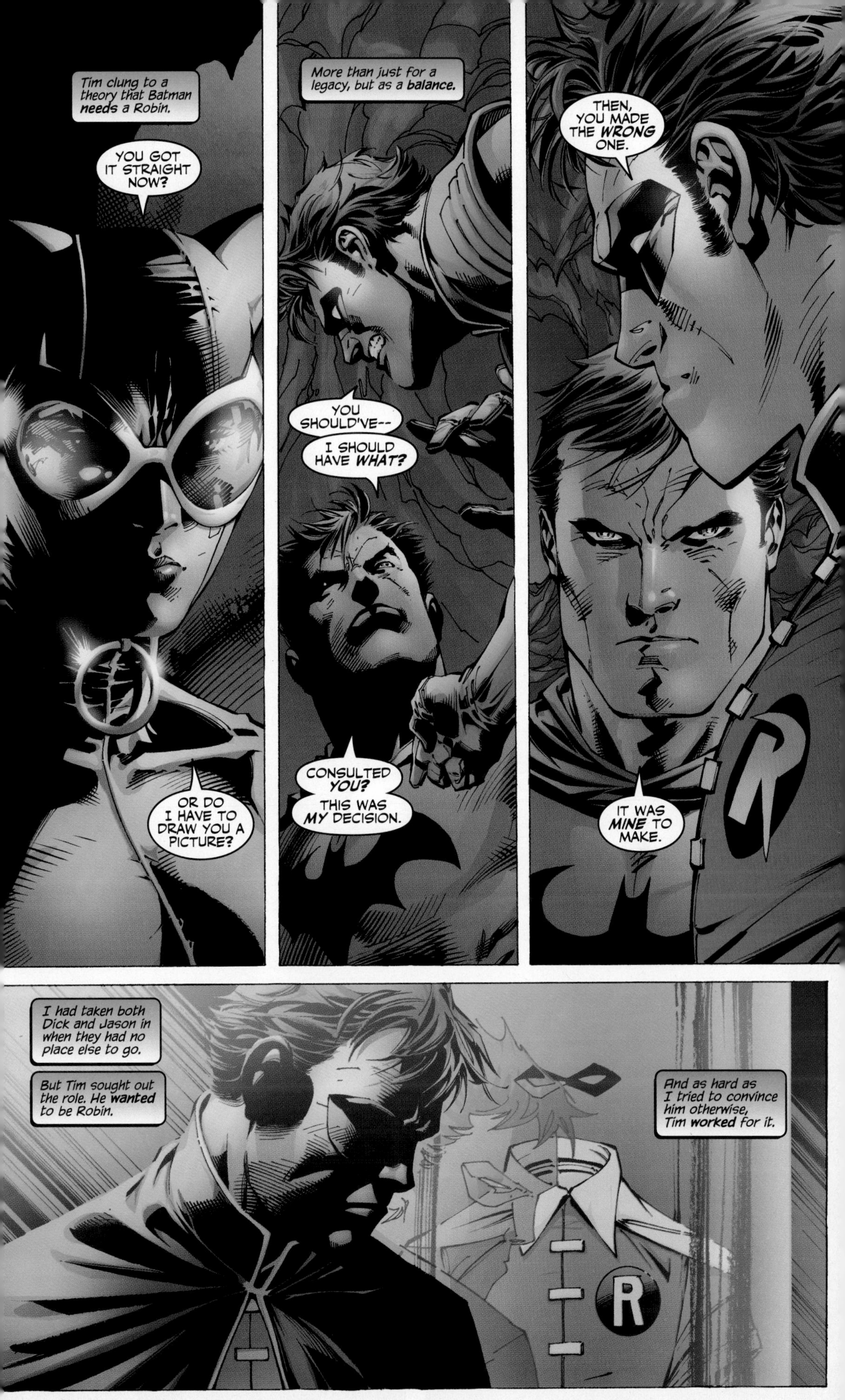

Tim clung to a theory that Batman **needs** a Robin.
YOU GOT IT STRAIGHT NOW?
OR DO I HAVE TO DRAW YOU A PICTURE?
More than just for a legacy, but as a **balance.**
YOU SHOULD'VE--
I SHOULD HAVE ***WHAT?***
CONSULTED ***YOU?***
THIS WAS ***MY*** DECISION.
THEN, YOU MADE THE ***WRONG*** ONE.
IT WAS ***MINE*** TO MAKE.
I had taken both Dick and Jason in when they had no place else to go.
But Tim sought out the role. He **wanted** to be Robin.
And as hard as I tried to convince him otherwise, Tim **worked** for it.

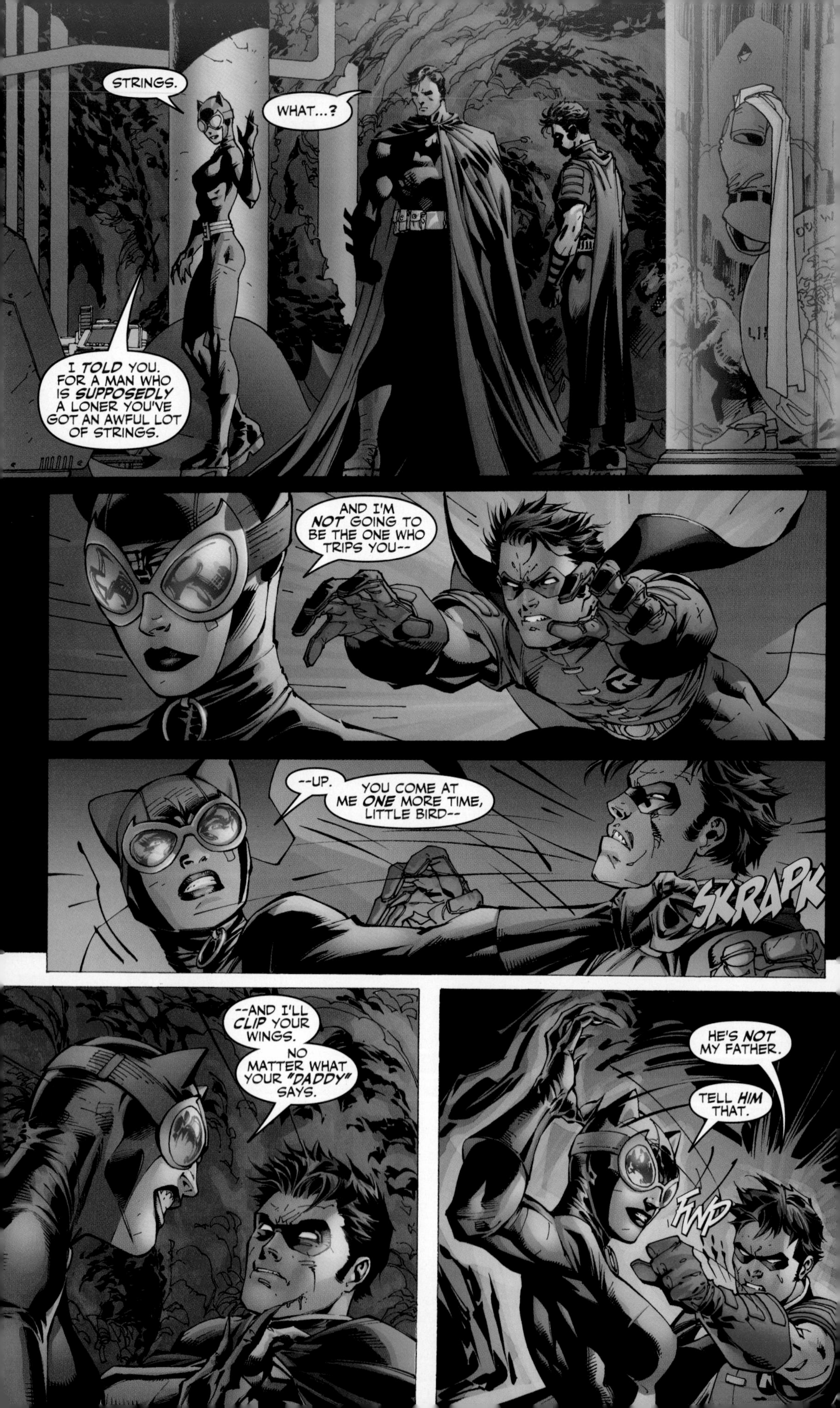
STRINGS.
WHAT...?
I TOLD YOU. FOR A MAN WHO IS SUPPOSEDLY A LONER YOU'VE GOT AN AWFUL LOT OF STRINGS.
AND I'M NOT GOING TO BE THE ONE WHO TRIPS YOU--
--UP.
YOU COME AT ME ONE MORE TIME, LITTLE BIRD--
SKRAPK
--AND I'LL CLIP YOUR WINGS.
NO MATTER WHAT YOUR "DADDY" SAYS.
HE'S NOT MY FATHER.
TELL HIM THAT.
FWP

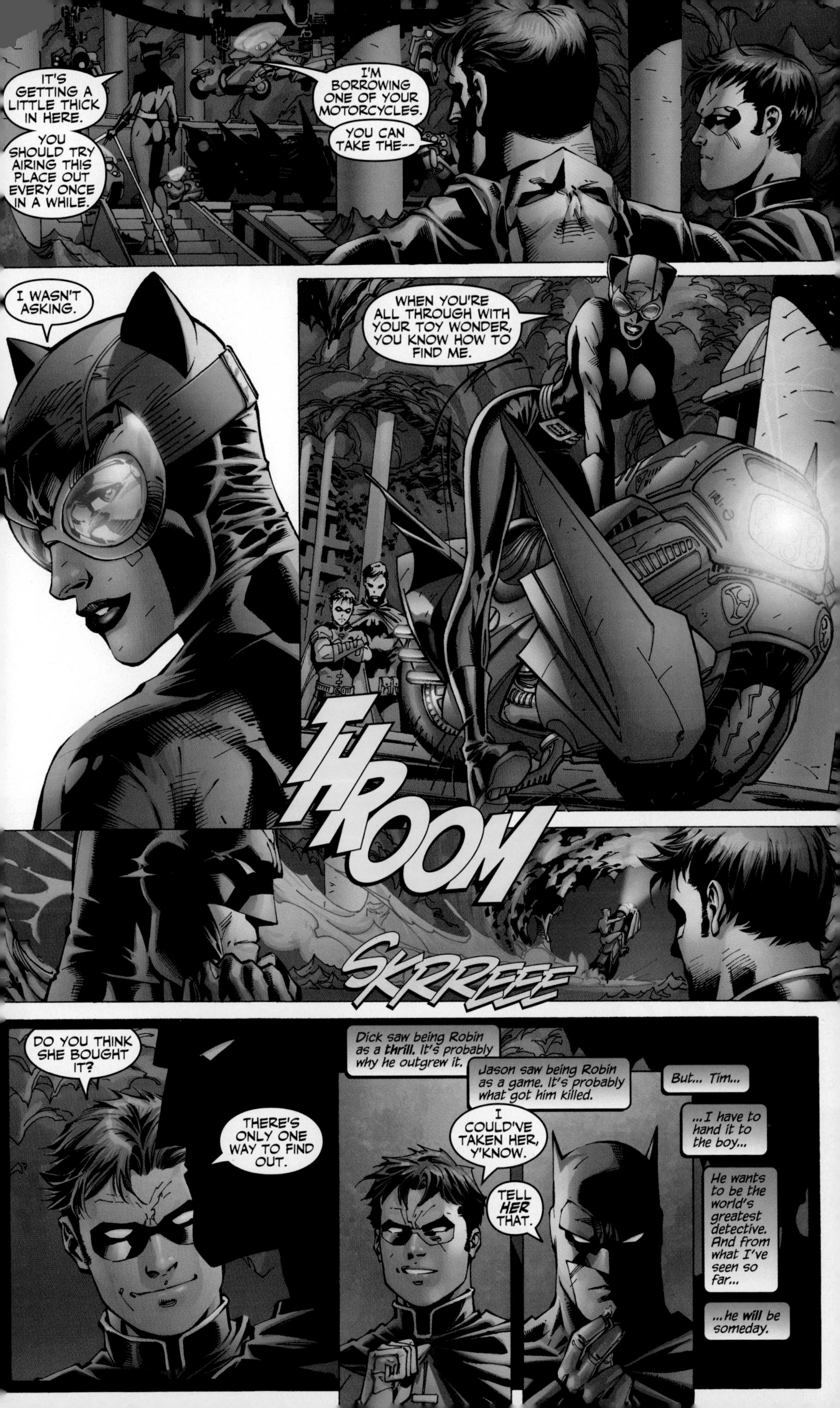

IT'S GETTING A LITTLE THICK IN HERE.
YOU SHOULD TRY AIRING THIS PLACE OUT EVERY ONCE IN A WHILE.
I'M BORROWING ONE OF YOUR MOTORCYCLES.
YOU CAN TAKE THE--
I WASN'T ASKING.
WHEN YOU'RE ALL THROUGH WITH YOUR TOY WONDER, YOU KNOW HOW TO FIND ME.
THROOM
SKRREEE
DO YOU THINK SHE BOUGHT IT?
THERE'S ONLY ONE WAY TO FIND OUT.
Dick saw being Robin as a thrill. It's probably why he outgrew it.
Jason saw being Robin as a game. It's probably what got him killed.
I COULD'VE TAKEN HER, Y'KNOW.
TELL HER THAT.
But... Tim...
...I have to hand it to the boy...
He wants to be the world's greatest detective. And from what I've seen so far...
...he will be someday.

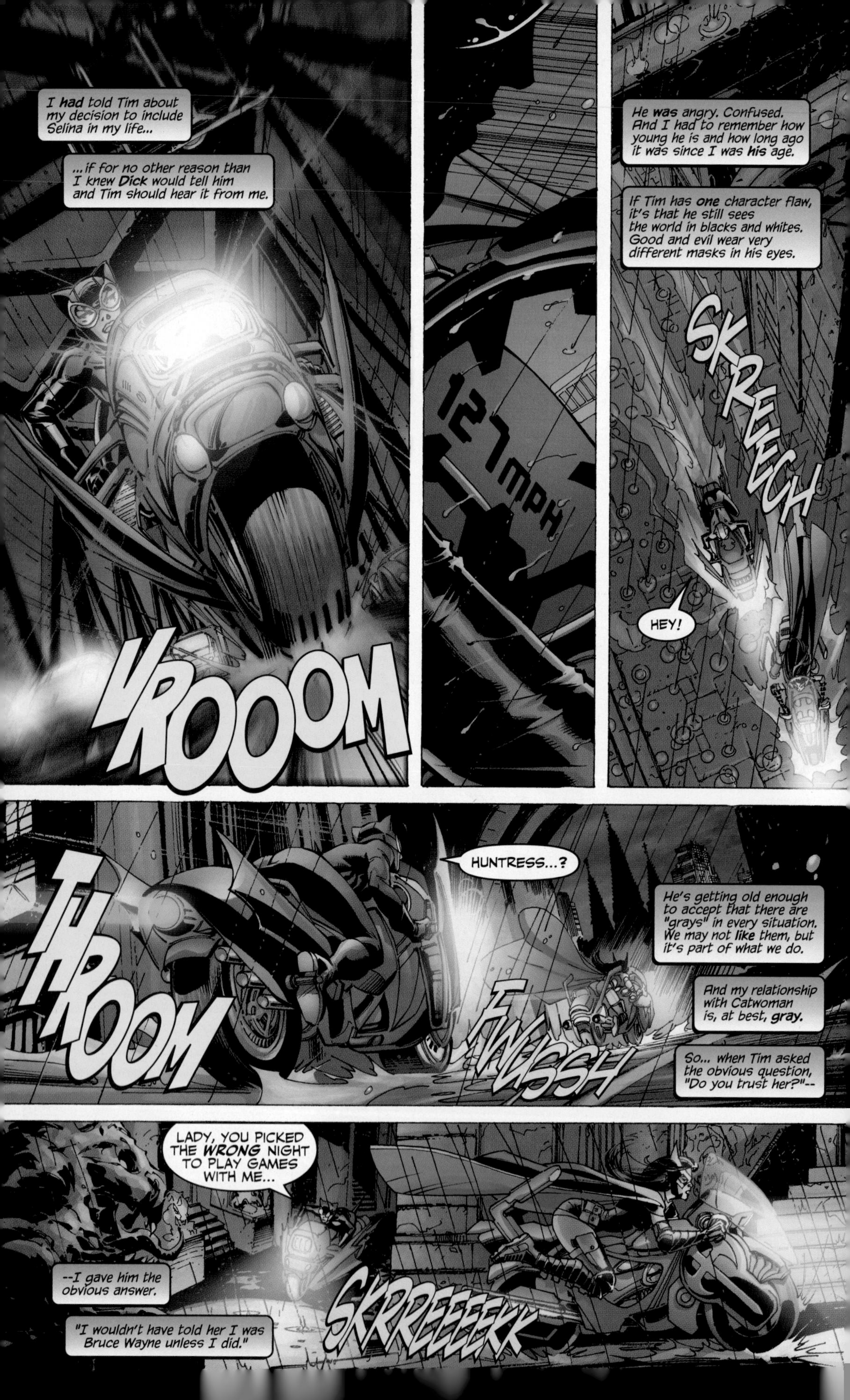

I had told Tim about my decision to include Selina in my life...
...if for no other reason than I knew Dick would tell him and Tim should hear it from me.
VROOOM
127 mph
He was angry. Confused. And I had to remember how young he is and how long ago it was since I was his age.
If Tim has one character flaw, it's that he still sees the world in blacks and whites. Good and evil wear very different masks in his eyes.
SKREEECH
HEY!
THROOM
HUNTRESS...?
He's getting old enough to accept that there are "grays" in every situation. We may not like them, but it's part of what we do.
And my relationship with Catwoman is, at best, gray.
FWUSSH
So... when Tim asked the obvious question, "Do you trust her?"--
LADY, YOU PICKED THE WRONG NIGHT TO PLAY GAMES WITH ME...
--I gave him the obvious answer.
"I wouldn't have told her I was Bruce Wayne unless I did."
SKRREEEEKK

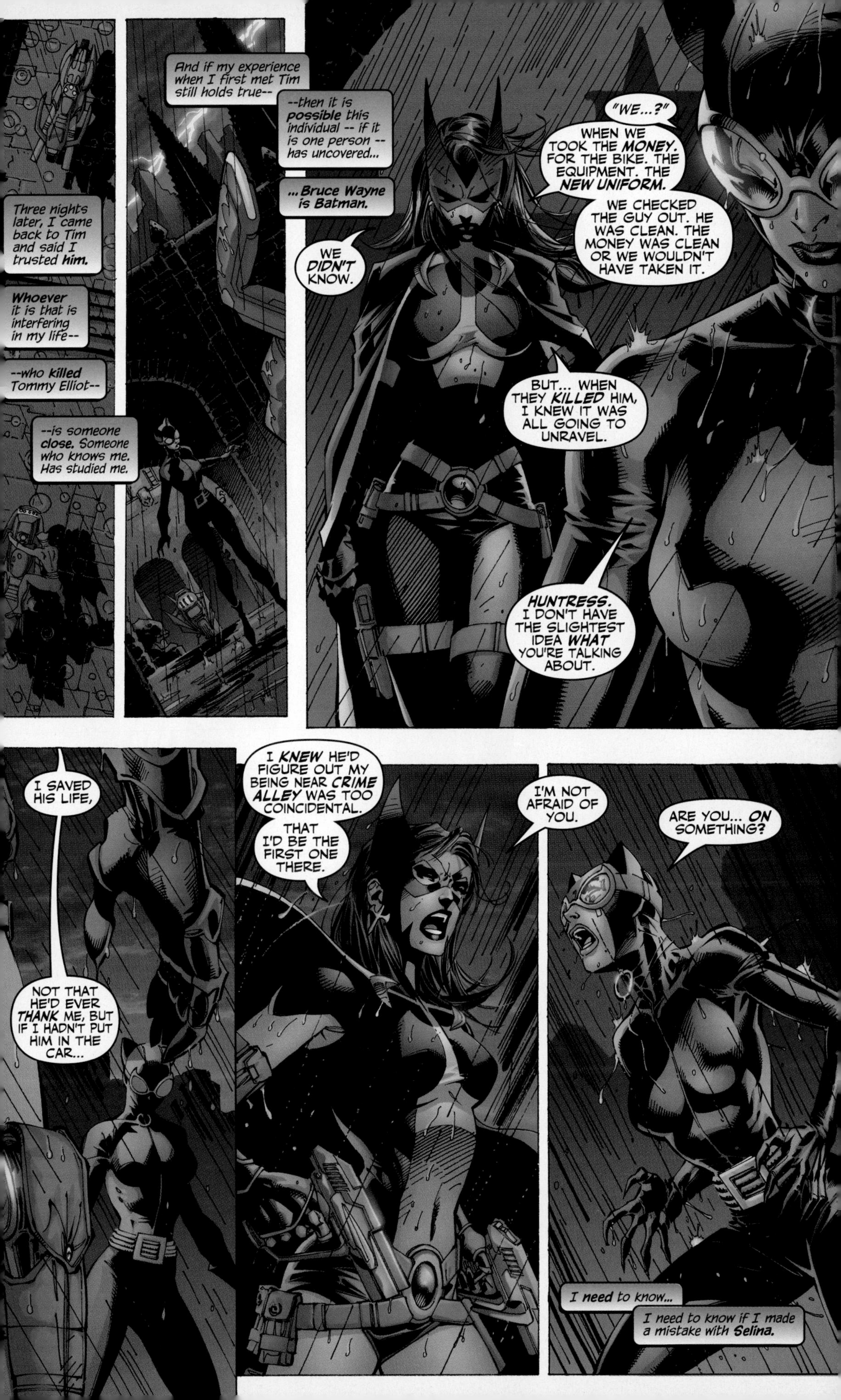
Three nights later, I came back to Tim and said I trusted **him.**
Whoever it is that is interfering in my life--
--who **killed** Tommy Elliot--
--is someone **close.** Someone who knows me. Has studied me.
And if my experience when I first met Tim still holds true--
--then it is **possible** this individual -- if it is one person -- has uncovered...
...**Bruce Wayne is Batman.**
WE **DIDN'T** KNOW.
"WE...?"
WHEN WE TOOK THE **MONEY.** FOR THE BIKE. THE EQUIPMENT. THE **NEW UNIFORM.**
WE CHECKED THE GUY OUT. HE WAS CLEAN. THE MONEY WAS CLEAN OR WE WOULDN'T HAVE TAKEN IT.
BUT... WHEN THEY **KILLED** HIM, I KNEW IT WAS ALL GOING TO UNRAVEL.
HUNTRESS. I DON'T HAVE THE SLIGHTEST IDEA **WHAT** YOU'RE TALKING ABOUT.
I SAVED HIS LIFE,
NOT THAT HE'D EVER **THANK** ME, BUT IF I HADN'T PUT HIM IN THE CAR...
I **KNEW** HE'D FIGURE OUT MY BEING NEAR **CRIME ALLEY** WAS TOO COINCIDENTAL.
THAT I'D BE THE FIRST ONE THERE.
I'M NOT AFRAID OF YOU.
ARE YOU... **ON** SOMETHING?
I **need** to know...
I need to know if I made a mistake with **Selina.**

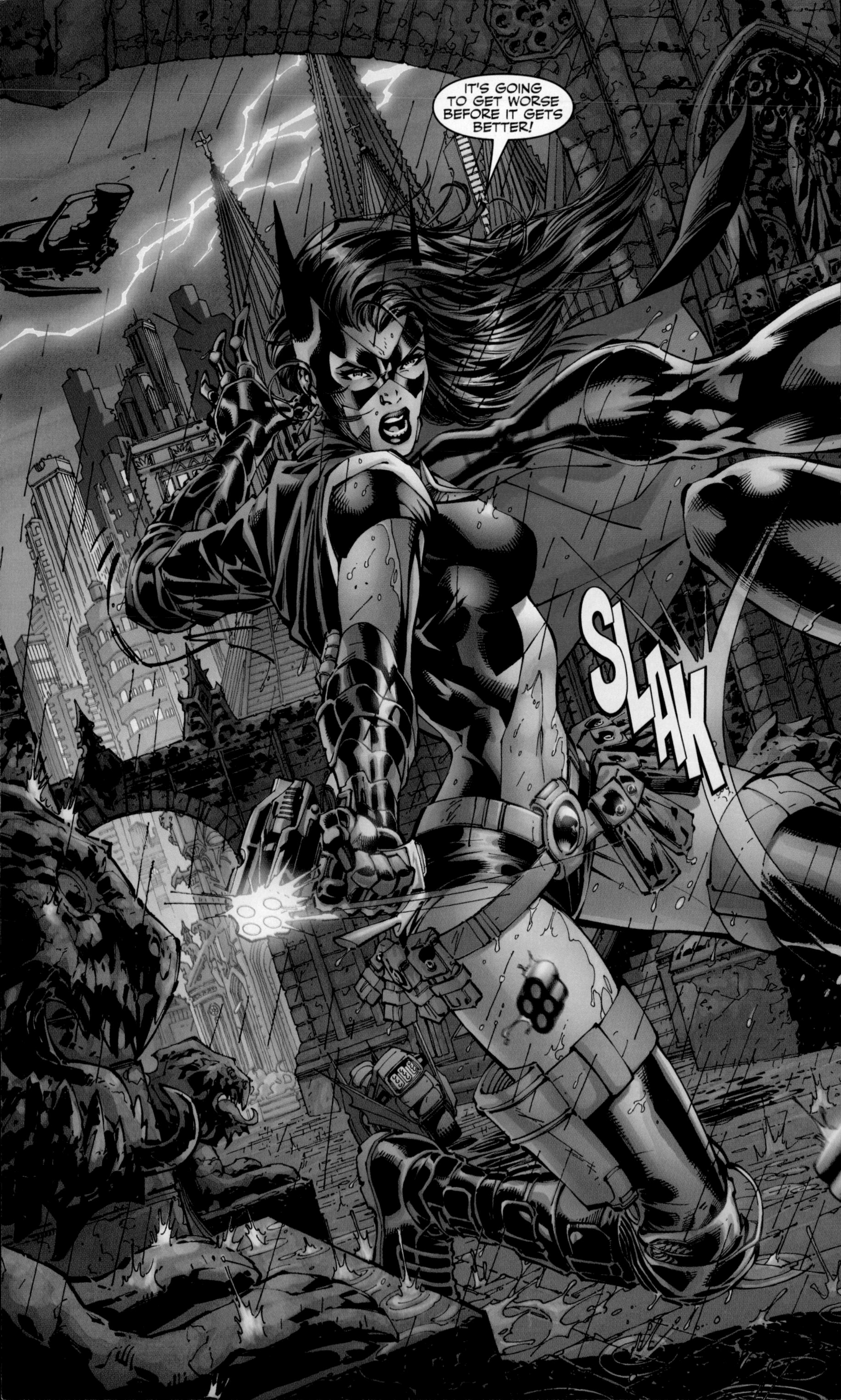
IT'S GOING TO GET WORSE BEFORE IT GETS BETTER!
SLAK

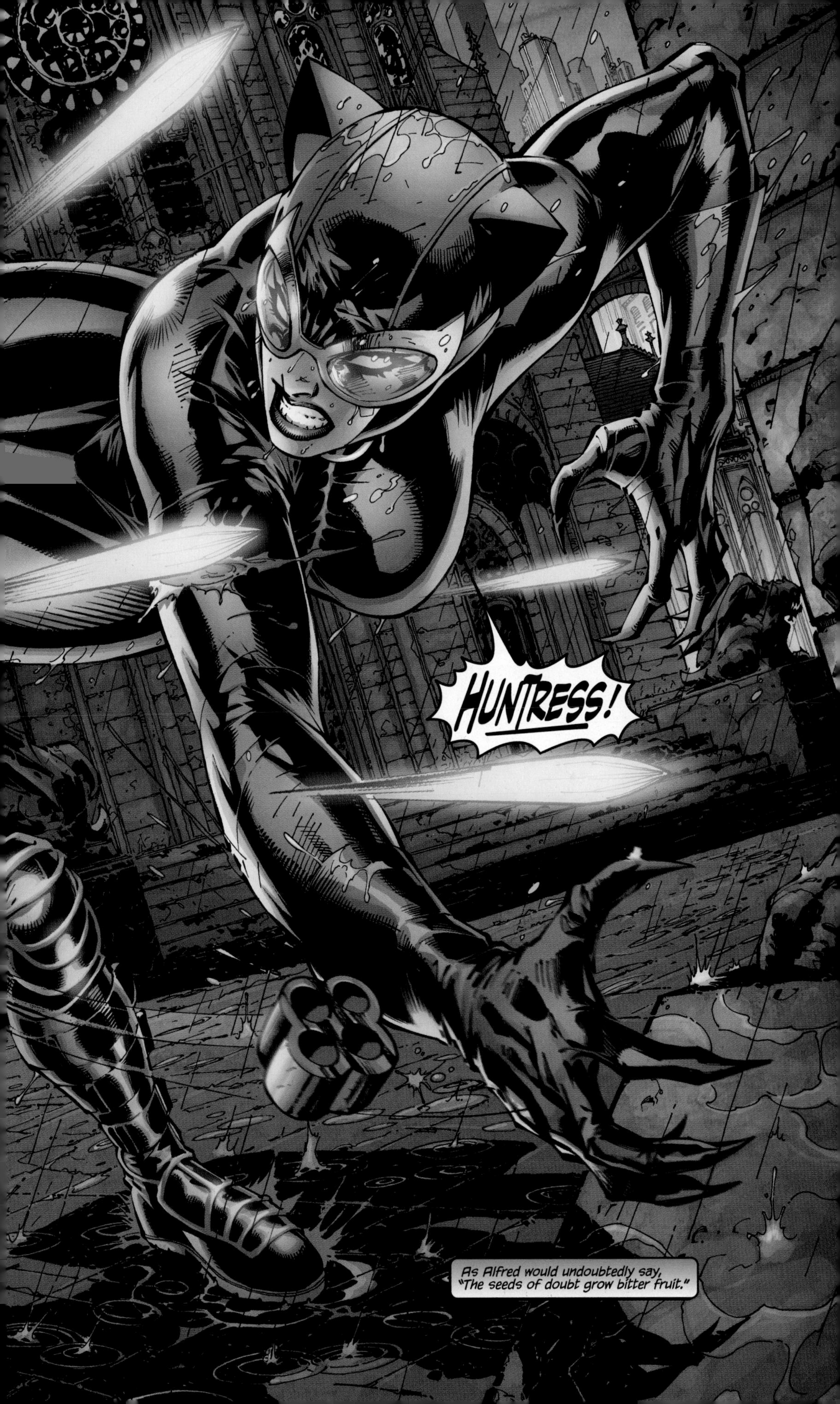
HUNTRESS!
As Alfred would undoubtedly say, "The seeds of doubt grow bitter fruit."

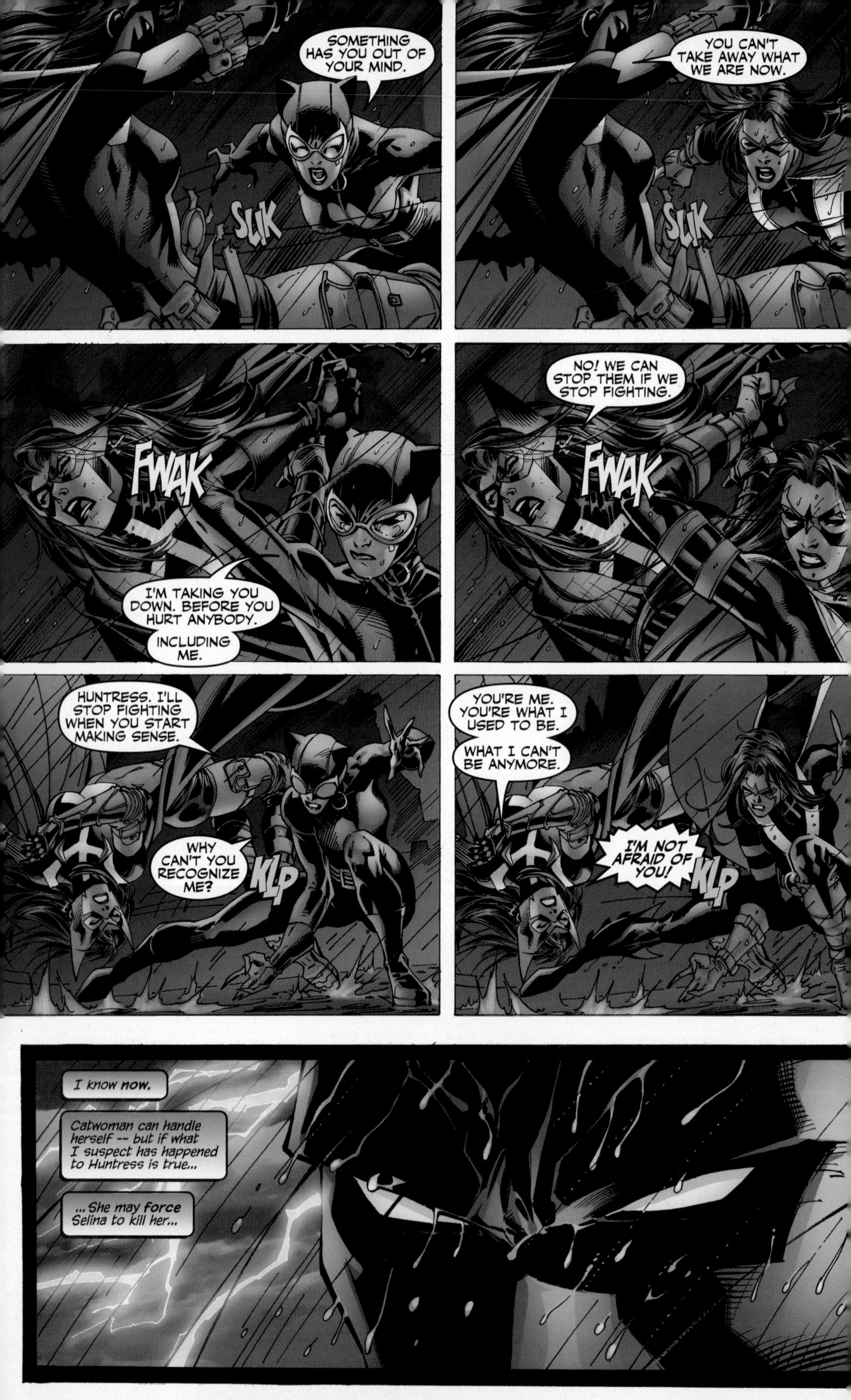
SOMETHING HAS YOU OUT OF YOUR MIND.
SLIK
YOU CAN'T TAKE AWAY WHAT WE ARE NOW.
SLIK
FWAK
I'M TAKING YOU DOWN. BEFORE YOU HURT ANYBODY.
INCLUDING ME.
NO! WE CAN STOP THEM IF WE STOP FIGHTING.
FWAK
HUNTRESS. I'LL STOP FIGHTING WHEN YOU START MAKING SENSE.
WHY CAN'T YOU RECOGNIZE ME?
KLIP
YOU'RE ME. YOU'RE WHAT I USED TO BE.
WHAT I CAN'T BE ANYMORE.
I'M NOT AFRAID OF YOU!
KLIP
I know now.
Catwoman can handle herself -- but if what I suspect has happened to Huntress is true...
...She may force Selina to kill her...

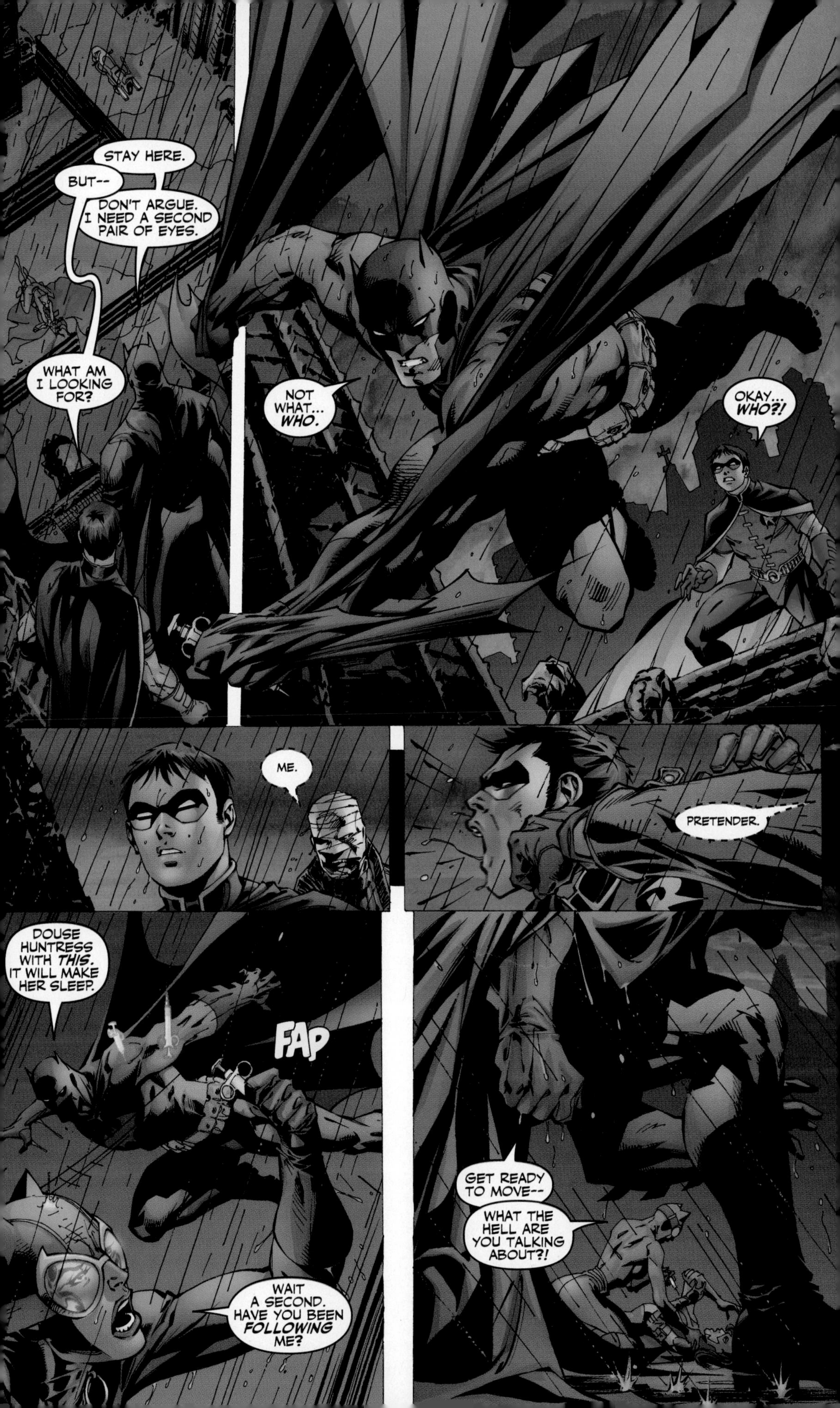

STAY HERE.
BUT--
DON'T ARGUE. I NEED A SECOND PAIR OF EYES.
WHAT AM I LOOKING FOR?
NOT WHAT... *WHO*.
OKAY... *WHO?!*
ME.
PRETENDER.
DOUSE HUNTRESS WITH *THIS*. IT WILL MAKE HER SLEEP.
FAP
WAIT A SECOND. HAVE YOU BEEN *FOLLOWING* ME?
GET READY TO MOVE--
WHAT THE HELL ARE YOU TALKING ABOUT?!

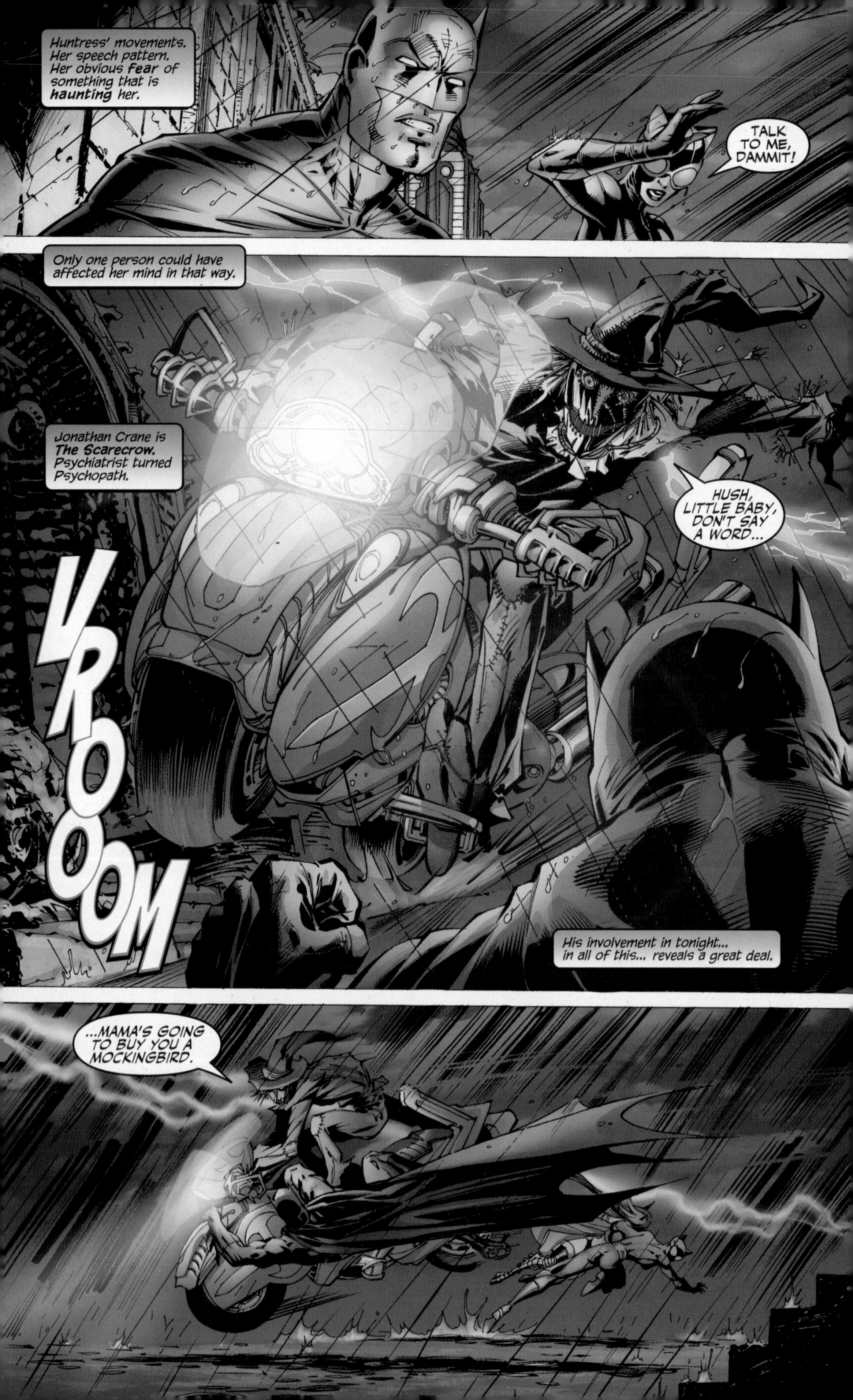
Huntress' movements. Her speech pattern. Her obvious fear of something that is haunting her.
TALK TO ME, DAMMIT!
Only one person could have affected her mind in that way.
Jonathan Crane is The Scarecrow. Psychiatrist turned Psychopath.
HUSH, LITTLE BABY, DON'T SAY A WORD...
VROOOOM
His involvement in tonight... in all of this... reveals a great deal.
...MAMA'S GOING TO BUY YOU A MOCKINGBIRD.

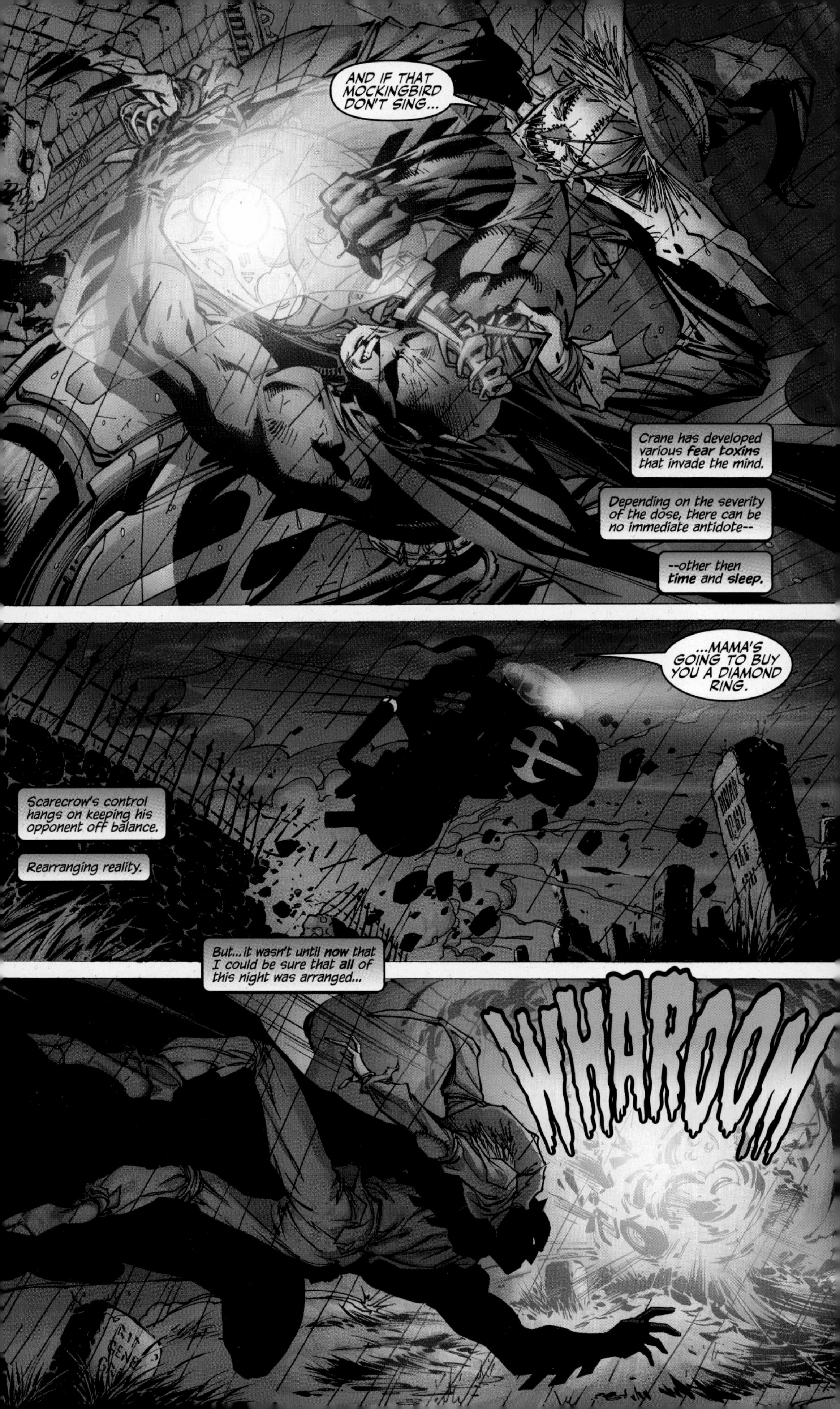

AND IF THAT MOCKINGBIRD DON'T SING...
Crane has developed various **fear toxins** that invade the mind.
Depending on the severity of the dose, there can be no immediate antidote--
--other then **time** and **sleep.**
...MAMA'S GOING TO BUY YOU A DIAMOND RING.
Scarecrow's control hangs on keeping his opponent off balance.
Rearranging reality.
But... it wasn't until now that I could be sure that **all** of this night was arranged...
WHAROOM

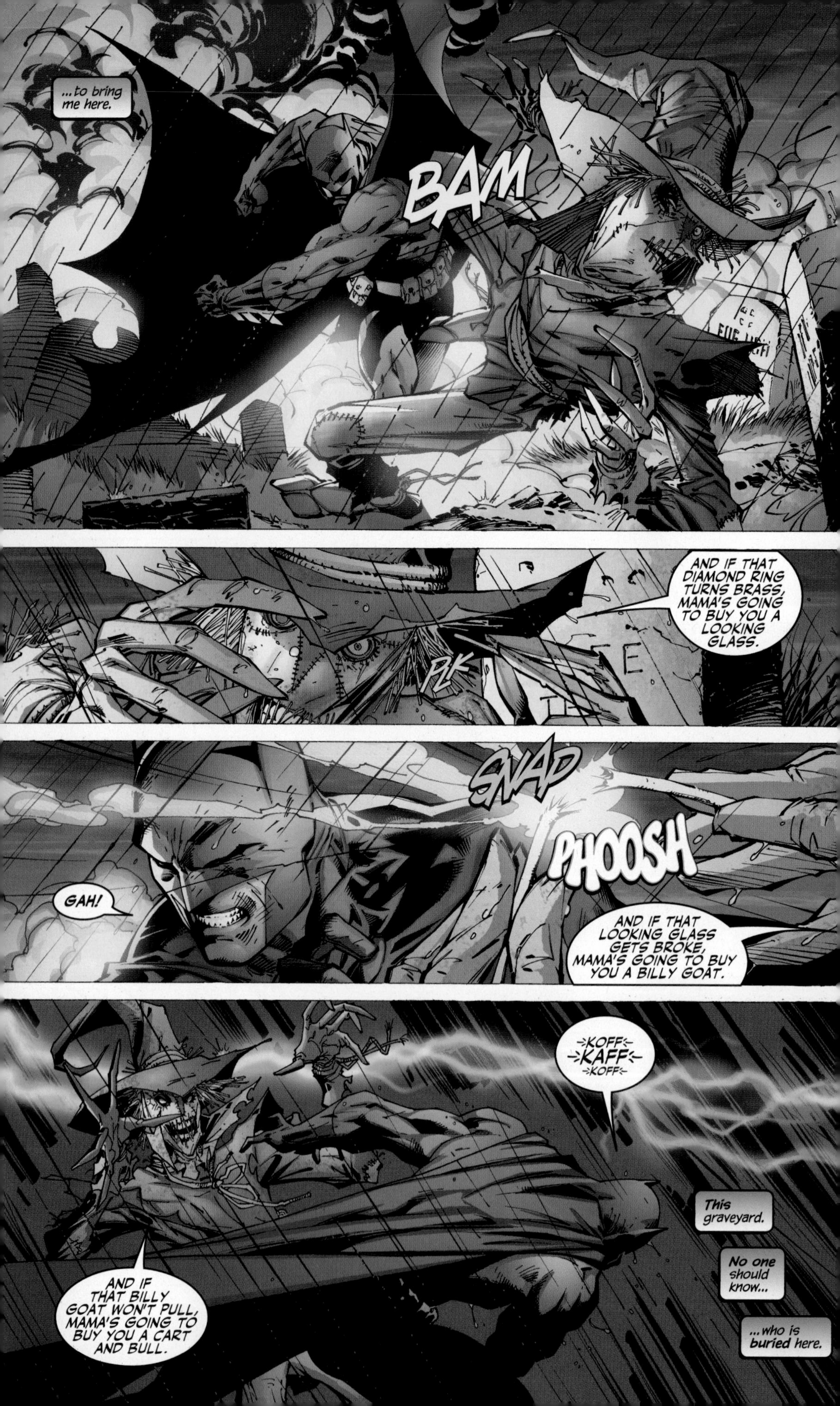
...to bring me here.
BAM
AND IF THAT DIAMOND RING TURNS BRASS, MAMA'S GOING TO BUY YOU A LOOKING GLASS.
PLK
SNAP
PHOOSH
GAH!
AND IF THAT LOOKING GLASS GETS BROKE, MAMA'S GOING TO BUY YOU A BILLY GOAT.
KOFF KAFF KOFF
AND IF THAT BILLY GOAT WON'T PULL, MAMA'S GOING TO BUY YOU A CART AND BULL.
This graveyard.
No one should know...
...who is buried here.

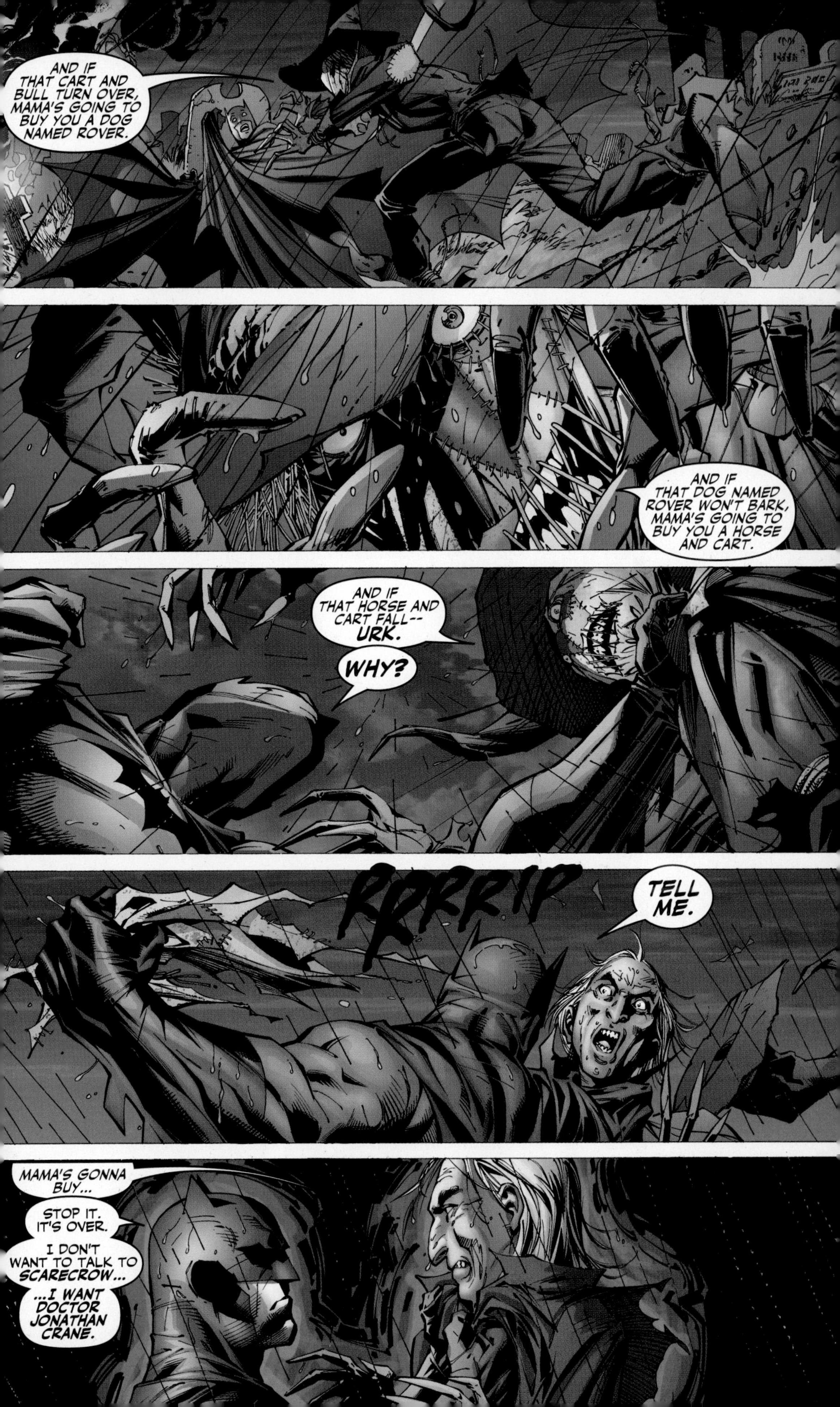
AND IF THAT CART AND BULL TURN OVER, MAMA'S GOING TO BUY YOU A DOG NAMED ROVER.
AND IF THAT DOG NAMED ROVER WON'T BARK, MAMA'S GOING TO BUY YOU A HORSE AND CART.
AND IF THAT HORSE AND CART FALL-- URK.
WHY?
RRRRIP
TELL ME.
MAMA'S GONNA BUY...
STOP IT. IT'S OVER.
I DON'T WANT TO TALK TO SCARECROW...
...I WANT DOCTOR JONATHAN CRANE.

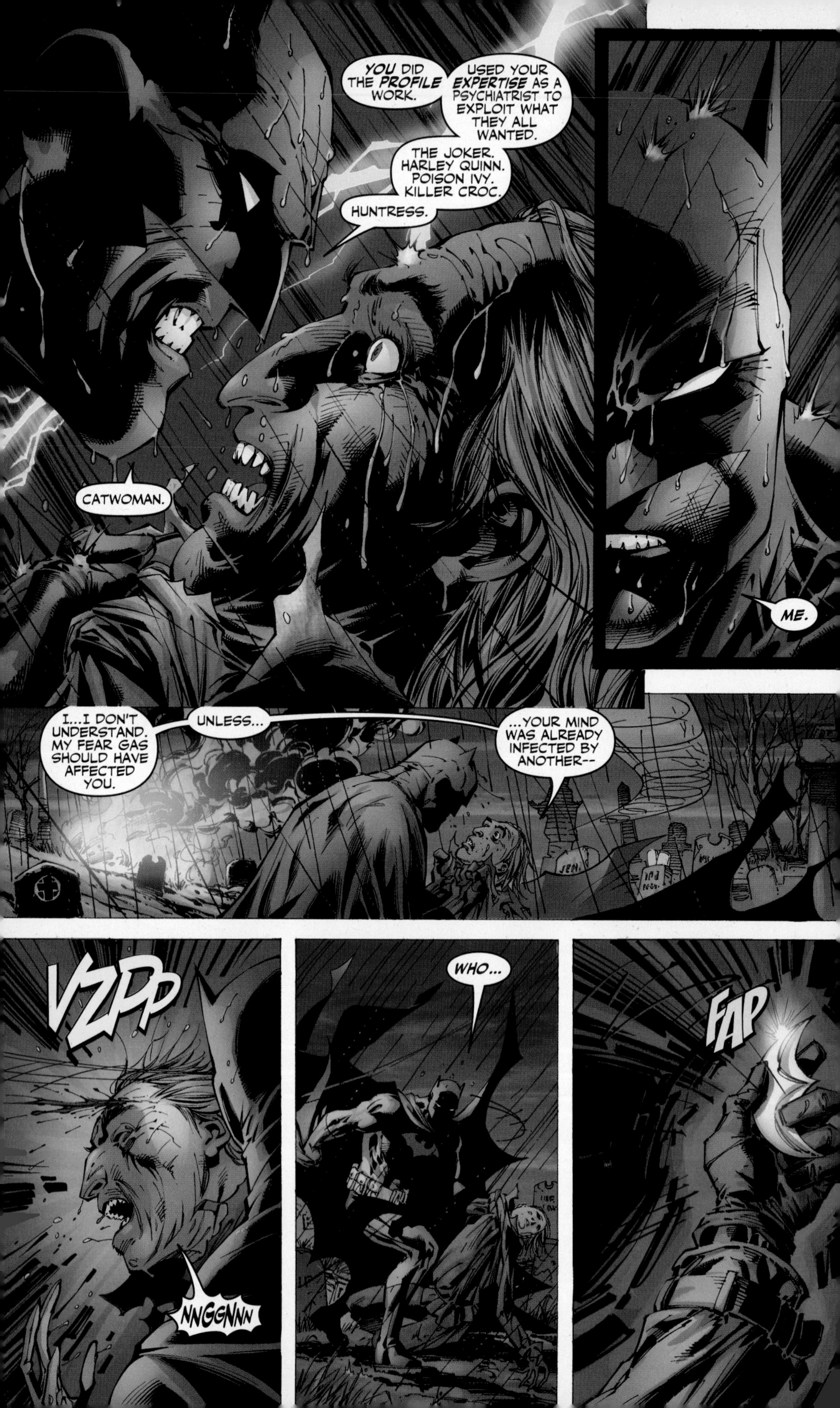
YOU DID THE PROFILE WORK.
USED YOUR EXPERTISE AS A PSYCHIATRIST TO EXPLOIT WHAT THEY ALL WANTED.
THE JOKER. HARLEY QUINN. POISON IVY. KILLER CROC.
HUNTRESS.
CATWOMAN.
ME.
I...I DON'T UNDERSTAND. MY FEAR GAS SHOULD HAVE AFFECTED YOU.
UNLESS...
...YOUR MIND WAS ALREADY INFECTED BY ANOTHER--
VZPP
NNGGNNN
WHO...
FAP

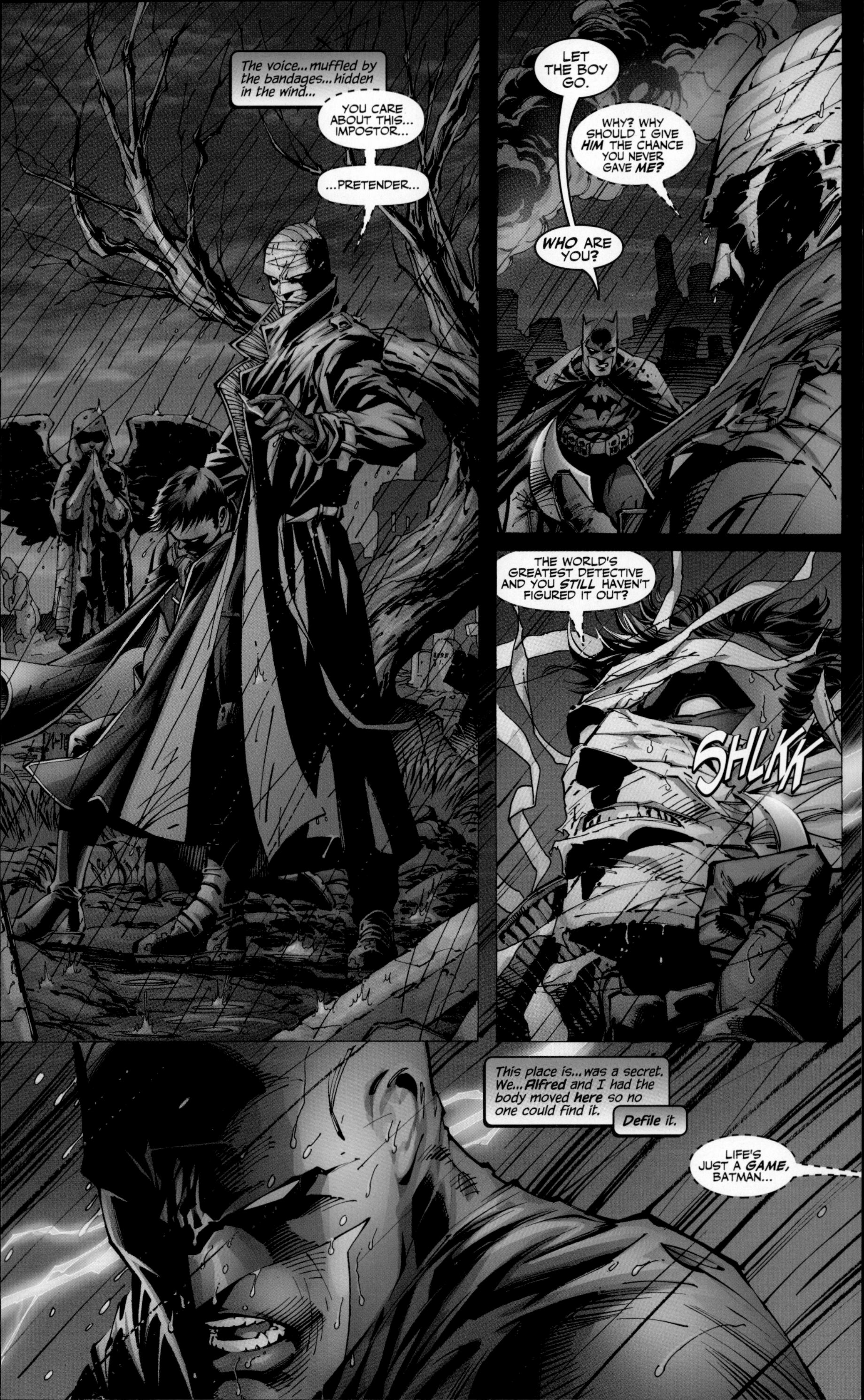

The voice... muffled by the bandages... hidden in the wind...
YOU CARE ABOUT THIS... IMPOSTOR...
...PRETENDER...
LET THE BOY GO.
WHY? WHY SHOULD I GIVE HIM THE CHANCE YOU NEVER GAVE ME?
WHO ARE YOU?
THE WORLD'S GREATEST DETECTIVE AND YOU STILL HAVEN'T FIGURED IT OUT?
SHLKK
This place is... was a secret. We... Alfred and I had the body moved here so no one could find it.
Defile it.
LIFE'S JUST A GAME, BATMAN...

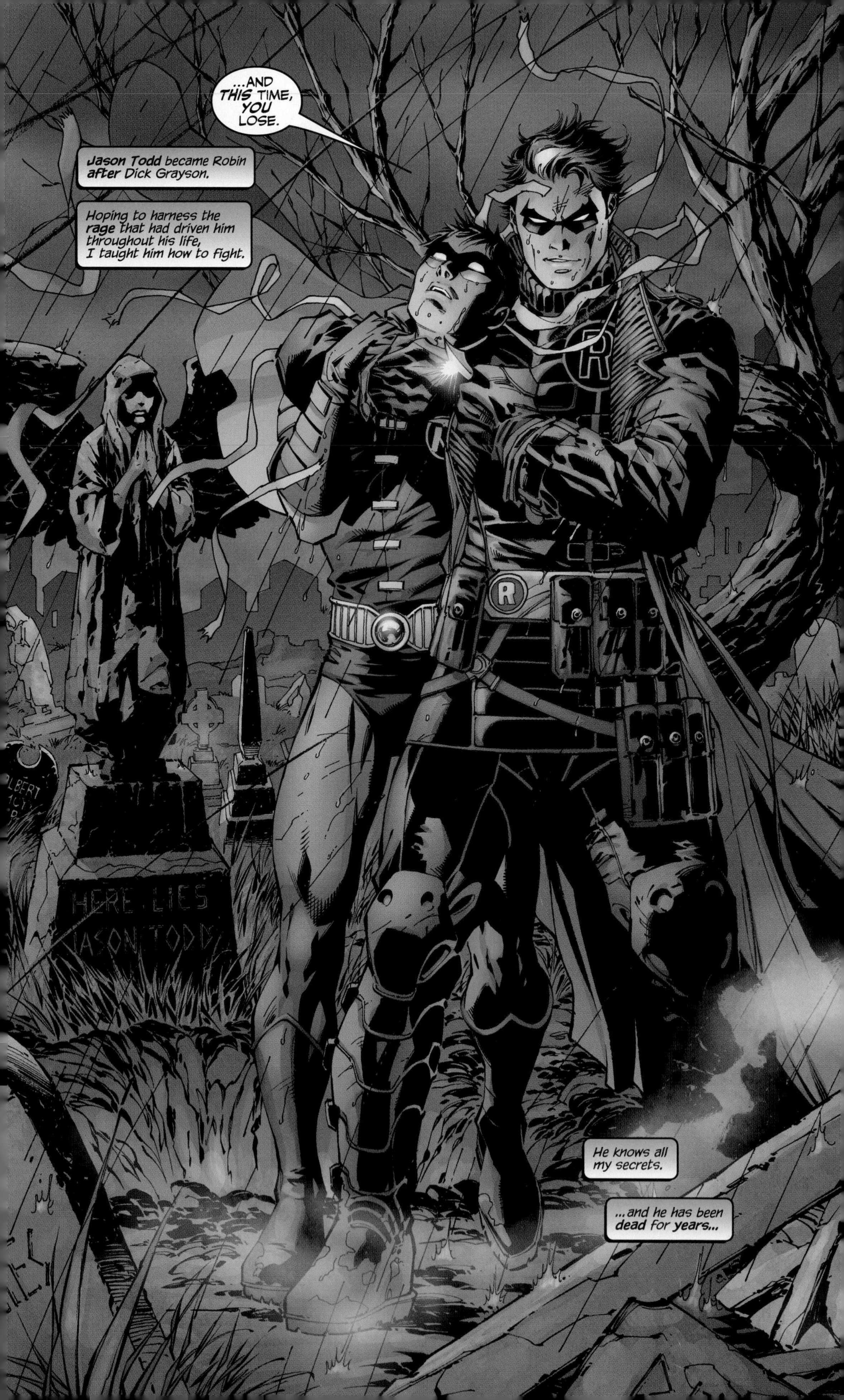
...AND THIS TIME, YOU LOSE.
Jason Todd became Robin after Dick Grayson.
Hoping to harness the rage that had driven him throughout his life, I taught him how to fight.
HERE LIES
He knows all my secrets.
...and he has been dead for years...

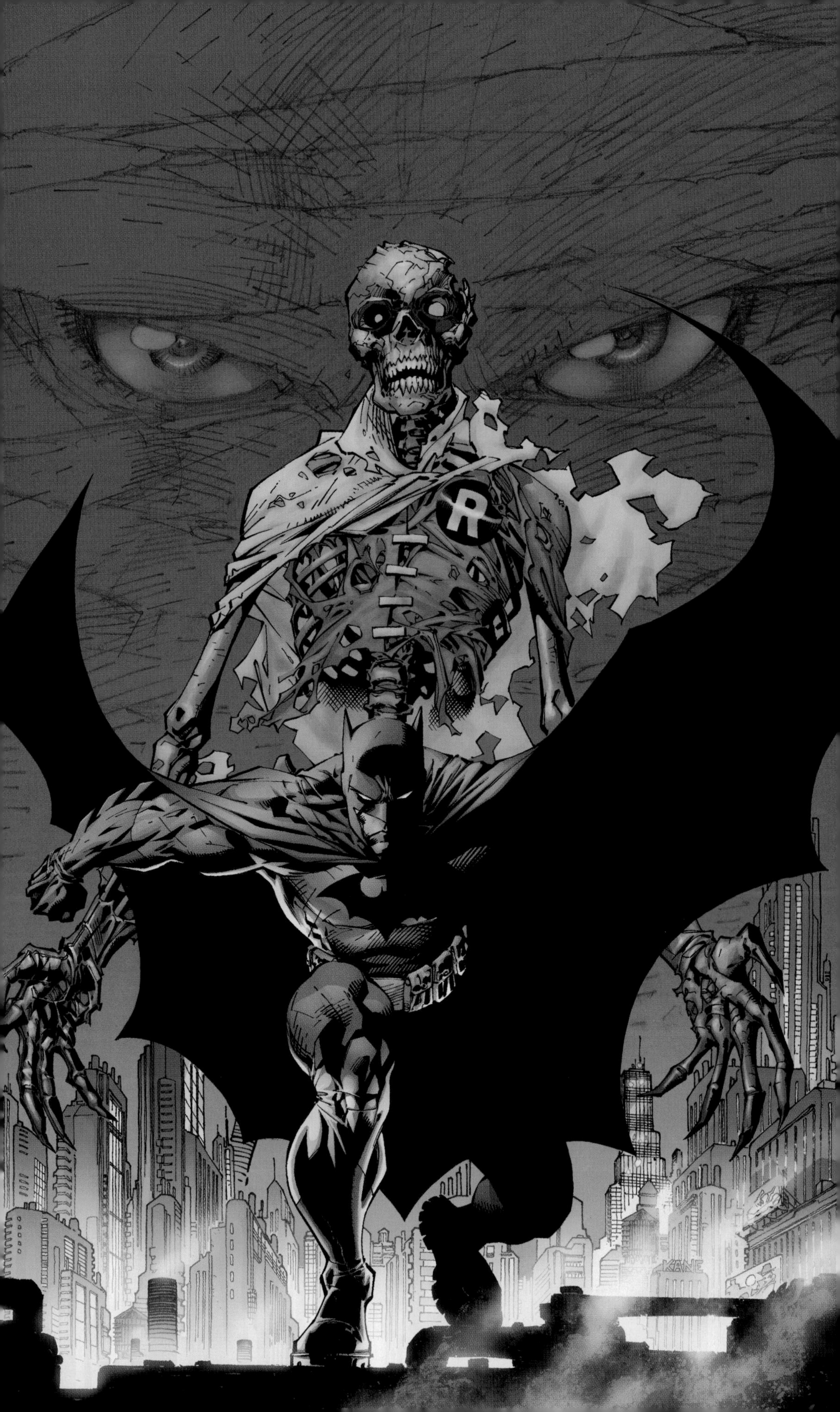
KANE

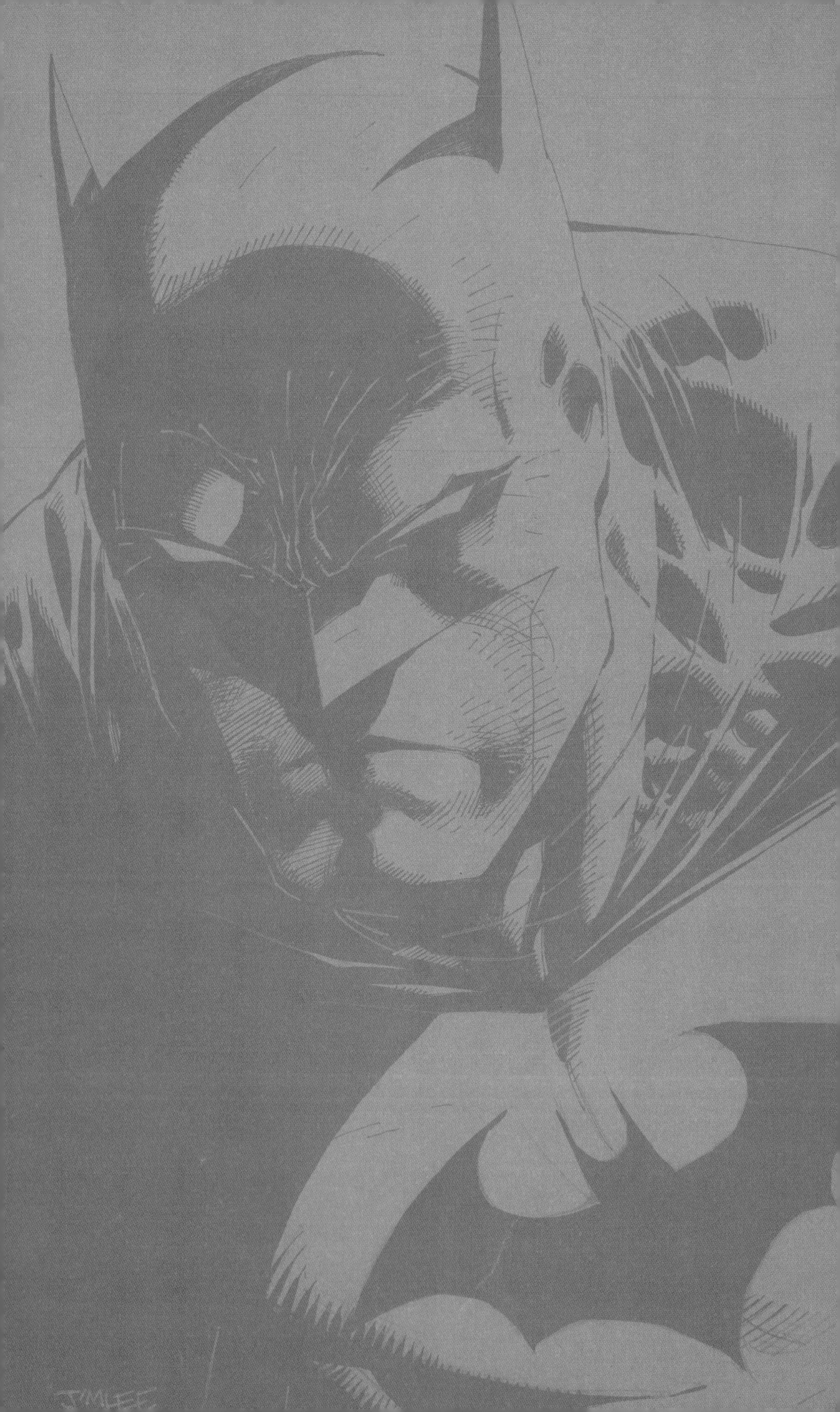

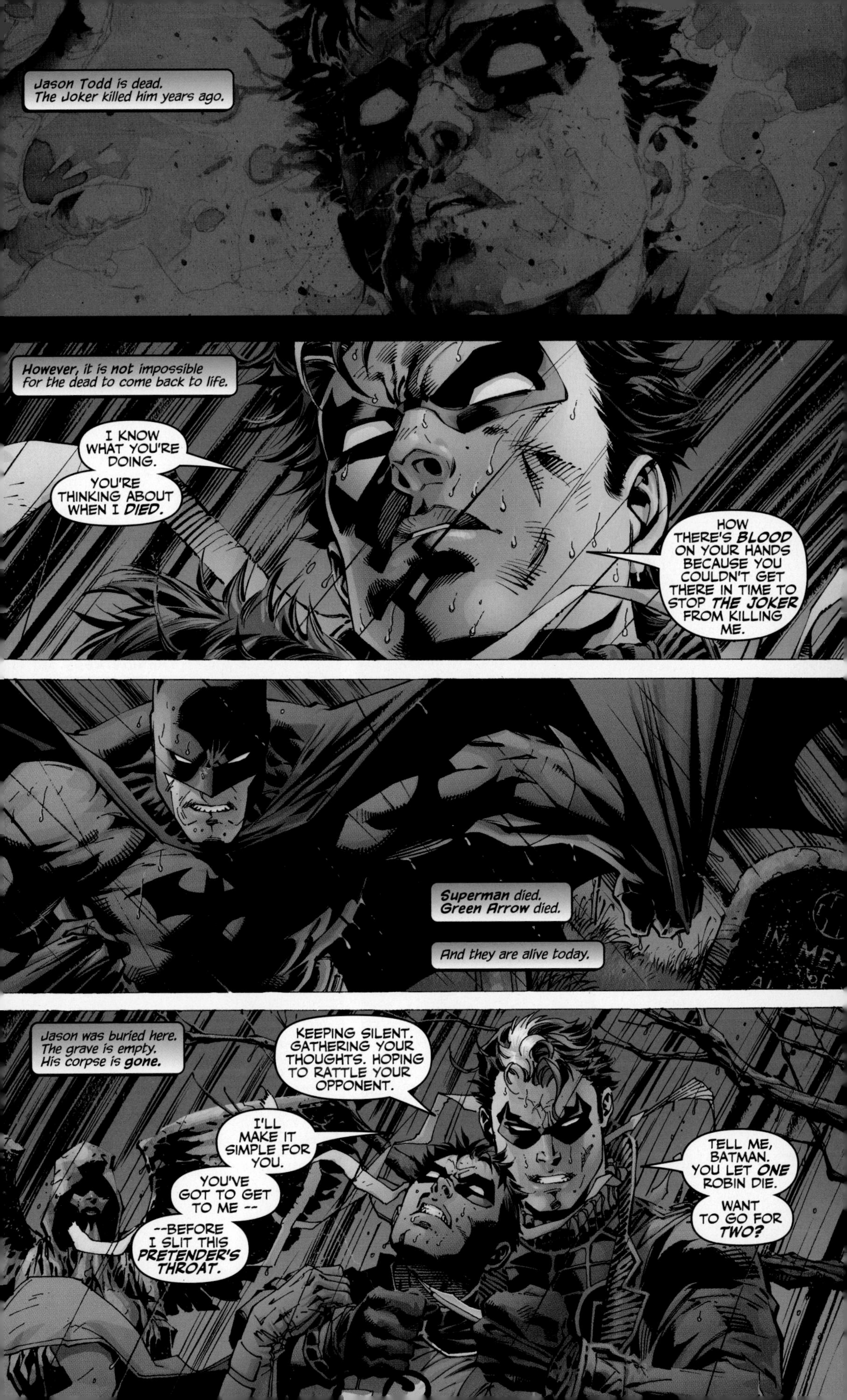
Jason Todd is dead. The Joker killed him years ago.
However, it is not impossible for the dead to come back to life.
I KNOW WHAT YOU'RE DOING.
YOU'RE THINKING ABOUT WHEN I DIED.
HOW THERE'S BLOOD ON YOUR HANDS BECAUSE YOU COULDN'T GET THERE IN TIME TO STOP THE JOKER FROM KILLING ME.
Superman died. Green Arrow died.
And they are alive today.
Jason was buried here. The grave is empty. His corpse is gone.
KEEPING SILENT. GATHERING YOUR THOUGHTS. HOPING TO RATTLE YOUR OPPONENT.
I'LL MAKE IT SIMPLE FOR YOU.
YOU'VE GOT TO GET TO ME --
--BEFORE I SLIT THIS PRETENDER'S THROAT.
TELL ME, BATMAN. YOU LET ONE ROBIN DIE.
WANT TO GO FOR TWO?

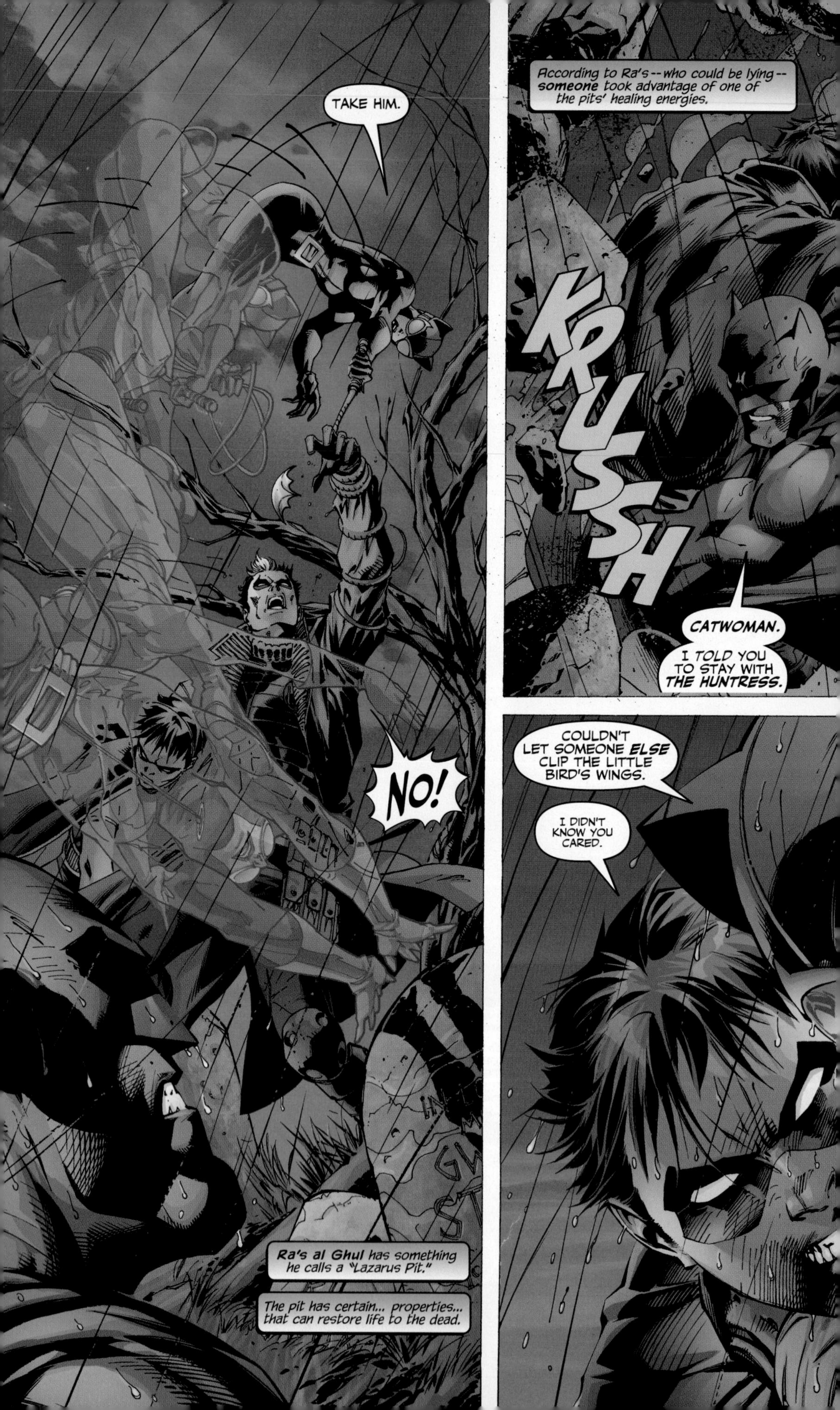

TAKE HIM.
NO!
Ra's al Ghul has something he calls a "Lazarus Pit."
The pit has certain... properties... that can restore life to the dead.
According to Ra's--who could be lying--someone took advantage of one of the pits' healing energies.
KRUSH
CATWOMAN.
I TOLD YOU TO STAY WITH THE HUNTRESS.
COULDN'T LET SOMEONE ELSE CLIP THE LITTLE BIRD'S WINGS.
I DIDN'T KNOW YOU CARED.

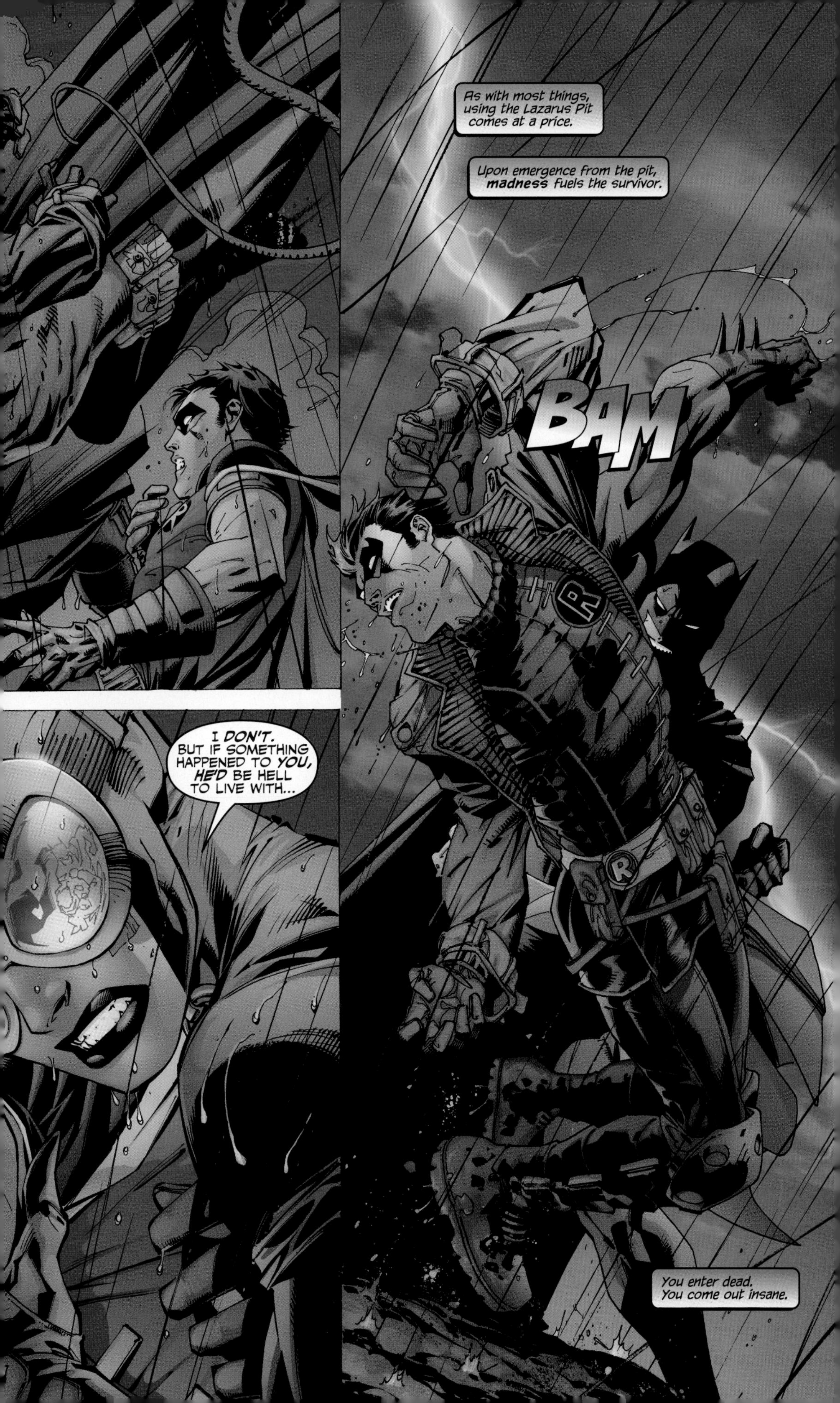
I DON'T. BUT IF SOMETHING HAPPENED TO YOU, HE'D BE HELL TO LIVE WITH...
As with most things, using the Lazarus Pit comes at a price.
Upon emergence from the pit, madness fuels the survivor.
BAM
You enter dead. You come out insane.

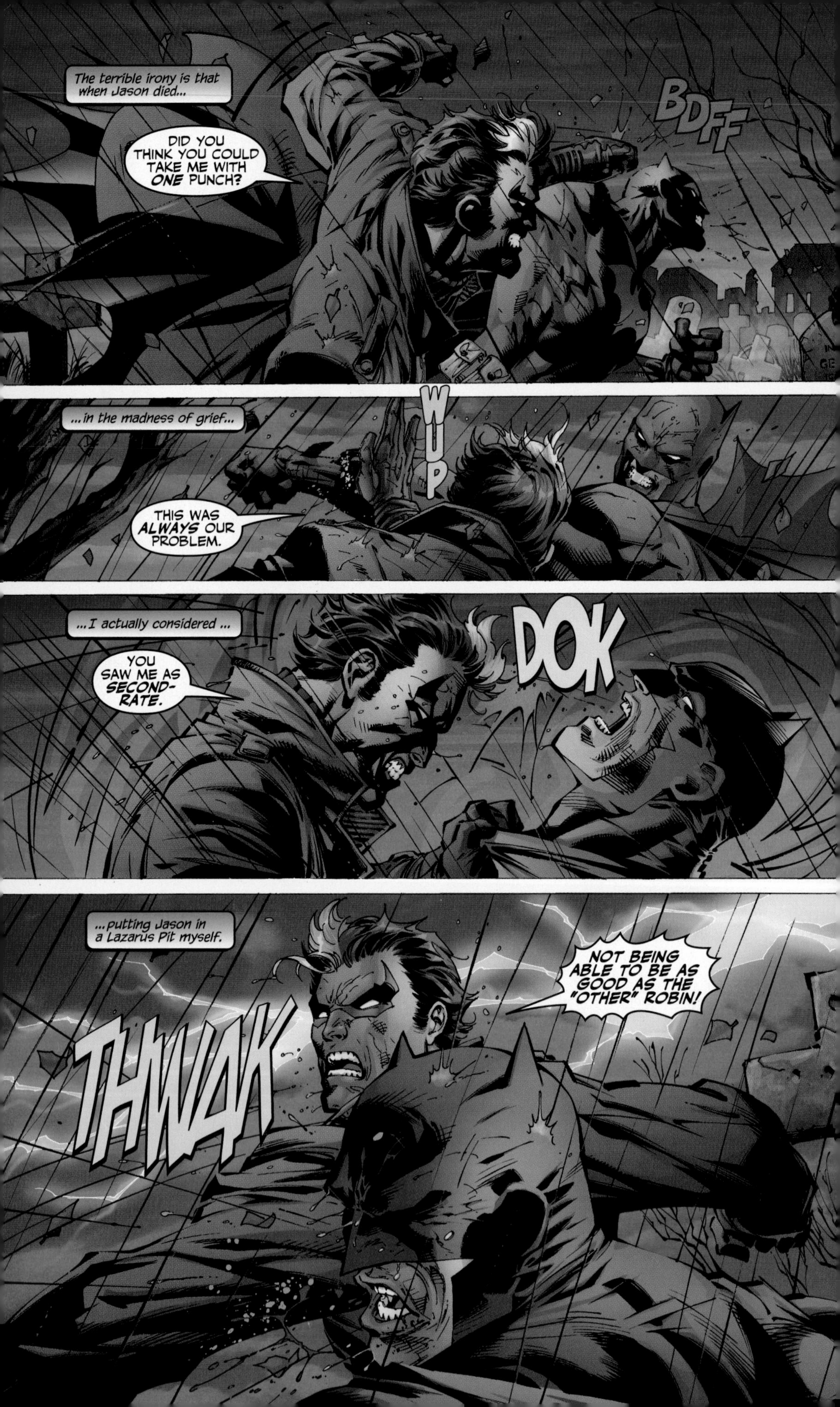

The terrible irony is that when Jason died...
DID YOU THINK YOU COULD TAKE ME WITH ONE PUNCH?
BDFF
...in the madness of grief...
WUP
THIS WAS ALWAYS OUR PROBLEM.
...I actually considered ...
YOU SAW ME AS SECOND-RATE.
DOK
...putting Jason in a Lazarus Pit myself.
NOT BEING ABLE TO BE AS GOOD AS THE "OTHER" ROBIN!
THWAK

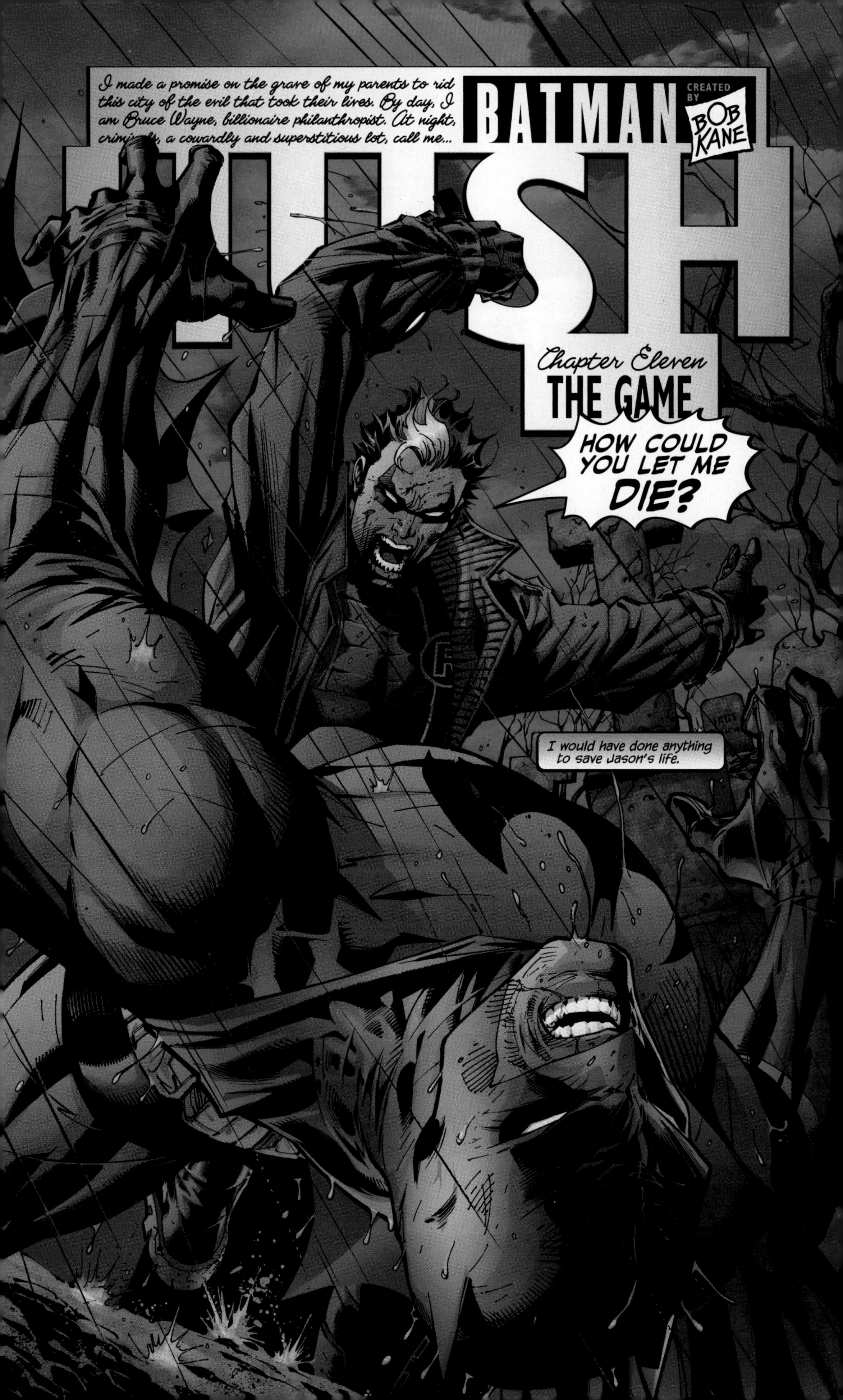
I made a promise on the grave of my parents to rid this city of the evil that took their lives. By day, I am Bruce Wayne, billionaire philanthropist. At night, criminals, a cowardly and superstitious lot, call me...
BATMAN
CREATED BY BOB KANE
HUSH
Chapter Eleven
THE GAME
HOW COULD YOU LET ME DIE?
I would have done anything to save Jason's life.

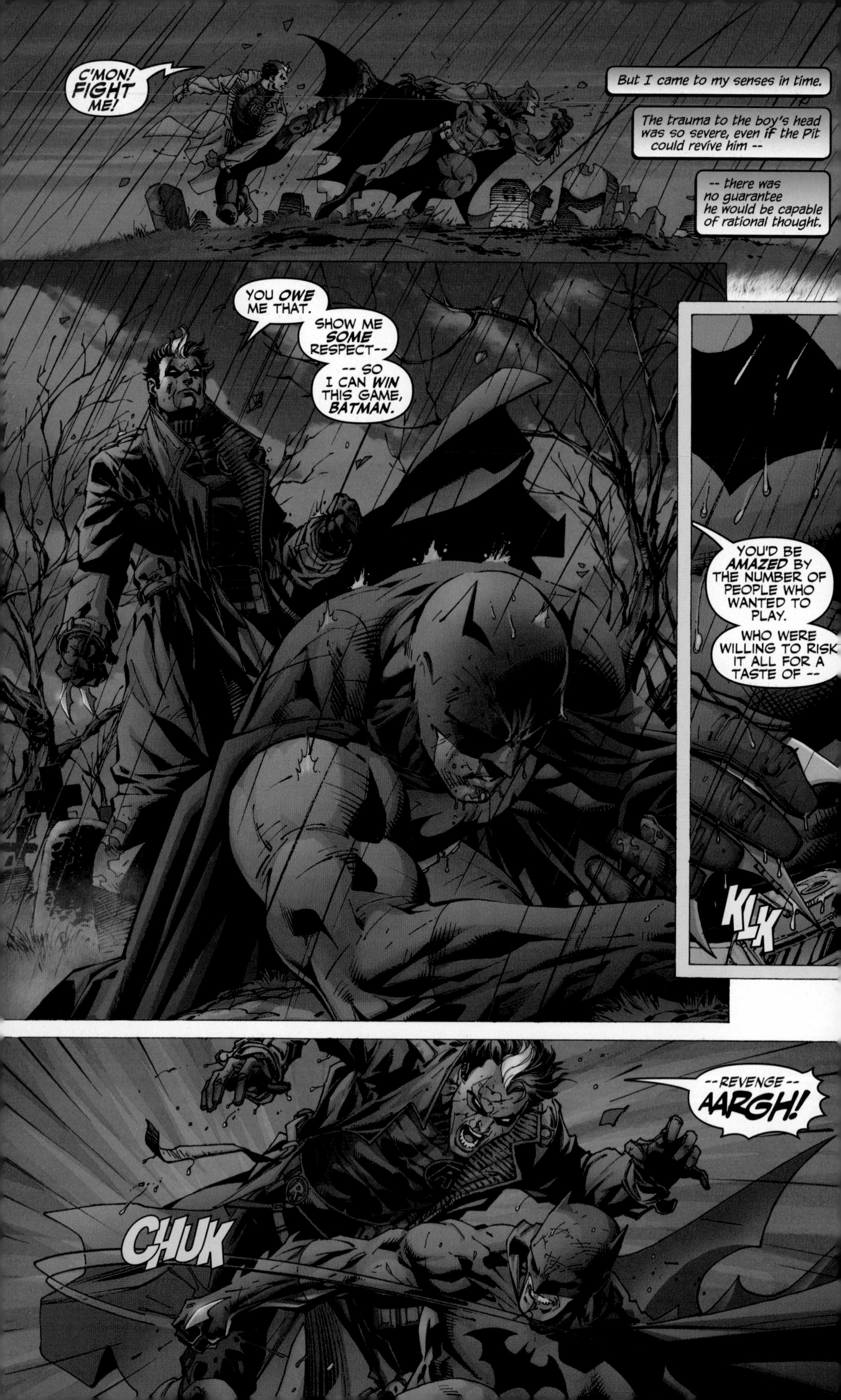

C'MON! FIGHT ME!
But I came to my senses in time.
The trauma to the boy's head was so severe, even if the Pit could revive him --
-- there was no guarantee he would be capable of rational thought.
YOU OWE ME THAT.
SHOW ME SOME RESPECT--
-- SO I CAN WIN THIS GAME, BATMAN.
YOU'D BE AMAZED BY THE NUMBER OF PEOPLE WHO WANTED TO PLAY.
WHO WERE WILLING TO RISK IT ALL FOR A TASTE OF --
KLIK
--REVENGE--
AARGH!
CHUK

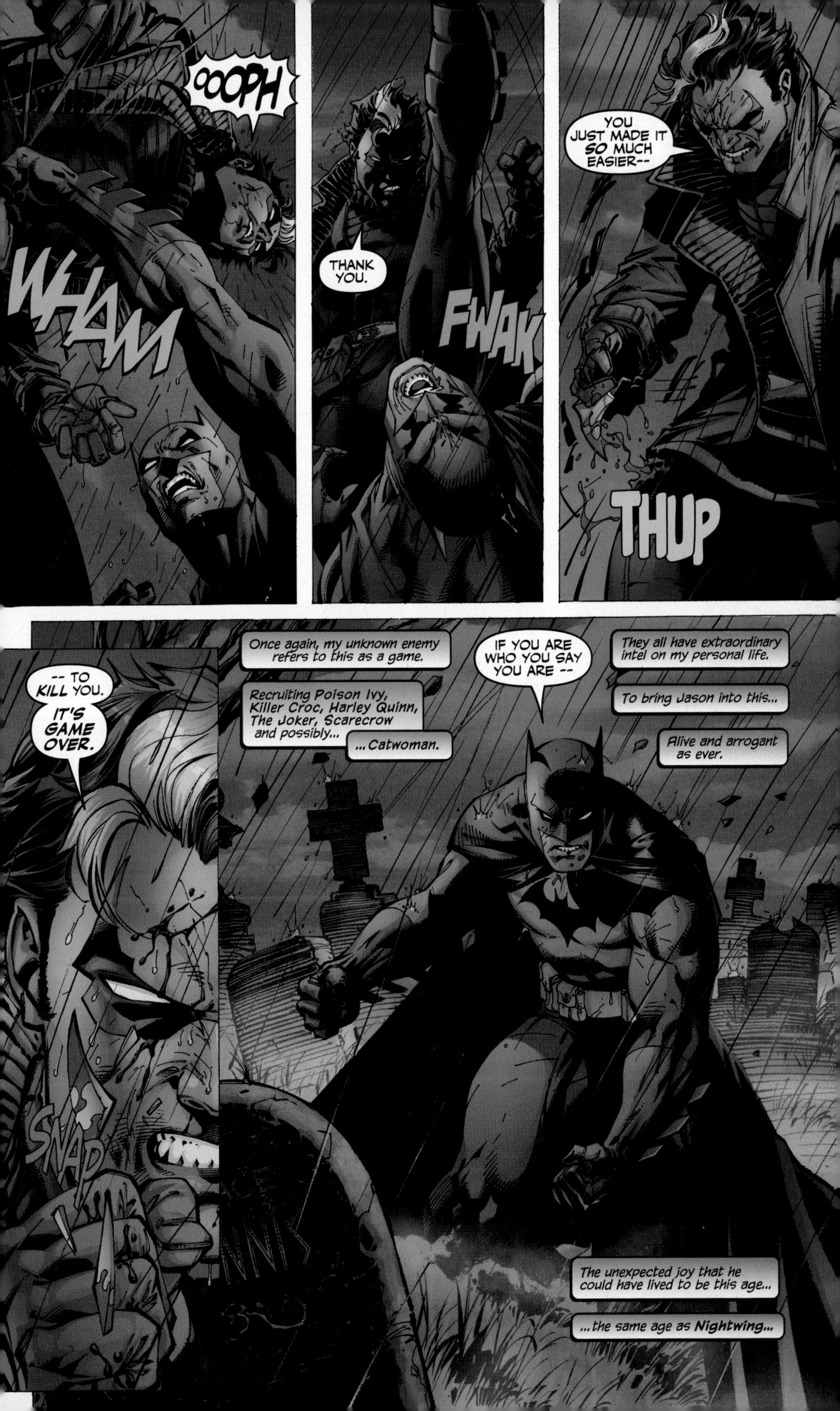
OOOPH
WHAM
THANK YOU.
FWAK
YOU JUST MADE IT SO MUCH EASIER--
THUP
-- TO KILL YOU.
IT'S GAME OVER.
SNAP
Once again, my unknown enemy refers to this as a game.
Recruiting Poison Ivy, Killer Croc, Harley Quinn, The Joker, Scarecrow and possibly...
...Catwoman.
IF YOU ARE WHO YOU SAY YOU ARE --
They all have extraordinary intel on my personal life.
To bring Jason into this...
Alive and arrogant as ever.
The unexpected joy that he could have lived to be this age...
...the same age as Nightwing...

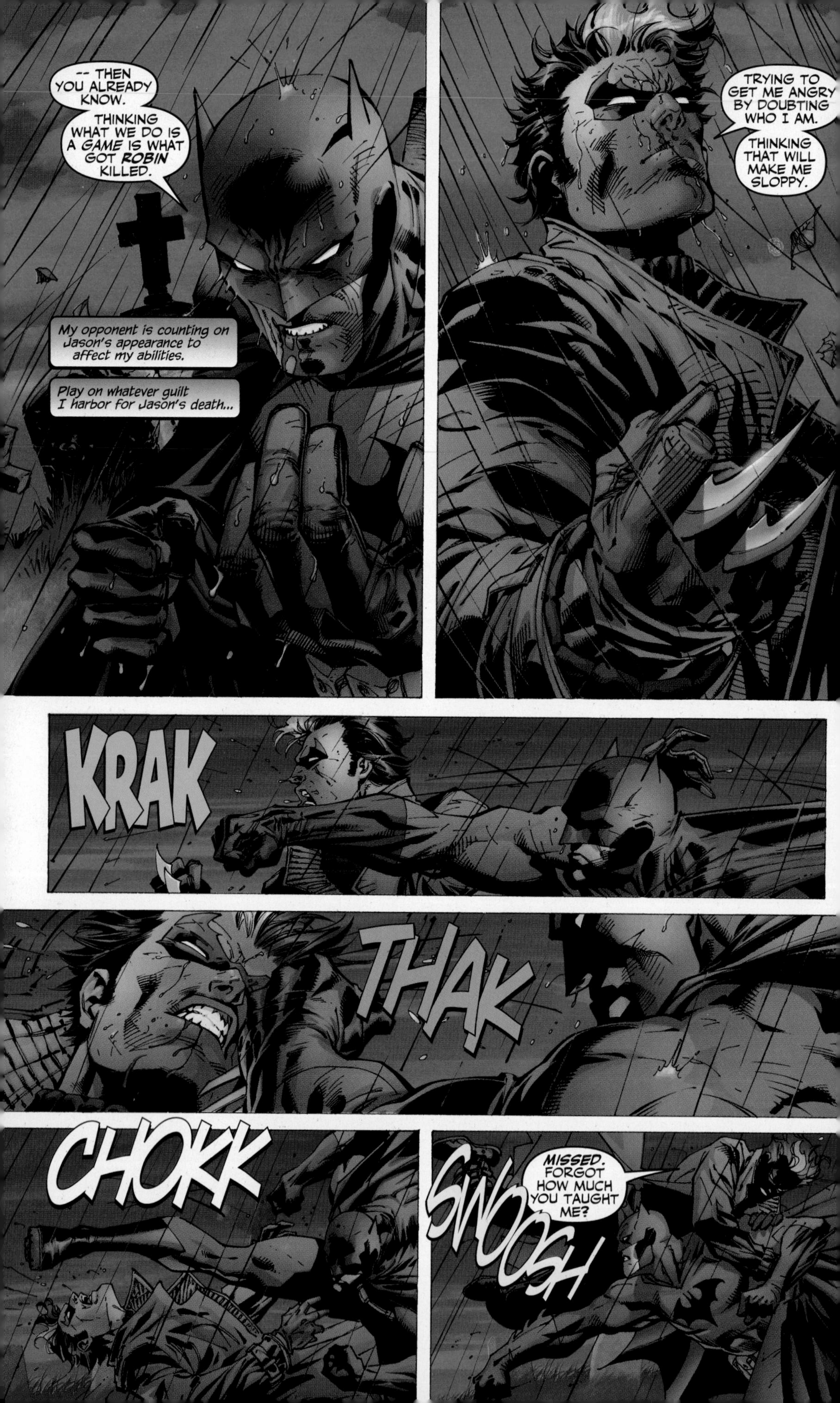
-- THEN YOU ALREADY KNOW.
THINKING WHAT WE DO IS A *GAME* IS WHAT GOT ***ROBIN*** KILLED.
My opponent is counting on Jason's appearance to affect my abilities.
Play on whatever guilt I harbor for Jason's death...
TRYING TO GET ME ANGRY BY DOUBTING WHO I AM.
THINKING THAT WILL MAKE ME SLOPPY.
KRAK
THAK
CHOKK
SWOOSH
MISSED. FORGOT HOW MUCH YOU TAUGHT ME?

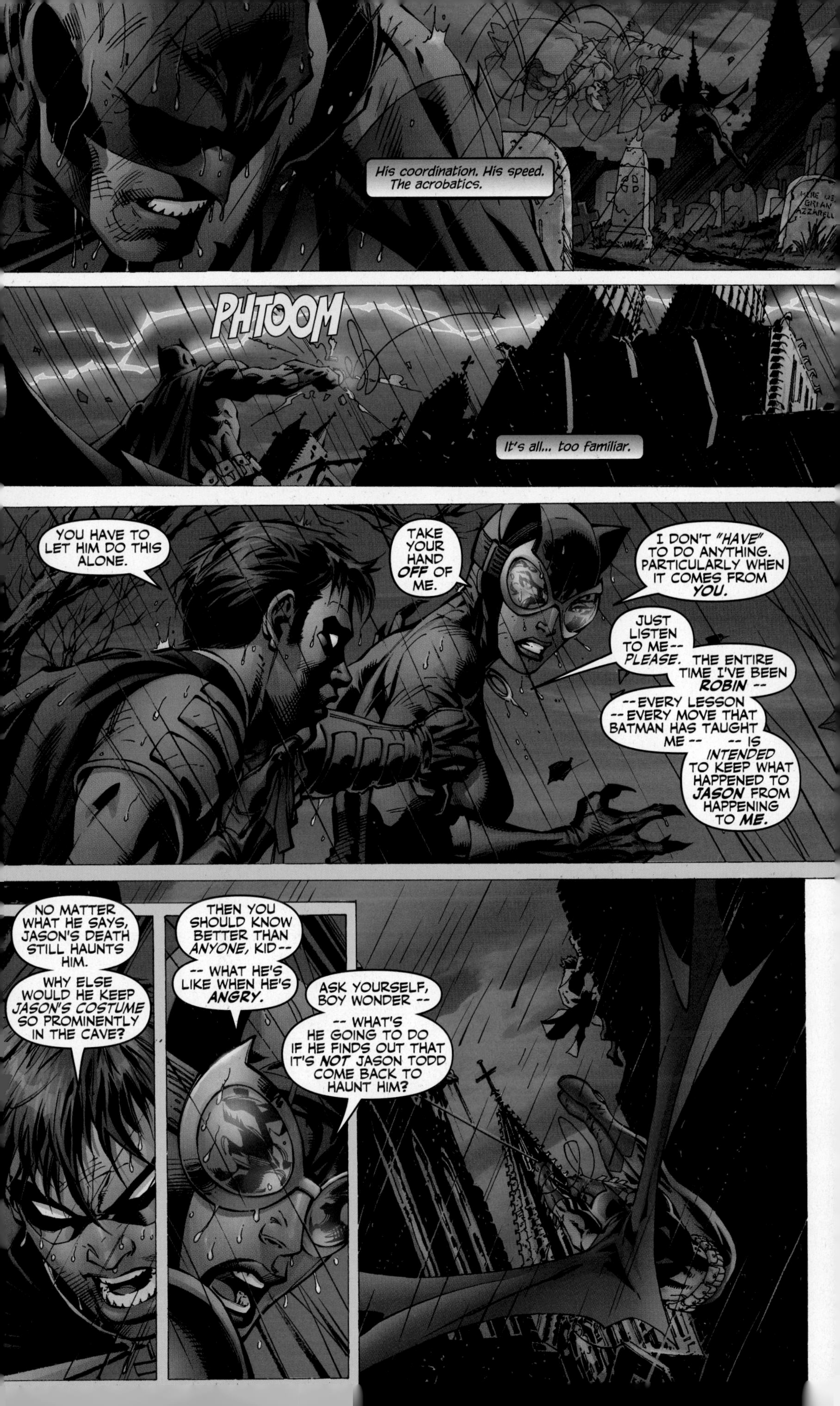

His coordination. His speed. The acrobatics.
PHTOOM
It's all... too familiar.
YOU HAVE TO LET HIM DO THIS ALONE.
TAKE YOUR HAND OFF OF ME.
I DON'T "HAVE" TO DO ANYTHING. PARTICULARLY WHEN IT COMES FROM YOU.
JUST LISTEN TO ME-- PLEASE. THE ENTIRE TIME I'VE BEEN ROBIN --
--EVERY LESSON --EVERY MOVE THAT BATMAN HAS TAUGHT ME --
-- IS INTENDED TO KEEP WHAT HAPPENED TO JASON FROM HAPPENING TO ME.
NO MATTER WHAT HE SAYS, JASON'S DEATH STILL HAUNTS HIM.
WHY ELSE WOULD HE KEEP JASON'S COSTUME SO PROMINENTLY IN THE CAVE?
THEN YOU SHOULD KNOW BETTER THAN ANYONE, KID--
-- WHAT HE'S LIKE WHEN HE'S ANGRY.
ASK YOURSELF, BOY WONDER --
-- WHAT'S HE GOING TO DO IF HE FINDS OUT THAT IT'S NOT JASON TODD COME BACK TO HAUNT HIM?

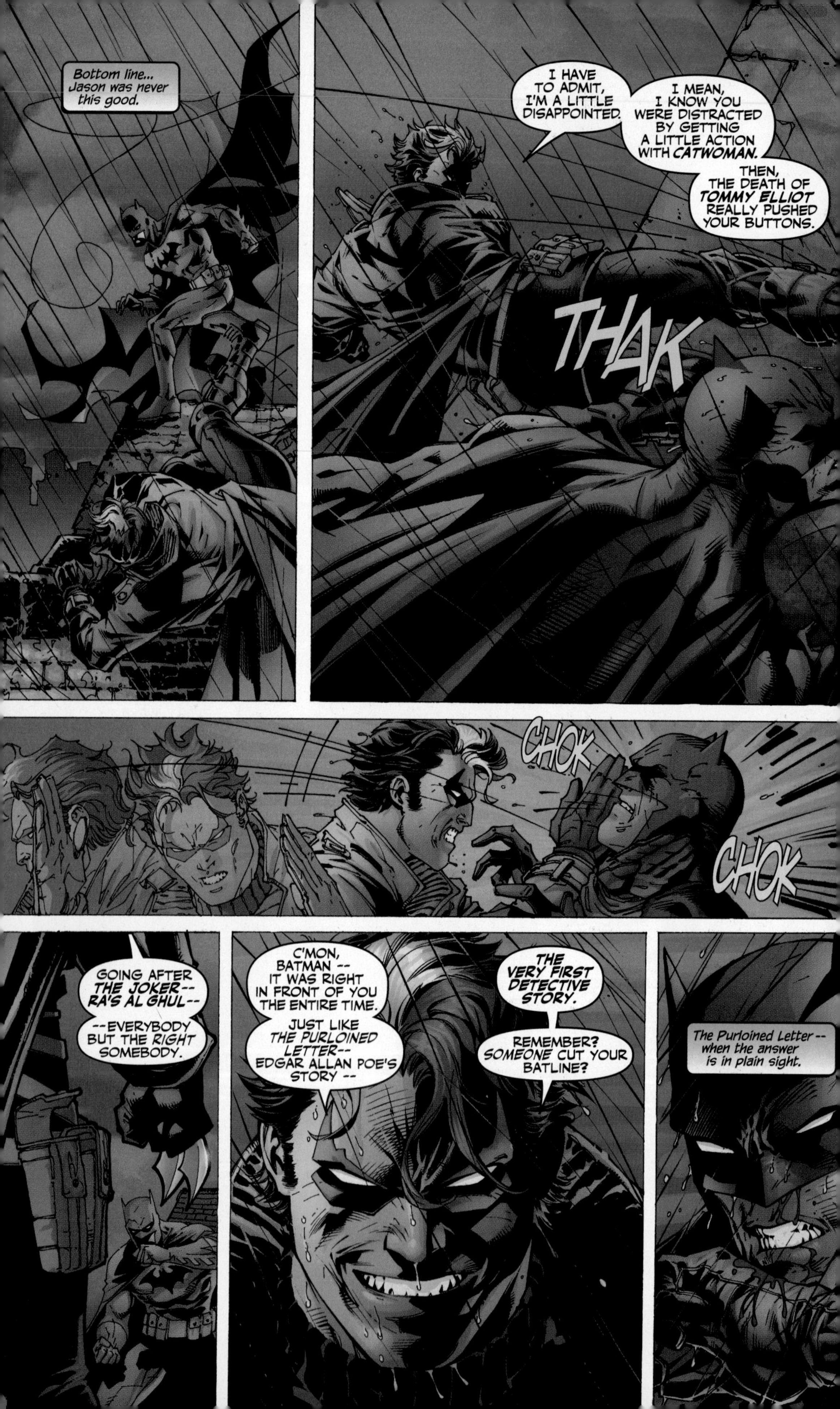
Bottom line... Jason was never this good.
I HAVE TO ADMIT, I'M A LITTLE DISAPPOINTED.
I MEAN, I KNOW YOU WERE DISTRACTED BY GETTING A LITTLE ACTION WITH CATWOMAN.
THEN, THE DEATH OF TOMMY ELLIOT REALLY PUSHED YOUR BUTTONS.
THAK
CHOK
CHOK
GOING AFTER THE JOKER-- RA'S AL GHUL--
--EVERYBODY BUT THE RIGHT SOMEBODY.
C'MON, BATMAN -- IT WAS RIGHT IN FRONT OF YOU THE ENTIRE TIME.
JUST LIKE THE PURLOINED LETTER-- EDGAR ALLAN POE'S STORY --
THE VERY FIRST DETECTIVE STORY.
REMEMBER? SOMEONE CUT YOUR BATLINE?
The Purloined Letter -- when the answer is in plain sight.

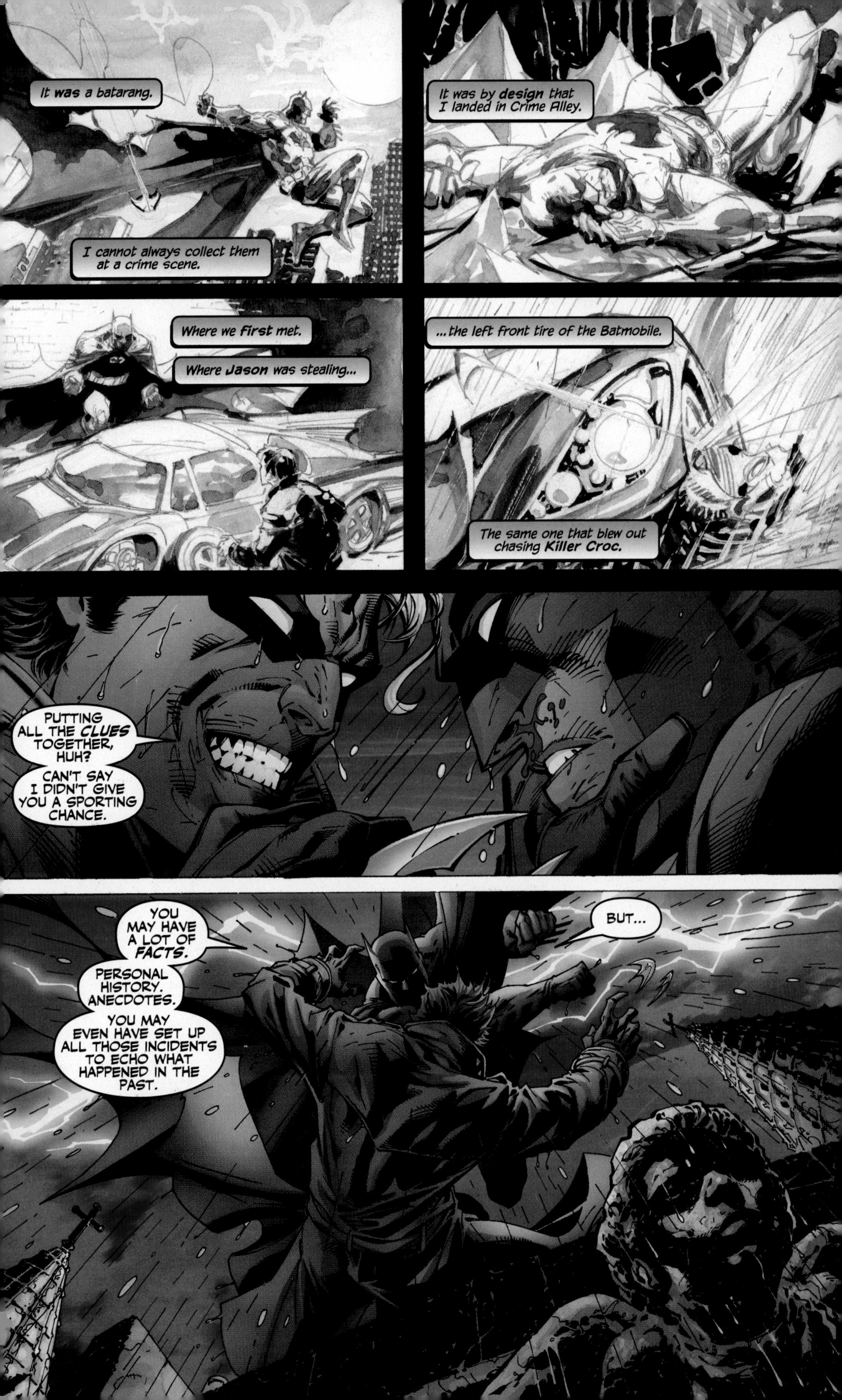
It was a batarang.
I cannot always collect them at a crime scene.
It was by design that I landed in Crime Alley.
Where we first met.
Where Jason was stealing...
...the left front tire of the Batmobile.
The same one that blew out chasing Killer Croc.
PUTTING ALL THE CLUES TOGETHER, HUH?
CAN'T SAY I DIDN'T GIVE YOU A SPORTING CHANCE.
YOU MAY HAVE A LOT OF FACTS.
PERSONAL HISTORY. ANECDOTES.
YOU MAY EVEN HAVE SET UP ALL THOSE INCIDENTS TO ECHO WHAT HAPPENED IN THE PAST.
BUT...

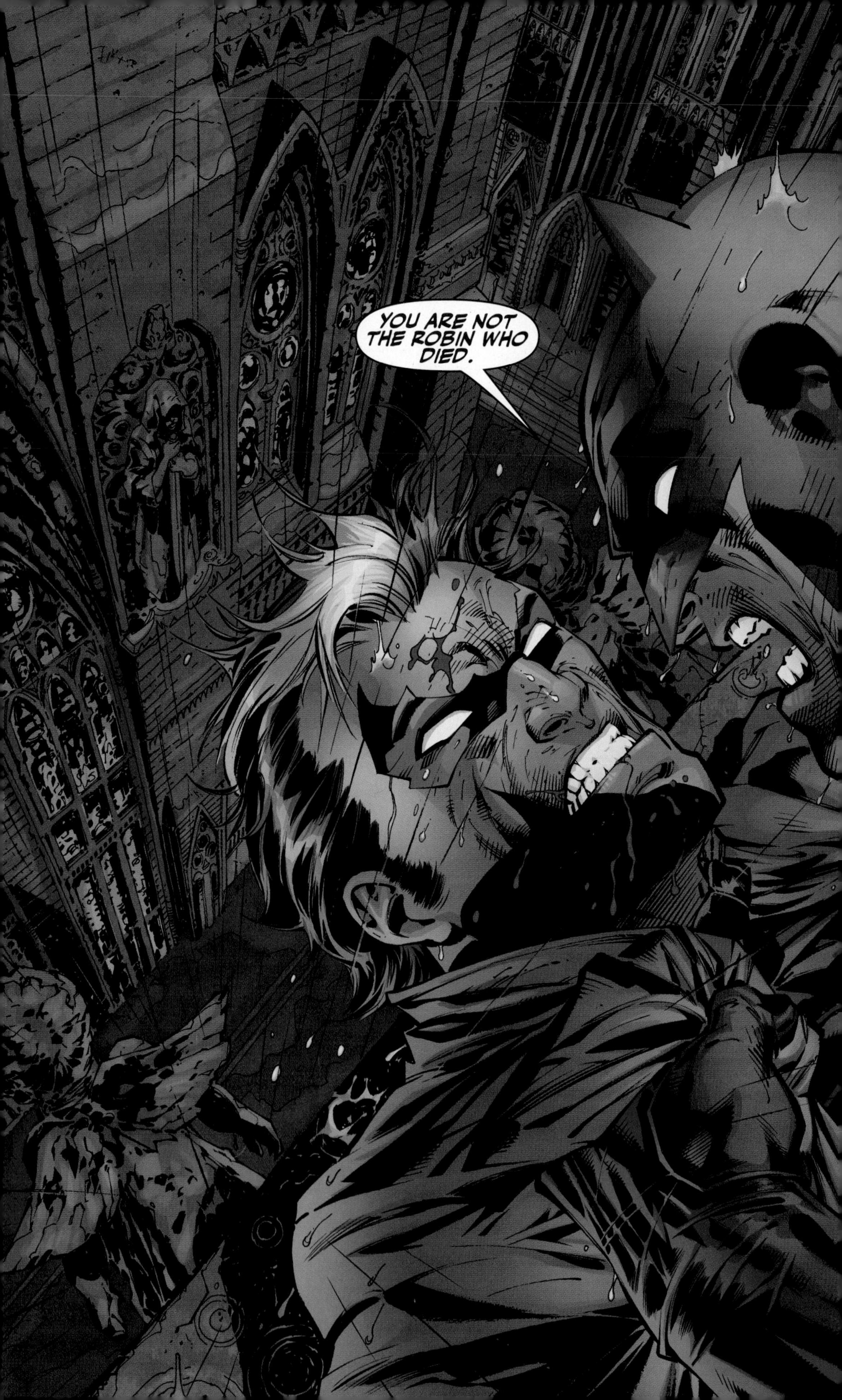
YOU ARE NOT THE ROBIN WHO DIED.

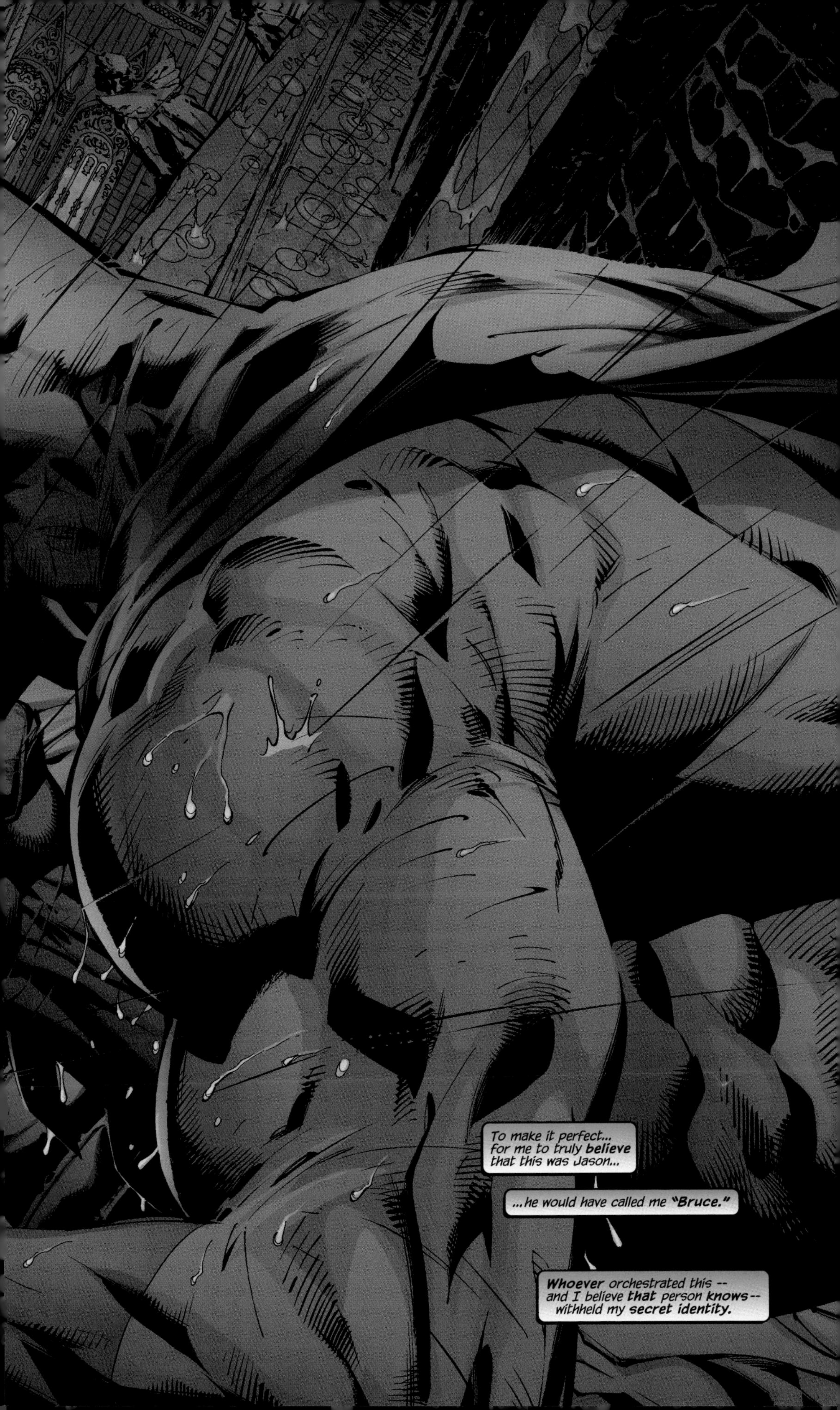
To make it perfect... for me to truly believe that this was Jason...
...he would have called me "Bruce."
Whoever orchestrated this -- and I believe that person knows-- withheld my secret identity.

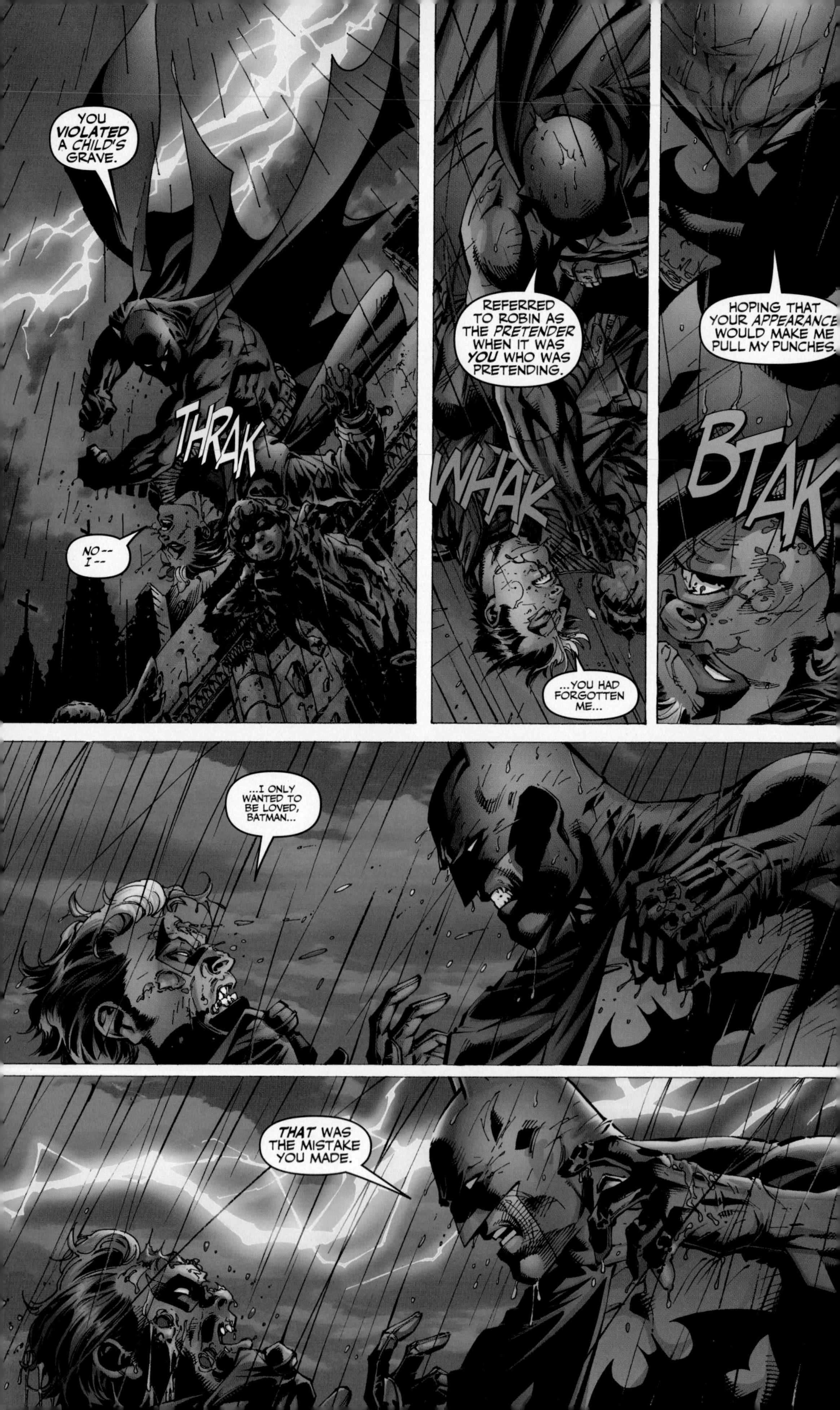
YOU VIOLATED A CHILD'S GRAVE.
THRAK
NO-- I--
REFERRED TO ROBIN AS THE PRETENDER WHEN IT WAS YOU WHO WAS PRETENDING.
WHAK
...YOU HAD FORGOTTEN ME...
HOPING THAT YOUR APPEARANCE WOULD MAKE ME PULL MY PUNCHES.
BTAK
...I ONLY WANTED TO BE LOVED, BATMAN...
THAT WAS THE MISTAKE YOU MADE.

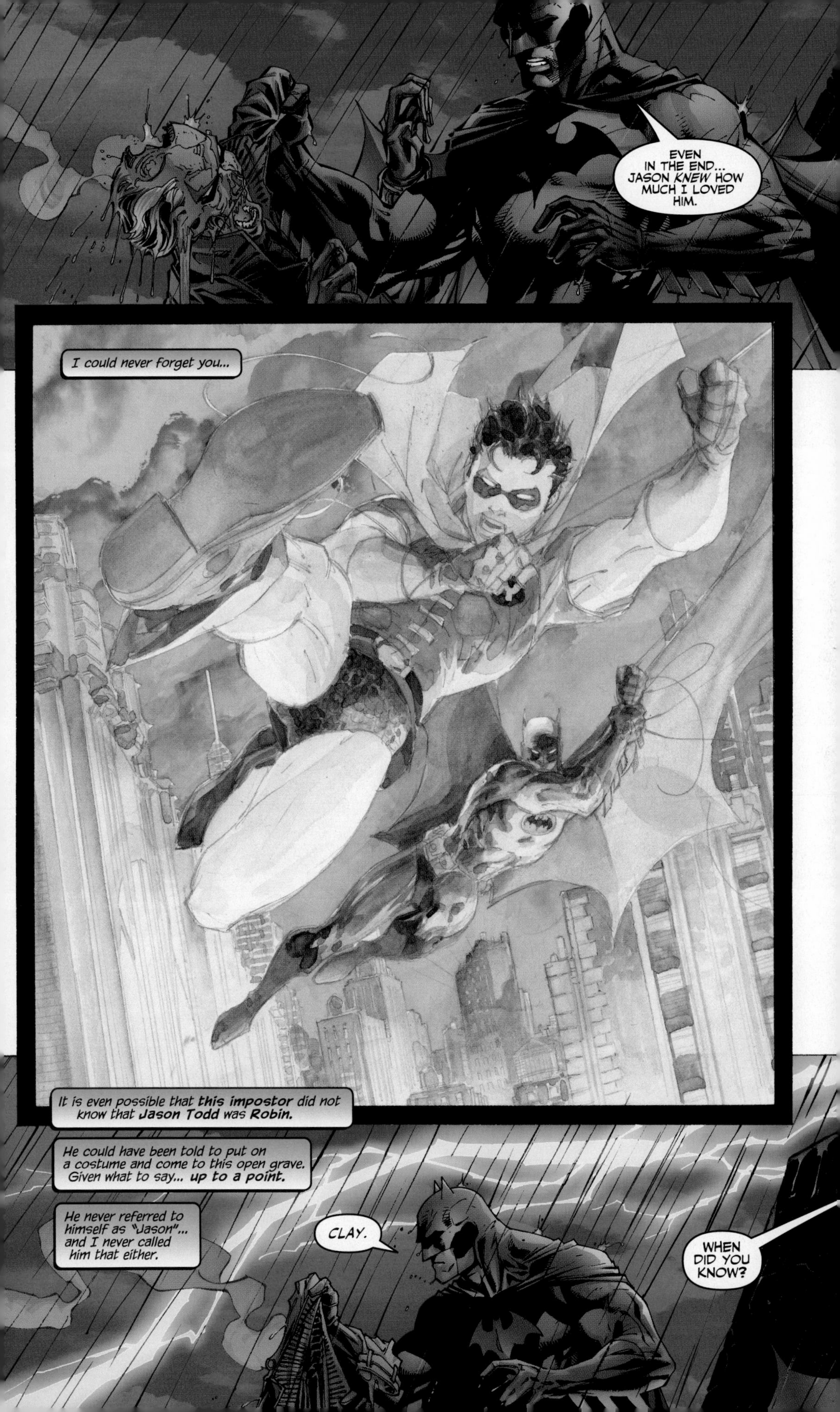
EVEN IN THE END... JASON *KNEW* HOW MUCH I LOVED HIM.
I could never forget you...
It is even possible that **this impostor** did not know that **Jason Todd** was **Robin.**
He could have been told to put on a costume and come to this open grave. Given what to say... **up to a point.**
He never referred to himself as "Jason"... and I never called him that either.
CLAY.
WHEN DID YOU KNOW?

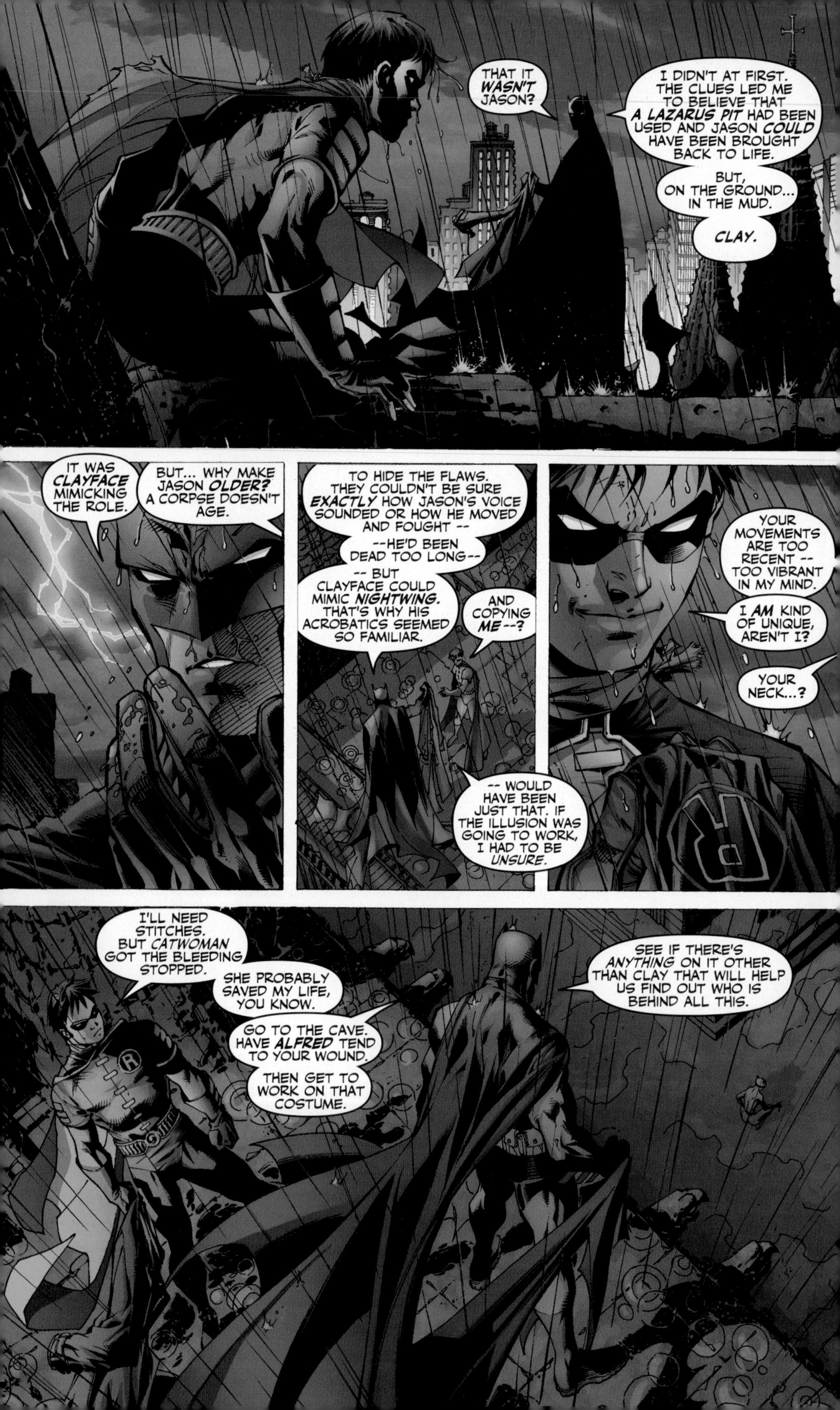
THAT IT WASN'T JASON?
I DIDN'T AT FIRST. THE CLUES LED ME TO BELIEVE THAT A LAZARUS PIT HAD BEEN USED AND JASON COULD HAVE BEEN BROUGHT BACK TO LIFE.
BUT, ON THE GROUND... IN THE MUD.
CLAY.
IT WAS CLAYFACE MIMICKING THE ROLE.
BUT... WHY MAKE JASON OLDER? A CORPSE DOESN'T AGE.
TO HIDE THE FLAWS. THEY COULDN'T BE SURE EXACTLY HOW JASON'S VOICE SOUNDED OR HOW HE MOVED AND FOUGHT --
--HE'D BEEN DEAD TOO LONG--
-- BUT CLAYFACE COULD MIMIC NIGHTWING. THAT'S WHY HIS ACROBATICS SEEMED SO FAMILIAR.
AND COPYING ME--?
-- WOULD HAVE BEEN JUST THAT. IF THE ILLUSION WAS GOING TO WORK, I HAD TO BE UNSURE.
YOUR MOVEMENTS ARE TOO RECENT -- TOO VIBRANT IN MY MIND.
I AM KIND OF UNIQUE, AREN'T I?
YOUR NECK...?
I'LL NEED STITCHES. BUT CATWOMAN GOT THE BLEEDING STOPPED.
SHE PROBABLY SAVED MY LIFE, YOU KNOW.
GO TO THE CAVE. HAVE ALFRED TEND TO YOUR WOUND.
THEN GET TO WORK ON THAT COSTUME.
SEE IF THERE'S ANYTHING ON IT OTHER THAN CLAY THAT WILL HELP US FIND OUT WHO IS BEHIND ALL THIS.

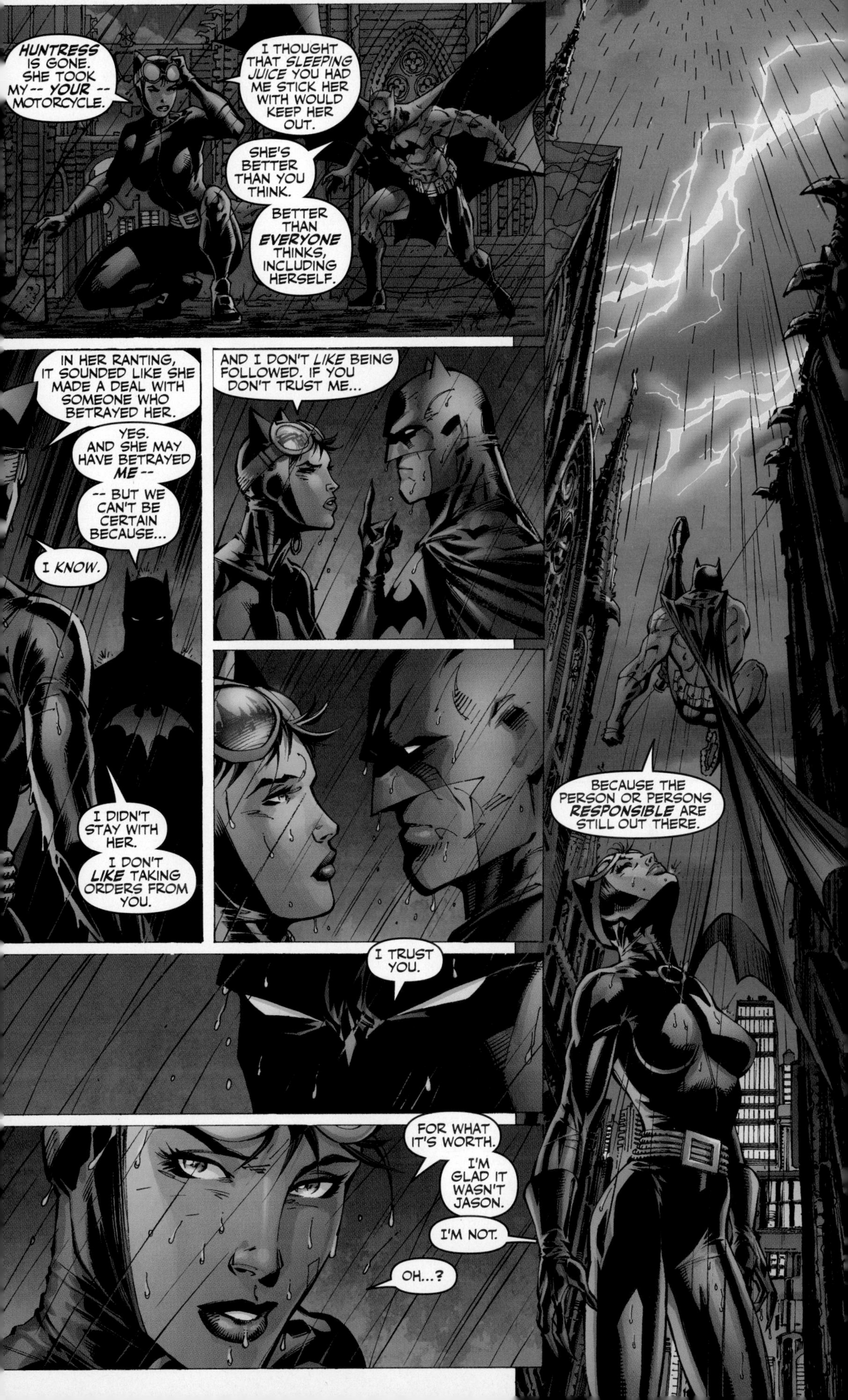
HUNTRESS IS GONE. SHE TOOK MY-- YOUR -- MOTORCYCLE.
I THOUGHT THAT SLEEPING JUICE YOU HAD ME STICK HER WITH WOULD KEEP HER OUT.
SHE'S BETTER THAN YOU THINK.
BETTER THAN EVERYONE THINKS, INCLUDING HERSELF.
IN HER RANTING, IT SOUNDED LIKE SHE MADE A DEAL WITH SOMEONE WHO BETRAYED HER.
YES. AND SHE MAY HAVE BETRAYED ME --
-- BUT WE CAN'T BE CERTAIN BECAUSE...
I KNOW.
I DIDN'T STAY WITH HER.
I DON'T LIKE TAKING ORDERS FROM YOU.
AND I DON'T LIKE BEING FOLLOWED. IF YOU DON'T TRUST ME...
I TRUST YOU.
FOR WHAT IT'S WORTH.
I'M GLAD IT WASN'T JASON.
I'M NOT.
OH...?
BECAUSE THE PERSON OR PERSONS RESPONSIBLE ARE STILL OUT THERE.

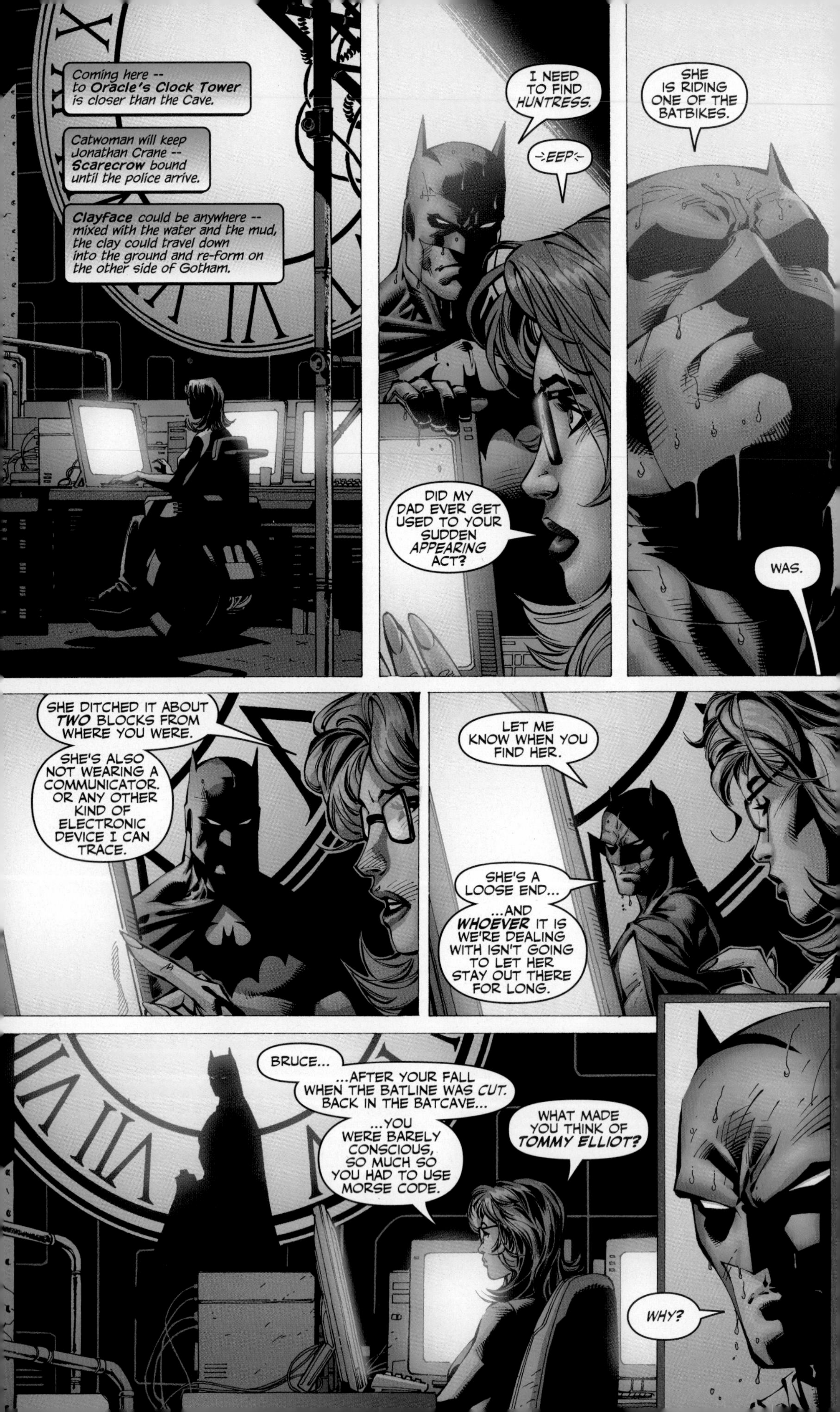
Coming here -- to Oracle's Clock Tower is closer than the Cave.
Catwoman will keep Jonathan Crane -- Scarecrow bound until the police arrive.
Clayface could be anywhere -- mixed with the water and the mud, the clay could travel down into the ground and re-form on the other side of Gotham.
I NEED TO FIND HUNTRESS.
EEP
SHE IS RIDING ONE OF THE BATBIKES.
DID MY DAD EVER GET USED TO YOUR SUDDEN APPEARING ACT?
WAS.
SHE DITCHED IT ABOUT TWO BLOCKS FROM WHERE YOU WERE.
SHE'S ALSO NOT WEARING A COMMUNICATOR. OR ANY OTHER KIND OF ELECTRONIC DEVICE I CAN TRACE.
LET ME KNOW WHEN YOU FIND HER.
SHE'S A LOOSE END...
...AND WHOEVER IT IS WE'RE DEALING WITH ISN'T GOING TO LET HER STAY OUT THERE FOR LONG.
BRUCE...
...AFTER YOUR FALL WHEN THE BATLINE WAS CUT. BACK IN THE BATCAVE...
...YOU WERE BARELY CONSCIOUS, SO MUCH SO YOU HAD TO USE MORSE CODE.
WHAT MADE YOU THINK OF TOMMY ELLIOT?
WHY?

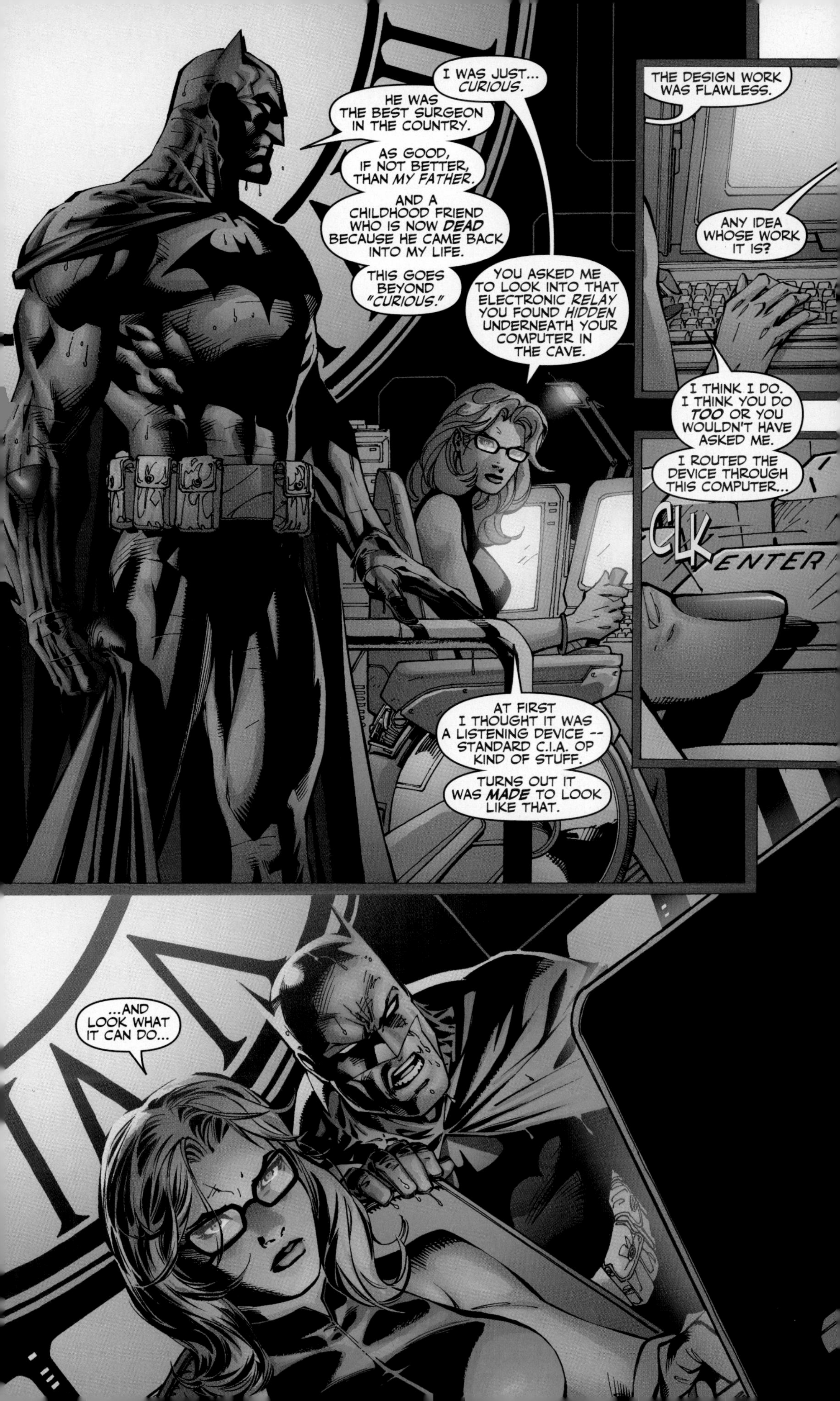

I WAS JUST... CURIOUS.
HE WAS THE BEST SURGEON IN THE COUNTRY.
AS GOOD, IF NOT BETTER, THAN MY FATHER.
AND A CHILDHOOD FRIEND WHO IS NOW DEAD BECAUSE HE CAME BACK INTO MY LIFE.
THIS GOES BEYOND "CURIOUS."
YOU ASKED ME TO LOOK INTO THAT ELECTRONIC RELAY YOU FOUND HIDDEN UNDERNEATH YOUR COMPUTER IN THE CAVE.
AT FIRST I THOUGHT IT WAS A LISTENING DEVICE -- STANDARD C.I.A. OP KIND OF STUFF.
TURNS OUT IT WAS MADE TO LOOK LIKE THAT.
THE DESIGN WORK WAS FLAWLESS.
ANY IDEA WHOSE WORK IT IS?
I THINK I DO. I THINK YOU DO TOO OR YOU WOULDN'T HAVE ASKED ME.
I ROUTED THE DEVICE THROUGH THIS COMPUTER...
CLK
ENTER
...AND LOOK WHAT IT CAN DO...

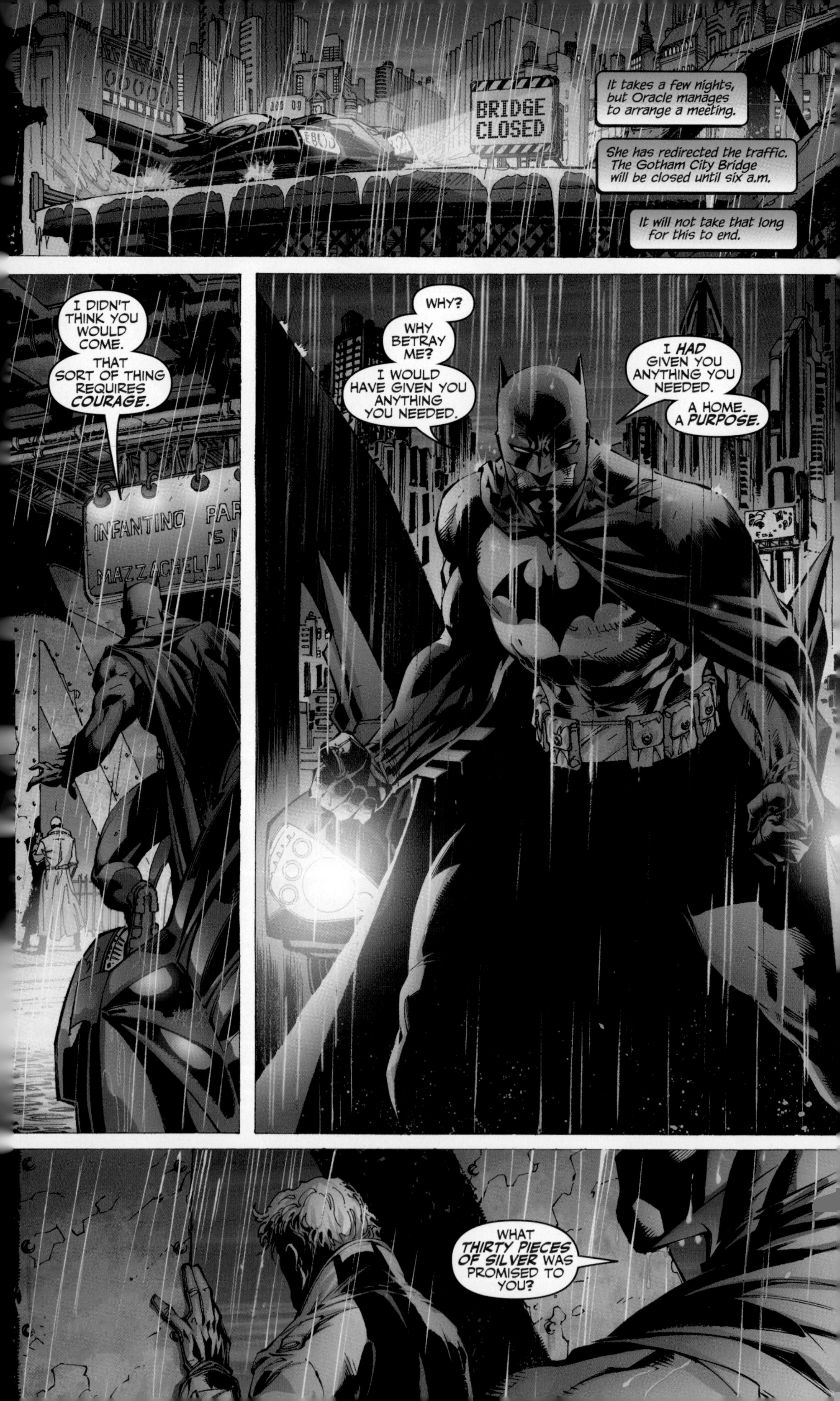

BRIDGE CLOSED
It takes a few nights, but Oracle manages to arrange a meeting.
She has redirected the traffic. The Gotham City Bridge will be closed until six a.m.
It will not take that long for this to end.
I DIDN'T THINK YOU WOULD COME.
THAT SORT OF THING REQUIRES COURAGE.
WHY?
WHY BETRAY ME?
I WOULD HAVE GIVEN YOU ANYTHING YOU NEEDED.
I HAD GIVEN YOU ANYTHING YOU NEEDED.
A HOME. A PURPOSE.
WHAT THIRTY PIECES OF SILVER WAS PROMISED TO YOU?

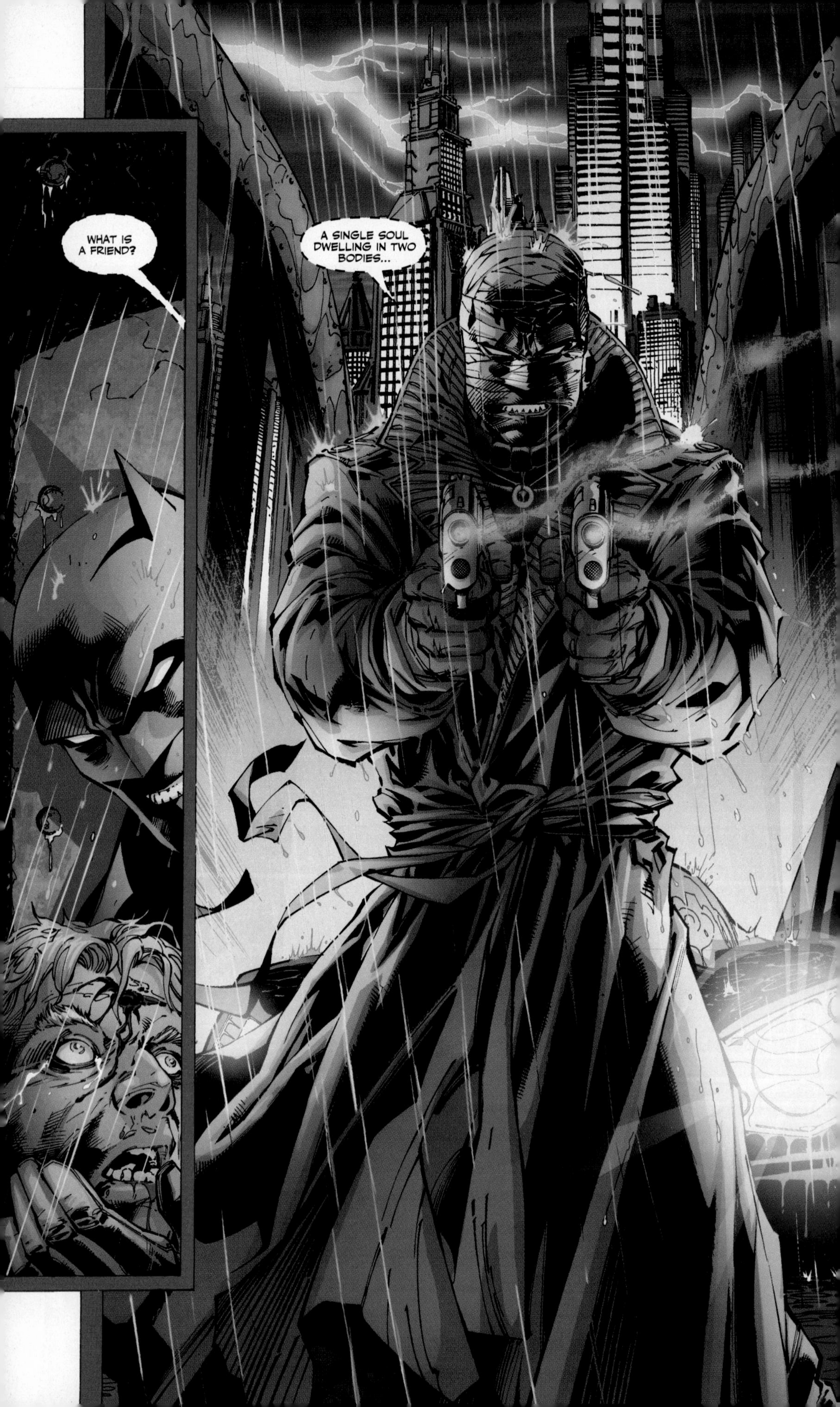
WHAT IS A FRIEND?
A SINGLE SOUL DWELLING IN TWO BODIES...

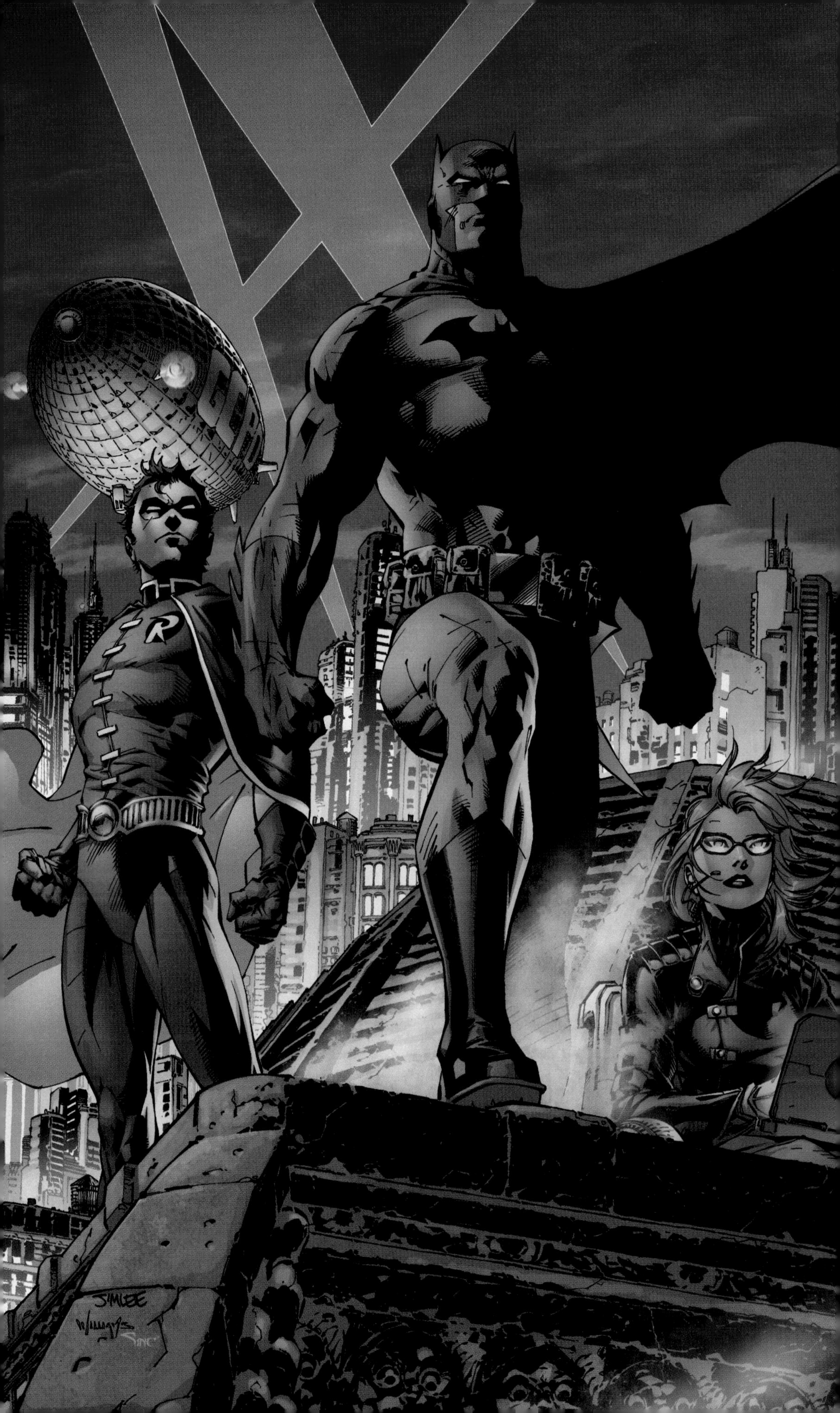

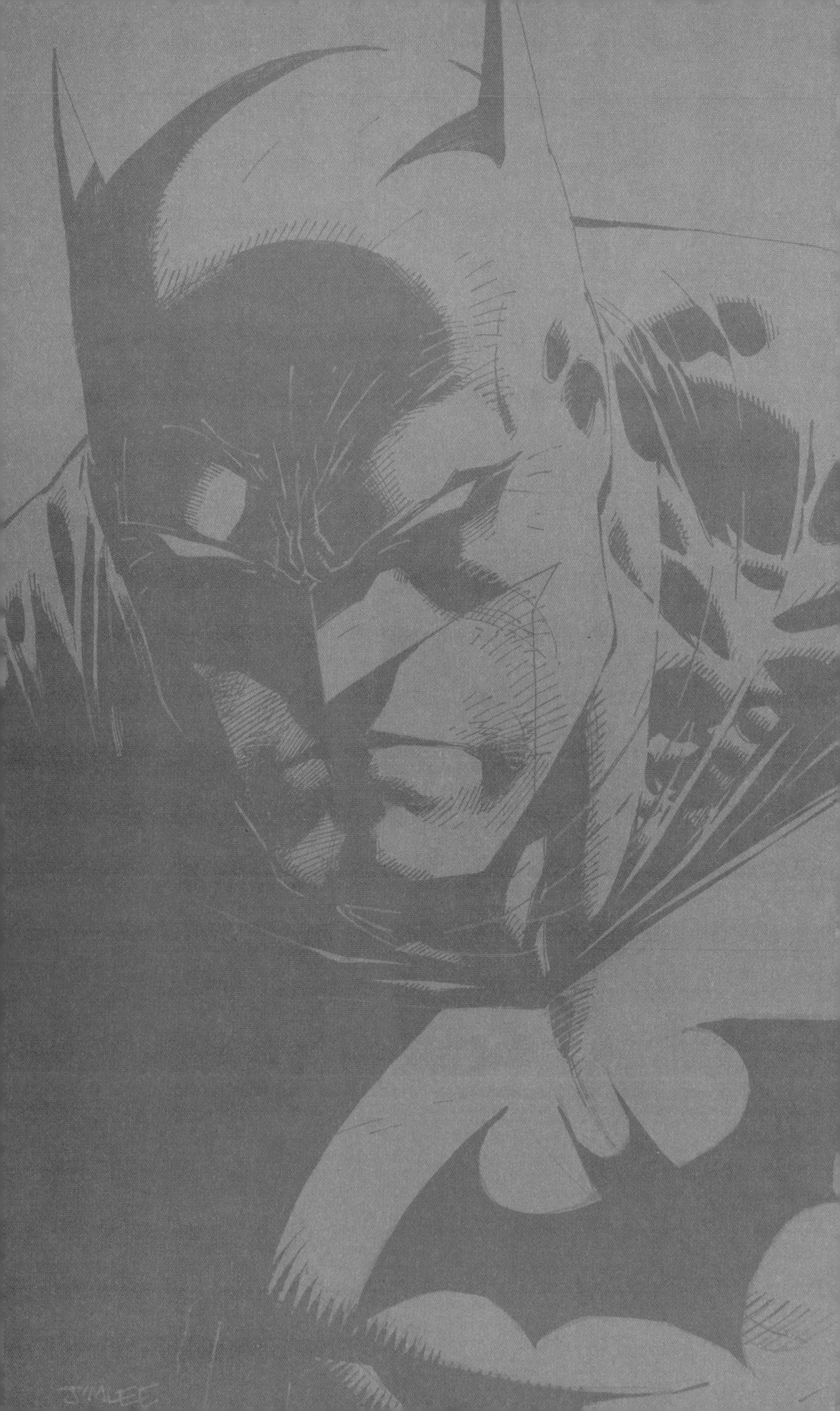
JIMLEE

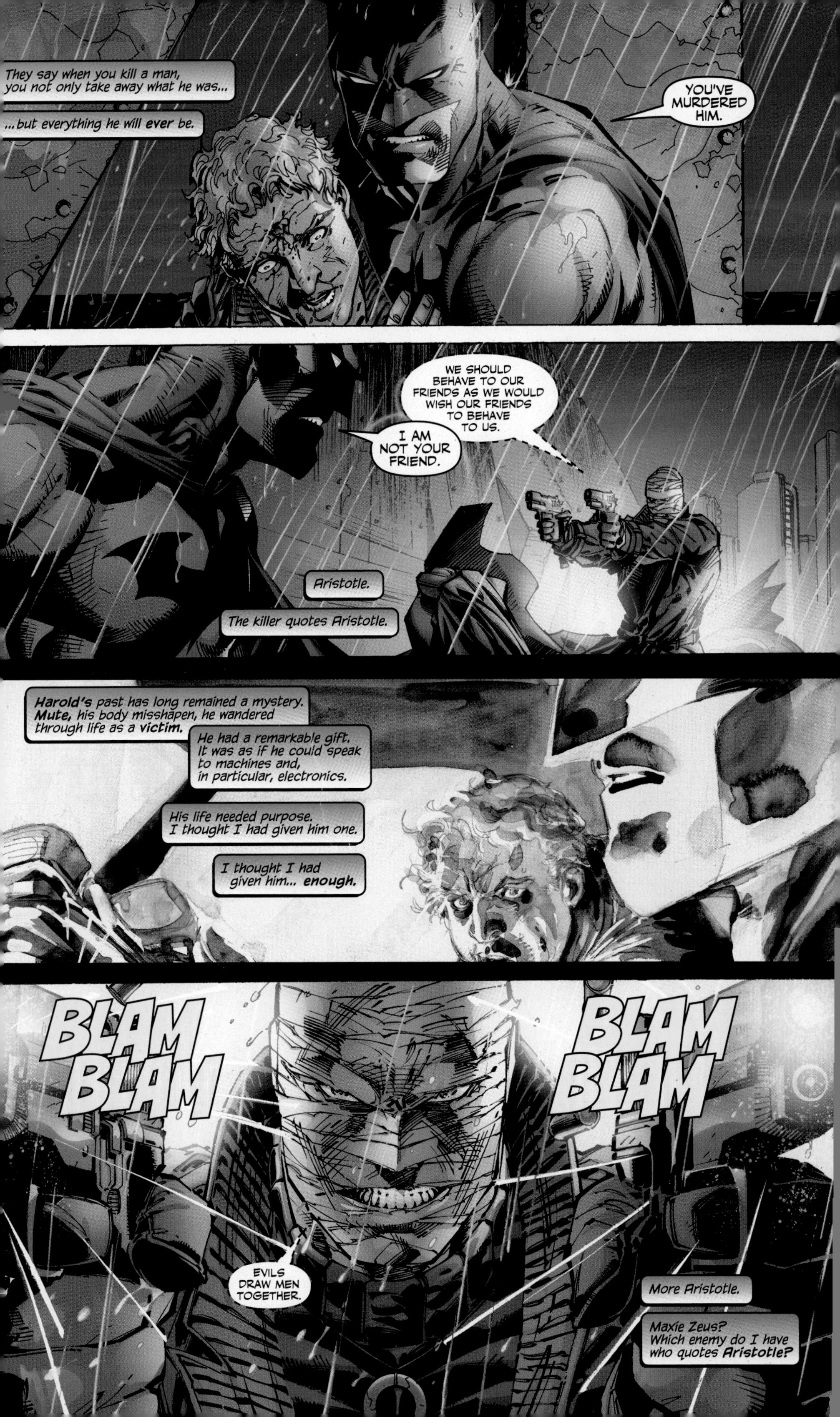
They say when you kill a man, you not only take away what he was...
...but everything he will ever be.
YOU'VE MURDERED HIM.
WE SHOULD BEHAVE TO OUR FRIENDS AS WE WOULD WISH OUR FRIENDS TO BEHAVE TO US.
I AM NOT YOUR FRIEND.
Aristotle.
The killer quotes Aristotle.
Harold's past has long remained a mystery. Mute, his body misshapen, he wandered through life as a victim.
He had a remarkable gift. It was as if he could speak to machines and, in particular, electronics.
His life needed purpose. I thought I had given him one.
I thought I had given him... enough.
BLAM BLAM
BLAM BLAM
EVILS DRAW MEN TOGETHER.
More Aristotle.
Maxie Zeus? Which enemy do I have who quotes Aristotle?

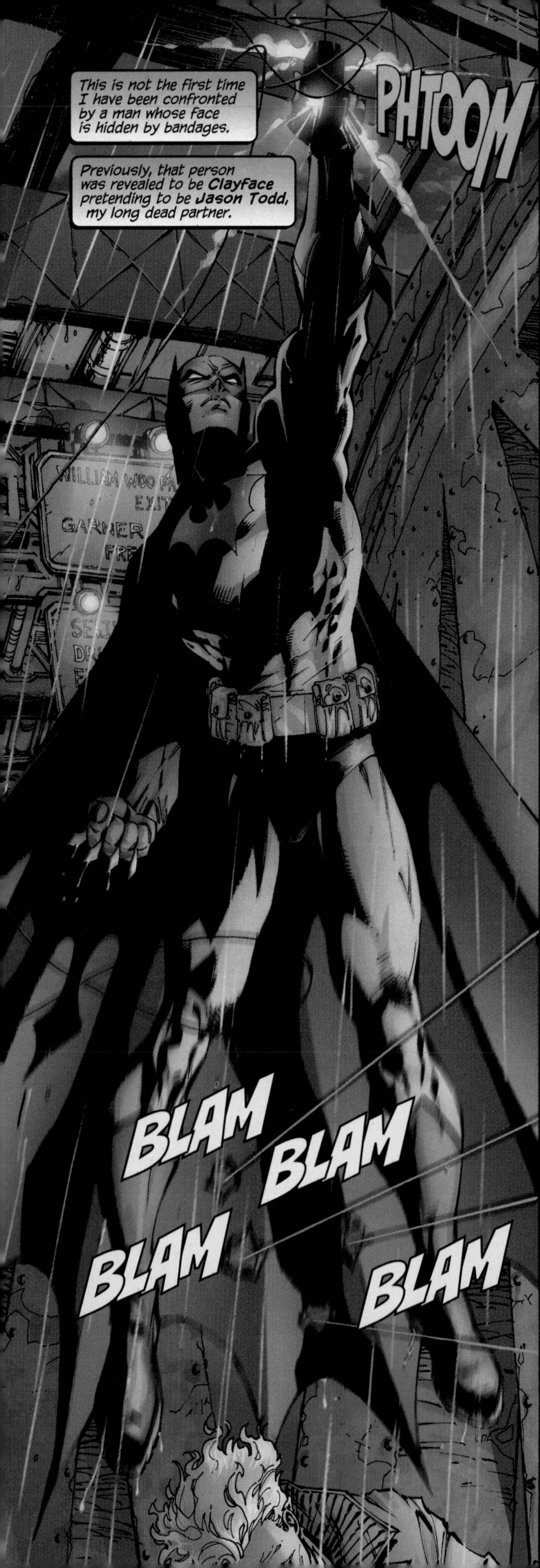
This is not the first time I have been confronted by a man whose face is hidden by bandages.
PHTOOM
Previously, that person was revealed to be **Clayface** pretending to be **Jason Todd**, my long dead partner.
GARNER
BLAM
BLAM
BLAM
BLAM

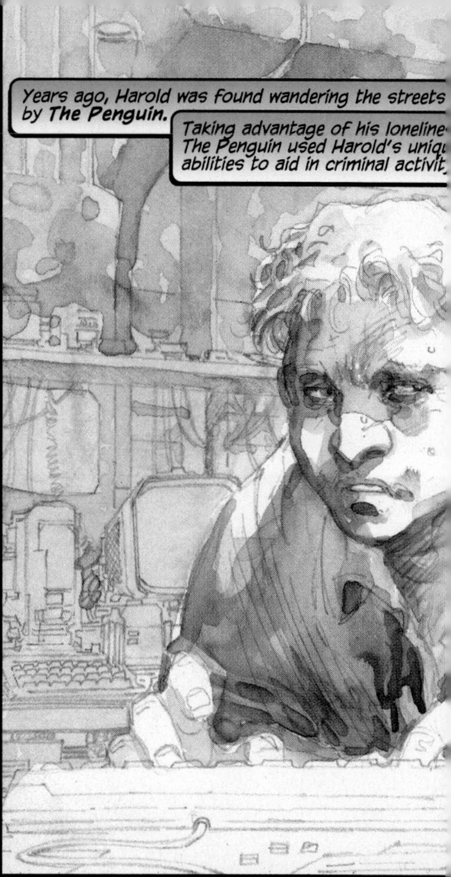
Years ago, Harold was found wandering the streets by **The Penguin.**
Taking advantage of his loneline The Penguin used Harold's uniq abilities to aid in criminal activit

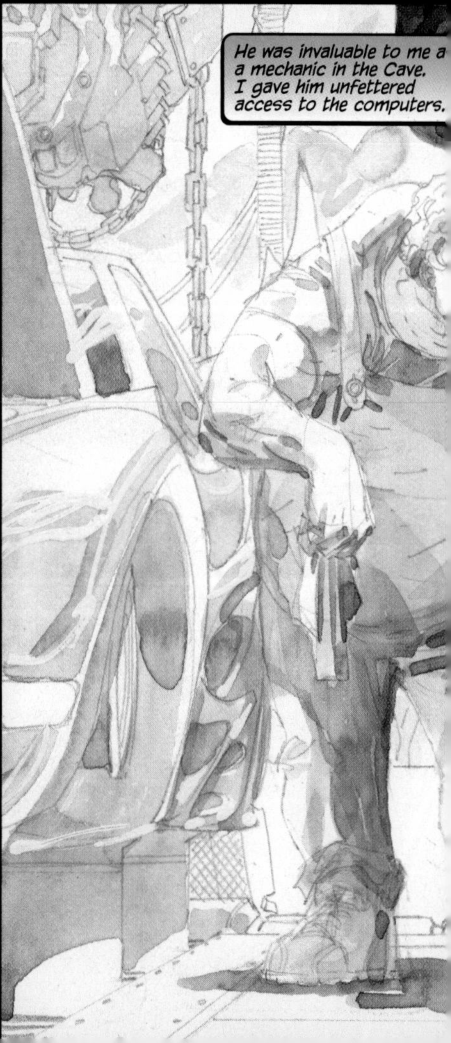
He was invaluable to me a a mechanic in the Cave. I gave him unfettered access to the computers.

I had hoped to have broken the pattern of Harold's trust in those who did not merit it.

But, in his silence, there was a yearning to repair his body and voice.

One which my *true* enemy took advantage of and Harold betrayed me.

It cost him his life.

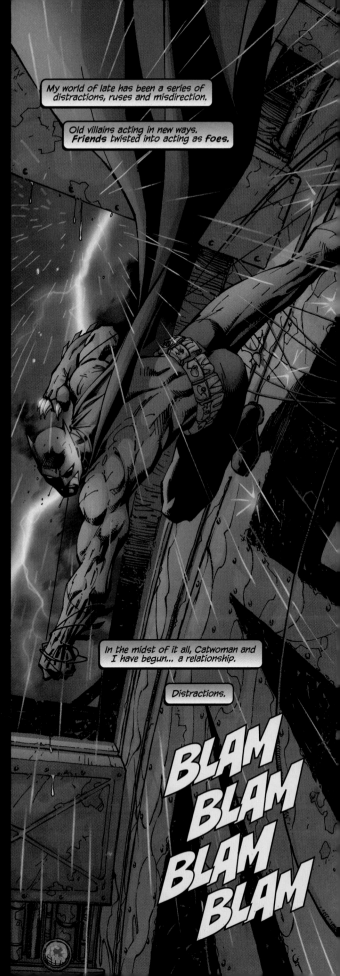

My world of late has been a series of distractions, ruses and misdirection.

Old villains acting in new ways. *Friends* twisted into acting as foes.

In the midst of it all, Catwoman and I have begun... a relationship.

Distractions.

BLAM
BLAM
BLAM
BLAM

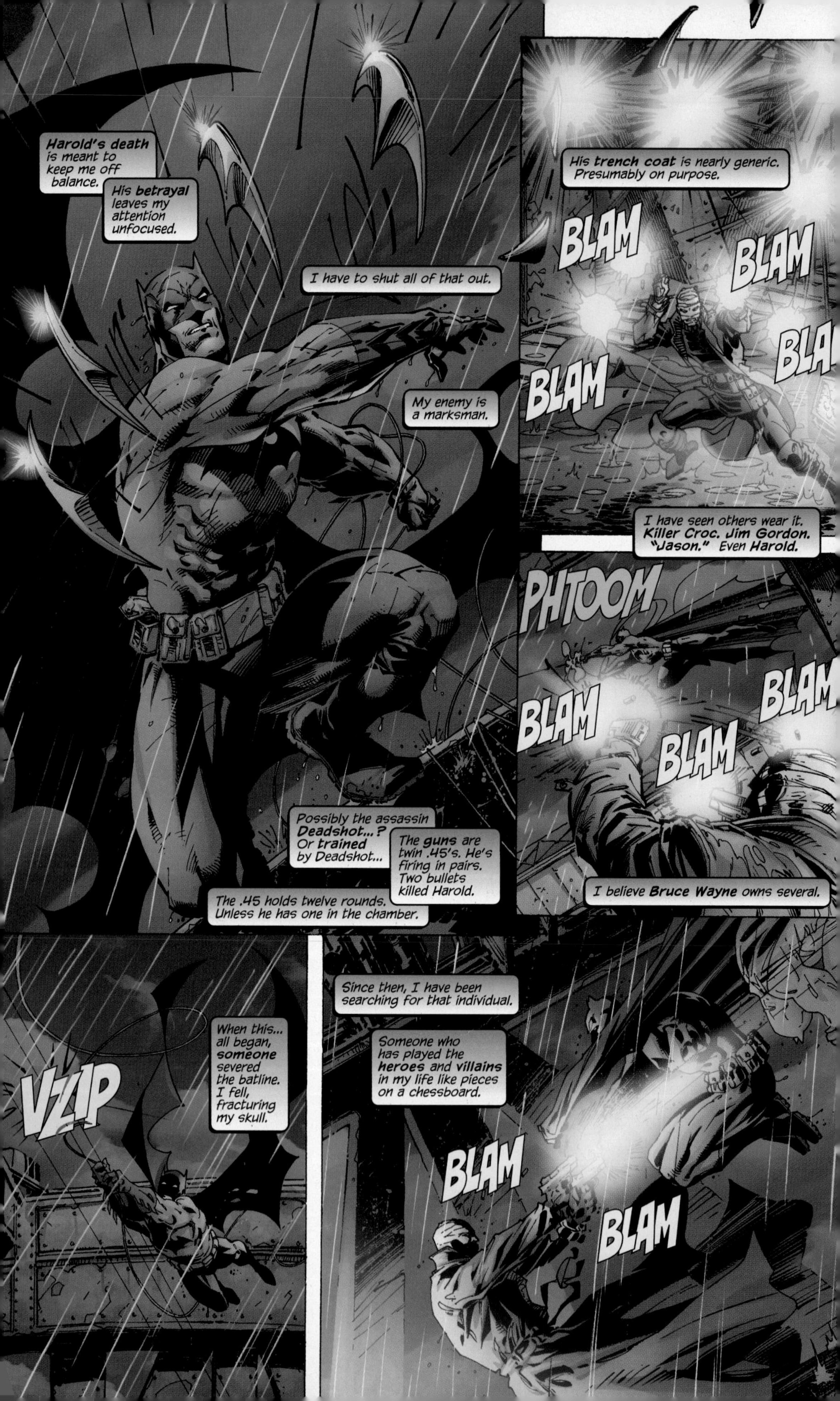

Harold's death is meant to keep me off balance.
His betrayal leaves my attention unfocused.
I have to shut all of that out.
My enemy is a marksman.
Possibly the assassin Deadshot...? Or trained by Deadshot...
The guns are twin .45's. He's firing in pairs. Two bullets killed Harold.
The .45 holds twelve rounds. Unless he has one in the chamber.
His trench coat is nearly generic. Presumably on purpose.
BLAM
BLAM
BLA
BLAM
I have seen others wear it. Killer Croc. Jim Gordon. "Jason." Even Harold.
PHTOOM
BLAM
BLAM
BLAM
I believe Bruce Wayne owns several.
VZIP
When this... all began, someone severed the batline. I fell, fracturing my skull.
Since then, I have been searching for that individual.
Someone who has played the heroes and villains in my life like pieces on a chessboard.
BLAM
BLAM

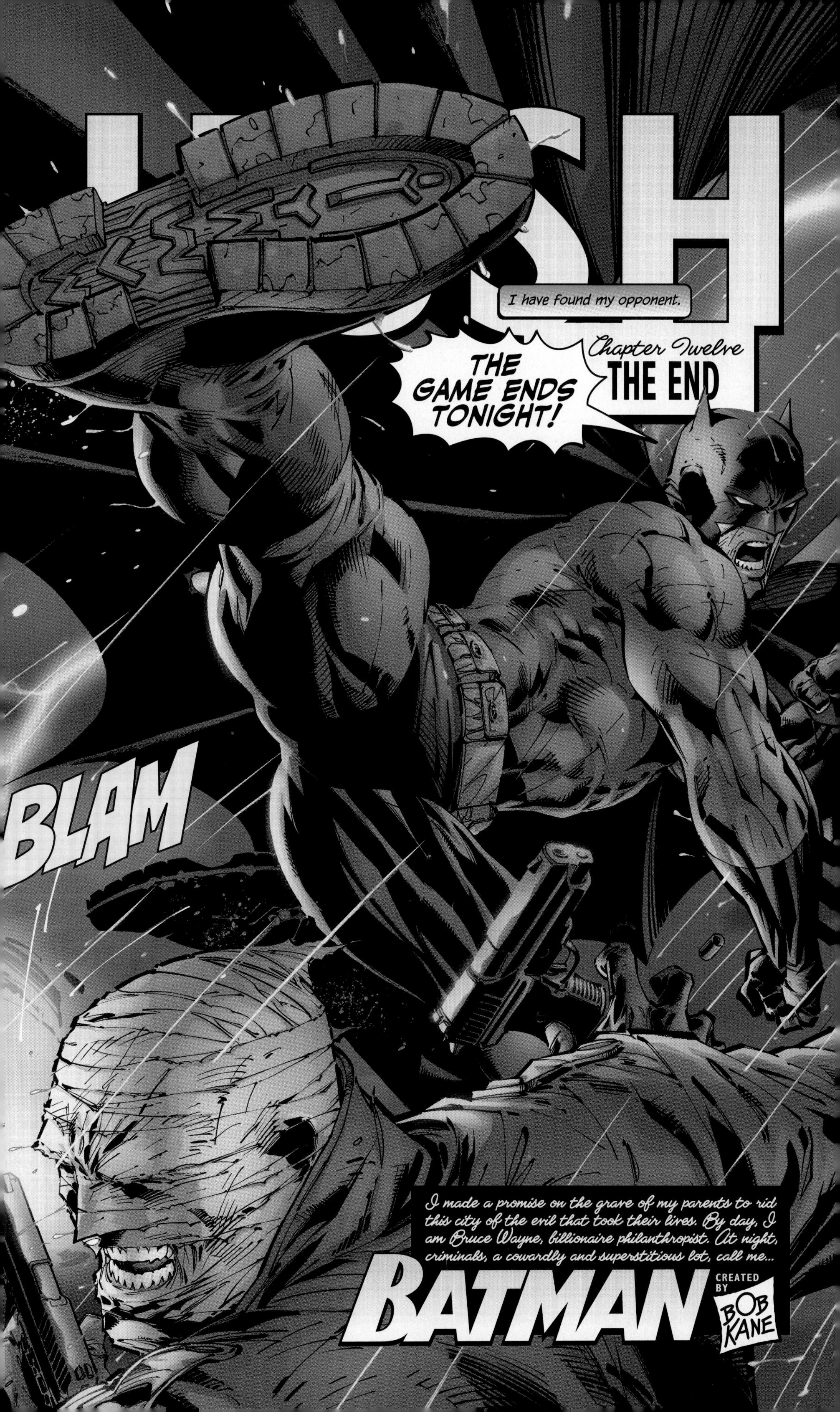
HUSH
I have found my opponent.
THE GAME ENDS TONIGHT!
Chapter Twelve
THE END
BLAM
I made a promise on the grave of my parents to rid this city of the evil that took their lives. By day, I am Bruce Wayne, billionaire philanthropist. At night, criminals, a cowardly and superstitious lot, call me...
BATMAN
CREATED BY BOB KANE

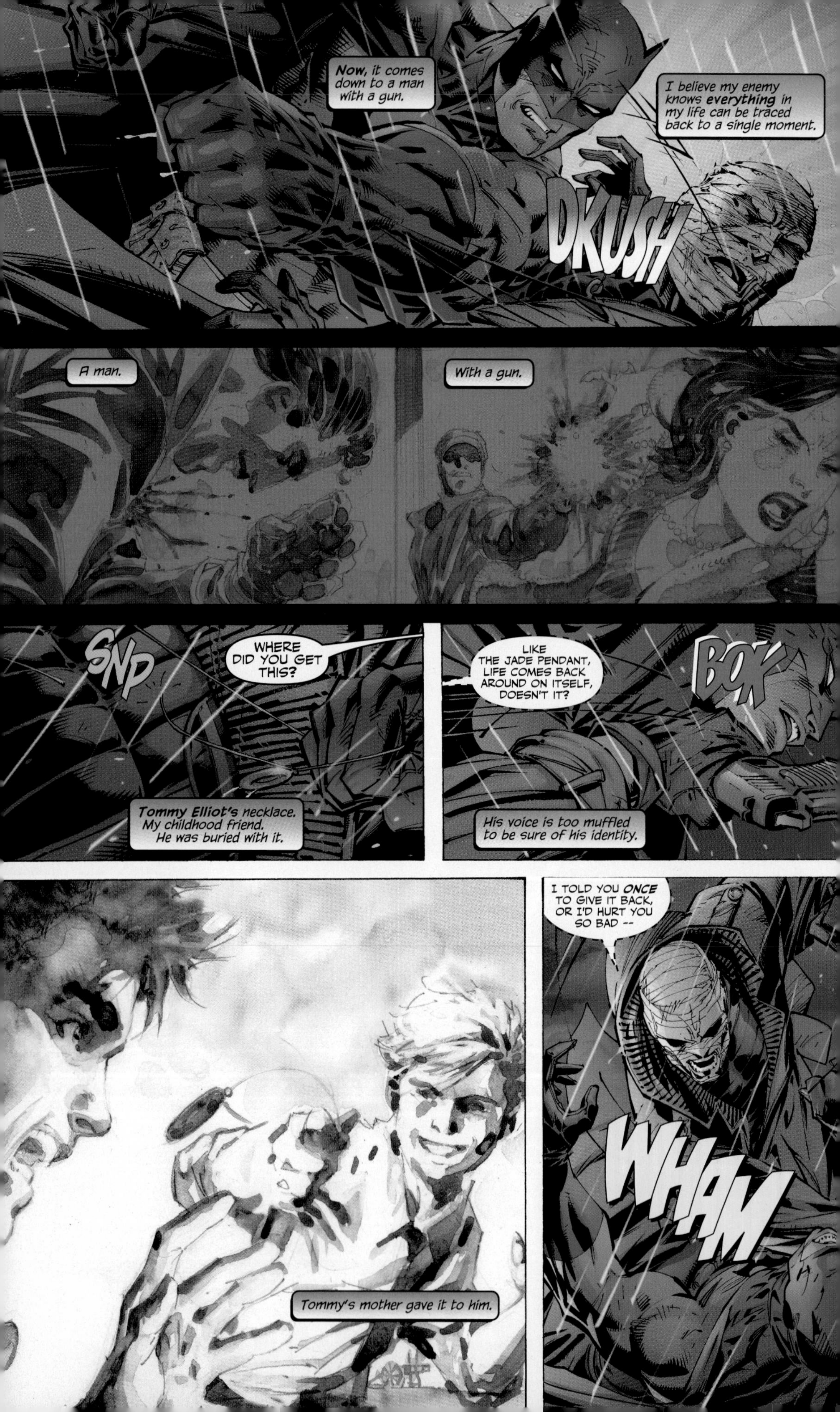

Now, it comes down to a man with a gun.
I believe my enemy knows everything in my life can be traced back to a single moment.
DKUSH
A man.
With a gun.
SNP
WHERE DID YOU GET THIS?
Tommy Elliot's necklace. My childhood friend. He was buried with it.
LIKE THE JADE PENDANT, LIFE COMES BACK AROUND ON ITSELF, DOESN'T IT?
BOK
His voice is too muffled to be sure of his identity.
Tommy's mother gave it to him.
I TOLD YOU ONCE TO GIVE IT BACK, OR I'D HURT YOU SO BAD --
WHAM

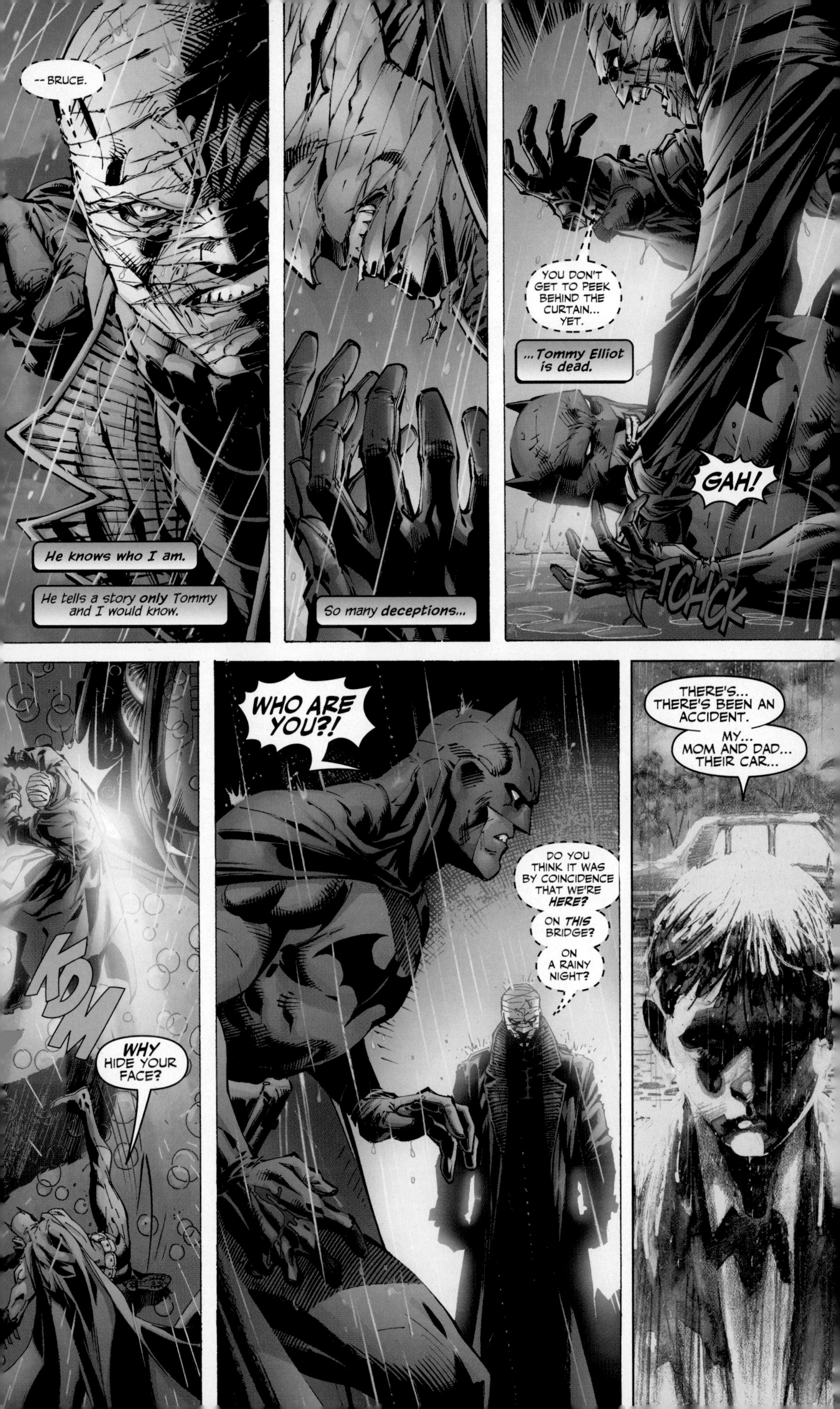

--BRUCE.
He knows who I am.
He tells a story only Tommy and I would know.
So many deceptions...
YOU DON'T GET TO PEEK BEHIND THE CURTAIN... YET.
...Tommy Elliot is dead.
GAH!
TCHCK
KOM
WHY HIDE YOUR FACE?
WHO ARE YOU?!
DO YOU THINK IT WAS BY COINCIDENCE THAT WE'RE HERE?
ON THIS BRIDGE?
ON A RAINY NIGHT?
THERE'S... THERE'S BEEN AN ACCIDENT.
MY... MOM AND DAD... THEIR CAR...

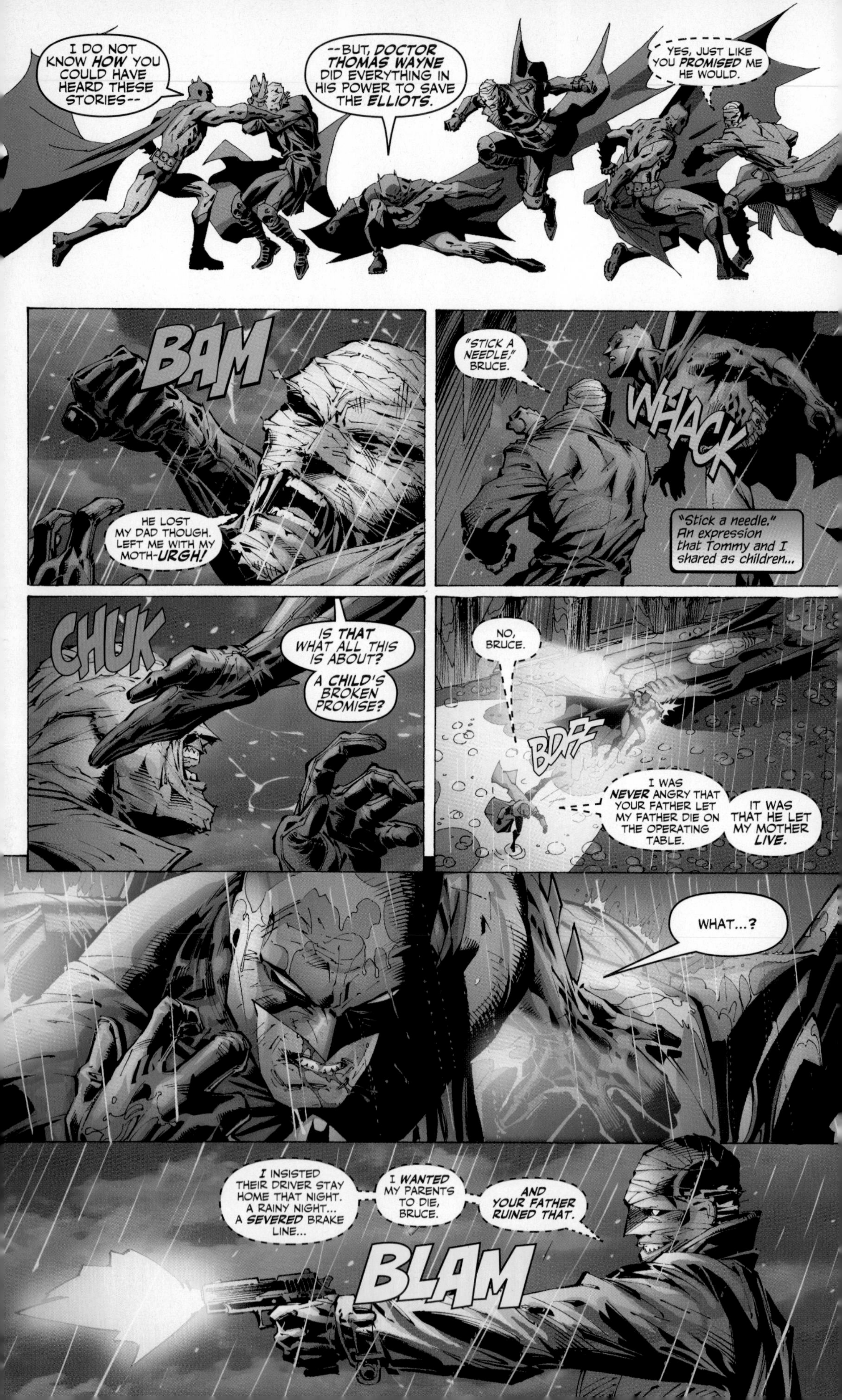

I DO NOT KNOW HOW YOU COULD HAVE HEARD THESE STORIES--
--BUT, DOCTOR THOMAS WAYNE DID EVERYTHING IN HIS POWER TO SAVE THE ELLIOTS.
YES, JUST LIKE YOU PROMISED ME HE WOULD.
BAM
HE LOST MY DAD THOUGH. LEFT ME WITH MY MOTH-URGH!
"STICK A NEEDLE," BRUCE.
WHACK
"Stick a needle." An expression that Tommy and I shared as children...
CHUK
IS THAT WHAT ALL THIS IS ABOUT?
A CHILD'S BROKEN PROMISE?
NO, BRUCE.
BDFF
I WAS NEVER ANGRY THAT YOUR FATHER LET MY FATHER DIE ON THE OPERATING TABLE.
IT WAS THAT HE LET MY MOTHER LIVE.
WHAT...?
I INSISTED THEIR DRIVER STAY HOME THAT NIGHT. A RAINY NIGHT... A SEVERED BRAKE LINE...
I WANTED MY PARENTS TO DIE, BRUCE.
AND YOUR FATHER RUINED THAT.
BLAM

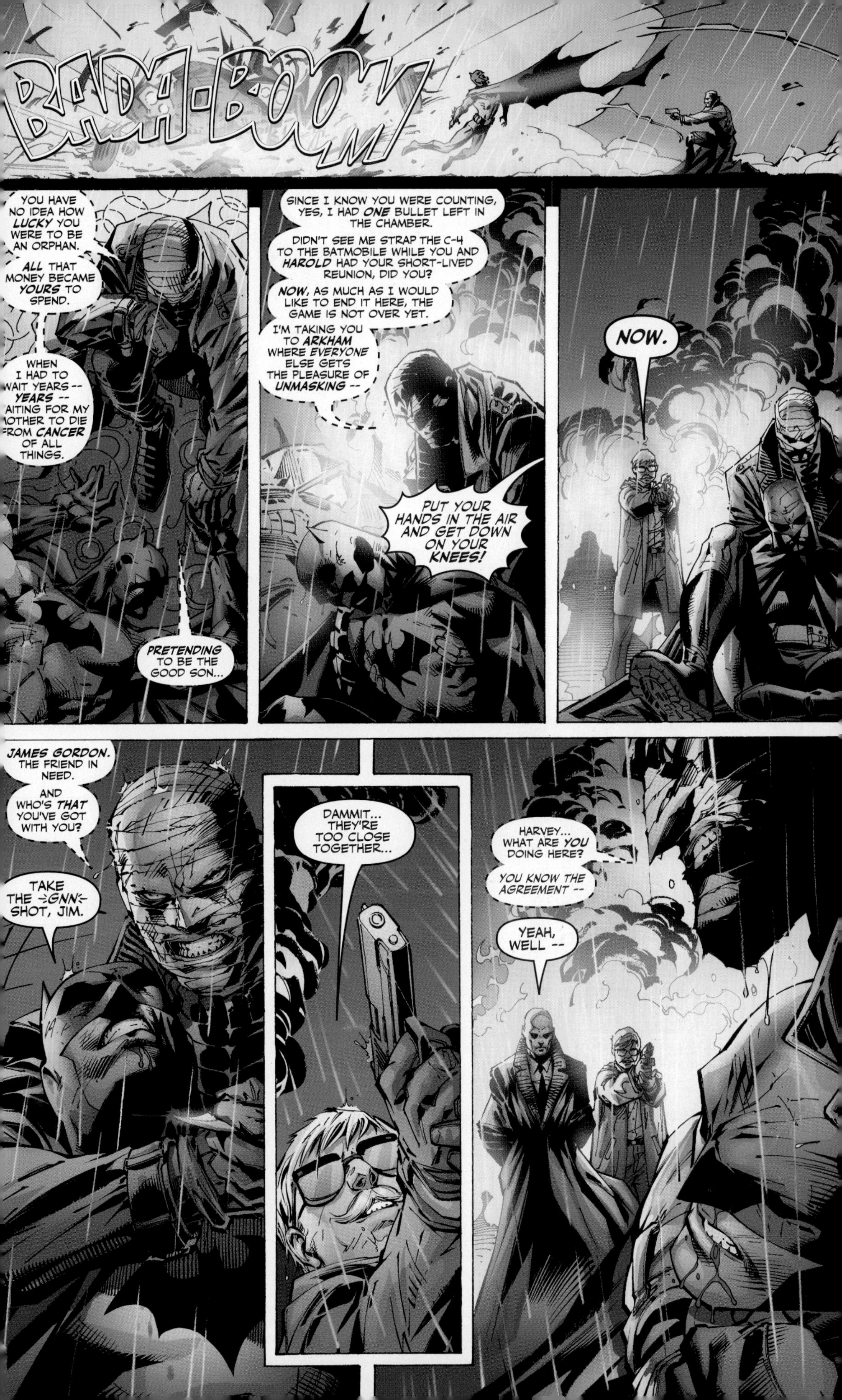

BADA-BOOM
YOU HAVE NO IDEA HOW LUCKY YOU WERE TO BE AN ORPHAN.
ALL THAT MONEY BECAME YOURS TO SPEND.
WHEN I HAD TO WAIT YEARS -- YEARS -- WAITING FOR MY MOTHER TO DIE FROM CANCER OF ALL THINGS.
PRETENDING TO BE THE GOOD SON...
SINCE I KNOW YOU WERE COUNTING, YES, I HAD ONE BULLET LEFT IN THE CHAMBER.
DIDN'T SEE ME STRAP THE C-4 TO THE BATMOBILE WHILE YOU AND HAROLD HAD YOUR SHORT-LIVED REUNION, DID YOU?
NOW, AS MUCH AS I WOULD LIKE TO END IT HERE, THE GAME IS NOT OVER YET.
I'M TAKING YOU TO ARKHAM WHERE EVERYONE ELSE GETS THE PLEASURE OF UNMASKING --
PUT YOUR HANDS IN THE AIR AND GET DOWN ON YOUR KNEES!
NOW.
JAMES GORDON. THE FRIEND IN NEED.
AND WHO'S THAT YOU'VE GOT WITH YOU?
TAKE THE -GNN- SHOT, JIM.
DAMMIT... THEY'RE TOO CLOSE TOGETHER...
HARVEY... WHAT ARE YOU DOING HERE?
YOU KNOW THE AGREEMENT --
YEAH, WELL --

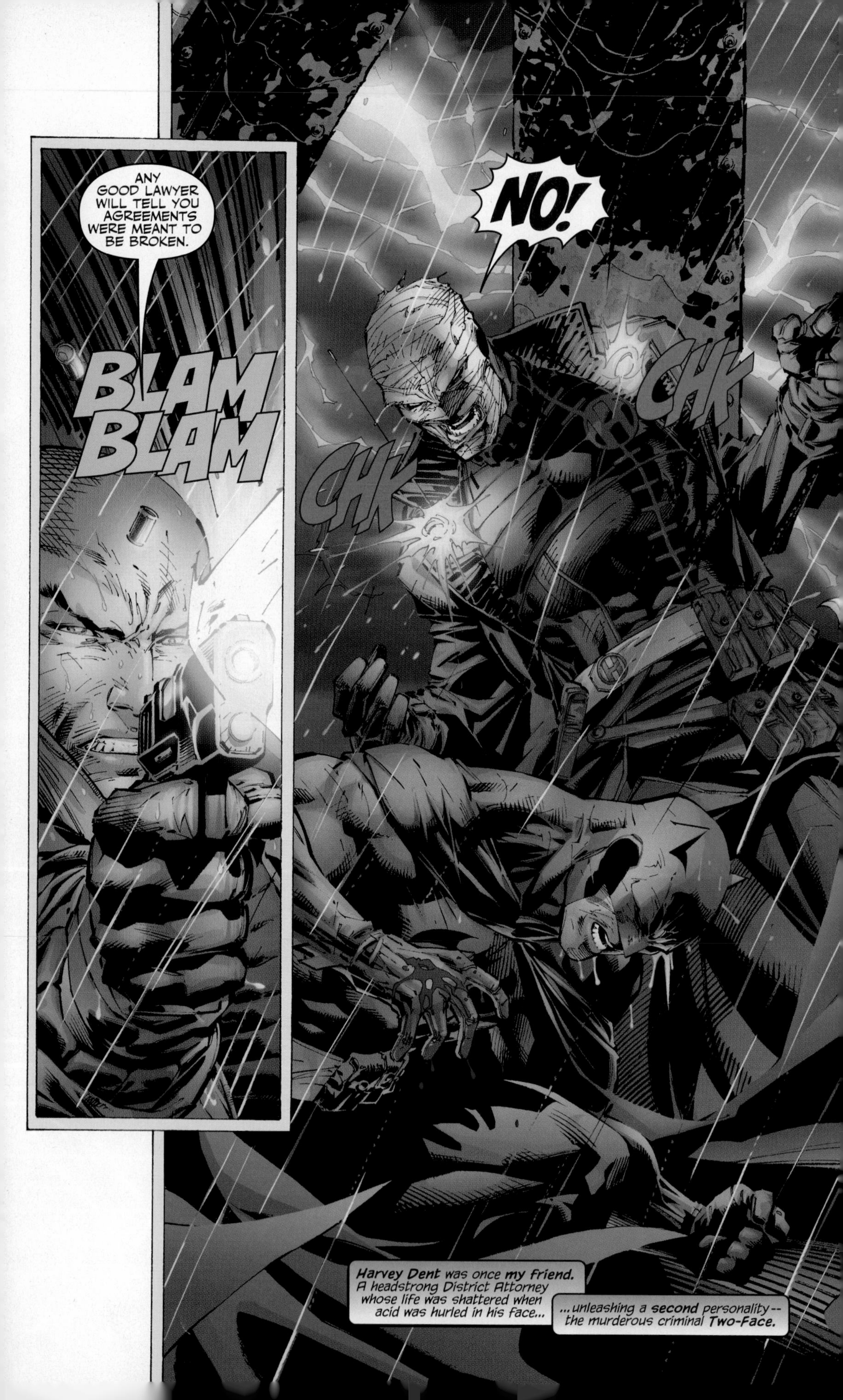
ANY GOOD LAWYER WILL TELL YOU AGREEMENTS WERE MEANT TO BE BROKEN.
BLAM BLAM
NO!
CHK
CHK
Harvey Dent was once my friend. A headstrong District Attorney whose life was shattered when acid was hurled in his face...
...unleashing a second personality-- the murderous criminal Two-Face.

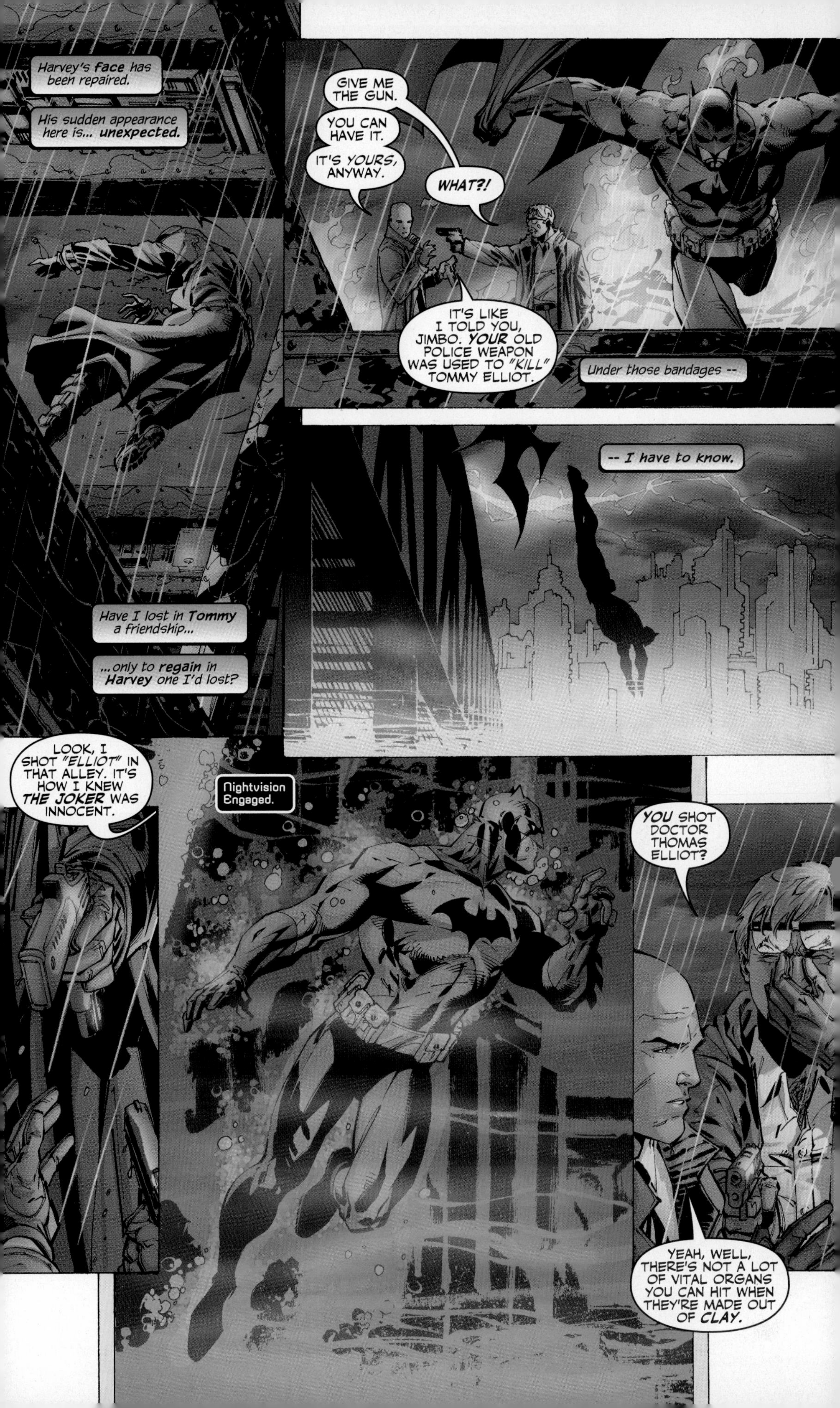
Harvey's face has been repaired.
His sudden appearance here is... unexpected.
GIVE ME THE GUN.
YOU CAN HAVE IT.
IT'S YOURS, ANYWAY.
WHAT?!
IT'S LIKE I TOLD YOU, JIMBO. YOUR OLD POLICE WEAPON WAS USED TO "KILL" TOMMY ELLIOT.
Under those bandages --
-- I have to know.
Have I lost in Tommy a friendship...
...only to regain in Harvey one I'd lost?
LOOK, I SHOT "ELLIOT" IN THAT ALLEY. IT'S HOW I KNEW THE JOKER WAS INNOCENT.
Nightvision Engaged.
YOU SHOT DOCTOR THOMAS ELLIOT?
YEAH, WELL, THERE'S NOT A LOT OF VITAL ORGANS YOU CAN HIT WHEN THEY'RE MADE OUT OF CLAY.

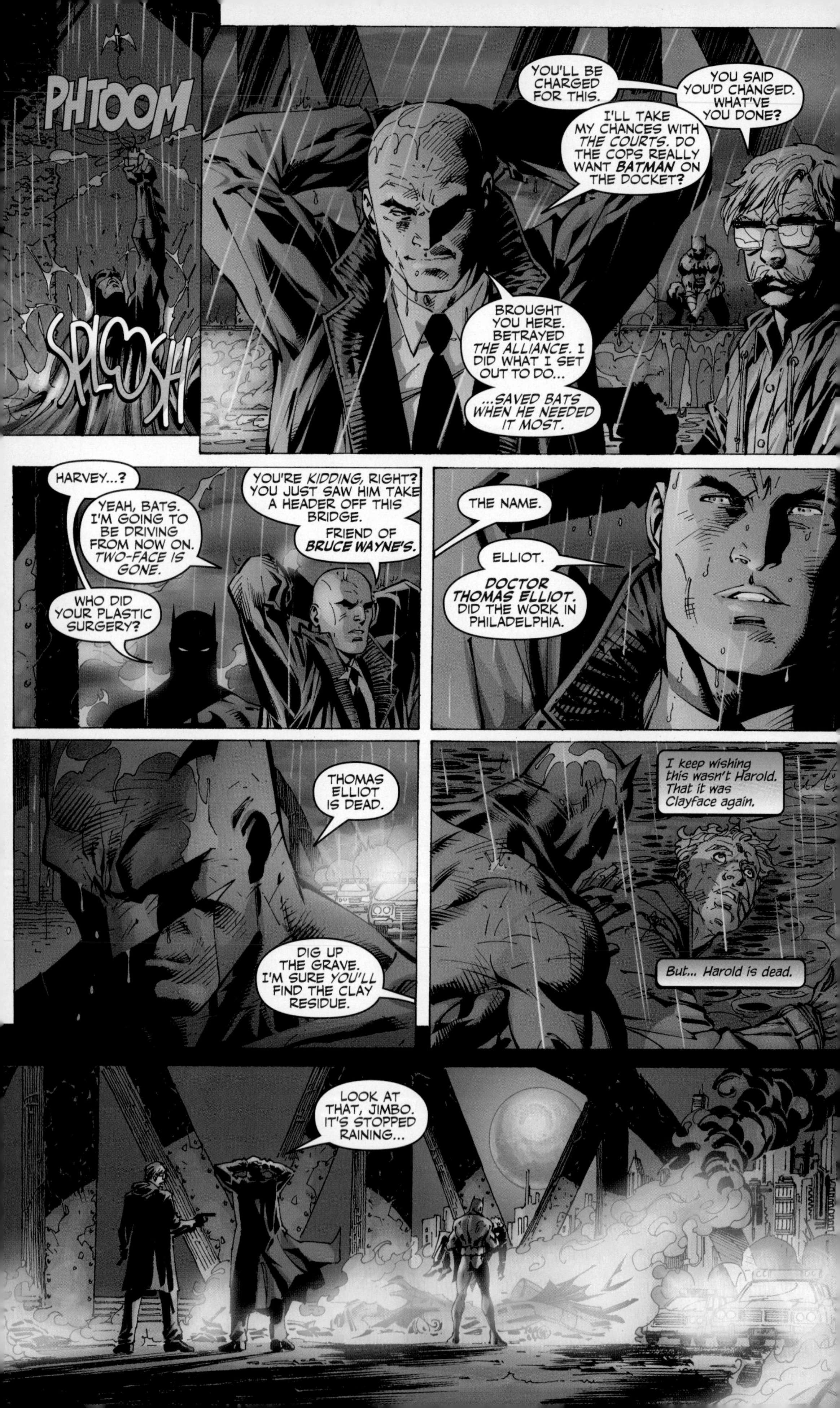
PHTOOM
SPLOOSH
YOU'LL BE CHARGED FOR THIS.
YOU SAID YOU'D CHANGED. WHAT'VE YOU DONE?
I'LL TAKE MY CHANCES WITH THE COURTS. DO THE COPS REALLY WANT BATMAN ON THE DOCKET?
BROUGHT YOU HERE. BETRAYED THE ALLIANCE. I DID WHAT I SET OUT TO DO...
...SAVED BATS WHEN HE NEEDED IT MOST.
HARVEY...?
YEAH, BATS. I'M GOING TO BE DRIVING FROM NOW ON. TWO-FACE IS GONE.
WHO DID YOUR PLASTIC SURGERY?
YOU'RE KIDDING, RIGHT? YOU JUST SAW HIM TAKE A HEADER OFF THIS BRIDGE.
FRIEND OF BRUCE WAYNE'S.
THE NAME.
ELLIOT.
DOCTOR THOMAS ELLIOT. DID THE WORK IN PHILADELPHIA.
THOMAS ELLIOT IS DEAD.
DIG UP THE GRAVE. I'M SURE YOU'LL FIND THE CLAY RESIDUE.
I keep wishing this wasn't Harold. That it was Clayface again.
But... Harold is dead.
LOOK AT THAT, JIMBO. IT'S STOPPED RAINING...

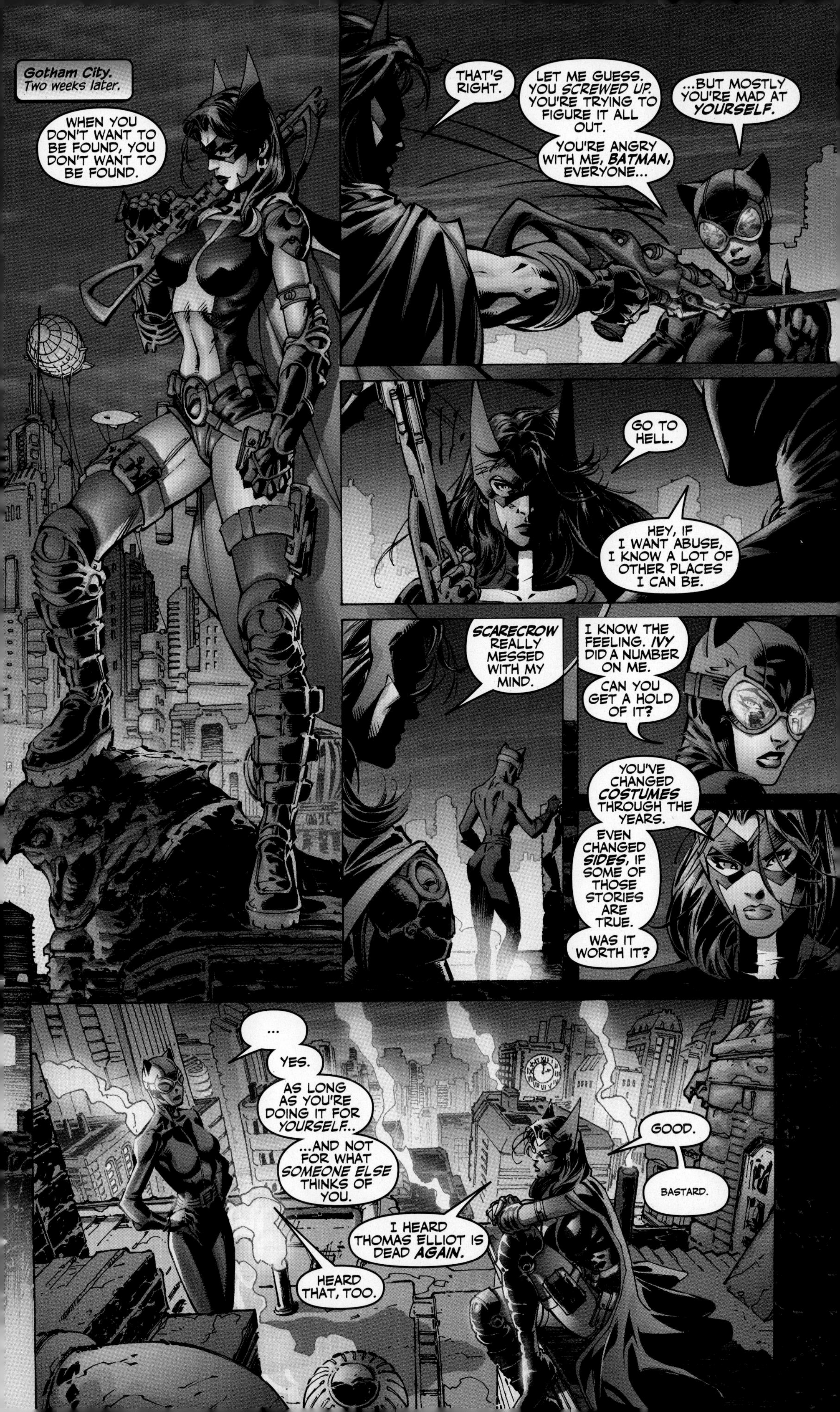
Gotham City. Two weeks later.
WHEN YOU DON'T WANT TO BE FOUND, YOU DON'T WANT TO BE FOUND.
THAT'S RIGHT.
LET ME GUESS. YOU SCREWED UP. YOU'RE TRYING TO FIGURE IT ALL OUT.
YOU'RE ANGRY WITH ME, BATMAN, EVERYONE...
...BUT MOSTLY YOU'RE MAD AT YOURSELF.
GO TO HELL.
HEY, IF I WANT ABUSE, I KNOW A LOT OF OTHER PLACES I CAN BE.
SCARECROW REALLY MESSED WITH MY MIND.
I KNOW THE FEELING. IVY DID A NUMBER ON ME.
CAN YOU GET A HOLD OF IT?
YOU'VE CHANGED COSTUMES THROUGH THE YEARS.
EVEN CHANGED SIDES, IF SOME OF THOSE STORIES ARE TRUE.
WAS IT WORTH IT?
...
YES.
AS LONG AS YOU'RE DOING IT FOR YOURSELF...
...AND NOT FOR WHAT SOMEONE ELSE THINKS OF YOU.
I HEARD THOMAS ELLIOT IS DEAD AGAIN.
HEARD THAT, TOO.
GOOD.
BASTARD.

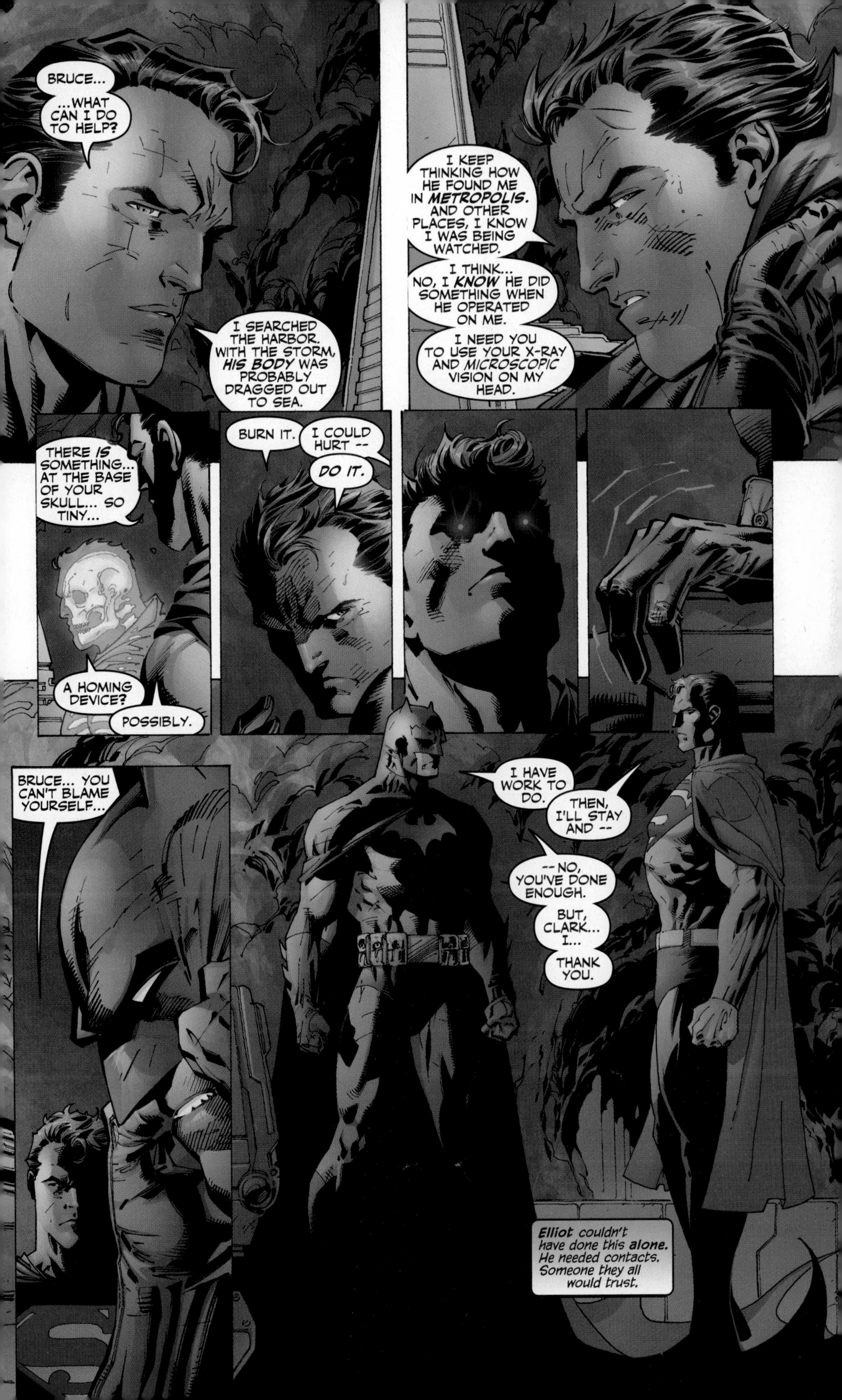
BRUCE...
...WHAT CAN I DO TO HELP?
I SEARCHED THE HARBOR. WITH THE STORM, HIS BODY WAS PROBABLY DRAGGED OUT TO SEA.
I KEEP THINKING HOW HE FOUND ME IN METROPOLIS. AND OTHER PLACES, I KNOW I WAS BEING WATCHED.
I THINK... NO, I KNOW HE DID SOMETHING WHEN HE OPERATED ON ME.
I NEED YOU TO USE YOUR X-RAY AND MICROSCOPIC VISION ON MY HEAD.
THERE IS SOMETHING... AT THE BASE OF YOUR SKULL... SO TINY...
A HOMING DEVICE?
POSSIBLY.
BURN IT.
I COULD HURT --
DO IT.
BRUCE... YOU CAN'T BLAME YOURSELF...
I HAVE WORK TO DO.
THEN, I'LL STAY AND --
-- NO, YOU'VE DONE ENOUGH.
BUT, CLARK... I...
THANK YOU.
Elliot couldn't have done this alone. He needed contacts. Someone they all would trust.

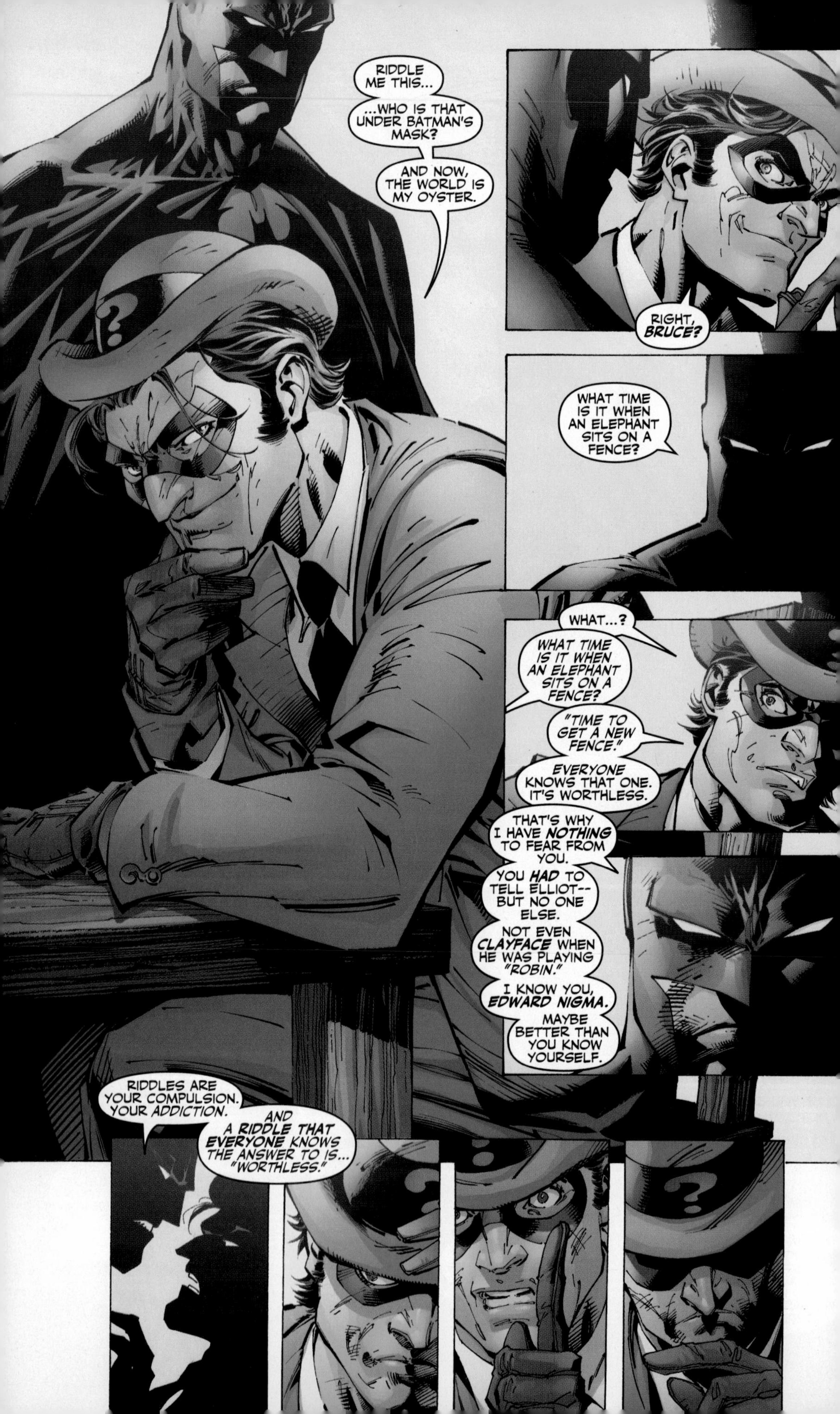
RIDDLE ME THIS...
...WHO IS THAT UNDER BATMAN'S MASK?
AND NOW, THE WORLD IS MY OYSTER.
RIGHT, BRUCE?
WHAT TIME IS IT WHEN AN ELEPHANT SITS ON A FENCE?
WHAT...?
WHAT TIME IS IT WHEN AN ELEPHANT SITS ON A FENCE?
"TIME TO GET A NEW FENCE."
EVERYONE KNOWS THAT ONE. IT'S WORTHLESS.
THAT'S WHY I HAVE NOTHING TO FEAR FROM YOU.
YOU HAD TO TELL ELLIOT-- BUT NO ONE ELSE.
NOT EVEN CLAYFACE WHEN HE WAS PLAYING "ROBIN."
I KNOW YOU, EDWARD NIGMA.
MAYBE BETTER THAN YOU KNOW YOURSELF.
RIDDLES ARE YOUR COMPULSION. YOUR ADDICTION.
AND A RIDDLE THAT EVERYONE KNOWS THE ANSWER TO IS... "WORTHLESS."

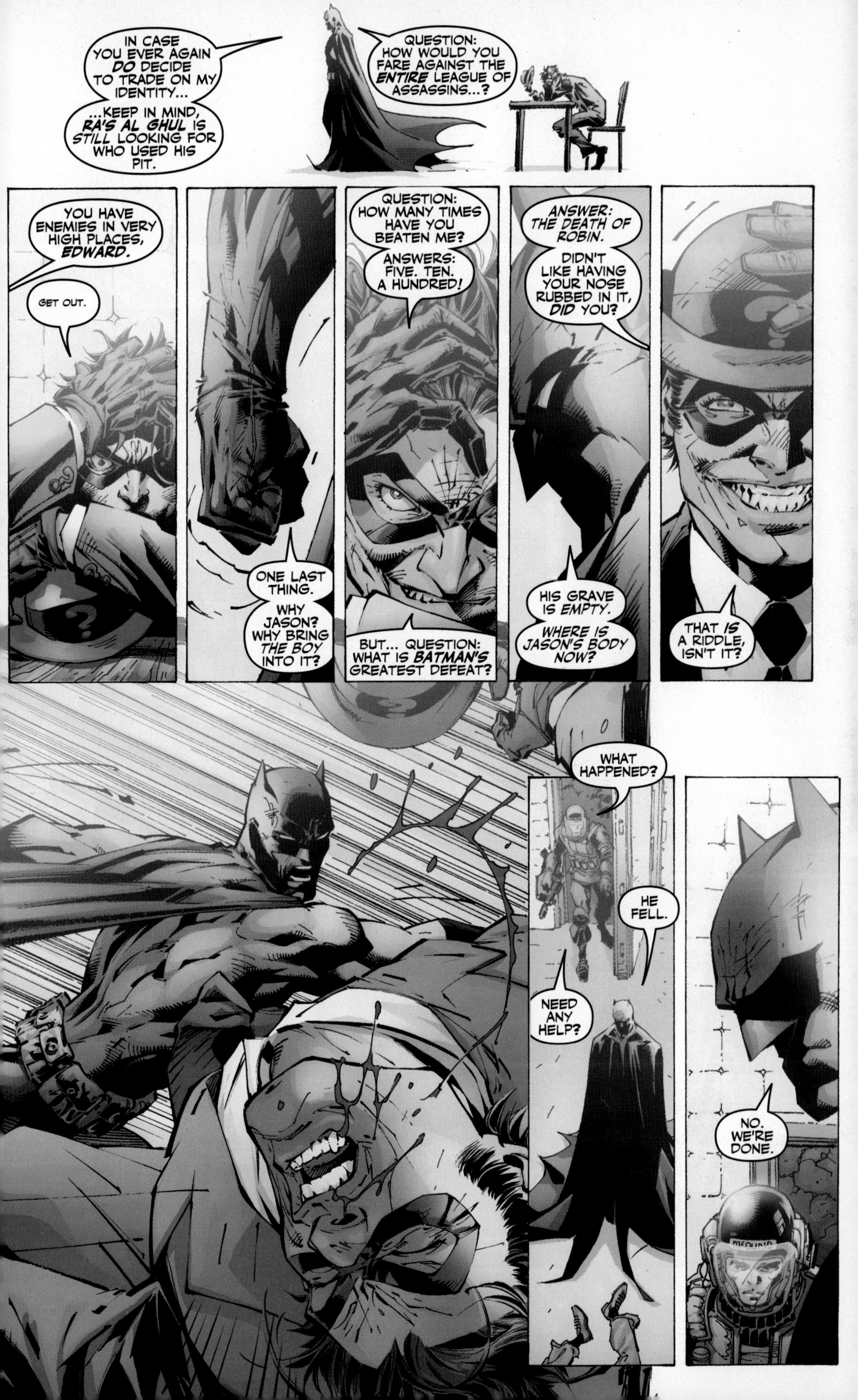

IN CASE YOU EVER AGAIN DO DECIDE TO TRADE ON MY IDENTITY...
...KEEP IN MIND, RA'S AL GHUL IS STILL LOOKING FOR WHO USED HIS PIT.
QUESTION: HOW WOULD YOU FARE AGAINST THE ENTIRE LEAGUE OF ASSASSINS...?
YOU HAVE ENEMIES IN VERY HIGH PLACES, EDWARD.
GET OUT.
ONE LAST THING.
WHY JASON? WHY BRING THE BOY INTO IT?
QUESTION: HOW MANY TIMES HAVE YOU BEATEN ME?
ANSWERS: FIVE. TEN. A HUNDRED!
BUT... QUESTION: WHAT IS BATMAN'S GREATEST DEFEAT?
ANSWER: THE DEATH OF ROBIN.
DIDN'T LIKE HAVING YOUR NOSE RUBBED IN IT, DID YOU?
HIS GRAVE IS EMPTY.
WHERE IS JASON'S BODY NOW?
THAT IS A RIDDLE, ISN'T IT?
WHAT HAPPENED?
HE FELL.
NEED ANY HELP?
NO. WE'RE DONE.

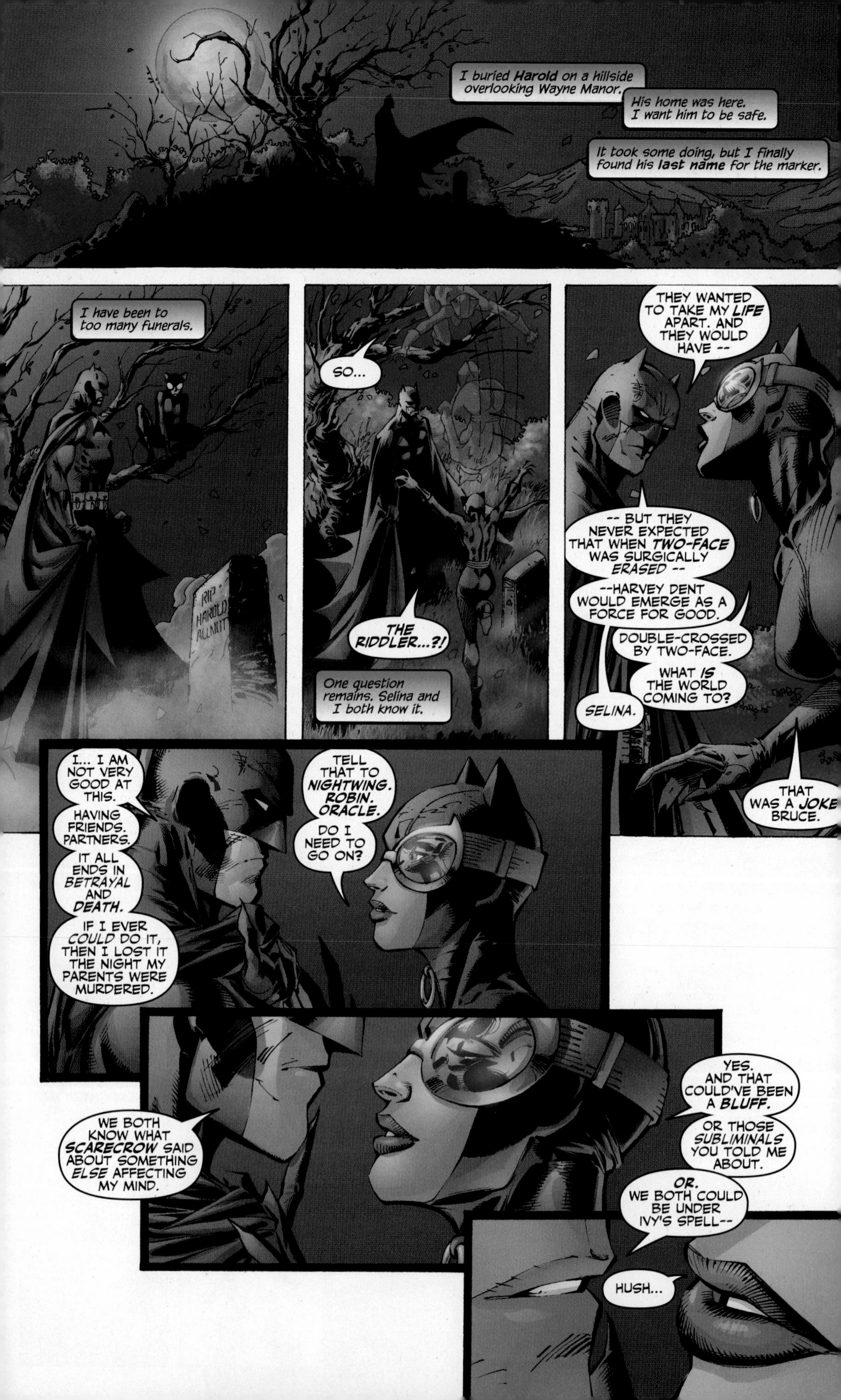

I buried Harold on a hillside overlooking Wayne Manor.
His home was here. I want him to be safe.
It took some doing, but I finally found his last name for the marker.
I have been to too many funerals.
RIP HAROLD ALLNUT
SO...
THE RIDDLER...?!
One question remains. Selina and I both know it.
THEY WANTED TO TAKE MY LIFE APART. AND THEY WOULD HAVE --
-- BUT THEY NEVER EXPECTED THAT WHEN TWO-FACE WAS SURGICALLY ERASED --
--HARVEY DENT WOULD EMERGE AS A FORCE FOR GOOD.
DOUBLE-CROSSED BY TWO-FACE.
WHAT IS THE WORLD COMING TO?
SELINA.
THAT WAS A JOKE BRUCE.
I... I AM NOT VERY GOOD AT THIS.
HAVING FRIENDS. PARTNERS.
IT ALL ENDS IN BETRAYAL AND DEATH.
IF I EVER COULD DO IT, THEN I LOST IT THE NIGHT MY PARENTS WERE MURDERED.
TELL THAT TO NIGHTWING. ROBIN. ORACLE.
DO I NEED TO GO ON?
WE BOTH KNOW WHAT SCARECROW SAID ABOUT SOMETHING ELSE AFFECTING MY MIND.
YES. AND THAT COULD'VE BEEN A BLUFF.
OR THOSE SUBLIMINALS YOU TOLD ME ABOUT.
OR. WE BOTH COULD BE UNDER IVY'S SPELL--
HUSH...

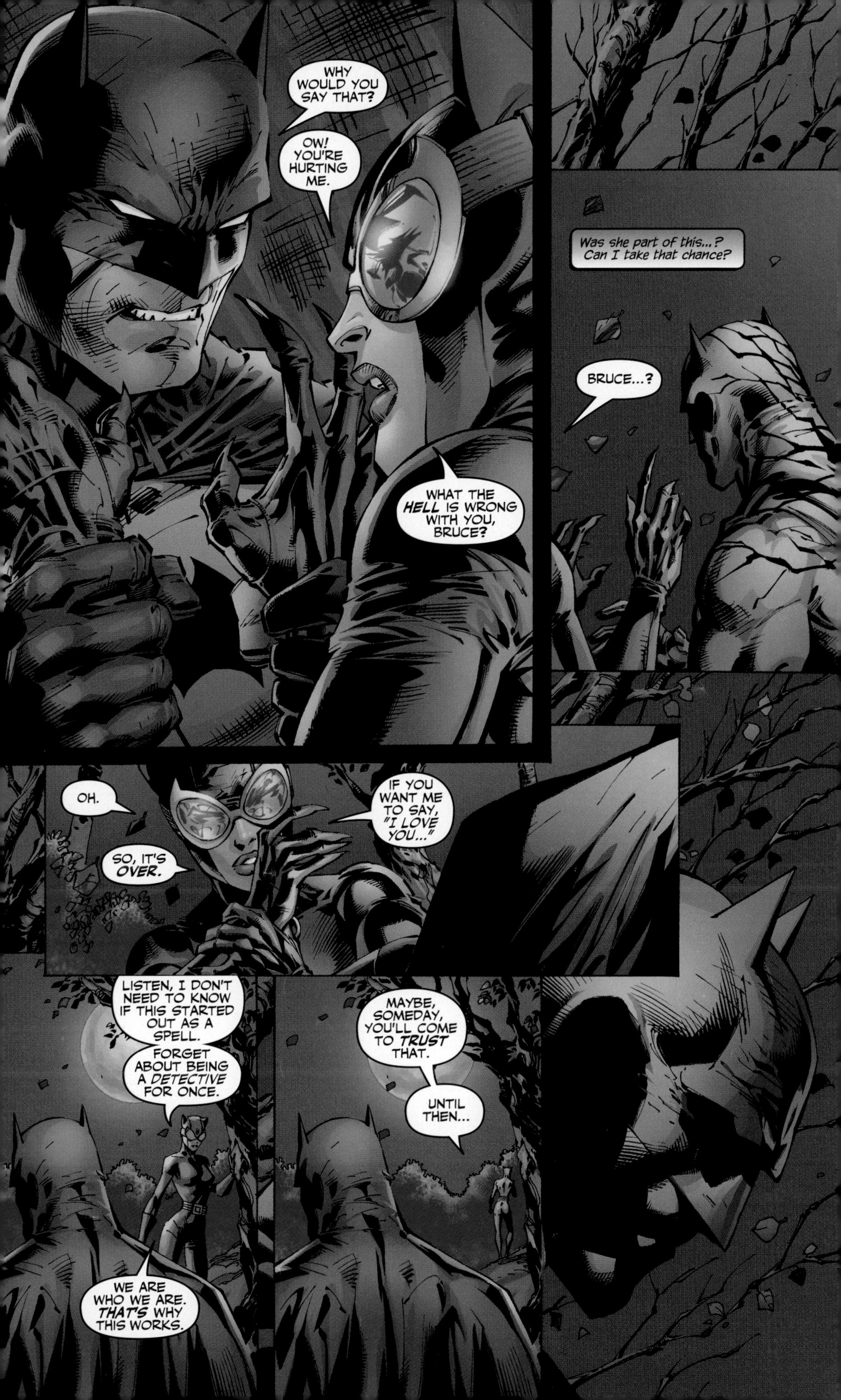
WHY WOULD YOU SAY THAT?
OW! YOU'RE HURTING ME.
WHAT THE *HELL* IS WRONG WITH YOU, BRUCE?
Was she part of this...? Can I take that chance?
BRUCE...?
OH.
SO, IT'S *OVER.*
IF YOU WANT ME TO SAY, *"I LOVE YOU..."*
LISTEN, I DON'T NEED TO KNOW IF THIS STARTED OUT AS A SPELL.
FORGET ABOUT BEING A *DETECTIVE* FOR ONCE.
WE ARE WHO WE ARE. *THAT'S* WHY THIS WORKS.
MAYBE, SOMEDAY, YOU'LL COME TO *TRUST* THAT.
UNTIL THEN...

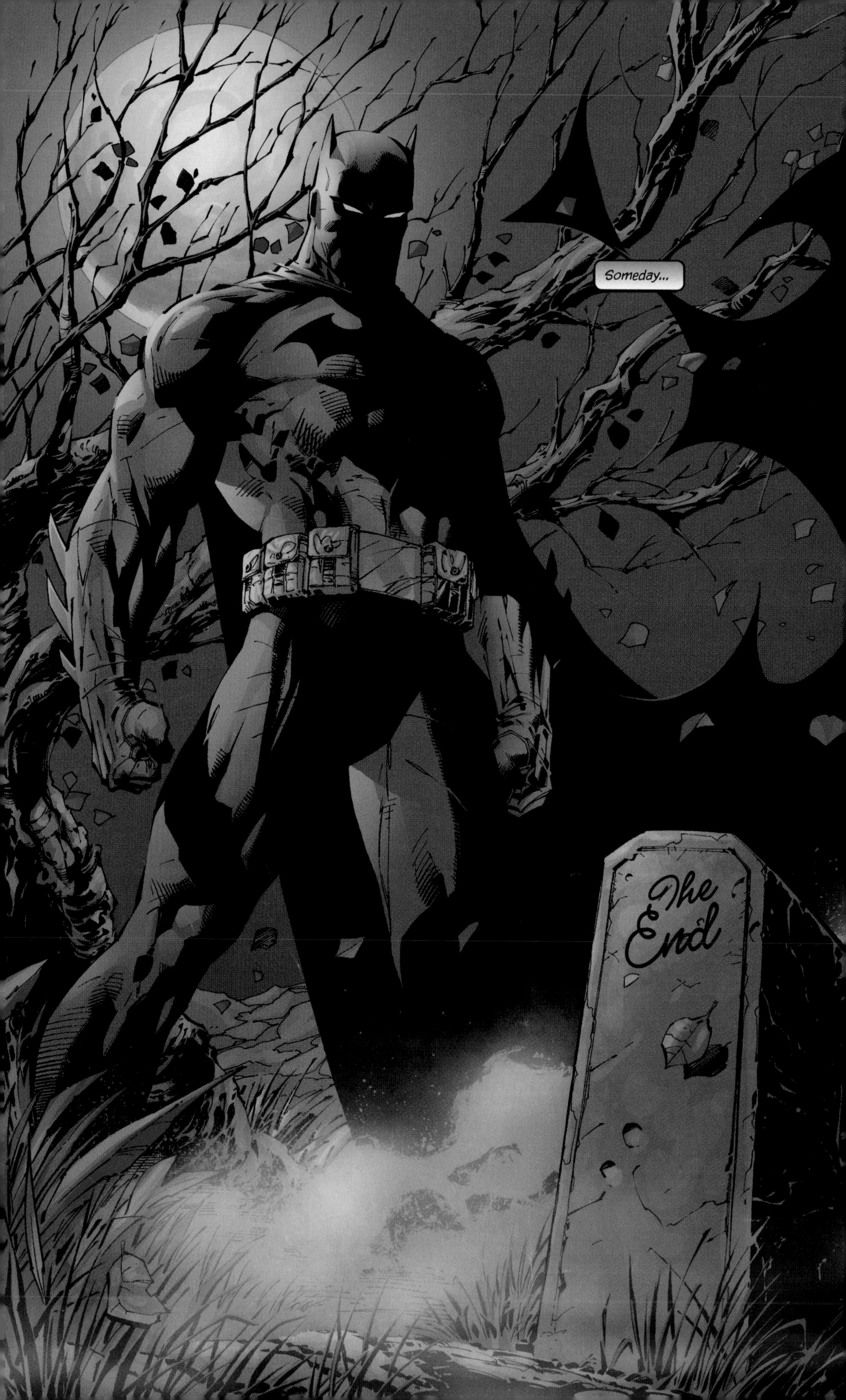
Someday...
The End

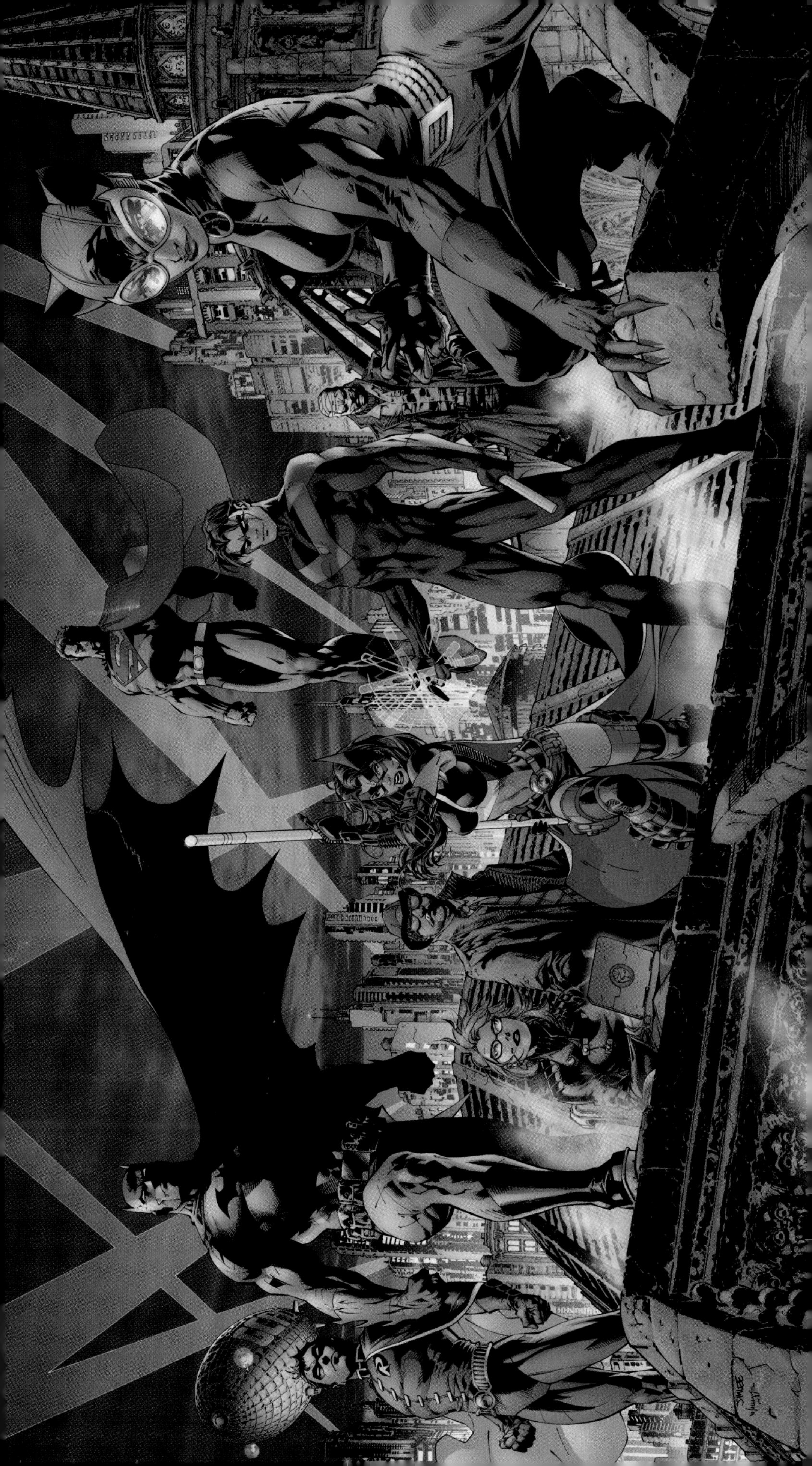

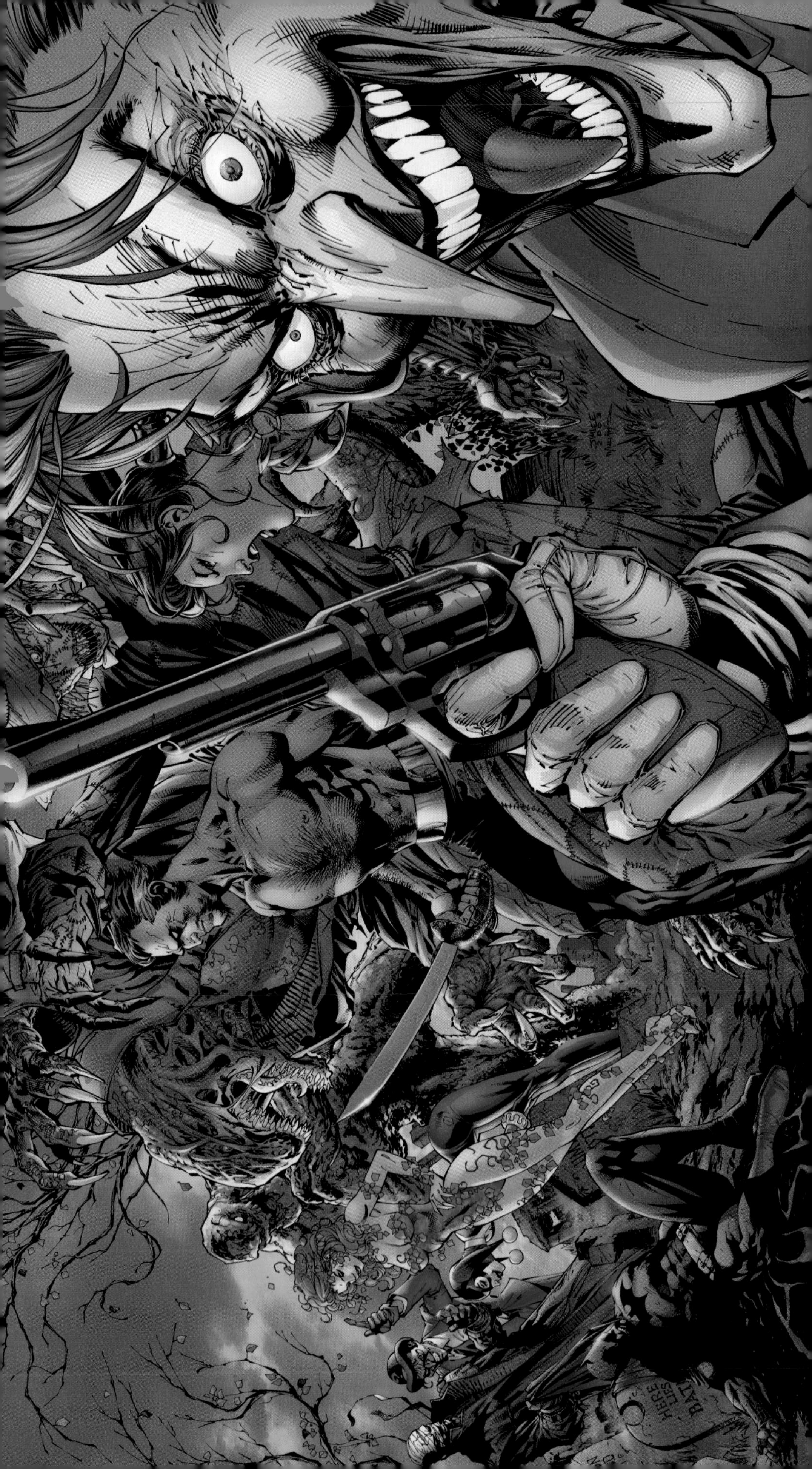
HERE LIES BAT

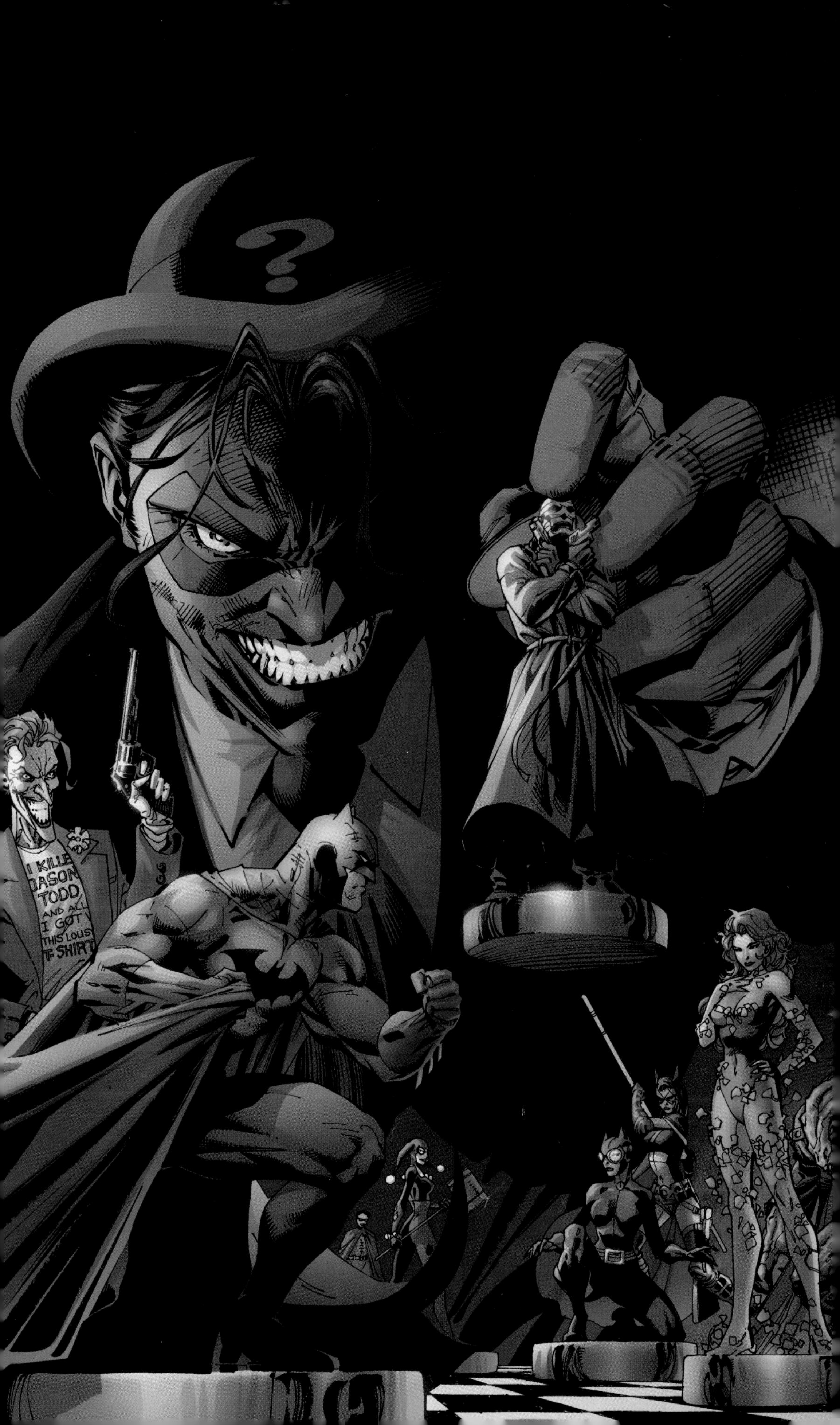
I KILLE
JASON
TODD
AND ALL
I GOT
THIS LOUSY
T-SHIRT

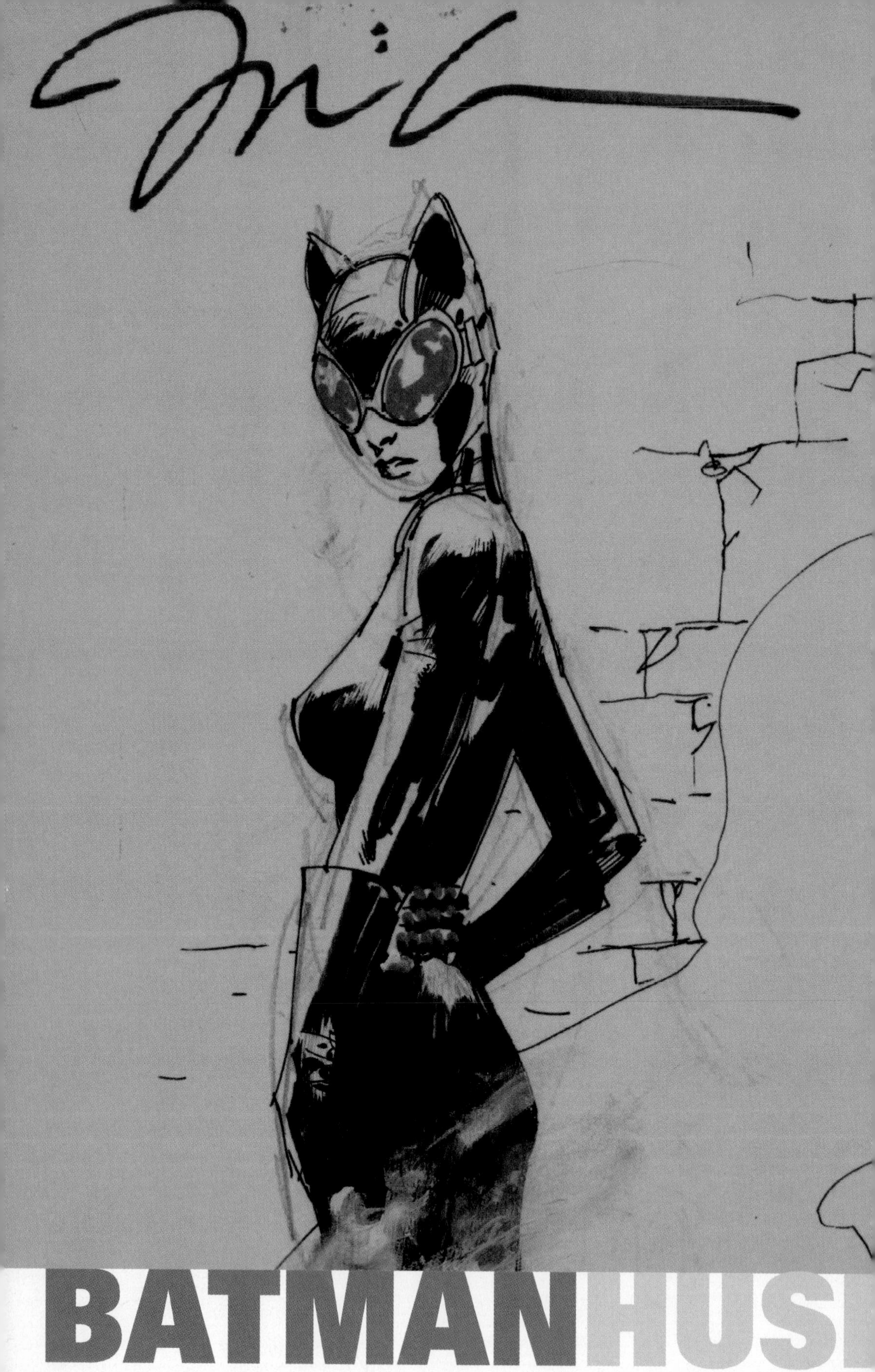

BATMANHUSH

SKETCHES

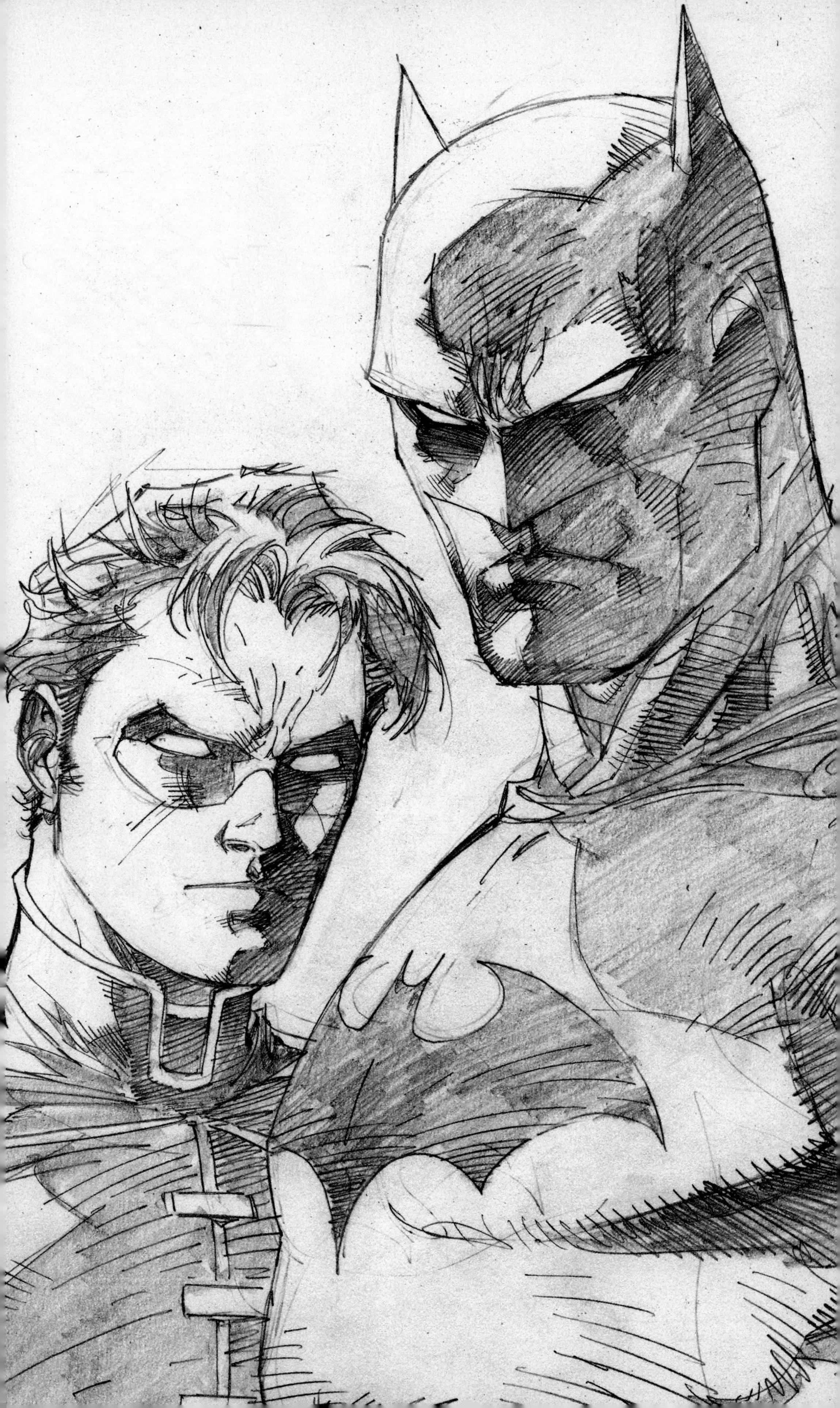

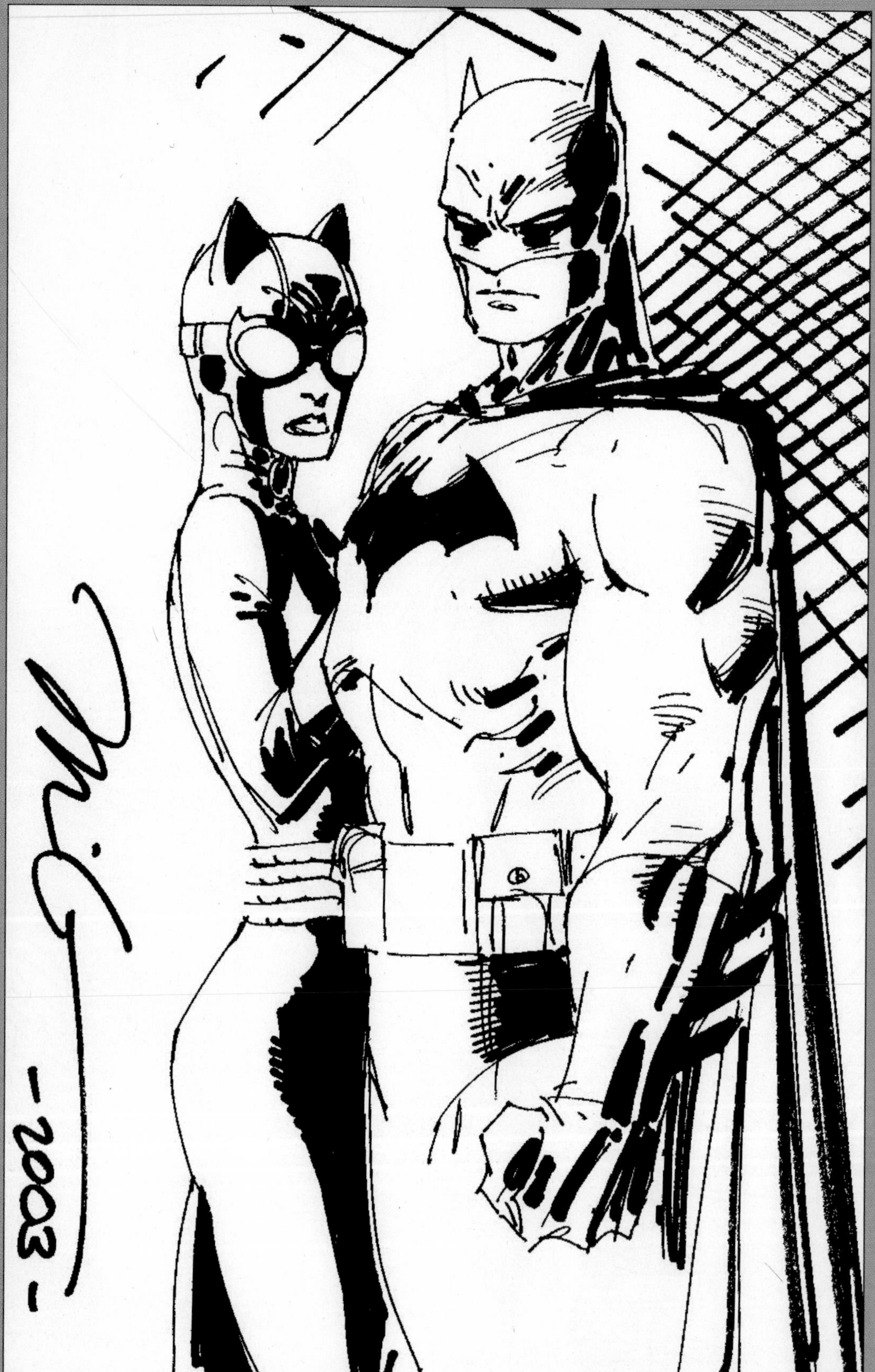
- 2003 -

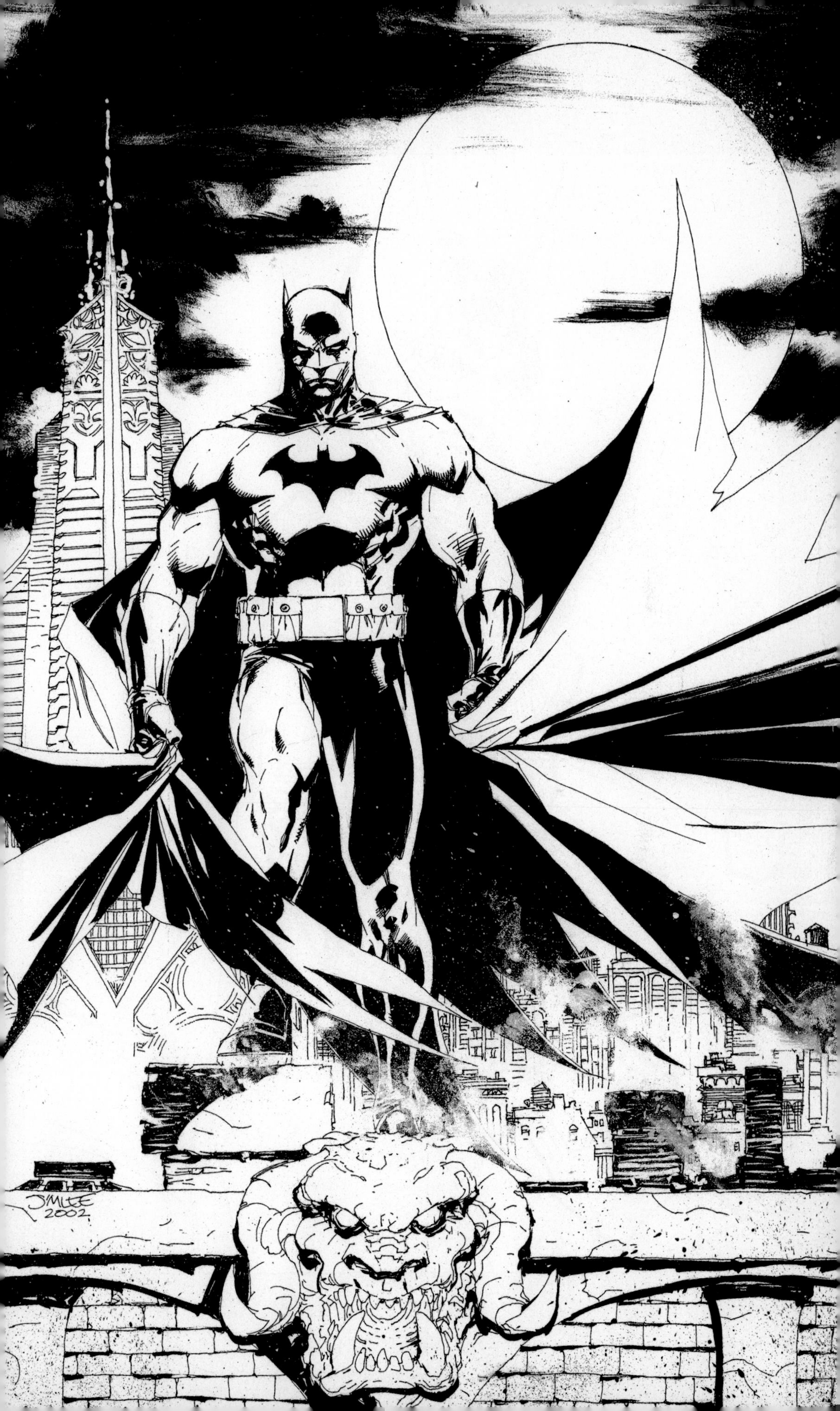
JIMLEE
2002

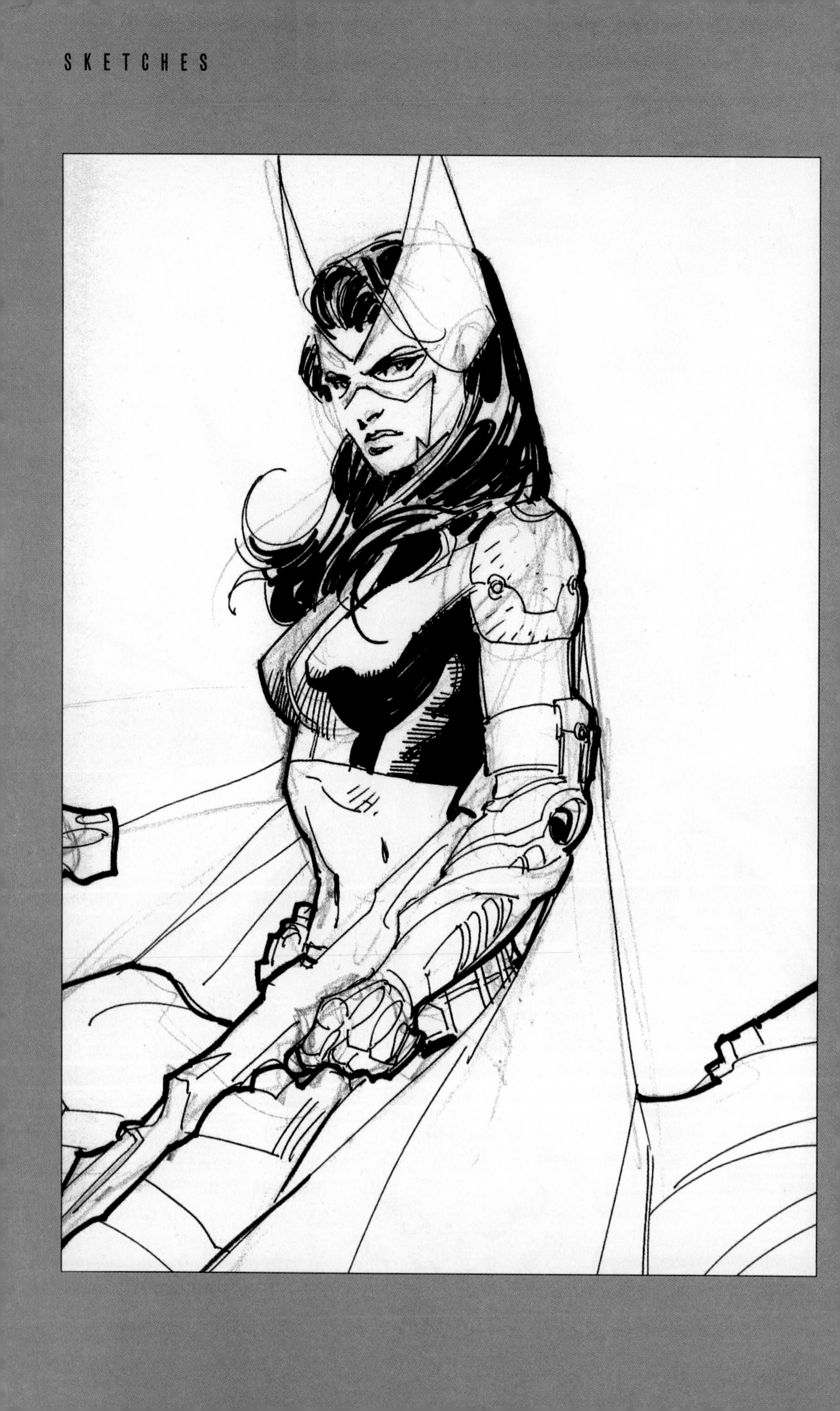

This one's for Mark Chiarello who took a very silly notion... that Jim Lee and I could actually put out a monthly Batman comic... and turned the dream into a reality. And along the way said some of the nicest things anyone has ever said about my work and for that, I am especially grateful.

—JEPH LOEB

In addition to the usual suspects mentioned before in the introduction, I would like to thank those "off-panel" who worked just as hard on HUSH but with far less fanfare. Much respect to designer Robbin Brosterman for making HUSH the classiest collection of my work (ever!); Robbin took great care with the smallest of details and made all the elements come together beautifully. Tip of the cap to Bob Greenberger for going the extra mile to make the collections chock-full of extras. Kudos to the marketing team — Bob Wayne, Patty Jeres, Matt Keller, and Adam Philips — who continually pushed HUSH to higher plateaus. Big thanks to the crew at *Wizard* — Casey, Brian and Matt — who believed from the start. A big ol' shout out to P Didi for hooking up the paper, and Alison Gill for checking out those rips and making sure the linework printed better with each passing issue. Two thumbs up to Mike Carlin, Richard Bruning and Scott Dunbier for the 1k of inspiration, and of course, Fletch for being so friendly with the fans. Last but certainly not least, I want to thank Ale, Carlos, Lee, Richard, Sandra and Trevor for the camaraderie, and my wife and kids for their sacrifices. Without their support and inspiration, none of this would have been possible.

—JIM LEE

A C K N O W L E D G M E N T S

Sometimes, everything just clicks. You know, the planets lining up, fate, or even dumb luck. I'm not sure which of these clichés might apply, but I do know that BATMAN: HUSH just clicked. I've worked on more than a few comic-book projects in my career, and this one was the most rewarding. It was probably also the most challenging. The creative bar was raised so high by Jim, Jeph, Alex and Richard, I struggled mightily to avoid being the weak link in the artistic chain. That struggle really forced me to take chances and stretch in ways I didn't think possible. And that, more than anything, is why I thank my colleagues for allowing me to be a part of something special.

A special thanks goes out to my family — Michael, Toffer and especially my beautiful wife Jennifer, who put up with an absentee dad and husband for the better part of a year while I put in the crazy hours at the drawing board. I owe you guys big time.

And finally a shout out to everyone who bought the comics and followed us along on our little adventure to the end. We're ALL fans of comics, and because of you, I don't have to go out and look for a real job.........

—SCOTT WILLIAMS

Thanks to Wes Abbott at Comicraft for his lettering assistance.

—RICHARD STARKINGS

I would like to thank Jim, Scott, Jeph and Richard for letting me be part of the team; Bob Schreck and Michael Wright for putting up with us; my wife Rebecca and daughters Grace, Blythe, Meredith and Harley for their continued support and inspiration; and the fans for making this a memorable run with one of the best characters in comics.

—ALEX SINCLAIR

JEPH LOEB is the author of BATMAN: THE LONG HALLOWEEN, BATMAN: DARK VICTORY, SUPERMAN FOR ALL SEASONS, *Spider-Man: Blue*, *Daredevil: Yellow* and *Hulk: Gray*. Currently, Jeph is writing SUPERMAN/BATMAN and CATWOMAN: WHEN IN ROME. A writer/producer living in Los Angeles, his credits include *Teen Wolf*, *Commando*, and *Smallville*.

Jim Lee was born in Seoul, South Korea in 1964. He graduated from Princeton University with a degree in medicine but decided to try his hand at comic-book art — his childhood fantasy. He found assignments at Marvel Comics, where his work quickly proved so popular that the company created a new X-Men title to showcase it. In 1992, Lee formed his own comics company, WildStorm Productions, which became one of the founding components of Image Comics. There, he launched the best-selling WILDC.A.T.S and introduced scores of characters such as GEN13. He also helped to discover and train a phalanx of writers, artists, and colorists. With its steady success, WildStorm as a business grew so demanding that Lee found he no longer had any time to draw, leading to his decision to sell the company to DC Comics. He remains WildStorm's editorial director but now concentrates on his first love, art. In 2004, he brings his vision to SUPERMAN. He lives in La Jolla, California with his wife Angie and his daughters Tyler, Kelsey and Siena.

BIOGRAPHIES

SCOTT WILLIAMS has worked with Jim Lee for more than ten years, and he was voted Favorite Inker for five years in a row (1990-94) in the *Comics Buyer's Guide* Fan Awards. His inking work can be found in WILDCATS, GEN13, JUST IMAGINE STAN LEE...WONDER WOMAN, WILDCATS/X-MEN, *X-Men: Mutant Genesis*, and *X-Men: X-Tinction Agenda*. In 2004, Scott reteams with Jim Lee on SUPERMAN.

ALEX SINCLAIR bought his first comic book — DETECTIVE COMICS #500 — with his brother, Celes, at their local convenience store. He immediately fell in love with comics and with Batman, who continues to be his favorite character. (Alex and Celes still argue over who would win in a fight between Batman and Superman.) He has previously worked on KURT BUSIEK'S ASTRO CITY, TOP 10, HARLEY QUINN, and, with Jim Lee and Scott Williams, on WILDC.A.T.S, GEN13, and DIVINE RIGHT. Sinclair lives in San Diego with his sidekick Rebecca and their four hench-girls: Grace, Blythe, Meredith, and Harley. He would love to fight crime, but the weather's too nice. Instead, Sinclair became an editor at WildStorm in the spring of 2003.

RICHARD STARKINGS is best known as the creator of the Comicraft studio, purveyors of unique design and fine lettering — and a copious catalogue of comic-book fonts — since 1992. He is less well known as the creator and publisher of *Hip Flask* and his semi-autobiographical cartoon strip, *Hedge Backwards*. He never seems to get tired of reminding people that he lettered BATMAN: THE KILLING JOKE with a pen.